# Lecture Notes in Computer Science 7378

Commenced Publication in 1973
Founding and Former Series Editors:
Gerhard Goos, Juris Hartmanis, and Jan van Leeuwen

## Editorial Board

Francisco J. Perales   Robert B. Fisher
Thomas B. Moeslund (Eds.)

# Articulated Motion
# and Deformable Objects

7th International Conference, AMDO 2012
Port d'Andratx, Mallorca, Spain, July 11-13, 2012
Proceedings

 Springer

Volume Editors

Francisco J. Perales López
UIB – Universitat de les Illes Balears
Dept. of Computer Science and Mathematics
C/ Valldemossa km 7.5, PC 07122, Palma de Mallorca, Spain
E-mail: paco.perales@uib.es

Robert B. Fisher
University of Edinburgh
School of Informatics
1.26 Informatics Forum, 10 Crichton St., Edinburgh, EH8 9AB, UK
E-mail: rbf@inf.ed.ac.uk

Thomas B. Moeslund
Aalborg University
Dept. for Architecture, Design and Media Technology
Niels Jernes Vej 14, 9220 Aalborg East, Denmark
E-mail: tbm@create.aau.dk

ISSN 0302-9743                          e-ISSN 1611-3349
ISBN 978-3-642-31566-4                  e-ISBN 978-3-642-31567-1
DOI 10.1007/978-3-642-31567-1
Springer Heidelberg Dordrecht London New York

Library of Congress Control Number: 2012940928

CR Subject Classification (1998): I.4, I.5, I.2.10, I.2, H.4-5, I.3

LNCS Sublibrary: SL 6 – Image Processing, Computer Vision, Pattern Recognition,
and Graphics

*Typesetting:* Camera-ready by author, data conversion by Scientific Publishing Services, Chennai, India

Printed on acid-free paper

Springer is part of Springer Science+Business Media (www.springer.com)

# Preface

The AMDO 2012 conference took place at the Hotel Mon Port, Port d'Andratx (Mallorca), during July 11–13, 2012, institutionally sponsored by MEC (Ministerio de Educación y Ciencia, Spanish Government), the Conselleria d'Economia, Hisenda i Innovació (Balearic Islands Government), the Consell de Mallorca, the AERFAI (Spanish Association in Pattern Recognition and Artificial Intelligence), the EG(Eurographics Association Spanish Section), the IEEE S.E (Advancing Technology for Humanity) and the Mathematics and Computer Science Department of the UIB. Important commercial and research sponsors also collaborated with practical demonstrations, and the main contributors were: Anima Information Technology, VICOM Tech, ANDROME Iberica, EDM (Expertise Cemtrum voor Digitale Media), INESCOP (Instituto Tecnologico del Calzado y Conexas), Aquateknica S.L.

The subject of the conference was the ongoing research on articulated motion in a sequence of images and sophisticated models for deformable objects. The goals of these areas are the understanding and interpretation of the motion of complex objects that can be found in sequences of images in the real world. The main topics considered as priority were: geometric and physical deformable models, motion analysis, articulated models and animation, modelling and visualization of deformable models, deformable model applications, motion analysis applications, single or multiple human motion analysis and synthesis, face modelling, tracking, recovering and recognition models, virtual and augmented reality, haptics devices, and biometrics techniques. The conference topics were grouped into four tracks: Track 1: Advanced Computer Graphics (Human Modelling and Animation), Track 2: Human Motion (Analysis, Tracking, 3D Reconstruction and Recognition), Track 3: Multimodal User Interaction and Applications, Track 4: Affective Interfaces (recognition and interpretation of emotions, ECAs - embodied conversational agents in HCI).

AMDO 2012 was the natural evolution of the six previous editions in this series and has been consolidated as a European reference for symposiums on the topics mentioned above. The main goal of this conference was to promote interaction and collaboration among researchers working directly in the areas covered by the main tracks. New perceptual user interfaces and emerging technologies increase the relation between areas involved with human–computer interaction. The new perspective of the AMDO 2012 conference was the strengthening of the relationship between the areas that share as key point the study of the human body using computer technologies as the main tool. The response to the Call for Papers for this conference was satisfactory. From 44 full papers submitted, 27 were accepted for oral presentation. The review process was carried out by the Program Committee, each paper being assessed by at least two reviewers. The conference included several sessions of oral presented papers and three tutorials. Also, the conference benefited from the collaboration of the invited speakers treating various aspects of the main topics. The invited speakers were: Thomas B. Moeslund (University of Aalborg, Denmark) Talk: Analyzing People in Thermal Imagery. Sergio Escalera (University of Barcelona, Spain) Talk: Human Behavior Analysis Using Depth Maps. Xianghua Xie (Swansea University, UK) Title: Deformable Model in Segmentation and Tracking.

July 2012                                                              F.J. Perales
                                                                        R. Fisher
                                                                  T.B. Moeslund

# Organization

AMDO 2012 was organized by the Computer Graphics, Vision and Artificial Intelligence team of the Department of Mathematics and Computer Science, Universitat de les Illes Balears (UIB) in cooperation AERFAI (Spanish Association for Pattern Recognition and Image Analysis) and EG S.E.(Eurograhics Association).

## Executive Committee

### General Conference Co-chairs

| | |
|---|---|
| F.J. Perales | UIB, Spain |
| R. Fisher | University of Edinburgh, UK |
| T.B. Moeslund | University of Aalborg, Denmark |

### Organizing Chairs

| | |
|---|---|
| M. González | UIB, Spain |
| R. Mas | UIB, Spain |
| A. Jaume | UIB, Spain |
| M. Mascaró Oliver | UIB, Spain |
| P. Palmer | UIB, Spain |
| C. Manresa | UIB, Spain |
| X. Varona | UIB, Spain |
| J.M. Buades | UIB, Spain |
| M. Miró | UIB, Spain |
| G. Fiol | UIB, Spain |
| A. Mir | UIB, Spain |
| G. Moyà | UIB, Spain |
| A. Delgado | UIB, Spain |
| S. Ramis | UIB, Spain |

### Tutorial Chairs

| | |
|---|---|
| M. González | UIB, Spain |
| J. Varona | UIB, Spain |
| F.J. Perales | UIB, Spain |

## Program Commitee

| | |
|---|---|
| Abasolo, M. | Universidad Nacional de La Plata, Argentina |
| Aloimonos, Y. | University of Maryland, USA |
| Bagdanov, A.D. | University of Florence, Italy |

| | |
|---|---|
| Baldassarri, S. | University of Zaragoza, Spain |
| Bartoli A. | CNRS-LASMEA, France |
| Baumela, L. | University of Technical of Madrid, Spain |
| Brunet, P. | Polytechnic University Catalonia, Spain |
| Bowden, R. | University of Surrey, UK |
| Campilho A. | University of Oporto, Portugal |
| Cerezo, E. | Universidad de Zaragoza, Spain |
| Coll, T. | DMI-UIB, Spain |
| Courty, N. | Université Bretagne Sud, France |
| Davis, L.S. | University of Maryland, USA |
| Del Bimbo, A. | Università di Firenze, Italy |
| Dogan, S. | I-Lab, University of Surrey, UK |
| Dugelay, J.L. | Eurecom, France |
| Escalera, S. | UB, Spain |
| Fernandez-Caballero, A. | CLM University, Spain |
| Fiol, G. | DMI-UIB, Spain |
| Flerackers, E. | LUC/EDM, Belgium |
| Flores, J. | Mar-USC, Spain |
| González, J. | CVC-UAB, Spain |
| González, M. | DMI-UIB, Spain |
| Hilton, A. | University of Surrey, UK |
| Iñesta, J.M. | University of Alicante, Spain |
| Kakadiaris, I.A. | University of Houston, USA |
| Komura, T. | IPAB University of Edinburgh, UK |
| Maia S. | University of Barcelona, Spain |
| Marcialis, G.L. | University of Cagliary, Italy |
| Mas, R. | DMI-UIB, Spain |
| Matey, L. | CEIT, Spain |
| Mir, A. | DMI-UIB, Spain |
| Medioni, G. | University of Southern California, USA |
| Pla, F. | University of Jaume I, Spain |
| Perez de la Blanca, N. | University of Granada, Spain |
| Radeva, P. | CVC-UB, Spain |
| Roca, X. | CVC-UAB, Spain |
| Qin, H | Stony Brook University, New York, USA |
| Salah, A.A. | University of Boğaziçi, Turkey |
| Sanfeliu, A. | IRI, CSIC-UPC, Spain |
| Santos-Victor, J. | IST, Portugal |
| Seron, F. | University of Zaragoza, Spain |
| Sigal, L. | Disney Research, USA |
| Skala V. | University of West Bohemia, Czech Republic |
| Susin, A. | Polytechnic University of Catalonia, Spain |
| Thalmann, D. | EPFL, Switzerland |

| | |
|---|---|
| Tavares J.M. | University of Porto, Portugal |
| Terzopoulos, D. | University of New York, USA |
| Van Reeth, F. | LUC/EDM, Belgium |
| Vitria J. | UB, Spain |
| Xianghua X. | Swansea University, UK |
| Wang, L. | NLPR, China |

## Sponsoring Institutions

AERFAI (Spanish Association for Pattern Recognition and Image Analysis)
EG S.E.(Eurograhics Association)
MEC (Ministerio de Educación y Ciencia, Spanish Government)
Conselleria d'Economia, Hisenda i Innovació (Balearic Islands Government)
Consell de Mallorca
Maths and Computer Science Department, Universitat de les Illes Balears (UIB)
Ajuntament d'Andratx. Sol de Ponent
Ajuntament de Palma
Sa Nostra. Caixa de Balears

## Commercial Sponsoring Enterprises

VICOM-Tech S.A., www.vicomtech.es
ANDROME Iberica S.A, www.androme.es
Aquateknica, http://www.aquateknica.com
Anima Information Technology, http://www.animabci.com/01/
EDM (Expertise Cemtrum voor Digitale Media), http://www.uhasselt.be/edm
INESCOP (Instituto Tecnologico del Calzado y Conexas), http://www.inescop.es/

# Table of Contents

# User Identification and Object Recognition in Clutter Scenes Based on RGB-Depth Analysis

Albert Clapés[1,2], Miguel Reyes[1,2], and Sergio Escalera[1,2]

[1] Dept. Matemàtica Aplicada i Anàlisi, Universitat de Barcelona, Gran Via de les Corts Catalanes 585, 08007, Barcelona, Spain
[2] Computer Vision Center, Campus UAB, Edifici O, 08193, Bellaterra, Spain
{aclapes,mreyes,sescalera}@cvc.uab.es

**Abstract.** We propose an automatic system for user identification and object recognition based on multi-modal RGB-Depth data analysis. We model a RGBD environment learning a pixel-based background Gaussian distribution. Then, user and object candidate regions are detected and recognized online using robust statistical approaches over RGBD descriptions. Finally, the system saves the historic of user-object assignments, being specially useful for surveillance scenarios. The system has been evaluated on a novel data set containing different indoor/outdoor scenarios, objects, and users, showing accurate recognition and better performance than standard state-of-the-art approaches.

**Keywords:** Multi-modal RGB-Depth data analysis, User identification, Object Recognition, Visual features, Statistical learning.

## 1 Introduction

In most monitoring surveillance scenarios a vast majority of video is permanently lost without any useful processing being gained from it. Several automatic approaches related to this topic has been published [1]. These works base on Computer Vision techniques to examine the video streams to determine activities, events, or behaviors that might be considered suspicious and provide an appropriate response when such actions occur. The detection of motion in many current tracking systems relies on the technique of background subtraction. The ability to represent multiple modes for the background values allows some techniques to model motion which is part of the background [2]. However, almost none of the state-of-the-art methods can adapt to quick image variations such as a light turning on or off.

Computer Vision techniques have been studied for decades in the surveillance scenario, and although huge improvements have been performed, still it is difficult to robustly identify users and objects in visual data. Some works have addressed the problem of developing complete vision systems for both object recognition and tracking in order to obtain a rough scene understanding [3]. However, still occlusions and noise can generate false object appearance in the scene.

F.J. Perales, R.B. Fisher, and T.B. Moeslund (Eds.): AMDO 2012, LNCS 7378, pp. 1–11, 2012.
© Springer-Verlag Berlin Heidelberg 2012

With the objective of improving the discriminability of relevant surveillance events in the scenes, some authors use calibrated cameras which are synchronized in order to obtain an approximation of the 3D representation of the scene. Although this approach can be useful in some situations, it requires from a perfect multi-camera synchronization, and a strategic location of each camera that could not be feasible in most real environments. Recently, with the appearance of the Depth maps introduced by the Kinect Microsoft device, a new source of information has emerged. With the use of depth maps, 3D information of the scene from a particular point of view is easily computed, and thus, working with consecutive frames, we obtain RGBDT information, from Red, Green, Blue, Depth, and Time data, respectively. This motivates the use of multi-modal data fusion strategies to benefit from the new data representation. In particular, Girshick and Shotton et al. [4] present one of the greatest advances in the extraction of the human body pose from depth images, that also forms the core of the Kinect human recognition framework. Through this technology are emerging work on reconstruction of dense surfaces and 3D object detection [5].

In this paper, we propose an automatic surveillance system for user identification and object recognition based on multi-modal RGB-Depth data analysis. We model a RGBD environment learning a pixel based background Gaussian distribution. Then, user and object candidate regions are detected and recognized using robust statistical approaches. The system robustly recognize users and update the system in an online way, identifying and detecting new actors in the scene. On the other hand, segmented regions of candidate objects are described, matched, and recognized using view-point 3D descriptions of normal vectors using spatial and depth information, being robust to partial occlusions and local 3D viewpoint rotations. Moreover, 3D object information is online updated as well as new views of the object are detected. Finally, the system saves the historic of user-object pick ups assignments, being specially useful for surveillance scenarios. The system has been evaluated on a novel data set containing different scenarios, objects, and users, showing accurate recognition results.

The rest of the paper is organized as follows: Section 2 presents the system for user identification and object recognition. Section 3 presents the results, and finally, Section 4 concludes the paper.

## 2   Muti-modal User Identification and Object Recognition

In this section, we present our system for automatic user-object interaction analysis using multi-modal RGBD data. The system is composed by four main modules which are described next. The control automata of the system that calls to the different module functionalities is summarized in Algorithm1. The scheme of the whole system is illustrated in Fig. 1.

### 2.1   Environment Modeling

Given the frame set $F = \{I, D\}$ containing a RGB image $I \in [0, 1]^{h \times w}$ and a depth map $D \in [0, \infty]^{h \times w}$ with the depth value of each pixel obtained by the

**Data:** $F_{\{1,..,T\}}$
1  Environment modeling of $F_{\{1,..,T\}}$ using pixel adaptive learning (section 2.1)
2  **while** *true* **do**
3     Acquire new frame $F_t = \{I_t, D_t\}$ composed by RGB image $I$ and depth map $D$ (section 2.1)
4     Segment new regions of $F_t$ based on environment modeling (section 2.1)
5     Look for subject/s and identification/s in $F_t$ (section 2.2)
6     Look for new objects or object removals in $F_t$ (section 2.3)
7     Look for getting/leaving objects in scene (section 2.4)
8     User-object association analysis
9  **end**

**Algorithm 1.** Control automata of the RGBD surveillance system

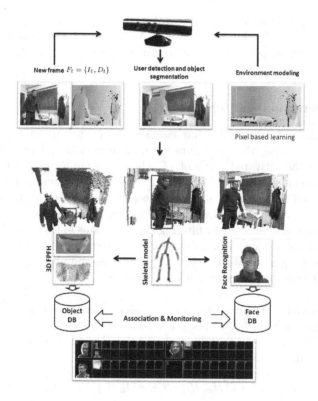

**Fig. 1.** Muti-modal user identification and object recognition surveillance system

Kinect infrared sensor, an adaptive model is learnt for each pixel. Supposing a RGBD Gaussian distribution for each pixel, the training procedure is performed as,

$$\mu_{\mathbf{X},t} = (1 - \alpha)\mu_{\mathbf{X},t-1} + \alpha \left( \frac{D_{\mathbf{X},t}}{\max D_t} \cup I_{\mathbf{X},t} \right), \tag{1}$$

$$\sigma^2_{\mathbf{X},t} = (1 - \alpha)\sigma^2_{\mathbf{X},t-1} + \alpha \left( \frac{D_{\mathbf{X},t}}{\max D_t} \cup I_{\mathbf{X},t} - \mu_{\mathbf{X},t} \right)^T \left( \frac{D_{\mathbf{X},t}}{\max D_t} \cup I_{\mathbf{X},t} - \mu_{\mathbf{X},t} \right), \tag{2}$$

where $\mu_{\mathbf{x},t}$ is the mean depth learnt at pixel $\mathbf{x} = (i,j)$ at frame $t$, $\alpha$ is a training weight of the parameters during learning, $D_{\mathbf{x},t}$ is the depth at pixel $\mathbf{x}$ at frame $t$, $I_{\mathbf{x},t}$ is the RGB values at pixel $\mathbf{x}$ at frame $t$, and $\sigma^2$ is the covariance. The computation of $\mu$ and $\sigma$ given a fixed $\alpha$ value is performed during a perfect stationary background composed of $T$ frames, so that $t \in [1,..,T]$. Once the background has been modeled, a new change of a pixel in the scene produced by the appearance/disappearance of items is detected as follows,

$$\sigma_{\mathbf{x},T} - \left| \frac{D_{\mathbf{x},t}}{\max D_t} \cup I_{\mathbf{x},t} - \mu_{\mathbf{x},T} \right| > \theta_S, \qquad (3)$$

where $|.|$ corresponds to the absolute value and $\theta_S$ is an experimentally set background segmentation hypothesis value. At the top of Fig. 1 one can see the background modeling procedure, a new frame $F$, and the detection of a new item corresponding to a user in the scene.

## 2.2   User Detection and Identification

Given the segmented image $M$ that contains 1 at those positions satisfying Eq. 3 and 0 otherwise, the procedure for user detection and identification is only applied on the activated pixels of $M$. The algorithm for user detection and identification is summarized in Algorithm 2. Note that we track each particular user based on its distance to previous detections in time, as well as the counter for the $n$ identifications is treated for each user independently. Moreover, temporal coherence is taken into account by filtering the detections in time based on region density and 3D coordinates, discarding isolated detections and recovering miss-detections, resulting in a reduction of false detections and allowing a continuous detection of objects and users within the sequence.

**User Identification Procedure.** For the user identification module we propose to use the combination of body color model $\mathcal{C}$ with the face recognition probability $\mathcal{F}$ based on the matching of visual features, defining the following energy functional,

$$E(c_i, u) = \mathcal{C}(H_u, H_i) \cdot \beta + \mathcal{F}(f_u, f_i) \cdot (1 - \beta), \qquad (4)$$

where $\beta$ is a trade-off energy parameter. Energy functional $E \in [0,1]$ is computed between a new test user $u = \{H_u, f_u\}$ and a candidate user class $c_i = \{H_i, f_i\}$, where $H_i$ is the set of RGB color histograms for user $i$, and $f_i$ is the set of face descriptions. Given a set of $k$ possible users $C = \{c_1,..,c_k\}$ learnt online by the system, using the energy functional of Eq. 4, the new user candidate $u$ is identified as follows,

$$\begin{array}{ll} i & \text{if} \quad E(c_i, u) > \theta_u, E(c_i, u) > E(c_j, u), \forall j \in [1,k], i \neq j \\ 0 & \text{otherwise} \end{array} \qquad (5)$$

**Data:** $M_t, F_t,$ count, $n$
1  **if** *count* $< n$ **then**
2  | a) User detection [4] on $D_t$ for the activated pixels in $M$
3  | **if** *Detected user* **then**
4  | | b) Skeletal model description [4] on the pixels corresponding to the detected user
5  | | c) Run Viola & Jones lateral and frontal face detectors on the surrounding areas to the detected head joint after background removal
6  | | **if** *Detected face* **then**
7  | | | d) Use Active Shape Model with a set of face landmark to align the detected face to the closest data set training sample for each subject based on the mesh fitting error
8  | | | e) Compute user body color histogram excluding face region (section 2.2)
9  | | | f) Perform user identification (section 2.2)
10 | | | g) Save the partial user identification $ID_{\text{count}}$ to the class of the closest user probability, or 0 if none of the possible users achieve a probability threshold $\theta_u$
11 | | | count++
12 | | **else**
13 | | | count=0
14 | | **end**
15 | **else**
16 | | count=0
17 | **end**
18 **else**
19 | h) Assign class label to subject based on majority voting of $ID$ or define new user if the majority vote is 0 count=0
20 **end**

**Algorithm 2.** User detection and identification algorithm

In the case that the new user defines a new model (classification label 0), it is used to update the user model $C$ with a new identifier $C = C \cup \{H_u, f_u\}$. In the case that the user has been identified as a previously learnt user, the user model can be updated if the energy $E$ for the classified user is bellow a particular update threshold parameter, so that if $E(c_i, u) < \theta_u$ for the identified user $i$, then $c_i = \{H_i, f_i\} \cup \{H_u, f_u\}$, subtracting the oldest data to reduce an uncontrolled growing of model information. Next, we describe the computation of the color and face models.

**Color Model Computation** $\mathcal{C}$. Once a new user is identified in the environment, a predefined number of color histograms is defined, computed, and saved in the histogram set $H_i$ for user $i$. Each histogram in this set is computed as a 62 bin normalized histogram (30-H and 32S) from HSV color representation (PDF of the HSV data for the subject) for each frame considered to model the user body color model, without considered the region of the subject detected as the face region. Once a new candidate user $u$ is detected by the system, its color model histogram is computed and compared with each learnt possible user $i$, defining the energy $\mathcal{C}(H_u, H_i)$ of Eq. 4. This energy is based on the Bhattacharyya distance of two histogram distributions $\mathcal{B}(h_u, h_i) = \sqrt{1 - \sum_j \frac{\sqrt{h_u^j \cdot h_i^j}}{\sqrt{\sum_j h_u^j \cdot \sum_j h_i^j}}}$, where $h_i^j$ is the $j$-th position of one of the histograms of the set $H_i$. Once this distance is computed among the candidate user $u$ and each histogram in the training set, the $m$ lowest distances for each user class are selected to compute the mean confidence for that class. Thus, the final color energy term is defined as $\mathcal{C}(H_u, H_i) = \frac{\sum_m 1 - \mathcal{B}(h_u, h_m)}{m}$ for the $m$ largest confidences (lowest Bhattacharyya distances) for candidate user $i$.

**Face Model Computation $\mathcal{F}$.** Describing in more detail lines 7-10 of Algorithm 2, our steps for face model computation are,

• We perform face alignment after face detection and background removal using Active Shape Model by means of linear transformation of position, rotation, and scale, computed using the mesh fitting changes.

• We use fast SURF point detection and description on the RGB user face $f_u$ and each candidate face $f_i$ for user $i$.

• We match SURF features between $f_u$ and $f_i$ using nearest neighbor assignments using a k-d tree with Best-bin-first search [6].

• We use RANSAC to discard final outliers based on the difference of the pair of features assignment to the computed linear transformation. Inliers are selected based on linear least squares.

• Using the initial set of $v$ descriptions and the $w$ final selected inliers, we compute a probabilistic membership of user model $f_u$ to face model $f_i$ for class $i$ as follows [7]: Let $P(y|\neg f_i)$ be the probability that the matched features $y$ would arise by accident if the model $f_i$ is not present. We assume the $w$ feature matches arose from $v$ possible features, each of which matches by accident with probability $p$. Therefore, we can use the cumulative binomial distribution for the probability of an event with probability $p$ occurring at least $w$ times out of $v$ trials $P(y|\neg f_i) = \sum_{j=w}^{v} \binom{v}{j} p^j (1-p)^{v-j}$. To compute $P(f_i|y)$ we use Bayes' theorem $P(f_i|y) = \frac{P(y|f_i) \cdot P(f_i)}{P(y|f_i) \cdot P(f_i) + P(y|\neg f_i) \cdot P(\neg f_i)}$. We approximate $P(y|f_i)$ as 1 as we normally expect to see at least $w$ features present when the model is present. We also approximate $P(\neg f_i)$ with the value 1 as there is a very low prior probability of a model appearing at a particular pose. Therefore, our face energy model $\mathcal{F}$ is computed as $\mathcal{F}(f_u, f_i) = P(f_i|y) \approx \frac{P(f_i)}{P(f_i) + P(y|\neg f_i)}$. As in the case of the color model $\mathcal{C}$, detected faces are used online to update the user model of faces either for the case of a new user or for the case of previously identified user. Figure 2 shows real application examples of the user identification approach based on the face energy $\mathcal{F}$.

## 2.3   Object Recognition

Each segmented region (connected component) of $M$ which has not been identified as a user is considered as a new object in case where the distance to the camera at those segmented pixels in $D$ are reduced from the modeled background, or as the absence of an object if depth values increase. The case where an object has been removed is straightforward to analyze since we saved the description of the object located at those positions from previous frame description. This means that if a user picks an object, we immediately know looking at the label of the object from the removed location which object it was.

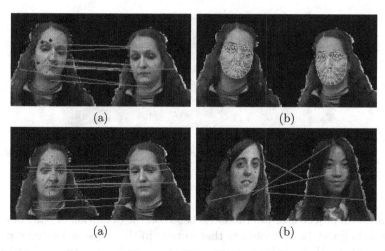

**Fig. 2.** Face identification analysis. Red dots: SURF candidate keypoints not matched based on descriptor distance. Blue dots: candidate keypoints discarded as outliers using RANSAC based on mesh transformation criteria. Green line: final matches considered for identification. (a) Example of images not aligned after face detection and background removal. Several outliers are detected using RANSAC (blue dots), reducing final identification probability of being the same user category (71.4% of probability in this example). (b) Shows the intermediate results of applying ASM meshes to both faces before alignment. (c) Applying the whole proposed process. Now the probability of identification increases up to 98.4%. (d) An example of alignment and identification for two different categories, with a result of 32.3% of probability.

In the case that a new object is located in a scene by a user, we take advantage of the 3D object information provided by the depth map $D$ to compute a normalized description of that particular 3D view [5]. For this task, we take use of the recently proposed Fast Point Feature Histogram (FPFH) to compute a 3D rotation invariant object description for each particular point of view of an object $\mathcal{P}$ in the scene. A visualization of the descriptors for a set of objects is shown in Fig. 3. This procedure is performed for each new object cluster in $M$, and the object description is compared to the data set of descriptions saved in memory as in the case of the user color model $\mathcal{C}$. In this case, $k$-NN are used to classify the new object view as a previous detected object if it achieves majority voting and a threshold value over object threshold $\theta_o$, being also used to update online the data set of object descriptions. In cases where two objects achieve high similarity with the new sample, we update the model and fuse two previous object descriptions. An example of object segmentation and 3D visual description using FPFH is shown in the middle of Fig. 1 for a detected object in the scene.

**Fig. 3.** Views of different objects and descriptions based on the normal components

## 2.4   User-Object Interaction

The analysis of object-user interaction is based on the definition of pairs of values (user,object) for those new objects that appear in the scene or those users that pick up an object, looking for past memberships in order to activate the required surveillance alerts. Some interface examples are shown in Fig. 5.

# 3   Results

In order to present the results of the proposed system, first, we discuss the data, methods and parameters, and evaluation measurements of the different experiments.

• **Data.** We defined a novel set of data recorded with the Kinect device. The data set consists of 10 videos of one minute each one in indoor scenes and 5 videos of one minute each one in outdoor scenes. The whole data set contains a total of 23600 semi-supervised labeled frames, containing a total of 8 different subjects and 11 different objects.

• **Methods and Parameters.** The values of our method parameters have been experimentally set via cross-validation. We also compare the proposed system with state-of-the-art methods: SURF and Bag-of-visual-words (BOVW) description, and the effect of background substraction and face alignment for user identification. Finally we also compare with RGB SIFT description in the case of object classification.

• **Evaluation Measurements.** We compute the performance of the system in terms of user detection, user identification, object detection, object classification, user-object association, and theft. For each of these evaluations we measure the number of true positives, false positives, and false negatives.

## 3.1   Surveillance System Evaluation

The mean global performance of the presented surveillance system is shown in Fig. 4. The Y-axis corresponds to the absolute value of true positives, false positives, and false negatives for each event category. One can see that we are able to correctly detect most of the events, corresponding to an accuracy upon 90%. Most true positives are detected. False positives are almost non existent except for the case of object detection, where small noisy regions of the image are sporadically detected as small objects. Only few false positives occur in the case of user identification and theft, where an error in the case of object or user

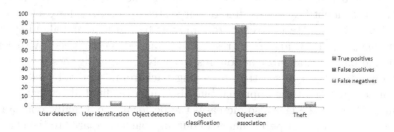

**Fig. 4.** Mean surveillance system performance

**Fig. 5.** (a) Outdoor scenario: user is identified, theft is recognized, and different objects, included a small cup are detected. (b) Users and object memberships are correctly identified and classified. Different users can be identified simultaneously by the system.

detection/recognition immediately propagates an error in the final theft detection step. Some qualitative results of the execution of the surveillance system are shown in Fig. 5.

## 3.2   User Identification Comparative

In Table 1 we show the identification accuracy of our method (Statistical Surf) and the standard SURF description using Bag of Visual Words (SURF BOVW) [8] for the user identification module of our system. Moreover, for each of these two configurations, we test the effect of removing background and aligning faces. In particular, A, $\overline{A}$, B, and $\overline{B}$ correspond to aligned, not aligned, with background, and background substraction, respectively. Comparing these approaches on the data set, one can see that removing background not only reduces the posterior complexity of the approach but also improves final identification performance. Aligning the face also increases the performance. Finally, one can see the robustness and better performance of our approach compared to the classical SURF BOVW technique, with a global mean improvement of 20% for the best configuration between both approaches.

**Table 1.** User identification performance results

| SURF BOVW | | | | STATISTICAL SURF | | | |
|---|---|---|---|---|---|---|---|
| $B + \overline{A}$ | $B + A$ | $\overline{B} + \overline{A}$ | $\overline{B} + A$ | $B + \overline{A}$ | $B + A$ | $\overline{B} + \overline{A}$ | $\overline{B} + A$ |
| 33.3% | 47.1% | 52.8% | 74.4% | 52.9% | 60.9% | 76.3% | 96.4% |

## 3.3   Object Recognition Comparative

In order to analyze the high discriminative power of the used FPFH descriptor encoding the normal vector distributions of a 3D object view, we compare the obtained recognition results with the standard object description using SIFT on the RGB segmented object region. The results are shown in Table 2. One can see that contrary to the state-of-the-art SIFT descriptor, the 3D-normal vector distributions improve classification results in 12% in the presented experiments.

**Table 2.** Object recognition performance results

| RGB SIFT | DEPTH FPFH |
|---|---|
| 86.2% | 98.5% |

## 4   Conclusion

We proposed an automatic system for user identification and object recognition based on multi-modal RGB-Depth data analysis. We modeled a RGBD environment learning a pixel based background Gaussian distribution. Then, user and object candidate regions were detected and recognized using robust statistical approaches. The system was evaluated on a novel data set containing different indoor and outdoor scenarios, objects, and users, showing accurate recognition results and better performance than classical approaches.

# References

1. Lipton, A.J., Fujiyoshi, H.: Moving target classification and tracking from real-time video. In: Proceedings of the Fourth IEEE Workshop on Applications of Computer Vision, WACV 1998, pp. 8–14 (1998)
2. Elgammal, A., Harwood, D., Davis, L.: Non-parametric Model for Background Subtraction. In: Vernon, D. (ed.) ECCV 2000. LNCS, vol. 1843, pp. 751–767. Springer, Heidelberg (2000)
3. Brown, L.M., Senior, A.W., Li Tian, Y., Connell, J., Hampapur, A., Fe Shu, C., Merkl, H., Lu, M.: Performance evaluation of surveillance systems under varying conditions. In: Proceedings of IEEE PETS Workshop, pp. 1–8 (2005)
4. Shotton, J., Fitzgibbon, A., Cook, M., Sharp, T., Finocchio, M., Moore, R., Kipman, A., Blake, A.: Real-time human pose recognition in parts from single depth images (2011)
5. Rusu, R.B.: Semantic 3D Object Maps for Everyday Manipulation in Human Living Environments. Articial Intelligence (KI - Kuenstliche Intelligenz) (2010)
6. Lowe, D.G.: Distinctive image features from scale-invariant keypoints. International Journal of Computer Vision 60, 91–110 (2004)
7. Lowe, D.G.: Local feature view clustering for 3d object recognition. In: IEEE Conference on Computer Vision and Pattern Recognition, pp. 682–688 (2001)
8. Csurka, G., Dance, C.R., Fan, L., Willamowski, J., Bray, C.: Visual categorization with bags of keypoints. In: Workshop on Statistical Learning in Computer Vision, ECCV, pp. 1–22 (2004)

# Compression Techniques
# for 3D Video Mesh Sequences

Margara Tejera and Adrian Hilton

Centre for Vision, Speech and Signal Processing
University of Surrey, Guildford, UK
{m.tejerapadilla,a.hilton}@surrey.ac.uk

**Abstract.** This paper approaches the problem of compressing temporally consistent 3D video mesh sequences with the aim of reducing the storage cost. We present an evaluation of compression techniques which apply Principal Component Analysis to the representation of the mesh in different domain spaces, and demonstrate the applicability of mesh deformation algorithms for compression purposes. A novel layered mesh representation is introduced for compression of 3D video sequences with an underlying articulated motion, such as a person with loose clothing. Comparative evaluation on captured mesh sequences of people demonstrates that this representation achieves a significant improvement in compression compared to previous techniques. Results show a compression ratio of 8-15 for an RMS error of less than $5mm$.

**Keywords:** compression, 3D video, PCA, Laplacian deformation.

## 1 Introduction

This paper addresses the problem of finding a compact representation of free-viewpoint video sequences, captured using a multi-camera set-up in a controlled studio environment [12,6,24,1]. These 3D video sequences are temporally aligned during a post-processing step [10], ensuring that all frames within a sequence share the same mesh connectivity. Therefore, the data under study is comprised of a set of temporally consistent mesh animations depicting articulated motion of an actor performance and surface deformation due to clothing.

We present a comparison of a set of compression techniques based on two different frameworks. On the one hand, we apply a commonly found technique in the compression literature, Principal Component Analysis, to the mesh sequences represented in various coordinate spaces. On the other hand, we encode a mesh as a reference mesh plus a set of constraints and decode it by the application of state-of-the art mesh deformation techniques, which allow the reconstruction of the original mesh. Although both of these approaches provide a lossy recovering of the mesh geometry, they offer the user total control over the trade-off between lost detail and storage cost.

To our knowledge, this is the first time that mesh deformation techniques are applied to compression of 3D video sequences. Moreover, we introduce a novel

F.J. Perales, R.B. Fisher, and T.B. Moeslund (Eds.): AMDO 2012, LNCS 7378, pp. 12–25, 2012.

layered mesh representation for articulated animation, comprised of an articulated base layer and an a detail layer representing remaining surface deformation. Comparative evaluation demonstrates that this gives significant improvement for compression of sequences with an underlying articulated structure. The approach accurately and efficiently represents non-rigid surface deformation due to loose clothing and hair as a local deformation basis on top of the underlying articulated motion, achieving an order of magnitude compression of 3D video sequences of people.

## 1.1   Related Work

Interest in mesh compression has been mainly motivated by the need for fast transmission of 3D animated sequences due to system-dependant bandwidth capacity and the production of high-quality (large-sized) animations. However, these techniques are also applicable to efficient storage of the data, which is the primary motivation in this work.

Two groups of mesh compression techniques can be distinguished, one that targets the compression of an individual mesh, and another which handles full mesh sequence animations. Although theoretically a mesh sequence could be compressed by applying single mesh compression techniques to every frame independently, this would ignore the temporal correlation present in the animation, which can be exploited to achieve further compression efficiency.

Touma and Gotsman [29] introduced one of the first mesh compression algorithms. It addresses the compression of both the connectivity and the geometry of the mesh and uses the "parallelogram" rule as a spatial predictor. *Progressive meshes*, which consist in the representation of a mesh by means of a coarse model and a set of details that progressively refine the reconstructed mesh, was first introduced by Hoppe [9]. This concept has been exploited by others: Lee *et al.* [17] encode surface deformation details as a set of scalar displacement maps; Cohen-Or *et al.* [20] compress the connectivity by an efficient colouring technique; and Khodakovsky *et al.* [15] construct a set of semi-regular approximations of the mesh and then use wavelet coefficients to express the difference between successive levels. Finally, Karni and Gotsman [13] compress the geometry of the mesh by analysing its spectral components to find an orthogonal basis of the Laplacian matrix (connectivity dependant) whose associated eigenvalues can be considered frequencies.

Lengyel [18] approached the compression of animated mesh sequences by means of affine transformations. This work takes advantage of the temporal correlation present in the sequence by clustering the vertices of the mesh in rigid bodies and then expresses the animation as a base mesh together with the set of transformations that these clusters undergo along the sequence. The same idea is applied by Collins and Hilton [7,8] on captured 3D video sequences. Shamir *et al.* [22] present a multi-resolution approach based on the construction of a Temporal Directed Acyclic Graph (T-DAG) which allows for changes of connectivity and topology of the meshes over time. This representation targets the compression of the connectivity component of the sequence and therefore is complementary to Lengyel's work.

The temporal correlation which is inherently linked to a mesh animation can also be exploited by the use of predictors that take into account the previously decoded meshes. Ibarria and Rossignac [11] introduced the use of two space-time extrapolating predictors, one suitable for translation and another which handles more complex transformations. Moreover, their technique only needs access to the previous frame, providing fast decompression. Müller *et al.* [19] go a step further by clustering the difference vectors resulting from subtracting the original and the predicted meshes and only process a representative vector of each of the clusters. Lastly, Stefanoski and Ostermann [25] decompose the sequence into spatial and temporal layers and develop a scalable predictive coding (SPC) algorithm in the space of rotation invariant coordinates, formed by representing Laplacian coordinates in a local reference frame associated with each spatial layer.

Alexa and Müller [2] pioneered the application of Principal Component Analysis (PCA) for compression of animated mesh sequences. They first align the sequence by removing the rigid motion component of all frames with respect to the first, and then apply PCA directly on vertex positions. Karni and Gotsman [14] broaden the method by applying Local Prediction Coding (LPC) to the PCA coefficients to exploit the temporal coherence of the animation. Sattler *et al.* [21] group the vertices that behave similarly over time by applying clustered PCA, which takes into account the total reconstruction error to find the best clusters. Clustering is also used by Amjoun and Straßer [3], who apply PCA to the vertex positions expressed with respect to a local reference frame associated with their corresponding cluster. Furthermore, they find the optimum number of basis vectors in order to avoid underfitting/overfitting.

These approaches consider compression and transmission of animated mesh sequences for arbitrary objects. In this paper we focus on the problem of compression of captured 3D video sequences of people with loose clothing. This presents a challenging problem due to the detailed surface deformation and inherent reconstruction and tracking noise in captured sequences. The underlying articulated structure can also be exploited to achieve improved compression.

## 2   Compression Techniques

### 2.1   Principal Component Analysis (PCA)

The application of PCA on a 3D video mesh sequence allows the extraction of an orthogonal basis that best represents the change of geometry of the sequence. In the following discussion we will consider that each data mesh is represented by a set of generic coordinates $(\mathbf{p}(\mathbf{x}), \mathbf{p}(\mathbf{y}), \mathbf{p}(\mathbf{z}))$. For a sequence of meshes $\{M(t_i)\}_{i=1}^{F}$, where $F$ is the number of frames, a data matrix $\mathbf{M}$ is built by placing the concatenated $(\mathbf{p}_i(\mathbf{x}), \mathbf{p}_i(\mathbf{y})$ and $\mathbf{p}_i(\mathbf{z}))$, $i \in [1, F]$, coordinates of each example in its rows:

$$M = \begin{pmatrix} \mathbf{p}_1^\top(\mathbf{x}) \; \mathbf{p}_1^\top(\mathbf{y}) \; \mathbf{p}_1^\top(\mathbf{z}) \\ \mathbf{p}_2^\top(\mathbf{x}) \; \mathbf{p}_2^\top(\mathbf{y}) \; \mathbf{p}_2^\top(\mathbf{z}) \\ \vdots \quad \vdots \quad \vdots \\ \mathbf{p}_F^\top(\mathbf{x}) \; \mathbf{p}_F^\top(\mathbf{y}) \; \mathbf{p}_F^\top(\mathbf{z}) \end{pmatrix} \tag{1}$$

The data matrix is centred obtaining $\mathbf{M_c} = \mathbf{M} - \bar{\mathbf{M}}$, where $\bar{\mathbf{M}}$ is a $F \times 3n$ matrix whose rows are the mean of the rows of the data matrix $\mathbf{M}$ and $n$ is the number of vertices of the meshes. In order to obtain a basis representing the mesh sequence a Singular Value Decomposition (SVD) is performed over the matrix $\mathbf{M_c}$: $\mathbf{M_c} = \mathbf{UDV}^\top$, where V is a $3n \times F$ matrix with a basis vector in each of its columns. By varying the number $l$ of basis vectors $\mathbf{e_k}$ we are able to represent the data maintaining a certain percentage of the variance. This gives a linear basis of the form:

$$\mathbf{p}(\mathbf{r}) = \bar{\mathbf{p}} + \sum_{k=1}^{l} r_k \mathbf{e}_k = \bar{\mathbf{p}} + \mathbf{Er}, \tag{2}$$

where $r_k$ are scalar weights for each basis vector, $\mathbf{r}$ is an $l$-dimensional weight vector and $\mathbf{E}$ is an $l \times 3n$ matrix whose rows are the first $l$ basis vectors of length $3n$. Applying PCA we are able to compress the representation of the original 3D video sequence: the whole sequence can be expressed by means of a basis matrix $\mathbf{E}$ of size $l \times 3n$, $F$ coefficients vectors (one per frame) of size $l$ and a mean vector $\bar{\mathbf{p}}$ of size $3n$.

## 2.2   Laplacian Deformation

Mesh editing techniques [27,23] allow deformation of a mesh following a set of positional constraints. They can be used, for example, to create novel mesh poses or to edit full 3D video sequences [30,16].

Laplacian mesh editing, based on the so-called Laplacian operator, manipulates the mesh in the space of differential coordinates $\delta$, which are computed by the simple multiplication of the Cartesian coordinates of the vertices by the Laplacian operator [23,5,26]: $\delta(\mathbf{x}) = \mathbf{Lx}$, $\delta(\mathbf{y}) = \mathbf{Ly}$ and $\delta(\mathbf{z}) = \mathbf{Lz}$. This new representation allows local mesh shape properties to be encoded.

Given a reference mesh and a set of sparse vertex positions, we can deform the reference mesh to fulfil these positional constraints. Therefore, we can think of reconstructing a full 3D video sequence by deforming a reference mesh and use this as a compression technique. Specifically, this process consists in the following steps:

1. Choose a reference mesh.
2. For each mesh, randomly sample a sparse set of vertex positions $(\mathbf{x_c}, \mathbf{y_c}, \mathbf{z_c})$ as constraints.

3. Reconstruct the original sequence by deforming the reference mesh, following the constraints found in step 2. The $\tilde{\mathbf{x}}$ absolute coordinates of the reconstructed mesh (the same applies for $\tilde{\mathbf{y}}$ and $\tilde{\mathbf{z}}$) can be computed in the least-square sense [23]:

$$\tilde{\mathbf{x}} = \arg\min_{x} \left( \|\mathbf{L}\mathbf{x} - \delta(\mathbf{x_o})\|^2 + \|\mathbf{W_c}(\mathbf{x} - \mathbf{x_c})\|^2 \right) \qquad (3)$$

Where $\mathbf{x_o}$ are the coordinates of the original mesh and $\mathbf{W_c}$ is a diagonal weight matrix.

Results of the reconstruction will depend on the suitability of the reference mesh and the number of sampled constraints. Applying this technique, we can express our original sequence by means of a reference mesh and a set of vertex constraints per frame, therefore compressing the data. The fewer constraints we use, the more efficient the compression will be, but the larger the error (difference between the original and the reconstructed sequence).

Laplacian deformation can be enhanced by the use of a learnt deformation space [28], which is constructed by taking each set of differential coordinates (one per frame) as a deformation example. This space is later taken into account in the minimisation process that takes place when deforming a mesh, ensuring that the resulting mesh lies within the learnt space, i.e., follows the same pattern of deformation as previously seen examples. The application of this modification implies the storage of a basis, which affects the efficiency of the compression. Let $\mathbf{r}$ be an $l$-dimensional weight vector which contains the scalar weights for each basis vector, then the least-square minimisation can be expressed as:

$$\bar{\mathbf{r}}, \bar{x} = \arg\min_{\mathbf{r},x}(\|\mathbf{L}\mathbf{x} - \delta(\mathbf{r})\|^2 + \|\mathbf{W_c}(\mathbf{x} - \mathbf{x_c})\|^2) \qquad (4)$$

## 3   Layered Articulated Representation

We present a novel layered representation of the mesh sequence, constructed in the following manner:

1. **Extraction of a Skeletal Sequence.** We use a 20-joint skeleton as seen in Figure 1. Firstly, 20 groups of vertices that best represent each of the joints are manually selected in a reference mesh (preferably, a T-pose), and secondly, the centroid of each group of vertices is computed, obtaining the position of the joints for the reference skeleton. Since the 3D video sequences under study are temporally consistent, we can use the same joint selection across the whole sequence, deriving a full skeletal sequence.

2. **Fixing the Size of the Skeleton.** Since the skeletal sequence obtained in the previous step follows the motion of the vertices of the meshes, it has the inconvenience of having limbs of different length in each of the frames. Therefore, it is converted into another skeletal sequence whose limbs are of the same length as the reference skeleton.

**Fig. 1.** Step 1: 20 joint areas are manually selected to extract a reference skeleton

3. **Skeletal Base Layer Animation.** We choose a base model and animate it following the fixed-length skeletal sequence found in the previous step, using a standard mesh animation technique and the skin attachment weights obtained by the Pinocchio framework [4]. The resulting sequence will be referred to as the *base sequence*. Figure 2 illustrates this process.

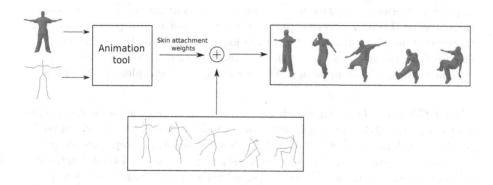

**Fig. 2.** Step 3: the base model is animated following the skeletal sequence and the skinning weights

4. **Detail Layer Extraction.** We find the *difference sequence* resulting from the subtraction of the *base sequence* from the original sequence. Finally, the original sequence has been decomposed into two layers: the *base sequence* and the *difference sequence*.

## 4    Description of the Experiments

In this section, a collection of compression techniques will be presented: three based on PCA applied to the representation of the mesh in different coordinate spaces, and two based on Laplacian deformation.

In order to express the storage cost of each approach, $S$, in bytes, we will follow this naming convention: $l$ is the number of eigenvectors kept for the basis, $F$ is the number of frames of the sequence, $n$ is the number of vertices of the meshes, $T$ the number of triangles, $C$ the number of constraints, $sizeOfInt$ the size in bytes of an integer value (4 bytes) and $sizeOfDouble$ the size in bytes of a double value (8 bytes).

## 4.1   PCA-Based Compression

*I - Direct PCA.* This method consists in applying PCA directly to the sequence, representing each mesh as the set of Cartesian coordinates of all of its vertices. Therefore, we have that $\mathbf{p}(\mathbf{x}) = \mathbf{x}$, $\mathbf{p}(\mathbf{y}) = \mathbf{y}$ and $\mathbf{p}(\mathbf{z}) = \mathbf{z}$.

$$S = basis + coefficients + mean$$
$$S = (l * 3 * n + l * F + 3 * n) * sizeOfDouble \tag{5}$$

*II - PCA Using Differential Coordinates.* In this method we use the Laplacian operator to derive a set of differential coordinates for each mesh of the sequence. Then, in this case $\mathbf{p}(\mathbf{x}) = \delta(\mathbf{x})$, $\mathbf{p}(\mathbf{y}) = \delta(\mathbf{y})$ and $\mathbf{p}(\mathbf{z}) = \delta(\mathbf{z})$. This representation allows the encoding of the local geometric features of the meshes and removes the dependency on the absolute position of the vertices, which is present in the previous approach. The storage cost is equivalent to Equation 5.

*III - PCA on a Layered Mesh Representation.* In order to perform compression of the data, we apply PCA on the *difference sequence* presented in Section 3. Taking into account that the reference skeleton is represented by the position of its joints and that we store rotations in the form of quaternions, the original sequence can then be reconstructed with the following storage cost:

$$S = basis + coefficients + mean + ref.\ skel + joint\ angles + base\ model$$
$$S = (l * 3 * n + l * F + 3 * n + 20 * 3 + 19 * 4 * F + 3 * n) * sizeOfDouble + 3 * T * sizeOfInt$$

## 4.2   Deformation-Based Compression

*IV - Laplacian Deformation.* The 3D video sequence is reconstructed within the Laplacian editing framework. For each mesh, a set of vertex indices are randomly sampled and their positions are fed to the mesh deformer in order to edit a reference mesh subject to those constraints.

$$S = constraints + reference\ mesh$$
$$S = (3 * C * F + 3 * n) * sizeOfDouble + 3 * T * sizeOfInt$$

**V - Laplacian Deformation with a Learnt Deformation Space.** This method uses an enhanced deformer with a learnt deformation basis. This ensures that the result lies within the space of deformations formed by the original sequence. Results of this technique depend on both the number of vectors kept for the basis and the number of constraints used for the deformation. Therefore, two sets of experiments have been undertaken: the first varies the number of constraints and keeps the number of vectors constant ($V_i$), while the second varies the number of vectors for a fixed number of constraints ($V_{ii}$). Specifically, for the former we keep 95% of the energy of the basis and for the latter we take 10% of the vertices as constraints.

$$S = basis + mean + constraints + reference\ mesh$$
$$S = (l * 3 * n + 3 * n + 3 * C * F + 3 * n) * sizeOfDouble + 3 * T * sizeOfInt$$

## 4.3   Statistical Error Measures

In order to characterise the reconstruction error caused by each of the compression techniques, a set of statistical measures are computed. For each mesh, an error vector whose elements contain the Euclidean distance between the original and the reconstructed vertices is constructed. The maximum error and the RMS is computed for each error vector, obtaining an *RMS vector* and a *maximum error vector*, both of length equal to the number of frames of the sequence. Finally, we average the elements of these vectors.

A Monte-Carlo simulation with 15 passes of random vertex samples is performed for each experiment of the deformation-based compression techniques.

**Fig. 3.** Original sequences. Selected frames from the walk sequence (top row), the dance sequence (middle row) and the twirl sequence (bottom row).

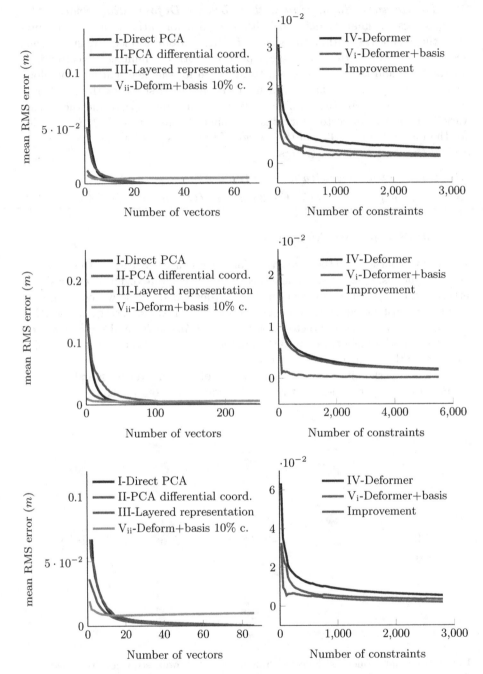

**Fig. 4.** Results for the walk (top), dance (middle) and twirl (bottom). On the left, results for the PCA-based approaches together with the deformation+basis technique with 10% of vertices as constraints and variable number of vectors for the basis. On the right, results of the Laplacian-based approaches.

# 5   Results and Discussion

Evaluation of the compression techniques introduced in this paper is performed on three reconstructed mesh sequences from a public 3D video database [24], depicting different characters and motions. Selected frames of these sequences are shown in Figure 3 and results can be found on Figures 4, 5 and Tables 1, 2.

Comparison between the PCA-based methods shows that representing the mesh in absolute coordinates (direct PCA) leads to the poorest results, since the global position of the mesh is taken into account. The use of differential coordinates provides a translational invariant local representation which is able to capture the spatial correlation of the meshes within a sequence, regardless of their global position. The proposed layered mesh representation provides the best compression results. The *difference sequence* can be considered as a set of displacement vectors between the original sequence and the animated model. This reduces the magnitude of the possible error considerably.

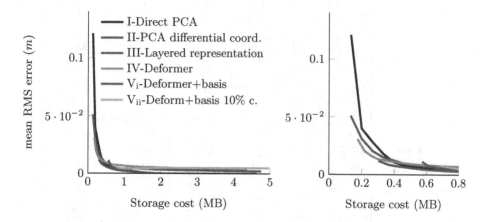

**Fig. 5.** Comparison of the storage cost *vs* committed error for all compression techniques presented in the paper, applied to the walk sequence. The figure on the right shows a close-up for the range 0-0.8MB.

**Table 1.** Compression ratios obtained for the layered mesh representation method when committing an RMS error of less than $5mm$

| Mesh sequence | RMS error (mm) | Original storage cost | Compressed storage cost | Compression ratio |
|---|---|---|---|---|
| Walk | 4.778 | 8.72MB | 0.57MB | 15.30 |
| Dance | 4.724 | 63.59MB | 6.49MB | 9.80 |
| Twirl | 4.741 | 11.23MB | 1.37MB | 8.21 |

**Table 2.** Results. Error is expressed in $mm$ and storage cost in MB. DirectPCA-$k$ = Direct PCA with $k$ basis vectors; LaplPCA-k = PCA using differential coordinates with $k$ basis vectors; LayeredPCA-$k$ = PCA on the *difference sequence* with $k$ basis vectors; Deformer-$c\%$ = Laplacian deformation using $c\%$ vertices as constraints for the deformation. DeformBasis-$c\%$ = Laplacian deformation plus learnt basis with 95% of the energy, using $c\%$ of the vertices as constraints; DeformConstr-$k$ = Laplacian deformation plus learnt space with $k$ basis vectors, using 10% of the vertices as constraints.

| Sequence | Techniques | Avg. RMS error | Avg. max error | Max max error | Storage cost |
|---|---|---|---|---|---|
| Walk 66 frames 2886 vertices 5772 triangles 8.72MB/seq. | DirectPCA-1 | 120.976 | 196.791 | 381.149 | 0.133 |
| | DirectPCA-5 | 10.676 | 11.994 | 31.0303 | 0.399 |
| | DirectPCA-10 | 3.998 | 4.791 | 3.984 | 0.732 |
| | LaplPCA-1 | 50.887 | 49.717 | 124.220 | 0.133 |
| | LaplPCA-5 | 12.214 | 16.294 | 33.911 | 0.399 |
| | LaplPCA-10 | 5.824 | 6.967 | 25.257 | 0.732 |
| | LayeredPCA-1 | 11.836 | 12.894 | 23.933 | 0.304 |
| | LayeredPCA-5 | 4.778 | 5.772 | 16.449 | 0.570 |
| | LayeredPCA-10 | 2.422 | 2.751 | 6.951 | 0.903 |
| | Deformer-5% | 12.434 | 16.907 | 31.897 | 0.344 |
| | Deformer-10% | 8.636 | 13.467 | 24.483 | 0.555 |
| | Deformer-50% | 4.964 | 9.148 | 16.637 | 2.247 |
| | DeformBasis-5% | 5.044 | 4.137 | 8.210 | 0.740 |
| | DeformBasis-10% | 4.147 | 4.065 | 8.074 | 0.951 |
| | DeformBasis-50% | 2.899 | 2.782 | 5.062 | 2.643 |
| | DeformConstr-1 | 7.774 | 5.512 | 4.699 | 0.687 |
| | DeformConstr-5 | 4.147 | 4.065 | 5.538 | 0.951 |
| | DeformConstr-10 | 4.213 | 3.817 | 11.768 | 1.282 |
| Dance 249 frames 5580 vertices 11156 triangles 63.59MB/seq. | DirectPCA-1 | 231.243 | 497.800 | 1303.04 | 0.257 |
| | DirectPCA-40 | 6.930 | 18.169 | 50.257 | 5.312 |
| | DirectPCA-80 | 2.536 | 6.804 | 17.558 | 10.497 |
| | LaplPCA-1 | 147.893 | 353.394 | 1143.910 | 0.257 |
| | LaplPCA-40 | 18.235 | 45.449 | 131.374 | 5.312 |
| | LaplPCA-80 | 8.030 | 19.214 | 50.877 | 10.497 |
| | LayeredPCA-1 | 40.857 | 61.628 | 154.965 | 0.658 |
| | LayeredPCA-40 | 5.701 | 16.118 | 52.839 | 5.713 |
| | LayeredPCA-80 | 2.354 | 6.870 | 19.511 | 10.897 |
| | Deformer-5% | 22.973 | 45.658 | 209.010 | 1.823 |
| | Deformer-10% | 5.983 | 35.429 | 104.905 | 3.390 |
| | Deformer-50% | 2.524 | 15.171 | 56.368 | 15.928 |
| | DeformBasis-5% | 7.022 | 29.112 | 116.499 | 2.589 |
| | DeformBasis-10% | 5.305 | 27.649 | 111.086 | 4.156 |
| | DeformBasis-50% | 2.288 | 11.047 | 53.720 | 16.694 |
| | DeformConstr-1 | 10.358 | 43.670 | 99.466 | 3.645 |
| | DeformConstr-40 | 5.314 | 27.122 | 110.756 | 8.626 |
| | DeformConstr-80 | 5.275 | 28.844 | 116.407 | 13.735 |
| Twirl 86 frames 2854 vertices 5704 triangles 11.23MB/seq. | DirectPCA-1 | 111.794 | 164.110 | 430.787 | 0.131 |
| | DirectPCA-7 | 22.863 | 23.235 | 59.3732 | 0.527 |
| | DirectPCA-14 | 7.165 | 7.237 | 27.146 | 0.989 |
| | LaplPCA-1 | 84.903 | 115.523 | 378.086 | 0.131 |
| | LaplPCA-7 | 22.050 | 19.075 | 36.443 | 0.527 |
| | LaplPCA-14 | 8.428 | 8.783 | 26.323 | 0.989 |
| | LayeredPCA-1 | 36.401 | 36.406 | 93.632 | 0.312 |
| | LayeredPCA-7 | 13.886 | 14.388 | 20.732 | 0.708 |
| | LayeredPCA-14 | 6.259 | 6.990 | 22.253 | 1.170 |
| | Deformer-5% | 21.208 | 31.494 | 117.428 | 0.406 |
| | Deformer-10% | 15.458 | 26.117 | 101.106 | 0.682 |
| | Deformer-50% | 7.543 | 17.286 | 77.156 | 2.886 |
| | DeformBasis-5% | 14.968 | 33.307 | 222.054 | 0.798 |
| | DeformBasis-10% | 9.230 | 10.497 | 53.120 | 1.074 |
| | DeformBasis-50% | 4.470 | 5.265 | 17.507 | 3.278 |
| | DeformConstr-1 | 19.472 | 28.840 | 87.401 | 0.812 |
| | DeformConstr-7 | 9.230 | 10.497 | 53.120 | 1.204 |
| | DeformConstr-14 | 8.188 | 9.793 | 50.643 | 1.662 |

The results of the Laplacian-based approaches demonstrate that the inclusion of the basis in the deformer reduces the compression error when the number of constraints is low, since the learnt space helps the algorithm to find a deformation that is closer to previous examples. Once the number of constraints increases certain threshold, the behaviour of the curves becomes more similar.

Although the deformation-based approaches provide a reduced range of error in comparison to those PCA-based, the decompression step has a much higher computational cost. While reconstructing the meshes using PCA consists in simple matrix multiplications, applying the deformation algorithm means running a costly least-square minimisation process whose complexity is increased with the number of vertices of the meshes involved. For instance, it takes 0.592s to reconstruct frame 20 of the walk sequence (2886 vertices) using 280 constraints.

Figure 5 depicts the error *vs.* the storage cost of all the techniques for the walk sequence. This shows that applying PCA on our layered mesh representation leads to the best compression results. Table 1 shows the compression ratio obtained with this method when committing an RMS error of less than $5mm$. Finally, Table 2 presents a detailed performance analysis for all methods.

## 6  Conclusions

This paper presents an evaluation of compression techniques for 3D video mesh sequences, based on PCA and Laplacian deformation. Deformer-based methods show better performance than the application of PCA on absolute and differential coordinates for high compression ratios. However, they provide a much slower decompression, since a least square minimisation has to be run for each mesh of the sequence.

A novel mesh layered representation which exploits the articulated nature of captured human performance is introduced. This significantly outperforms the previous mesh sequence compression approaches achieving a compression ratio of 8-15 with RMS error $< 5mm$ for captured 3D video sequences of people. It is important to note that although this representation is based on an articulated structure, it can be employed to represent arbitrary surface deformation (such as the loose skirt in the twirl of Figure 3), but will give good compression for sequences with an underlying anatomical articulated motion.

This paper focuses on the shape component of 3D video, future research should also address the compression of multiple view appearance information.

## References

1. de Aguiar, E., Stoll, C., Theobalt, C., Ahmed, N., Seidel, H.P., Thrun, S.: Performance capture from sparse multi-view video. In: ACM SIGGRAPH 2008 Papers (2008)
2. Alexa, M., Müller, W.: Representing Animations by Principal Components. In: EUROGRAPHICS (2000)
3. Amjoun, R., Straßer, W.: Efficient compression of 3D dynamic mesh sequences. Journal of the WSCG 15, 99–106 (2007)

4. Baran, I., Popović, J.: Automatic rigging and animation of 3D characters. ACM Trans. Graph. 26 (2007)
5. Botsch, M., Sorkine, O.: On Linear Variational Surface Deformation Methods. IEEE Trans. on Visualization and Computer Graphics 14(1), 213–230 (2008)
6. Carranza, J., Theobalt, C., Magnor, M.A., Seidel, H.P.: Free-viewpoint video of human actors. In: ACM SIGGRAPH 2003 Papers, pp. 569–577 (2003)
7. Collins, G., Hilton, A.: A rigid transform basis for animation compression and level of detail. In: Vision, Video and Graphics (2005)
8. Collins, G., Hilton, A.: Spatio-Temporal Fusion of Multiple View Video Rate 3D Surfaces. In: Proceedings of the Fifth International Conference on 3-D Digital Imaging and Modeling, pp. 142–149. IEEE Computer Society (2005)
9. Hoppe, H.: Progressive meshes. In: ACM SIGGRAPH 1996 Papers, pp. 99–108 (1996)
10. Huang, P., Budd, C., Hilton, A.: Global temporal registration of multiple non-rigid surface sequences. In: IEEE CVPR 2011, pp. 3473–3480 (2011)
11. Ibarria, L., Rossignac, J.: Dynapack: space-time compression of the 3D animations of triangle meshes with fixed connectivity. In: Proceedings of the 2003 ACM SIGGRAPH/Eurographics Symposium on Computer Animation, pp. 126–135 (2003)
12. Kanade, T., Rander, P., Narayanan, P.J.: Virtualized Reality: Constructing Virtual Worlds from Real Scenes. IEEE MultiMedia 4(1), 34–47 (1997)
13. Karni, Z., Gotsman, C.: Spectral compression of mesh geometry. In: ACM SIGGRAPH 2000 Papers, pp. 279–286 (2000)
14. Karni, Z., Gotsman, C.: Compression of soft-body animation sequences. Computers & Graphics 28(1), 25–34 (2004)
15. Khodakovsky, A., Schröder, P., Sweldens, W.: Progressive geometry compression. In: SIGGRAPH 2000 Papers, pp. 271–278 (2000)
16. Kircher, S., Garland, M.: Free-form motion processing. ACM Trans. Graph. 27(2), 1–13 (2008)
17. Lee, A., Moreton, H., Hoppe, H.: Displaced subdivision surfaces. In: ACM SIGGRAPH 2000 Papers, pp. 85–94 (2000)
18. Lengyel, J.E.: Compression of time-dependent geometry. In: Proceedings of the 1999 Symposium on Interactive 3D Graphics, New York, NY, USA, pp. 89–95 (1999)
19. Muller, K., Smolic, A., Kautzner, M., Eisert, P., Wiegand, T.: Predictive compression of dynamic 3D meshes. In: IEEE International Conference on Image Processing, vol. 1, pp. I–621–4 (2005)
20. Or, D.C., Levin, D., Remez, O.: Progressive Compression of Arbitrary Triangular Meshes. In: Proceedings of the 10th IEEE Visualization 1999 Conference, VIS 1999 (1999)
21. Sattler, M., Sarlette, R., Klein, R.: Simple and efficient compression of animation sequences. In: Proceedings of the 2005 ACM SIGGRAPH/Eurographics Symposium on Computer Animation, pp. 209–217 (2005)
22. Shamir, A., Pascucci, V., Bajaj, C.: Multi-Resolution Dynamic Meshes with Arbitrary Deformations. In: Procs. of the Conference on Visualization 2000, pp. 423–430 (2000)
23. Sorkine, O.: Differential Representations for Mesh Processing. Computer Graphics Forum 25(4), 789–807 (2006)
24. Starck, J., Hilton, A.: Surface Capture for Performance-Based Animation. IEEE Computer Graphics and Applications 27(3), 21–31 (2007)
25. Stefanoski, N., Ostermann, J.: SPC: Fast and Efficient Scalable Predictive Coding of Animated Meshes. Computer Graphics Forum 29(1), 101–116 (2010)

26. Stoll, C., de Aguiar, E., Theobalt, C., Seidel, H.P.: A Volumetric Approach to Interactive Shape Editing. Tech. rep., Max-Planck-Institut fur Informatik (2007)
27. Sumner, R.W., Zwicker, M., Gotsman, C., Popović, J.: Mesh-based inverse kinematics. In: ACM SIGGRAPH 2005 Papers, pp. 488–495 (2005)
28. Tejera, M., Hilton, A.: Space-time editing of 3D video sequences. In: Conference on Visual Media Production, pp. 148–157 (2011)
29. Touma, C., Gotsman, C.: Triangle mesh compression. In: Graphics Interface (1998)
30. Xu, W., Zhou, K., Yu, Y., Tan, Q., Peng, Q., Guo, B.: Gradient domain editing of deforming mesh sequences. ACM Trans. Graph. 26 (2007)

# Spatial Measures between Human Poses for Classification and Understanding

Søren Hauberg[1] and Kim Steenstrup Pedersen[2]

[1] Max Planck Institute for Intelligent Systems, Perceiving Systems
Spermannstrasse, 72076 Tübingen, Germany
soren.hauberg@tue.mpg.de
[2] Dept. of Computer Science, University of Copenhagen
Universitetsparken 1, 2100 Copenhagen, Denmark
kimstp@diku.dk

**Abstract.** Statistical analysis of humans, their motion and their behaviour is a very well-studied problem. With the availability of accurate motion capture systems, it has become possible to use such analysis for animation, understanding, compression and tracking of human motion. At the core of the analysis lies a measure for determining the distance between two human poses; practically always, this measure is the Euclidean distance between joint angle vectors. Recent work [7] has shown that articulated tracking systems can be vastly improved by replacing the Euclidean distance in joint angle space with the geodesic distance in the space of joint positions. However, due to the focus on tracking, no algorithms have, so far, been presented for measuring these distances between human poses.

In this paper, we present an algorithm for computing geodesics in the Riemannian space of joint positions, as well as a fast approximation that allows for large-scale analysis. In the experiments we show that this measure significantly outperforms the traditional measure in classification, clustering and dimensionality reduction tasks.

## 1 Modelling Human Poses

For many years researchers in different research fields have studied image sequences of moving humans and tried to reason about human behaviour. Examples of such reasoning include *articulated tracking* of the individual limbs in the human body [1,6,18,22], *clustering* to e.g. learn a discrete vocabulary of human motion *(visual words)* [5,13], *action recognition* [25] and *dimensionality reduction* [9,19,23]. We also note a focus on statistical analysis of humans in animation [4,21,24] and robotics [17]. Due to the complexity of the human body it is common to use a rather simple body model consisting of only a few selected mass-less bones, which gives the *kinematic skeleton* [3]. This "stick figure" (see fig. 1a) is complex enough to capture many aspects of human behaviour, but simple enough to give tractable algorithms. In the kinematic skeleton, bone lengths are assumed constant such that the *joint angles* between connected bones constitute the only degrees of freedom in the model. It is, thus, common to learn models directly in the space of these joint angles, which can be treated as a Euclidean space. This is computationally efficient, but, as we shall later see, leads to an unnatural distance measure. Alternatively, we can model humans in the space of joint positions, which is more

F.J. Perales, R.B. Fisher, and T.B. Moeslund (Eds.): AMDO 2012, LNCS 7378, pp. 26–36, 2012.

similar to what is actually observed in images of humans. However, the space of joint positions is a non-trivial Riemannian manifold [6], which complicates analysis. In this paper, we provide an algorithm for computing geodesics on this manifold as well as a very efficient approximation scheme. This allows us to perform larger studies, which show that changing the distance measure has profound impact on the performance of the learned models.

## 1.1 Related Work

As previously stated, most of the work concerning analysis of human movement represents the human body with the kinematic skeleton. For a given skeleton, a human pose can be represented by a vector of all joint angles; this vector is often assumed to be Euclidean such that standard techniques apply. From the vector of joint angles, we can compute joint positions by recursively orienting each bone in the skeleton according to the angle vector. This process is known as *forward kinematics* [3]. From a geometric point of view, we can think of forward kinematics as recursively selecting a point on a 2-sphere with centre corresponding to the previous bone end-point and radius corresponding to the bone length.

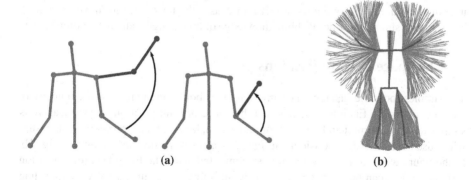

**Fig. 1.** Different distance measures. (a) Two motions of equal size (90°) under the joint angle metric. The example is adapted from [7]. (b) The mean pose and data from a *jumping jack* sequence under the Euclidean joint position distance measure. The resulting mean pose does not respect the skeleton structure of the data.

Letting $\theta$ denote the joint angles of the kinematic skeleton we define the joint angle metric as

$$\text{dist}_\theta(\theta_1, \theta_2) = \|\theta_1 - \theta_2\|_2 \ , \tag{1}$$

i.e. the Euclidean metric in joint angle space. This metric appears frequently in the literature [4, 9, 12, 17–19, 22–24].

In articulated tracking, i.e. sequential pose estimation, the joint angle metric is often used as part of a Gaussian prior to ensure smooth motion estimates, see e.g. [8, 11, 12,

18]. When learning activity specific priors, the angle metric is also used for comparing training data, e.g. for learning Gaussian Process Latent Variable Models [22–24] and for manifold learning techniques [9,19]. Furthermore, these learning schemes also often use the angle metric for regularisation purposes.

The angle metric is often used due to its simplicity, but, as pointed out by Hauberg et al. [7], it has little relation to the *visual* size of the motion. Fig. 1a shows two different motions that all have the same size under the joint angle metric, as only one joint angle has been changed 90 degrees. The motions, however, appear to have different size, with the motion on the left appearing larger than the motion on the right. This behaviour is due to the fact that the angle metric ignores the structure of the skeleton, i.e. the size of the bones as well as how they are connected to each other.

In robotics and computer vision it is common to use *twists and exponential maps* [1, 10] instead of joint angles. This has great practical impact on, e.g., optimisation, but the underlying distance measure still ignores bone lengths and connectivity. The same can be said for *quaternion* [3] representations.

An alternative metric was suggested by Tournier et al. [21] for the purpose of *motion compression*. This measure treats the kinematic skeleton as a product of one sphere per bone, such that the metric is the sum of distances on $SO(3)$. This measure incorporates knowledge of bone lengths and has a simple physical interpretation as it works in the world coordinate system. The measure, however, ignores how bones are connected, i.e. it cannot capture that moving the upper arm causes the lower arm to move as well. A better metric should incorporate both knowledge of bone lengths and bone connectivity.

## 2   The Space of Joint Positions

The simplest possible distance measure that takes both bone lengths and connectivity into account is the Euclidean distance in the space of joint positions. This measure is simple, easy to interpret and fast to compute. It can, however, be a problematic measure when used for statistics; consider the *jumping jacks* sequence data shown in fig. 1b. In the figure we also show the mean pose computed using the Euclidean joint position distance and as can be seen the limbs of the mean pose are substantially smaller than those found in the original data. Clearly, the choice of distance measure has resulted in statistics that fail to preserve the skeleton structure.

The immediate solution is to perform analysis in the Euclidean space, but with the restriction that only parts of space corresponding to a valid skeleton configuration is allowed. The *kinematic manifold* [6] is exactly this part of the Euclidean space. The manifold $\mathcal{M}$ is defined as the space of all possible joint positions,

$$\mathcal{M} = \{F(\theta) \mid \theta \in \Theta\} \ , \tag{2}$$

where $F$ is the *forward kinematics function*, i.e. the function that maps from joint *angles* to joint *positions*, and $\Theta$ is the set of legal joint angles, i.e. it encodes joint constraints. This is a Riemannian manifold embedded in $\mathbb{R}^{3L}$, where $L$ is the number of joints in the skeleton [6]. As such, $F(\theta)$ is simply the vector containing the position of all joints at the pose $\theta$. The manifold structure arises due to the constraint that connected joints have a fixed distance between them. This means that any point on $\mathcal{M}$ will be a valid skeleton, i.e. it will respect both bone lengths and joint constraints. If we confine our statistics to this manifold, we avoid the problems of working directly in the Euclidean space of joint positions.

As discussed in [7], the geodesic distance on $\mathcal{M}$ between two poses $\theta_0$ and $\theta_N$ is the visually natural measure of the length of the spatial curves $c$ that joints move along, i.e.

$$\text{dist}_{\mathcal{M}}(\theta_0, \theta_N) = \min_{\substack{c(\tau) \in \mathcal{M}, \\ c(0) = F(\theta_0), \\ c(1) = F(\theta_N)}} \mathcal{L}(c) \ , \tag{3}$$

where $\mathcal{L}$ denotes the length of a curve $c$, i.e.

$$\mathcal{L}(c) = \int_0^1 \left\| \frac{\partial c(\tau)}{\partial \tau} \right\| d\tau \ , \tag{4}$$

As the geodesic curve $c$ is restricted to $\mathcal{M}$ any point on the curve is a valid skeleton, which makes the measure different from the ordinary Euclidean measure in joint position space.

While the distance measure in eq. 3 provides a natural notion of the "size" of a movement between two poses, no practical algorithms have yet been provided for computing this distance and the corresponding geodesics.

## 2.1 Computing Geodesics and Distances

In order to compute geodesics, and hence distances, between two poses, we need to minimise the integral in eq. 4. This can be vastly simplied by utilising that extremal points of eq. 3 coincides with extremal points of the *curve energy* [2],

$$\mathcal{E}(c) = \int_0^1 \left\| \frac{\partial c(\tau)}{\partial \tau} \right\|^2 d\tau \ . \tag{5}$$

To compute a geodesic, we can, thus, iteratively evolve an initial curve $c$ towards a curve minimizing eq. 5. To do this, we discretise a given initial curve $c$ connecting $\theta_0$ and $\theta_N$ by sampling $N - 1$ points between $\theta_0$ and $\theta_N$. The curve is, thus, approximated by $\hat{c} = \{\theta_0 : \theta_N\} = \{\theta_0, \ldots, \theta_N\}$. We can then compute the energy of this discrete curve as

$$\mathcal{E}(\theta_0 : \theta_N) \approx \sum_{n=1}^{N} \|F(\theta_{n-1}) - F(\theta_n)\|^2 \ , \tag{6}$$

which is a straight-forward discretisation of the integral in eq. 5. In order to minimise eq. 6 we then seek the set of intermediate points $\theta_1 : \theta_{N-1}$ that minimises $\mathcal{E}$.

The derivative of the approximate curve energy can be computed in closed-form as (derived in appendix A)

$$\frac{\partial \mathcal{E}}{\partial \theta_i} = 2\big(F(\theta_{i-1}) - F(\theta_{i+1})\big)^T \mathbf{J}_{\theta_i} \ , \tag{7}$$

where $\mathbf{J}_{\theta_i} = \frac{\partial F}{\partial \theta_i}$ is the Jacobian of $F$ evaluated in $\theta_i$, which can easily be computed in closed-form, cf. [26]. With this, we perform minimisation using a trust-region gradient descent algorithm.

## 2.2    Approximations and the Geometry of the Kinematic Manifold

One problem with the presented algorithm for computing geodesics is that it can be rather time consuming due to its iterative nature. In most statistical computations we need to repeatedly calculate distances, so this quickly becomes a bottleneck. We, thus, look for fast alternatives that do not rely on an iterative optimisation. For this we take a closer look at the geometry of the kinematic manifold.

The strength of the joint angle metric is that it is just the Euclidean metric in joint angle space, which makes it fast and easy to compute. As discussed above, and as will be illustrated by our experiments, this metric does, however, not model human pose data well. Another issue with this metric is that it is dependent on the choice of root node in the kinematic skeleton, whereas the joint position metric is not.

Our approximation of the geodesic curve on the kinematic manifold utilizes the simplicity of computing the joint angle metric for a particular choice of root node in the kinematic skeleton. As we shall see, this choice turns out to be a good approximation for the geodesic *curve* in joint position space, even though the corresponding *distances* – joint angle distance and joint position distance – are vastly different. This choice of approximation rests on the following geometric considerations.

The simplest case of a kinematic manifold is when the skeleton only has one bone. In this case the kinematic manifold reduces to the well-known 2-sphere in $\mathbb{R}^3$, as is illustrated in the left of fig. 2. When the sphere is parametrised using angles, it is well-known that geodesics in the joint position metric will form straight lines in the angle space.

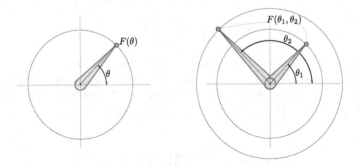

**Fig. 2.** Illustrations of the kinematic manifold for simple skeletons. *Left:* for skeletons with only one bone, the kinematic manifold is a sphere, where the centre coincides with the root of the skeleton. *Right:* for skeletons with two bones we can place the root of the skeleton at the joint connecting the two bones. The kinematic manifold then corresponds to the product of two spheres with a shared centre.

The situation is similarly simple when the skeleton has two bones. If we pick the root of the skeleton as the joint that connects the two bones, then the kinematic manifold is the product of two spheres with a shared centre that coincides with the root, see the right of fig. 2. If we consider geodesics in the joint position metric, then it is again clear that it will consist of straight lines in the joint angle space representing the two spheres.

These observations provide us with the hint that many geodesics in the joint position metric form straight lines in joint angle space. As the kinematic manifold is Riemannian, we know that the metric tensor varies smoothly, such that we most often will see smooth changes in geodesics when the end-points move. Hence, we will use the straight line in joint angle space connecting the end-points as an approximation of the geodesic, i.e. $c_{\text{line}} = \{\theta_0, \frac{1}{N}\theta_0 + \frac{N-1}{N}\theta_N, \ldots, \theta_N\}$. This path is a geodesic under the joint angle metric and the $SO(3)$ product metric suggested by Tournier et al. [21], but the actual geodesic lengths differ. It is worth noting that when using the length of non-geodesic curves as a distance measure, we are not guaranteed that the measure satisfies the triangle inequality. In many practical scenarios this is, however, acceptable; see e.g. the work on metric learning by Ramanan and Baker [14] where straight lines are also used to approximate geodesics.

As we shall see in sec. 3.1, the suggested curve turns out to be a very good approximation of the true geodesic. As this approximation does not require any iterative optimisation it can be computed very fast, which allows for large scale experiments.

## 3    Experiments

The purpose of the experiments is to show that the approximate spatial geodesic distance improves different machine learning tasks, such as dimensionality reduction, clustering and classification. Here we focus on rather simple techniques as these are most well-understood, allowing us to easier analyse the impact of changing the distance measure. We will use data collected with an optical motion capture system as large datasets with different people and activities are readily available online[1].

In all experiments we only consider the human pose and disregard global position and orientation.

### 3.1    Quality of Geodesic Approximation

Our first experiment is concerned with how well the approximate geodesic curve, described in sec. 2.2, approximates the true geodesic. This turns out to be a good approximation of the true geodesic, but it is much faster to compute.

As a first qualitative experiment we pick two random poses from a *walking* sequence, form the approximate geodesic curve $c_{\text{line}}$ as described in sec. 2.2, and compute the length minimising geodesic curve $c_{\text{geodesic}}$ using the approach described in sec. 2.1. We discretise the curves using 10 sample points and compute the first two principal components of the discrete points, which allows us to visualise the curves, cf. fig. 3a. In the figure, the background is colour coded with the trace of the local metric tensor, which can be considered a measure of the local curvature of $\mathcal{M}$. The expression for the metric tensor is derived in appendix B. We visually see that the approximate geodesic curve is very similar to the length-minimising geodesic.

---

[1] We use the Carnegie Mellon dataset from http://mocap.cs.cmu.edu/

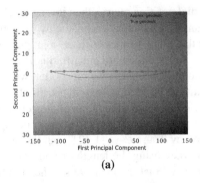 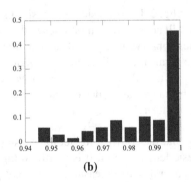

(a)                                              (b)

**Fig. 3.** (a) A visualisation of the geodesic path and the straight-line approximation. The coordinate system are the first two principal components of the sample points along the curves expressed in joint angles. Notice the size of the $y$-axis compared to the $x$-axis; this is an indication that the two curves are very similar. The background colouring of each point is proportional to the trace of the local metric tensor expressed in joint angles, i.e. a measure of the local curvature of $\mathcal{M}$. (b) A histogram over the ratio in eq. 8. Notice that the smallest observed value of this ratio is 0.94, which tells us that the approximation is quite good.

Next, we seek to quantify the above observations. Given an approximate geodesic and a length minimising geodesic between two poses, we can measure how much they differ as

$$r = \frac{\mathcal{L}(c_{\text{geodesic}})}{\mathcal{L}(c_{\text{line}})} \ . \tag{8}$$

As the length of the true geodesic is shorter than or equal to the length of the approximate curve $r \in [0, 1]$. In fig. 3b we show a histogram of the ratios for 100 random pairs of poses. As can be seen, the ratio is always very close to 1, and the lowest observed ratio is 0.94, which tells us that the approximation curve is indeed quite good. In practice, the true geodesic distance is too expensive to compute in large studies, so we only consider the approximation in the remaining parts of the paper.

### 3.2 Dimensionality Reduction

One of the most basic machine learning tasks is to learn a low-dimensional model from high-dimensional data. The most basic model for such dimensionality reduction tasks is *principal component analysis*, which can be generalised to metric spaces, such as Riemannian manifolds, with *multidimensional scaling (MDS)* [15]. This algorithm finds the Euclidean representation of a set of points that preserve pair-wise distances of the original data as well as possible.

As a first *qualitative* experiment we consider two sequences corresponding to the walk cycles of two people. We then compute the first two principal components of this data according to the angular metric and the geodesic approximation of the joint position metric. In fig. 4a we show the results for the angular metric. As can be seen, the learned model is essentially bimodal, where each mode corresponds to the two different persons. As such, the model fails to capture any similarity between the walking styles, i.e. we cannot expect this model to generalise to new people. In fig. 4b we show the comparable results for the geodesic approximation of the joint position metric. We see that the resulting model is essentially unimodal, which indicates that the learned model has captured the similarities between the two different walking styles.

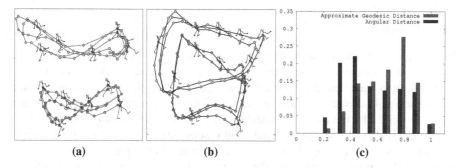

**(a)**            **(b)**            **(c)**

**Fig. 4.** (a)–(b) Illustration of results attained for the different metrics when using multidimensional scaling for dimensionality reduction; (a) show results for the angular metric and (b) the spatial distance. The colours indicate different persons. Note how the angular metric fails to capture any similarity between the different walking styles. (c) A histogram of the percentage of data explained by the first principal component under the two different metrics. The approximate geodesic distance significantly outperforms the angular distance measure according to a Mann–Whitney $U$-test. *These figures are best viewed in colour.*

In order to quantify the above observations, we measure how large a percentage of the data is captured by the first principal component under the different distance measures. We do this for 673 independent sequences and show a histogram of these percentages in fig. 4c. For the results under the joint angle metric we see a mode of explaining 40% of the data, whereas the mode is at 80% under the approximate joint position geodesic distance. Using a Mann–Whitney $U$-test we see that the approximate joint position geodesic distance model significantly explains more of the data in the first component than the angular distance model ($p$-value below $10^{-6}$). This is a strong indication that the approximate geodesic distance is better for dimensionality reduction than the angular distance measure. It is worth noting that we have performed similar experiments with other dimensionality reduction techniques, such as Isomap [20], and see similar behaviour.

### 3.3 Classification

Another classical machine learning task is that of classification. To illustrate the impact of the choice of distance measure, we pick a simple two-class problem consisting of distinguishing *walking* from *running*. As we use motion capture data, we can expect little noise, so we expect this problem to be easily solved. We randomly select 10 walking and 10 running sequences, and, in a leave-one-out fashion, test on 1 walking sequence and train on the 19 remaining. We down-sample the sequences to 12Hz such that we in total use 1096 data points. We choose to use the nearest neighbour classifier to maximum stress on the choice of metric.

For this trivial classification problem, the approximate geodesic distance achieves 100% success rate, which clearly illustrates that the problem is not particularly hard. The angular metric, on the other hand, only achieves a 90% success rate, which is a very disappointing result that shows the limits of the joint angle metric.

## 3.4  Clustering

The last classical machine learning task we consider is that of clustering. Again, the choice of distance measure can potentially have a large impact on the results attained as this is often what determines whether two data points belong to the same cluster. We pick a simple clustering technique that introduces little extra knowledge other than what is provided by the metric. Specifically, we use the *medioid–shift* algorithm [16] with a Gaussian kernel, where the bandwidth is selected to achieve the correct number of clusters. We use the same data as in the classification example, i.e. 10 walking sequences and 10 running sequences. We combine all pairs of sequences from different classes, which gives us 100 clustering tasks with two clusters. We then measure the percentage of data points assigned to the correct class and report the average. When using the angle metric we assign 60% of the data to the correct class and 65% when using the approximate joint position geodesic distance, which is a small but noticeable improvement.

## 4  Discussion

In this paper, we have provided a novel algorithm for computing geodesics on the kinematic manifold for representing joint positions in human skeleton models. This provides a mathematically well-founded and visually natural distance measure for comparing human poses. This algorithm, however, depends on iterative optimisation, which can make it impractical for large studies. For this reason, we have also provided a fast and accurate algorithm for approximating the geodesics. In our experiments this approximation only differs slightly from the true geodesic. More thorough experiements in this direction would, however, be interesting.

In the experimental part of the paper, we perform a number of comparisons of the new metric with the standard joint angle measure, which is used practically everywhere else in the literature. The experiments included the classical machine learning tasks clustering, classification and dimensionality reduction. In all cases we saw improved results. Sometimes the improvements are drastic, as in the case of dimensionality reduction, and other times the improvements are minor, as in the case of clustering. However, in general we see improvements in all experiments. As the suggested measure can be computed efficiently, we see little reason to use the standard joint angle measure in the future.

**Acknowledgements.** S.H. would like to thank the Villum Foundation for financial support.

# References

1. Bregler, C., Malik, J., Pullen, K.: Twist based acquisition and tracking of animal and human kinematics. International Journal of Computer Vision 56, 179–194 (2004)
2. Carmo, M.P.D.: Differential Geometry of Curves and Surfaces. Prentice Hall (1976)
3. Erleben, K., Sporring, J., Henriksen, K., Dohlmann, H.: Physics Based Animation. Charles River Media (August 2005)
4. Grochow, K., Martin, S.L., Hertzmann, A., Popović, Z.: Style-based inverse kinematics. ACM Transaction on Graphics 23(3), 522–531 (2004)
5. Guerra-Filho, G., Aloimonos, Y.: A language for human action. Computer 40, 42–51 (2007)
6. Hauberg, S., Sommer, S., Pedersen, K.S.: Gaussian-Like Spatial Priors for Articulated Tracking. In: Daniilidis, K., Maragos, P., Paragios, N. (eds.) ECCV 2010, Part I. LNCS, vol. 6311, pp. 425–437. Springer, Heidelberg (2010)
7. Hauberg, S., Sommer, S., Pedersen, K.S.: Natural metrics and least-committed priors for articulated tracking. In: Image and Vision Computing (2011)
8. Kjellström, H., Kragić, D., Black, M.J.: Tracking people interacting with objects. In: IEEE CVPR (2010)
9. Lu, Z., Carreira-Perpinan, M., Sminchisescu, C.: People Tracking with the Laplacian Eigenmaps Latent Variable Model. In: NIPS, vol. 20, pp. 1705–1712. MIT Press (2008)
10. Murray, R.M., Li, Z., Sastry, S.S.: A Mathematical Introduction to Robotic Manipulation. CRC Press (March 1994)
11. Poon, E., Fleet, D.J.: Hybrid monte carlo filtering: Edge-based people tracking. In: IEEE Workshop on Motion and Video Computing, p. 151 (2002)
12. Poppe, R.: Vision-based human motion analysis: An overview. Computer Vision and Image Understanding 108(1-2), 4–18 (2007)
13. Priyamvada, K.K., Kahol, K., Tripathi, P., Panchanathan, S.: Automated gesture segmentation from dance sequences. In: Int. Conf. on Automatic Face and Gesture Recognition (2004)
14. Ramanan, D., Baker, S.: Local distance functions: a taxonomy, new algorithms, and an evaluation. TPAMI (4) (2011)
15. Ripley, B.D.: Pattern recognition and neural networks. Cambridge University Press (1996)
16. Sheikh, Y.A., Khan, E.A., Kanade, T.: Mode-seeking by medoidshifts. In: IEEE 11th International Conference on Computer Vision, pp. 1–8 (2007)
17. Shon, A.P., Grochow, K., Rao, R.P.: Robotic imitation from human motion capture using Gaussian processes (2005)
18. Sidenbladh, H., Black, M.J., Fleet, D.J.: Stochastic Tracking of 3D Human Figures Using 2D Image Motion. In: Vernon, D. (ed.) ECCV 2000, Part II. LNCS, vol. 1843, pp. 702–718. Springer, Heidelberg (2000)
19. Sminchisescu, C., Jepson, A.: Generative modeling for continuous non-linearly embedded visual inference. In: ICML 2004, pp. 759–766. ACM (2004)
20. Tenenbaum, J.B., Silva, V., Langfor, J.C.: A global geometric framework for nonlinear dimensionality reduction. Science 290(5500), 2319–2323 (2000)
21. Tournier, M., Wu, X., Courty, N., Arnaud, E., Reveret, L.: Motion compression using principal geodesics analysis. Computer Graphics Forum 28(2), 355–364 (2009)
22. Urtasun, R., Fleet, D.J., Fua, P.: 3D People Tracking with Gaussian Process Dynamical Models. In: IEEE CVPR, pp. 238–245 (2006)
23. Urtasun, R., Fleet, D.J., Hertzmann, A., Fua, P.: Priors for people tracking from small training sets. In: ICCV, vol. 1, pp. 403–410 (2005)
24. Wang, J.M., Fleet, D.J., Hertzmann, A.: Gaussian Process Dynamical Models for Human Motion. IEEE PAMI 30(2), 283–298 (2008)

25. Yao, A., Gal, J., Fanelli, G., van Gool, L.: Does human action recognition benefit from pose estimation? In: BMVC (2011)
26. Zhao, J., Badler, N.I.: Inverse kinematics positioning using nonlinear programming for highly articulated figures. ACM Transaction on Graphics 13(4), 313–336 (1994)

## A    Derivative of Curve Energy

We remind the reader that the energy of a curve on $\mathcal{M}$ is approximated as

$$\mathcal{E}(\theta_0 : \theta_N) \approx \sum_{n=1}^{N} \|F(\theta_{n-1}) - F(\theta_n)\|^2 . \tag{9}$$

As this function only depends on $\theta_1 : \theta_{N-1}$, the gradient can be written as

$$\nabla \mathcal{E} = \begin{pmatrix} \frac{\partial \mathcal{E}}{\partial \theta_1} \\ \vdots \\ \frac{\partial \mathcal{E}}{\partial \theta_{N-1}} \end{pmatrix} . \tag{10}$$

Each of these partial derivatives can easily be computed using the chain rule, which gives us

$$\frac{\partial \mathcal{E}}{\partial \theta_i} = \frac{\partial}{\partial \theta_i} \|F(\theta_{i-1}) - F(\theta_i)\|^2 + \frac{\partial}{\partial \theta_i} \|F(\theta_i) - F(\theta_{i+1})\|^2 \tag{11}$$

$$= 2\big((F(\theta_{i-1}) - F(\theta_i)) + (F(\theta_i) - F(\theta_{i+1}))\big)^T \mathbf{J}_{\theta_i} \tag{12}$$

$$= 2\big(F(\theta_{i-1}) - F(\theta_{i+1})\big)^T \mathbf{J}_{\theta_i} , \tag{13}$$

where $\mathbf{J}_{\theta_i} = \frac{\partial F}{\partial \theta_i}$ is the Jacobian of $F$ evaluated in $\theta_i$. This can easily be computed in closed-form, cf. [26].

## B    The Metric Tensor of $\mathcal{M}$ in Angle Space

The background colour of fig. 3a is the trace of the metric tensor of $\mathcal{M}$ expressed in the joint angle space. The metric tensor is in itself an interesting object so we derive it here.

The length of a curve $c(t) : [0, 1] \to \Theta$ measured on $\mathcal{M}$ is defined as

$$\mathcal{L}(c) = \int_0^1 \left\| \frac{\partial F(c(t))}{\partial t} \right\| dt = \int_0^1 \left\| \frac{\partial F(c(t))}{\partial c(t)} \frac{\partial c(t)}{\partial t} \right\| dt \tag{14}$$

$$= \int_0^1 \|\mathbf{J}_{c(t)} c'(t)\| dt = \int_0^1 \sqrt{c'(t)^T \mathbf{J}_{c(t)}^T \mathbf{J}_{c(t)} c'(t)} dt , \tag{15}$$

where $\mathbf{J}_{c(t)}$ is the Jacobian of $F$ evaluated at $c(t)$ and $c'(t)$ is the derivative of $c$ with respect to $t$. Eq. 15 tells us that the metric tensor of $\mathcal{M}$ at a point $\theta$ in joint angle space is given by $\mathbf{J}_\theta^T \mathbf{J}_\theta$.

# Real-Time Pose Estimation
# Using Constrained Dynamics

Rune Havnung Bakken[1] and Adrian Hilton[2]

[1] Faculty of Informatics and e-Learning,
Sør-Trøndelag University College, Trondheim, Norway
`rune.h.bakken@hist.no`
[2] Centre for Vision, Speech and Signal Processing,
University of Surrey, Guildford, UK
`a.hilton@surrey.ac.uk`

**Abstract.** Pose estimation in the context of human motion analysis is
the process of approximating the body configuration in each frame of a
motion sequence. We propose a novel pose estimation method based on
fitting a skeletal model to tree structures built from skeletonised visual
hulls reconstructed from multi-view video. The pose is estimated independently in each frame, hence the method can recover from errors in
previous frames, which overcomes some problems of tracking. Publically
available datasets were used to evaluate the method. On real data the
method performs at a framerate of ~ 14 fps. Using synthetic data the
positions of the joints were determined with a mean error of ~6 cm.

**Keywords:** Pose estimation, real-time, model fitting.

## 1 Introduction

Human motion capture is the process of registering human movement over a
period of time. Accurately capturing human motion is a complex task with
many possible applications, like automatic surveillance, input for animation in
the entertainment industry and biomechanical analysis.

In some application areas it is important that the data aquisition is unconstrained by the markers or wearable sensors tradionally used in commercial motion capture systems. Furthermore, there is a need for low latency and real-time
performance in some applications, for instance in perceptive user interfaces and
gait recognition.

Computer vision-based motion capture is a highly active field of research, as
recent surveys by Moeslund et al. [11] and Poppe [13] show. Within the computer vision community the shape-from-silhouette approach has been popular
for multi-camera setups. The visual hull is an overestimate of the volume oc-
cupied by the subject, and is reconstructed from silhouette images covering the
scene from different viewpoints.

Moeslund et al. [11] define pose estimation as the process of approximating
the configuration of the underlying skeletal structure that governs human motion

F.J. Perales, R.B. Fisher, and T.B. Moeslund (Eds.): AMDO 2012, LNCS 7378, pp. 37–46, 2012.
© Springer-Verlag Berlin Heidelberg 2012

in one or more frames. The curve-skeleton is a simplified 1D representation of a 3D object, and skeletonisation yields an approximation of the curve-skeleton. By skeletonising the visual hull and fitting a kinematic model to the resulting skeleton the pose of the subject can be estimated.

In a tracking framework temporal correspondences between body parts from one frame to the next are found, and information from previous frames can be used to predict configurations in future frames. A problem with many tracking approaches is that they can get stuck in invalid configurations and not automatically recover.

**Goal:** the overall goal of the research presented in this paper is to develop a robust, real-time pose estimation method.

**Contribution:** we present a pose estimation method based on fitting a skeletal model to skeletonised voxel data. The joint configuration of the model is independently estimated in each frame, which overcomes limitations of tracking, and fascilitates automatic initialisation and recovery from erroneous estimates. The method achieves real-time performance on a variety of motion sequences.

This paper is organised as follows: in Sect. 2 relevant work by other researchers is examined. The proposed pose estimation method is detailed in section 3. Results of experiments with the proposed method are presented in Sect. 4, and the strengths and limitations of the approach are discussed in Sect. 5. Sect. 6 concludes the paper.

## 2   Related Work

The motion of the human body is governed by the skeleton, a rigid, articulated structure. Recovering this structure from image evidence is a common approach in computer vision based motion capture, and fitting a kinematic model to skeletal data is an approach taken by several researchers.

The pose estimation framework described by Moschini and Fusiello [12] used the hierarchical iterative closest point algorithm to fit a stick figure model to a set of data points on the skeleton curve. The method can recover from errors in matching, but requires manual initialisation. The approach presented by Menier et al. [9] uses Delauney triangulation to extract a set of skeleton points from a closed surface visual hull representation. A generative skeletal model is fitted to the data skeleton points using maximum a posteriori estimation. The method is fairly robust, even for sequences with fast motion. A tracking and pose estimation framework where Laplacian Eigenmaps were used to segment voxel data and extract a skeletal structure consisting of spline curves was presented by Sundaresan and Chellappa [15]. These approaches do not achieve real-time performance.

A comparison of real-time pose estimation methods was presented by Michoud et al. [10]. Their findings were that real-time initialisation was a feature lacking from other approaches. Michoud et al.'s own approach has automatic initialisation and pose estimation with a framerate of around 30 fps. Their approach relies on finding skin-coloured blobs in the visual hull to identify the face and hands. This places restrictions on the clothing of the subject and the start pose, as well as requiring the camera system to be colour calibrated.

The real-time tracking framework presented by Caillette et al. [4] used variable length Markov models. Basic motion patterns were extracted from training sequences and used to train the classifier. The method includes automatic initialisation and some degree of recovery from errors, but as with all training based approaches it is sensitive to over-fitting to the training data, and recognition is limited by the types of motion that were used during the training phase.

Straka et al. [14] recently presented a real-time skeletal graph based pose estimation approach. Using distance matrices they identified the extremities, and used an automated skinning procedure to fit a skeletal model to the graph. This method will be discussed further in Sect. 5.

# 3 Approach

In this section, we will detail the steps in the proposed pose estimation method, starting with the input data, and ending up with a skeletal model with a joint configuration representing the subject's pose during the motion sequence.

## 3.1 Data Aquisition

It is natural to represent the human body using a tree structure. The head, torso and limbs form a tree-like hierarchy. If the nodes in the tree are given positions in Euclidean space the tree describes a unique pose. We employ the data aquisition procedure described in [2]. A volumetric visual hull is skeletonised, and a tree structure is built from the skeleton voxels. Next, the extremities (hands, feet, and head) are identified, and the tree segmented into body parts. Finally, a vector pointing forward is estimated and used to label the hands and feet as left or right. An example labelled data tree is shown in Fig. 1a.

## 3.2 Skeletal Model

In a fashion similar to [5] we build a model of the human skeleton by parsing the data in the CMU motion capture database (mocap.cs.cmu.edu). The CMU database contains 2605 motion capture sequences of 144 subjects. All the skeleton files in the database are parsed, and the mean lengths for a subset of the bones calculated. The skeletal model consists of a bone hierarchy where the length of each bone is calculated by multiplying the bone ratio with an estimate of the stature of the subject. The skeletal model and bone ratios are shown in Fig. 1b and 1c, respectively.

During model fitting the length of each bone is computed by multiplying the ratios with an estimate of the subject's stature. The geodesic distance from toe tip to the top of the head would be an overestimate of the stature. Instead the tree is traversed upwards, and node groups corresponding to each bone created. The stature is calculated by summing up the Euclidean distances between the first and last nodes in each node group.

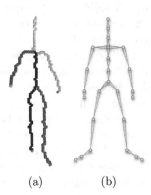

| Bone | Ratio | Bone | Ratio |
|---|---|---|---|
| Head | 0.042 | Upper spine | 0.050 |
| Upper neck | 0.042 | Lower spine | 0.050 |
| Lower neck | 0.042 | Hip | 0.061 |
| Shoulder | 0.085 | Thigh | 0.172 |
| Upper arm | 0.124 | Lower leg | 0.184 |
| Lower arm | 0.121 | Foot | 0.050 |
| Hand | 0.029 | Toe | 0.025 |
| Thorax | 0.050 | | |

(a)        (b)                              (c)

**Fig. 1.** (a) Labelled data tree. (b) Skeletal model. (c) Ratios between limb lengths and estimated stature.

### 3.3   Model Fitting

As discussed in Sect. 2 fitting a model to skeletal data is not a completely novel idea, however, it is in general not achieved in real-time. An optimisation approach that minimises some cost function between the model and the data is typically too computationally expensive.

A possible alternative to the optimisation approach is to use an inverse kinematics (IK) type method to align the model with the data. The end effectors could be placed at the positions of the extremities in the data tree, and the intermediate joints placed as close to their respective branches as possible. Commonly used IK techniques [3], however, offers poor control of intermediate joints, and are difficult to adapt for this purpose. Tang et al. [16] demonstrated that constrained dynamics is a viable alternative to IK for handling intermediate joints in motion capture data.

**The SHAKE Constraint Algorithm.** Constraints on bodies that obey the Newtonian laws of motion can be satisfied using a constraint algorithm. One possible approach is to introduce explicit constraint forces and minimise them using Lagrange multipliers. A stiff bond between two bodies $i$ and $j$ is called a holonomic constraint and has the form:

$$\sigma(t) = |r_{ij}(t)|^2 - l_{ij}^2 = 0 \tag{1}$$

where $r_{ij}$ is the vector between the two bodies and $l$ is the desired distance between them.

Lagrange-type constraint forces are assumed to act along the interbody vectors from the previous time step $r_{ij}^k$, and are used to update the position $r_i''$ at time $k + 1$ after unconstrained motion has displaced a body to $r_i'$. The constraint satisfaction procedure can be seen in Alg. 1. For more details on the SHAKE algorithm, see Kastenmeier and Vesely [8] and Tang et al. [16].

---

**Algorithm 1.** SHAKE

---

1: **while** $\sigma_c > \varepsilon_{local}$ and $\dfrac{1}{n}\displaystyle\sum_{c=1}^{n}\sigma_c > \varepsilon_{global}$ and $k < max\_iter$ **do**

2:   **for** each constraint $c$ **do**

3:     Compute $\sigma'_c \equiv \sigma_c(r'_{ij}) \equiv |r'_{ij}|^2 - l_{ij}^2$.

4:     Compute the Lagrange factor $a$ from the requirement $\sigma''_c = 0$:

$$a = \frac{\sigma'_c \mu}{2r^k_{ij} \cdot r'_{ij}}, \text{ where } 1/\mu \equiv 1/m_i + 1/m_j.$$

5:     Adjust the positions of $i$ and $j$ using:

$$r''_i = r'_i + \frac{a}{m_i}r^k_{ij}$$

$$r''_j = r'_j - \frac{a}{m_j}r^k_{ij}$$

6:   **end for**

7: **end while**

---

Tang et al. [16] demonstrated that SHAKE requires few iterations to converge, and the computational complexity is $O(n)$, where $n$ is the number of constraints. We propose to extend the SHAKE method with constraints that keep the intermediate joints close to their corresponding positions in the data.

**Model Fitting Algorithm.** Distance constraints are created for each pair of neighbouring joints in the model, and their lengths are calculated using the ratios in Fig. 1c. Additionally, constraints are needed to place each joint at its approximate location in the data.

Fitting a straight line to a set of data points with orthogonal distance regression (ODR) is a computationally inexpensive operation. Constraining a joint to lie on a line fitted to the data points around the joint's location in the data is a reasonable approximation to the optimal fit of the joint.

A line constraint is simulated by introducing a dummy rigid body with infinite mass and using a distance constraint with unit length, as seen in Fig. 2. For the line constraints the vector $r'_{ij}$ is replaced with $\rho v$ (where $j$ is the dummy rigid body, $\rho$ is a constant, and $v$ is the unit normal from $i$ to the line), and the position of $i$ is adjusted using:

$$\sigma'_c = |\rho v|^2 - 1, \quad a = \frac{\sigma'_c}{2v \cdot (\rho v)}, \quad r''_i = r'_i + av$$

This has the effect of gradually moving the joint $i$ towards the line, while the normal distance constraints between joints are satisfied. The constant $\rho$ controls the rate of change from one iteration to the next. Since the mass of the dummy rigid body is infinite its position is not explicitly updated.

The data around the shoulders and hips is not reliable. Due to artefacts of skeletonisation, the limbs can be shortened if the legs are close together or the arms close to the torso. To compensate for the missing shoulder and hip data, lines are fitted to the torso instead and displaced along the mediolateral axis.

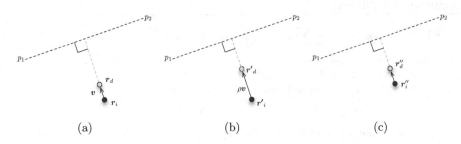

**Fig. 2.** Simulating a line constraint using a dummy rigid body $r_d$ and distance constraint. (a) The constraint vector $v$ is a unit vector in the direction of the normal from the joint $i$ to the line. (b) The unconstrained inter-body vector is set to $\rho v$, essentially moving the dummy rigid body towards the line. (c) SHAKE updates the position of $i$ moving it towards the line.

Since the torso can be twisted, two mediolateral axes are needed. A forward vector is provided with the data tree and used to find the hip mediolateral axis. A plane is fitted to the data around the upper torso, and the plane normal is used to find the shoulder mediolateral axis.

To achieve faster convergence of SHAKE, the model is first roughly aligned with the data. The model is rotated to face the direction of the forward vector, and translated so the chest joint in the model is at the position of the top of the torso in the data. To overcome errors in the data tree labelling, the pose from the previous frame is used if the tree is marked as invalid, or the change in pose from one frame to the next exceeds a threshold value. The difference in pose is calculated by summing up the Euclidean distance between estimated positions for each joint. The complete model fitting procedure can be seen in Alg. 2.

## 4    Results

A number of experiments have been conducted using the proposed method. Both real and synthetic data were used, and reconstruction was done with a resolution of $128 \times 128 \times 128$ voxels, resulting in a voxel size of 15.6 mm.

The accuracy of the method was evaluated using synthetic data generated with the toolset presented in [1]. An avatar was animated using motion capture data from the CMU dataset. Silhouette images of the sequence were rendered with eight virtual cameras at a resolution of $800 \times 600$, seven placed around the avatar and one in the ceiling pointing down.

Two dance sequences, *dance-whirl* and *lambada*, totalling around 1000 frames (subject 55, trial 1 and 2) were used. The joint locations from the motion capture data were used as a basis for comparison. Box and whisker plots (1.5 IQR convention) of the two sequences can be seen in Fig. 3. The distances between the upper and lower quartiles are within the size of two voxels, suggesting that the errors are caused by differences between the bone lengths of the model and

**Algorithm 2.** Model fitting

```
 1: for each frame n do
 2:     if tree is valid then
 3:         Fit shoulder plane.
 4:         for each joint j do
 5:             Fit line l to nodes corresponding to j using ODR.
 6:             Set up line constraint between j and l.
 7:         end for
 8:         Roughly align model with tree using rotation and translation.
 9:         Run the SHAKE algorithm to refine pose^(n).
10:         if diff(pose^(n), pose^(n−1)) > τ then
11:             Set pose^(n) ← pose^(n−1).
12:         end if
13:     else
14:         Set pose^(n) ← pose^(n−1).
15:     end if
16: end for
```

the underlying skeletal structure. The right finger tip joints are particularly inaccurate, and generally the extremities have higher errors than internal joints.

The mean positional errors of the joints over the entire sequences were 60.8 mm (st. dev. 26.8 mm) and 67.0 mm (st. dev. 31.0 mm), respectively. If an invalid labelling of the tree structure is detected the estimated pose from the previous frame will be reused. This happened in 1.6 % of the frames of the *dance-whirl* sequence, and 2.9 % of the frames of the *lambada* sequence.

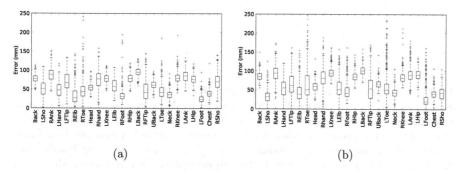

(a)                                             (b)

**Fig. 3.** Box and whisker plots of two sequences of synthetic data, (a) *dance-whirl* consists of 451 frames (subject 55, trial 1), (b) *lambada* has 545 frames (subject 55, trial 2)

The computational cost of the method was evaluated using real data drawn from the i3DPost dataset [6]. This is a publically available multi-view video dataset of a range of different motions captured in a studio environment. Four sequences of varying complexity were tested, and the results can be seen in

Table 1. The method achieves near real-time performance of $\sim 14$ fps. The model fitting is highly efficient, and skeletonising the volume is the main bottleneck. Some frames from the *ballet* and *dance-whirl* sequences can be seen in Fig. 4.

**Table 1.** Comparison of mean processing times for four sequences from the i3DPost dataset. All times are in milliseconds, with standard deviations in parentheses.

| | Data aq. | Line fitting | SHAKE | Sum | Framerate |
|---|---|---|---|---|---|
| *Walk*, seq. 013 | 65.16 (2.67) | 0.09 (0.01) | 2.93 (0.06) | 68.18 (2.68) | 14.67 |
| *Walk-spin*, seq. 015 | 67.95 (4.06) | 0.10 (0.02) | 2.95 (0.08) | 70.33 (3.96) | 14.22 |
| *Run-jump*, seq. 017 | 67.33 (3.97) | 0.09 (0.01) | 2.90 (0.08) | 68.54 (3.76) | 14.59 |
| *Ballet*, seq. 023 | 68.53 (5.53) | 0.09 (0.01) | 2.90 (0.11) | 71.12 (5.60) | 14.06 |

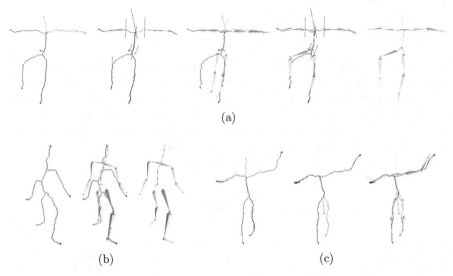

(a)

(b)                         (c)

**Fig. 4.** Some frames from the *ballet* and *dance-whirl* sequences. In (a) the steps of the model fitting are shown: the labelled tree structure with forward vector, lines fitted to the data, rough alignment, joints constrained to lines, and fitted model. An example of an invalid tree is shown in (b), where the model configuration from the previous frame is reused. In (c) two consecutive frames, where the second tree labelling is valid, but still incorrect. The difference between the two estimated poses is above a threshold, and the first pose is reused in the second frame.

## 5   Discussion and Future Work

In the previous section we demonstrated the proposed method on several sequences where it robustly recovers a segmented skeletal structure. There are, however, some limitations to using a skeletonisation based approach, and we will discuss them here, and how these issues can be resolved in the future.

Skeletonisation based pose estimation methods have problems recovering the skeletal structure in frames where the limbs are close together, or close to the torso. A significant advantage of the proposed method is that frames are processed individually, and thus the method can recover after detecting invalid poses.

Straka et al. [14] recently presented a similar approach and also used synthetic data from the CMU database for quantitative evaluation. Section 4 shows that the accuracy and processing time of the proposed method is on a par with a state-of-the-art skeletonisation based method using similar data for evaluation. The method presented in [14], however, requires the head to be the highest point for the duration of a sequence, and labelling of left and right limbs is not automatic. These are limitations that the proposed approach does not suffer from.

Similarly to Kastenmeier and Vesely [8], we experimented with combining SHAKE with simulated annealing to refine the model fitting. Several different cost functions were tested, but the improvement in accuracy was negligible at the cost of $> 30$ ms extra processing time. It is possible, however, that a cost function could be found that significantly improves the accuracy, further experimentation is required to evaluate the benefit of adding simulated annealing.

Some of the extreme outliers in the toe positions in Fig. 3 are caused by poor 3D reconstruction resulting in a reversal of the foot direction. The currently used model does not include joint angle limits, so in these cases the model is brought into what should be illegal configurations. Using a model representation that includes joint angles, such as the one presented by Guerra-Filho [7], would prevent the model fitting from resulting in illegal configurations and improve accuracy.

## 6    Concluding Remarks

We have presented a novel pose estimation method based on fitting a model to labelled tree structures that are generated from skeletonised sequences of visual hulls. The SHAKE algorithm was used to constrain the model to straight lines fitted to the data trees. This is intended to be a real-time approach for pose estimation, the results for the pose tree computation back this up and demonstrate good model fitting across multiple sequences of complex motion with framerates of around 14 fps. The approach can recover from errors or degeneracies in the initial volume/skeletal reconstruction which overcomes inherent limitatons of many tracking approaches which cannot re-initialise. Ground-truth evaluation on synthetic data indicates correct model fitting in $\sim 97\%$ of frames with rms errors $\sim 6$ cm.

## References

1. Bakken, R.H.: Using Synthetic Data for Planning, Development and Evaluation of Shape-from-Silhouette Based Human Motion Capture Methods. In: Proceedings of ISVC (2012)

2. Bakken, R.H., Hilton, A.: Real-Time Pose Estimation Using Tree Structures Built from Skeletonised Volume Sequences. In: Proceedings of VISAPP, pp. 181–190 (2012)
3. Buss, S.R.: Introduction to Inverse Kinematics with Jacobian Transpose, Pseudoinverse and Damped Least Squares Methods (2004) (unpublished manuscript), http://math.ucsd.edu/~sbuss/ResearchWeb
4. Caillette, F., Galata, A., Howard, T.: Real-time 3-D human body tracking using learnt models of behaviour. Computer Vision and Image Understanding 109(2), 112–125 (2008)
5. Chen, Y.-L., Chai, J.: 3D Reconstruction of Human Motion and Skeleton from Uncalibrated Monocular Video. In: Zha, H., Taniguchi, R.-i., Maybank, S. (eds.) ACCV 2009, Part I. LNCS, vol. 5994, pp. 71–82. Springer, Heidelberg (2010)
6. Gkalelis, N., Kim, H., Hilton, A., Nikolaidis, N., Pitas, I.: The i3DPost multi-view and 3D human action/interaction database. In: Proceedings of the Conference for Visual Media Production, pp. 159–168 (2009)
7. Guerra-Filho, G.: A General Motion Representation - Exploring the Intrinsic Viewpoint of a Motion. In: Proceedings of GRAPP, pp. 347–352 (2012)
8. Kastenmeier, T., Vesely, F.: Numerical robot kinematics based on stochastic and molecular simulation methods. Robotica 14(03), 329–337 (1996)
9. Menier, C., Boyer, E., Raffin, B.: 3D Skeleton-Based Body Pose Recovery. In: Proceedings of 3DPVT, pp. 389–396 (2006)
10. Michoud, B., Guillou, E., Bouakaz, S.: Real-Time and Markerless 3D Human Motion Capture Using Multiple Views. In: Elgammal, A., Rosenhahn, B., Klette, R. (eds.) Human Motion 2007. LNCS, vol. 4814, pp. 88–103. Springer, Heidelberg (2007)
11. Moeslund, T.B., Hilton, A., Krüger, V.: A survey of advances in vision-based human motion capture and analysis. Computer Vision and Image Understanding 104, 90–126 (2006)
12. Moschini, D., Fusiello, A.: Tracking Human Motion with Multiple Cameras Using an Articulated Model. In: Gagalowicz, A., Philips, W. (eds.) MIRAGE 2009. LNCS, vol. 5496, pp. 1–12. Springer, Heidelberg (2009)
13. Poppe, R.: Vision-based human motion analysis: An overview. Computer Vision and Image Understanding 108(1-2), 4–18 (2007)
14. Straka, M., Hauswiesner, S., Rüther, M., Bischof, H.: Skeletal Graph Based Human Pose Estimation in Real-Time. In: Proceedings of BMVC (2011)
15. Sundaresan, A., Chellappa, R.: Model-driven segmentation of articulating humans in Laplacian Eigenspace. IEEE Transactions on Pattern Analysis and Machine Intelligence 30(10), 1771–1785 (2008)
16. Tang, W., Cavazza, M., Mountain, D., Earnshaw, R.: A constrained inverse kinematics technique for real-time motion capture animation. The Visual Computer 15(7-8), 413–425 (1999)

# An NVC Emotional Model for Conversational Virtual Humans in a 3D Chatting Environment

Junghyun Ahn[1], Stéphane Gobron[1,2], David Garcia[3],
Quentin Silvestre[1], Daniel Thalmann[1,4], and Ronan Boulic[1]

[1] Immersive Interaction Group (IIG), EPFL, Lausanne, Switzerland
[2] Information and Communication Systems (ISIC), HE-Arc, St-Imier, Switzerland
[3] Chair of Systems Design (CSD), ETHZ, Zurich, Switzerland
[4] Institute for Media Innovation (IMI), NTU, Singapore

**Abstract.** This paper proposes a new emotional model for Virtual Humans (VHs) in a conversational environment. As a part of a multi-users emotional 3D-chatting system, this paper focus on how to formulate and visualize the flow of emotional state defined by the Valence-Arousal-Dominance (VAD) parameters. From this flow of emotion over time, we successfully visualized the change of VHs' emotional state through the proposed *emoFaces* and *emoMotions*. The notion of Non-Verbal Communication (NVC) was exploited for driving plausible emotional expressions during conversation. With the help of a proposed interface, where a user can parameterize emotional state and flow, we succeeded to vary the emotional expressions and reactions of VHs in a 3D conversation scene.

**Keywords:** Emotional model and dynamics, facial expressions.

## 1   Introduction

Effective control and visualization of Non-Verbal Communication (**NVC**) is essential for development of a plausible industrial [1,2] or academic [3,4] application, involving 3D social communication. As illustrated in Figure 1, the NVC consists of complex emotional events such as facial expression, head orientation, gaze, emotional body motion, breathing, and etc. Since a large part of these emotional information is transmitted in an unconscious manner, it is not easy to be fully controlled by a user. Moreover, a Virtual Human (**VH**) acting as a user's avatar or conversational agent involves understanding of emotion, which is also not an easy task as this concept is shown to be difficult to define [5,6]. In this context, we propose an efficient emotional model that facilitates user's control for visualizing affective conversational VHs.

The basic emotional state of VH is interpreted by using three dimensional emotion axes, **V**alence, **A**rousal, and **D**ominance (**VAD**) [7,8,9]. These VAD parameters simplify task of designing user interface and easily transfers emotional states through conversational VHs. From our proposed emotional model and dynamics, the VAD parameters vary over time and visualize the NVC attributes from interactive emotional events. A *demo video* is provided for more detail of each process described in this paper (see also Section 5).

F.J. Perales, R.B. Fisher, and T.B. Moeslund (Eds.): AMDO 2012, LNCS 7378, pp. 47–57, 2012.

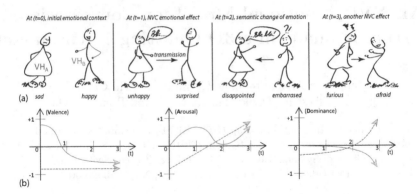

**Fig. 1.** (a) time-line of complex emotion variations highlighting NVC; (b) corresponding VAD variations

## 2    Related Works

A number of researches on conversational VH have been presented so far. A behavior expression animation toolkit (BEAT) that allows animators to input typed text to be spoken by an animated human figure was introduced [10]. Later, a dialog agent "Max" was developed as museum guide [11] and a gaming opponent [12]. Two virtual agents was also presented in an interactive poker game [13]. They applied the RFID technique to understand real world situation with speech recognition. Recently, two museum guide agents "Ada" and "Grace" [14] and a bartender agent was also introduced within an interdisciplinary VR architecture [15]. The VA and VAD parameters were also applied in [16,15] and [11,12]. However, they mainly focused on dialog agents, system design, speech recognition, and a single user environment. The transmission of avatar's emotion in a multi-users scene was not considered.

A model of behavior expressivity using a set of six parameters that act as modulation of behavior animation has been developed [17] as well. Recently, a constraint-based approach to the generation of multi-modal emotional displays was introduced [18]. Those works offer a good insight about how to derive sequential behavior including emotions. However, our approach gives more weight to the NVC emotional dynamics and its visualization in a conversational scene.

## 3    Emotional Model

The emotional face and body expressions influence the whole conversation even if a spoken sentence is short. We have developed a model where a single utterance produces continuous changes of emotion as depicted in Figure 1.

### 3.1    Types of Emotions

To parameterize the emotion of a **VH**, we choose the **VAD** coordinate system, as it allows any emotions to be simulated. The corresponding flow of emotion is influenced by users' typed sentences, users' direct emotional command, memory towards a VH, time attenuation functions, direction of dialog, and etc. Therefore, in the context of social communication, at least three aspects of emotions have to be taken into account: (1) short term emotions; (2) long term emotions; and (3) inter-personal emotions (*i.e.* individual opinion towards encountered VHs). These aspects are presented in the following paragraphes.

**Short Term Emotions (STE).** We process the messages (typed by a user, generated by a computer, or scripted) to extract information about the most recent emotional content in terms of polarity and VAD. Each VH taking part of the conversation is influenced by this extracted information. Moreover, users' direct VAD input also influences the change of emotional flow. As the core of the proposed model, more details on STE (*emotional dynamics*) will be explained later in Section 4. Facial expressions generated from VAD value (see Sub-section 3.2) and breathing rhythm from the arousal are the main outputs generated by STE.

**Long Term Emotions (LTE).** The model of internal emotion dynamics provides us with a data-driven estimation of the LTE of a user, given the set of STE expressed and perceived by the user. Emotional body motions (see Sub-section 3.3) is triggered from the interpretation of this LTE.

**Inter-Personal Emotions (IPE).** Another type of emotion is related at individual level, *i.e.* how "we" appreciate people at individual scale. To simulate this aspect, we memorize all conversations received from every individual separately, and we keep updated a special variable that stores the current state of the emotions between each pair of VH. Then, if we want to know the emotional appreciation that a specific VH has towards another, we can access this variable, which relaxes on time the same way as internal emotions do. Accumulated average VAD toward a VH is added as an offset to the current STE VAD state.

We believe that this classification can be also useful to simulate *autonomous agents* with emotions.

## 3.2   Facial Expressions: *emoFaces*

Based on an internal survey (11 subjects, one woman and 10 men from 25 to 43 years old), we derived 27 emotional words potentially corresponding to the VAD space as presented in Figure 2. We defined three different areas, *i.e.* negative, neutral, and positive for each axis and attribute 27 emotional adjectives for each spatial region. Those words were referred to analyze facial expressions (*emoFaces*) and emotional body movements (*emoMotions*).

As a main output of the STE, facial expression is continuously updated by the VAD value obtained from each simulation loop. Therefore, it was necessary to design a framework that generates *emoFaces* from any VAD coordinate point. In this context, we exploited 7 face parts and 11 face-part actions (see Table 1), which are extracted from Facial Action Coding System (FACS)'s Action Unit (AU)s [19] and Facial Animation Parameter (FAP) [20]. We cross referenced each face-part actions with the emotional words in the VAD model and exploited

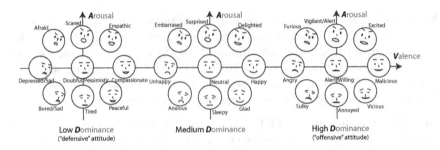

**Fig. 2.** A VAD model with emotional terms and its facial expressions

the dependency of each action on emotional axes as presented in Table 1. Each facial expression of emotional words has been explored from our internal observation and related researches in social psychology [21,22,23]. Besides expressions, the *emoFace* also controls a simple text-to-visual-speech and head turn motions.

**Table 1.** Dependency of each face-part action on **VAD** axes. Related axis to the action is mark with an 'o'. Detailed *emoFaces* are illustrated in Figure 2.

| Face parts | Face-part actions | Related AUs (FAPs) | V | A | D |
|---|---|---|---|---|---|
| 1. Eyebrows | Tilt left and right | AU 1,2 (FAP 31,32,35,36) | o | | |
| | Move up and down | AU 4 (FAP 33,34) | o | o | |
| 2. Eyelids | Move up and down | AU 5,7 (FAP 19,20) | | o | |
| 3. Upper lip | Move up and down | AU 10 | | | o |
| 4. Lip corners | Tilt left and right | AU 12,15 (FAP 12,13) | o | | |
| | Stretch and Pull | AU 18,20 (FAP 6,7) | o | | o |
| 5. Mouth | Open and Close | AU 17,26 | | o | o |
| 6. Head | Turn left or right | AU 51 or 52 | o | | o |
| | Head up and down | AU 53,54 | | o | |
| | Tilt left or right | AU 55 or 56 | o | | o |
| 7. Eye | Look at | AU 61-64 (FAP 23-26) | | o | o |

### 3.3    Emotional Body Movements: *emoMotions*

From the emotional words defined in Figure 2 and with the participation of a professional actor, we associated emotional body movements to fit all 27 areas of the VAD model. Each full-body motion (including fingers movement and facial animation) was captured around 5 seconds.

Unlike *emoFace*, and as an output of LTE, an *emoMotion* is triggered from the analysis of emotions over a longer temporal window (*e.g.* 10 seconds). A recently peaked VAD area is interpreted as a recent emotion and is updated in each simulation loop. The peak is measured by the norm of VAD and the *emoMotion* activates when the current VAD hits again this area.

Another type of body movements, the breathing motion is related to STE rather than LTE. It shares the control of five joints (left/right sternoclavicular, left/right acromioclavicular, and head) during the whole simulation loop. Therefore, any activated motion such as *emoMotions*, conversational motion, or etc is combined with the background breathing motion, which it adds an angular contribution given by $\sin(\omega t + \phi)$, where $t$ is the current simulation time. The angular frequency is $\omega = (a+1)^3 + 1$, where $a$ is the current arousal value, resulting in a range of breathing frequencies within $[0.15, 1.43]$ *Hz*. Then, the phase is updated by an equation $\phi = \phi + \omega \Delta t$, for the purpose of smoothing the sine curve upon change of $\omega$. Figure 3 shows examples of *emoFaces* and *emoMotions*.

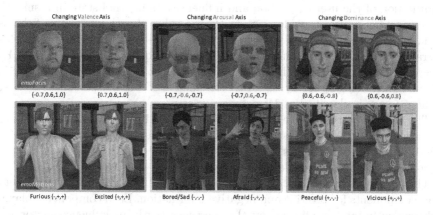

**Fig. 3.** The effect of changing one dimension applied to *emoFaces* and *emoMotions*. The *emoFaces* need exact VAD coordinate, since each VAD state has different facial expression. The *emoMotions* are presented with emotional words depicted in Figure 2.

## 4   Short Term Emotions (STE)

The STE model contains two different types of input from the users: text message ($S_i$) and an external VAD ($U_i$) input, which is also described in the companion paper [24]. The $S_i$ is processed to extract three types of values: (1) sentiment polarity from a lexicon-based classification [25]; (2) VAD from averaged ANEW values [26]; and (3) target of the emotion in terms of grammatical person ("I", "you", "it") from LIWC word frequency analysis [27].

The *emoFaces* and *emoMotions* are driven by the internal state of the *agent* as part of a data-driven simulation of our agent-based model, which is designed within the framework for collective emotions [28,29]. Therefore, in this section, we use the *Systems Design* notation of the term *agent* [30] instead of the term VH. Each *agent* has an emotional state composed of the VAD variables: $v_i$, $a_i$, and $d_i$. Each one of these variables $x_i$ of *agent* $A_i$ changes continuously over time through an equation of the form $\dot{x}_i = -\gamma_x x_i + \mathcal{F}_x(x_i, h)$.

The first term models an exponential decay of parameter $\gamma_x$ that makes the emotional states relax to the neutral in the absence of input. The second term models the effect of communication and user input on the variable, given the communication fields present in the simulation, as explained below. Each one of these fields is subject to a decay of the same type as the emotional states of the *agents*, of the form $\dot{h} = -\gamma_h h$. This decay of the field represents the aging of emotional information and the vanishing memory of the system.

The first process that defines the changes in the internal state of an *agent* is a refinement process based on the user input and messages. This type of information is stored in the self-influence field ( *VAD field*) $h_{ii}$ of *agent* $A_i$, with a component for each of the VAD axes. This individual field receives the discrete information of the user expression and influences its internal state in a smooth manner. When a user provides a $S_i$ or $U_i$, the value of each one of this fields is updated to a weighted average between its previous value and the input. This averaging depends on the input type and follows the equation $h = (1-s_y)h + s_y Y_i$, where $Y_i$ can be $S_i$ or $U_i$. The weight of the change in the field $s_y$ will depend on the input, being $s_u$ for $U_i$, $s_s$ for $S_i$ classified as $2^{nd}$ or $3^{rd}$ person, or $s_i > s_s$ if the message is classified as $1^{st}$ person.

The second process is the simulation of changes in emotional states due to message exchanges in the system. This information, extracted from the polarity classification of the messages, aggregates in two different kinds of fields, related to conversation and social identity (*signed field*).

The conversation field $h_{ij\pm}$ between the *agents* $A_i$ and $A_j$ has two independent components for positive and negative information. Each component relaxes independently, and is affected by the messages (with an influence factor $s_d$) coming from the conversation *agents* through equation $\dot{h}_\pm = -\gamma_h h_\pm + s$.

The social identity field $h_{i\pm}$ keeps the importance of *agent* $A_i$ in the community, aggregating all the information related to each conversation it has been involved in. The size of the change in these conversation fields will depend on whether the messages taken as input were classified as $2^{nd}$ person ($s_t$), being then larger than if they were classified as $1^{st}$ or $3^{rd}$.

**Valence** of an *agent* is affected by the conversation fields with an asymmetric effect depending on its sign. The second change comes from the self-influence fields, forcing the attractors to particular values stated by the user or inferred from the expression. When $v \geq 0$, the $\mathcal{F}_v$ is defined as Equation 1. Otherwise, when $v < 0$, $h_{ij+}$ and $h_{ij-}$ are switched. The attention parameter $\alpha$ defines the asymmetry of positive and negative emotions, $b_0$ is the bias towards positive emotions and $b_3$ is the saturation that avoids infinite valences. $\beta_v$ is the strength factor of the update to known values of the state from utterances or user input, compared with the rest of the dynamics. When $v = 0$, the term $sgn(v)$ is 1.

$$\mathcal{F}_v = (\alpha h_{ij+} + (1-\alpha)h_{ij-})(b_0 \, sgn(v) - b_3 v^3) + \beta_v(h_{iiv} - v) \qquad (1)$$

*Arousal* increases with all the information present in the system, regardless of its valence but depending on how relevant it is for the individual. This way, the arousal will increase with all the fields and decrease only based in relaxation or internal assessments of low arousal, coming from the $S_i$ or $U_i$. The parameter $\eta$ balances how stronger is the identity field rather than the conversation, and $d_0$ and $d_1$ work similarly as their valence counterparts but with a linear saturation. The weight $\beta_a$ is the importance of the self-field as for the valence.

$$\mathcal{F}_a = ((1 - \eta)h_{ij} + \eta h_i)(d_0 - d_1 a) + \beta_a(h_{iia} - a) \tag{2}$$

*Dominance* dynamics are based on the social identity fields, and how the information directed to the individual changes its power regarding emotions. The parameters $g_+$ and $g_-$ represent the asymmetric effect on the dominance, if a fearful reaction is supposed to be fast, $g_- > g_+$.

$$\mathcal{F}_d = g_+ h_{i+} - g_- h_{i-} + \beta_d(h_{iid} - d) \tag{3}$$

## 5  Parameterizations and Results

The proposed emotional model includes various parameters and variables, which define the emotional state and enable to differentiate the flow of emotion. In this section, we describe how we parameterized these values and show the result.

**Table 2.** A description of the short term emotions parameters and their values

| Category | Par. | Description | Val. | Category | Par. | Description | Val. |
|---|---|---|---|---|---|---|---|
| | $\alpha$ | attention shift | 0.5 | | $g+$ | pos influence speed | 0.7 |
| | $b_0$ | direct influence | 0.9 | Dominance | $g-$ | neg influence speed | 0.7 |
| **Valence** | $b_3$ | saturation | 0.9 | ($\mathcal{F}_d$) | $\beta_d$ | update strength | 0.8 |
| ($\mathcal{F}_v$) | $\beta_v$ | update strength | 0.8 | | $\gamma_d$ | decay | 0.1 |
| | $\gamma_v$ | decay | 0.1 | | $\gamma_h$ | general decay | 0.1 |
| | $\eta$ | identity strength | 0.5 | Signed | $s_d$ | discussion influence | 0.4 |
| | $d_0$ | direct influence | 0.8 | Field ($h_\pm$) | $s_t$ | targeted influence | 0.4 |
| **Arousal** | $d_1$ | saturation | 0.8 | | $s_s$ | baseline influence | 0.3 |
| ($\mathcal{F}_a$) | $\beta_a$ | update strength | 0.8 | VAD | $s_i$ | "I" influence | 0.5 |
| | $\gamma_a$ | decay | 0.1 | ($h$) | $s_u$ | user input influence | 0.8 |

Twenty different parameters (see Table 2) are assigned for a VH, and through the parametrization, we could vary the emotional attributes of each conversational VH. The influence functions $\mathcal{F}$ of each VAD can be parameterized independently and different social behaviors can be observed from the parametrization of signed and VAD fields. For example, the increment of decays causes a VH to lose its emotional feelings more or less quickly. The decrement of update strengths makes a VH

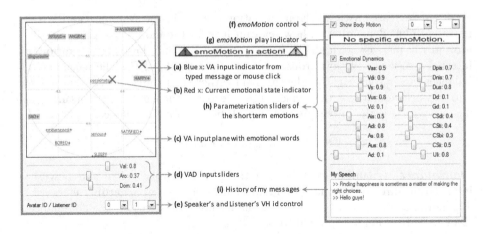

**Fig. 4.** The UI for emotional VH control. A message "Finding happiness is sometimes a matter of making the right choices" was typed in from a user. (a) and (d) show the goal VAD state {0.80,0.37,0.41} extracted from the typed message. The detail of (h) short term emotions parameters are described in Table 2.

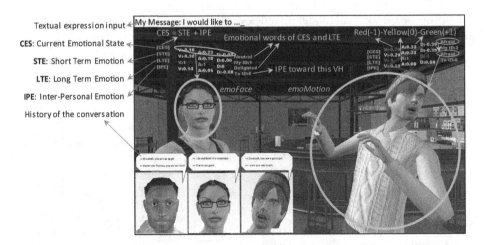

**Fig. 5.** Three-VH conversation simulated and rendered by our proposed model

less emotional from the coming events. According to our observation, parameter values in Table 2 simulated a plausible animation of VHs conversation. These STE parameters was controlled by a User Interface (UI) introduced in Figure 4.

Our simulated conversation scene is illustrated in Figure 5 and the details of our results can be seen at the following link: http://youtu.be/UGbW8nDNO24. Another demo video of our companion paper can also be found *here*.

# 6  Conclusion

In this paper, we presented a new emotional model for text-based conversational environment. This approach adds a new dimension to animation applicable to virtual worlds where resulting conversations enable to create more natural direct and indirect exchanges. Original contributions introduced in this paper were: (a) multiple levels of emotion for each VH (STE, LTE, and IPE); (b) the *emoFaces* and *emoMotions* associated with VAD model.

However, there are still some issues to be considered: First, the model can be improved by considering heterogeneous effects of *when* text utterances were exchanged. Second, the STE parameters have a potential to find interesting results on the personality of emotional VH. Third, in the case of avatar, this automatic method can be contested as it implies that the user and his/her avatar can have different opinions towards the same encountered VH. Nevertheless, when dealing with NVC, the user cannot control all possible parameters. The proposed direct VAD input could be served as a solution of this issue.

**Acknowledgments.** The authors wish to thank O. Renault, M. Clavien, and J. Conus for their collaboration on the mocap, modeling, and algorithm. This work was supported by a EU FP7 CYBEREMOTIONS Project (Contract 231323).

# References

1. GUILE3D: Virtual assistant denise, http://guile3d.com/en/products/
2. Boellstorff, T.: Coming of Age in Second Life: An Anthropologist Explores the Virtually Human. Princeton University Press (2008)
3. Cassell, J., Pelachaud, C., Badler, N., Steedman, M., Achorn, B., Becket, T., Douville, B., Prevost, S., Stone, M.: Animated conversation: rule-based generation of facial expression, gesture and spoken intonation for multiple conversational agents. In: SIGGRAPH 1994, pp. 413–420. ACM (1994)
4. Becker, C., Kopp, S., Wachsmuth, I.: Simulating the Emotion Dynamics of a Multimodal Conversational Agent. In: André, E., Dybkjær, L., Minker, W., Heisterkamp, P. (eds.) ADS 2004. LNCS (LNAI), vol. 3068, pp. 154–165. Springer, Heidelberg (2004)
5. Ekman, P.: Emotions revealed. Henry Holt and Company, LLC, New York (2004)
6. Kappas, A.: Smile when you read this, whether you like it or not: Conceptual challenges to affect detection. IEEE Transactions on Affective Computing 1(1), 38–41 (2010)
7. Bush, L.E.: Individual differences multidimensional scaling of adjectives denoting feelings. Journal of Personality and Social Psychology 25(1), 50–57 (1973)
8. Russell, J.A.: A circumplex model of affect. Journal of Personality and Social Psychology 39(6), 1161–1178 (1980)
9. Scherer, K.R.: What are emotions? and how can they be measured? Social Science Information 44(4), 695–729 (2005)
10. Cassell, J., Vilhjálmsson, H.H., Bickmore, T.: Beat: Behavior expression animation toolkit. In: SIGGRAPH 2001, pp. 477–486 (2001)

11. Kopp, S., Gesellensetter, L., Krämer, N.C., Wachsmuth, I.: A Conversational Agent as Museum Guide – Design and Evaluation of a Real-World Application. In: Panayiotopoulos, T., Gratch, J., Aylett, R.S., Ballin, D., Olivier, P., Rist, T. (eds.) IVA 2005. LNCS (LNAI), vol. 3661, pp. 329–343. Springer, Heidelberg (2005)

12. Becker, C., Nakasone, A., Prendinger, H., Ishizuka, M., Wachsmuth, I.: Physiologically interactive gaming with the 3d agent max. In: Intl. Workshop on Conversational Informatics, pp. 37–42 (2005)

13. Gebhard, P., Schröder, M., Charfuelan, M., Endres, C., Kipp, M., Pammi, S., Rumpler, M., Türk, O.: IDEAS4Games: Building Expressive Virtual Characters for Computer Games. In: Prendinger, H., Lester, J.C., Ishizuka, M. (eds.) IVA 2008. LNCS (LNAI), vol. 5208, pp. 426–440. Springer, Heidelberg (2008)

14. Swartout, W., Traum, D., Artstein, R., Noren, D., Debevec, P., Bronnenkant, K., Williams, J., Leuski, A., Narayanan, S., Piepol, D., Lane, C., Morie, J., Aggarwal, P., Liewer, M., Chiang, J.-Y., Gerten, J., Chu, S., White, K.: Ada and Grace: Toward Realistic and Engaging Virtual Museum Guides. In: Safonova, A. (ed.) IVA 2010. LNCS, vol. 6356, pp. 286–300. Springer, Heidelberg (2010)

15. Gobron, S., Ahn, J., Silvestre, Q., Thalmann, D., Rank, S., Skoron, M., Paltoglou, G., Thelwall, M.: An interdisciplinary vr-architecture for 3d chatting with nonverbal communication. In: EG VE 2011: Proceedings of the Joint Virtual Reality Conference of EuroVR. ACM (September 2011)

16. Ahn, J., Gobron, S., Silvestre, Q., Thalmann, D.: Asymmetrical facial expressions based on an advanced interpretation of two-dimensional russell's emotional model. In: ENGAGE 2010 (2010)

17. Pelachaud, C.: Studies on gesture expressivity for a virtual agent. Speech Commun. 51(7), 630–639 (2009)

18. Niewiadomski, R., Hyniewska, S.J., Pelachaud, C.: Constraint-based model for synthesis of multimodal sequential expressions of emotions. IEEE Transactions on Affective Computing 2(3), 134–146 (2011)

19. Ekman, P., Friesen, W.V.: Facial action coding system. Consulting Psychologists Press, CA (1978)

20. Magnenat-Thalmann, N., Thalmann, D.: Handbook of Virtual Humans. Wiley (2004)

21. Ekman, P.: Universals and cultural differences in facial expressions of emotions. In: Nebraska Symposium on Motivation, pp. 207–283. University of Nebraska Press (1971)

22. Ekman, P.: About brows: Emotional and conversational signals. In: von Cranach, M., Foppa, K., Lepenies, W., Ploog, D. (eds.) Human Ethology, pp. 169–248. Cambridge University Press, Cambridge (1979)

23. Ekman, P., Friesen, W.V., Ancoli, S.: Facial signs of emotional experience. Journal of Personality and Social Psychology 39(6), 1125–1134 (1980)

24. Gobron, S., Ahn, J., Garcia, D., Silvestre, Q., Thalmann, D., Boulic, R.: An Event-Based Architecture to Manage Virtual Human Non-Verbal Communication in 3D Chatting Environment. In: Perales, F.J., Fisher, R.B., Moeslund, T.B. (eds.) AMDO 2012. LNCS, vol. 7378, pp. 58–68. Springer, Heidelberg (2012)

25. Paltoglou, G., Gobron, S., Skowron, M., Thelwall, M., Thalmann, D.: Sentiment analysis of informal textual communication in cyberspace. In: ENGAGE 2010, pp. 13–15 (2010)

26. Bradley, M.M., Lang, P.J.: Affective norms for english words (ANEW): Stimuli, instruction manual and affective ratings. Technical report, The Center for Research in Psychophysiology. University of Florida (1999)

27. Pennebaker, J., Francis, M., Booth, R.: Linguistic Inquiry and Word Count, 2nd edn. Erlbaum Publishers (2001)
28. Schweitzer, F., Garcia, D.: An agent-based model of collective emotions in online communities. The European Physical Journal B - Condensed Matter and Complex Systems 77, 533–545 (2010)
29. Garcia, D., Schweitzer, F.: Emotions in product reviews empirics and models. In: IEEE SocialCom 2011 and PASSAT 2011, 483–488 (2011)
30. Schweitzer, F.: Brownian Agents and Active Particles. Collective Dynamics in the Natural and Social Sciences, 1st edn. Springer Series in Synergetics. Springer (2003)

# An Event-Based Architecture to Manage Virtual Human Non-Verbal Communication in 3D Chatting Environment

Stéphane Gobron[1,2], Junghyun Ahn[2], David Garcia[3],
Quentin Silvestre[2], Daniel Thalmann[2,4], and Ronan Boulic[2]

[1] Information and Communication Systems Institute (ISIC), HE-Arc, St-Imier, Switzerland
[2] Immersive Interaction Group (IIG), EPFL, Lausanne, Switzerland
[3] Chair of Systems Design (CSD), ETHZ, Zurich, Switzerland
[4] Institute for Media Innovation (IMI), NTU, Singapore

**Abstract.** Non-verbal communication (NVC) makes up about two-thirds of all communication between two people or between one speaker and a group of listeners. However, this fundamental aspect of communicating is mostly omitted in 3D social forums or virtual world oriented games. This paper proposes an answer by presenting a multi-user 3D-chatting system enriched with NVC relative to motion. This event-based architecture tries to recreate a context by extracting emotional cues from dialogs and derives virtual human potential body expressions from that event triggered context model. We structure the paper by expounding the system architecture enabling the modeling NVC in a multi-user 3D-chatting environment. There, we present the transition from dialog-based emotional cues to body language, and the management of NVC events in the context of a virtual reality client-server system. Finally, we illustrate the results with graphical scenes and a statistical analysis representing the increase of events due to NVC.

**Keywords:** Affective architecture, Social agents, Virtual reality, Non-verbal communication, 3D-chatting, Avatars.

## 1 Introduction

Non-verbal communication (NVC) is a wordless process of communication that mainly consists of the following animations: gaze, facial expressions, head and body orientation, and arm and hand movements. One exception to animation is changes of voice tone that are not considered in this paper as we focus on the exchange of text messages. In particular, facial expression plays an important role in the process of empathy [18], and emotional contagion [10], *i.e.* unconscious sharing of the emotions of conversation members. This conscious or unconscious way of communicating influences emotional state of all characters involved in a conversation [2]. NVC is triggered by emotional states, social customs, and personal attributes. In the context of 3D-chatting they should strongly influence character animation, making the conversation alive, the scenarios more consistent, and the virtual world simulation more *ecologically valid*.

Entertainment and industrial applications involving 3D social communication –for instance *Second LIFE* [15,5]– start looking for solutions to simulate this key aspect of

F.J. Perales, R.B. Fisher, and T.B. Moeslund (Eds.): AMDO 2012, LNCS 7378, pp. 58–68, 2012.
© Springer-Verlag Berlin Heidelberg 2012

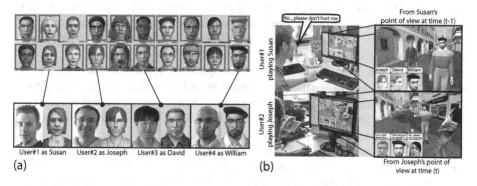

**Fig. 1.** (a) user's choice of avatar; (b) 3D-chatting scenario involving animated NVC

communication. The main issue is that trying to simulate NVC involves understanding "emotion", which is not an easy task as this concept is shown to be difficult to define even by specialists [8,12]. Another issue arises in a context of virtual world, it is not possible for users to control all the attributes of their avatars [9]. In the real world face to face communication, a large part of the information transmitted is done in a unconscious manner, through cues such as facial expressions or voice intonation. For this reason, users of a virtual world cannot consciously control those communication attributes, and then simulation techniques has to provide a way to fill this gap in virtual communication. In this paper we propose the event-based architecture of a working system –the emotional dynamic model being presented in a companion paper. This system proposes a "walkable 3D world environment enriched with facial and full body animation of every user's avatar consistent with the potential emotion extracted from the exchanged dialog. We believe that this approach simulates the most important NVC attributes, *i.e.*: (a) Virtual human (VH) emotional mind including a dimensional representation of emotions in three axes –*i.e.* valence, arousal, and dominance– and facial animation and "emoMotions" that predefined full-body VH animations corresponding to emotional attitudes –*e.g.* fear (Susan, user 1), anger (William, user 4), and empathy (David, user 3) illustrated Figure 1(b); (b) A virtual reality client-server architecture to manage in real-time events and induced NVC events mainly produced by the emotional dynamic model –see Figure 6; (c) Avatar's internal emotion dynamics by enabling short term emotions, long-term emotions, and emotional memory towards encountered VHs; (d) Automatic gazing, speech target redirection, and breathing rhythm according to arousal level.

## 2 Related Works

Previous research has explored NVC in different ways. In psychology, non-verbal behavior and communication [20] are widely studied. Virtual reality researches oriented towards psychology give motivations to simulate natural phenomenon of human conversation. NVC contains two different elements: human posture and relative positioning, and they have been analyzed to simulate interpersonal relationship between two virtual humans [2]. The evaluation of conversational agent's non-verbal behavior has also been conducted in [14].Communication over the internet by various social platforms was also explored. They specified what they learned regarding how people communicate face-to-face in a cyberworld [11].

A number of researches about 3D chatting or agent conversational system have been presented so far. A behavior expression animation toolkit entitled "BEAT" that allows animators to input typed text to be spoken by an animated human figure was also propose by Cassell in [6]. A few years later, emotional dynamics for conversational agent has been presented in [3]. Similarly to our approach, their architecture of an agent called "Max" used an advanced representation of emotions. Instead of a restricted set of emotions a dimensional representation with three dimension *i.e.* v,a,d for *valence-arousal-dominance*. Later, an improved version of agent "Max" has been also presented as a museum guide [13] and as a gaming opponent [4]. A model of behavior expressivity using a set of six parameters that act as modulation of behavior animation has been developed [17] as well. Very recently [16] proposed to study constraint-based approach to the generation of multimodal emotional displays.

For what concerns the cooperation between agents and humans, and in [7] people appreciate to cooperation with a machine when the agent expresses gratitude by means of artificial facial expression were found. For this reason, adding emotional NVC to virtual realities would not only enhance user experience, but also foster collaboration and participation in online communities. An interdisciplinary research was proposed late 2011 in [9] that merges data-mining, artificial intelligence, psychology and virtual reality. Gobron *et al.* demonstrated an architecture of 3D chatting system available only for one to one conversation and their approach did not allow free virtual world navigation.

## 3   NVC Architecture

Compared to the literature presented in the previous section, our NVC real 3D-chatting approach is original in terms of aims (i.e. NVC enriched 3D-chatting), structure (i.e. building context with events), time related management of events. The process pipeline is especially novel as it enables multiple users chatting with NVC represented on their respective avatars –see Sections 3.1 and 3.4. Different types of events (potential client events, certified server events, secondary server events) play a key role allowing a consistent NVC to be simulated –see Section 3.3 and Figures 2 and 3). As induced NVC events cannot simply be sorted into a FIFO pile, we propse an event management allowing time shifting and forecasting for all types of event –see Section 3.2. The heart of the emotional model, described in details via the formalization of the short term emotional dynamics –this model is proposed in a companion paper. This section details a virtual human [VH] conversation architecture that uses semantic and emotional communication, especially suited for entertainment applications involving a virtual world. Similarly to [9] and [3], our emotional model uses the dimensional representation v,a,d for valence, arousal and dominance that allow any emotion to be represented. The basic idea behind our architecture is that dialogs trigger emotions, emotions and user interruptions trigger events, and events trigger NVC visual output. During the software design of this work, we realized that the key-links between interacting avatars and their potential emotions were events. Indeed, depending of context, different types of events could, should, or would happen generating waves of emotion, changing avatars' attitudes, and influencing back perceptions and therefore dialogs.

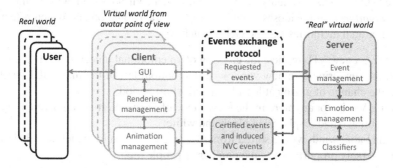

**Fig. 2.** Global interaction between users, associated clients, and the unique server

This is why, as shown in Figures 2 and 3, we propose an event-based architecture system to manage NVC for 3D-chatting. A relatively large number of aspects have to be presented to cover such virtual reality simulation. In the following subsections, we present how user commands influence NVC graphics in a context of client-server architecture; next, we describe the management of events; and finally, we propose relationships between client and server.

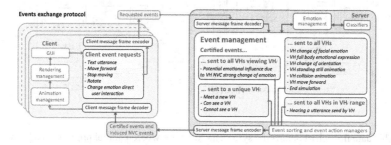

**Fig. 3.** Events exchange protocol between clients and server: events requested by clients (representing VHs) produce direct and indirect events of different nature such as induced-events

## 3.1 Building a Context

The Figure 4 details the 3D-chatting simulation with NVC. As shown, users interact in the virtual world through their individual client environment with a graphical user interface (GUI). User's input and commands to the 3D chatting system are collected via the GUI using keyboard and mouse on two windows. The first one presenting the virtual world from the point of view of the avatar (1st person view). The second window being the representation of emotional states of the avatar including also interruption command buttons for immediate change of emotion. The user can input text for verbal communication, he can move forward, rotate while standing still, and, at will, adjust the avatar emotion manually. The server puts the received events in a history list according to their arrival time. When the server executes an event, it sends the corresponding message to the concerned clients. As a VH travels in the virtual world, it meets unknown VHs (*encounters*) and/or looses sight (see Figure 7(a)) some others, which affect the avatar emotional memories and the GUI in such way:

- Meeting a new VH implies: the creation of an emotional object in the avatar memory; the rendering of a new window–at the bottom left of the main GUI window; and the change of gazing at least for a very short period;
- (b) if a VH is not anymore in the view range of an avatar, it is kept in memory but not animated and displayed in black and white;
- (c) the facial windows are sorted from most recently seen in the left and their sizes are inversely proportional to the number of people met.

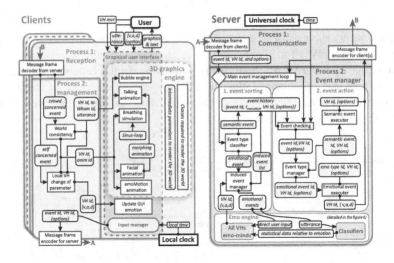

**Fig. 4.** This data flow chart details the system architecture where parallel processes on both server and clients are necessary to manage NVC events

Notification of any VH NVC have to be sent to every client but the users are aware of such change only if their coordinates and orientation allow it. Similarly, whenever a VH is animated for any reason, walking, re-orientating or communicating non-verbally, all clients are also notified in order to animate the corresponding VH if it is in the client field of view. Furthermore, the emotion influence is also sent to all the VHs that see the concerned VH which can lead to multiple emotion exchanges without any exchange of word. However, as messages are instantaneous, when a VH communicates a text utterance, only the ones that can "hear", *e.g.* the ones that are in the field of view, will receive the message.

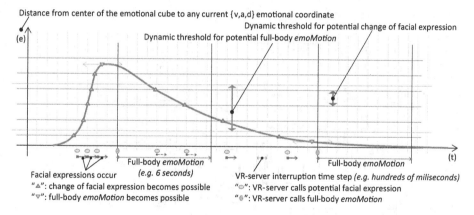

Distance from center of the emotional cube to any current {v,a,d} emotional coordinate

**Fig. 5.** Example of events chain reaction that an emotional peek (blue wave) that the VR-server produce which involve new facial expressions and full-body *emoMotions*

## 3.2    From Dialog to NVC Motions

Collected data is transmitted from the client to the server which processes it using the event manager. In a context of virtual reality client-server, one major difficulty is probably to animate VH corresponding to their potential emotions without sending too many events between VR-server and VR-clients. For that purpose, we defined different thresholds (see Figure 5) for synchronizing and differentiating simultaneous changes of facial expressions and full-body movements (mainly arms movements, torso posture, and head orientation). Another way to relax the streaming and to avoid computational explosion at the server level, is to make the assumption that minor changes of emotion can be simulated only by facial expression (low cost NVC–in term of interruption delay), and full-body emotional motions (high cost NVC) occur only as major change of emotional events. The figure 5 illustrates how an emotional peak (computed by the short term emotional model) is interrupted in term of indirect events at server's level. These emotional events will produce other interruptions at client's level for VH facial and full-body emotional animations. In that figure, the blue line represents a sudden change of emotion, triangles indicate that the VR-server identifies a potential graphical action relative to emotion (*i.e.* an event is created and stored inside a dynamic chain of events depending of its time priority), and ellipses represent actual emotional animation orders from server to clients.

## 3.3    VR Event Manager

In the context of simulation involving virtual worlds, avoiding a break in presence is an absolute priority. Considering that NVC related events occurring before triggered verbal events is a serious threat to the simulation consistency. Therefore, we have designed an event-driven architecture at the server level. The *event manager* is then probably the most important part of the system as it guarantees: first, the correctness of time sequences; second, the coherence production of non-verbal induced-events; and third, the information transmission to clients (*e.g.* dialog, movements, collisions, self emotional states, others visible emotional change of emotion).

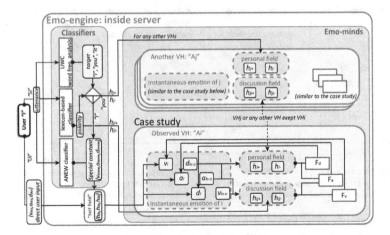

**Fig. 6.** Data flow chart presenting the core of the emotional model for NVC: the short term emotions model based from [19]; details of this model are proposed in a companion paper [1]

In this system, an event is anything that can happen in the virtual world. It can be a VH movement as well as a semantic transmission (*i.e.* text utterance) or a user emotional interruption command. Events can be sorted into two categories, events requested by the user input at GUI level and events generated by the server. The first category represents a request from a VR-client, not what will happen for sure. For instance, the "move forward" user command is not possible if a wall is obstructing the avatar's path. The second category represents factual consequences produced by the server that occur in the virtual world. Notice that from a single client-event, multiple induced-events can occur. For instance, a user inputs a text utterance: specific personal emotional cues can be identify that will imply changes of facial and body expression. Then, depending on the avatar world coordinate and orientation, multiple VHs can receive the change of emotion (at $t + \epsilon$, *i.e.* as fast as server can handle an event) and the text utterance (at $t + \delta t$, *i.e.* slightly later so that emotions are presented before possible semantic interpretation, *e.g.* 350 milliseconds). Naturally, the body behavior of an avatar has also consequences on the emotional interpretation of any VH that can see it –*i.e.* purpose of NVC– which will produce other induced-events.

Multiple threads are needed to simulate the above mentioned effects. The event manager stores induced events in a dynamic history list depending on their time occurrence (present or future). Simultaneously, the event manager also un-stacks all events that are stored in the past. In both cases, the process consists of defining from what could happen and what should happen in the virtual world. This management of events must then be centralized which is why the VR-server level represent the *reality* and the VR-client levels its *potential projections* only.

### 3.4  VR Client-Server Tasks

As seen in previous paragraphs, the server defines the reality of the virtual world as it is the only element that dynamically forecasts events. It runs two threads: one for the event management, connecting to database and emotional engines and the other to execute events, communicating to specific clients corresponding information that runs animation and rendering engines (lips, facial expression, motion capture emotional full-body sequences, interactive text bubbles, etc.). VR-clients also run two parallel processes: one for the communication with the server and the other for the GUI. The data flow chart Figure 4 left depicts main processes of the VR-client which basically is: (a) communicating user requests and context to server, and (b) execute server semantical and induced events valid from the point of view of the local avatar. Every VR-client receives all information relative to physical world and only part of events relative to utterance. One part of these data is stored in the crowd data structures, the other part in the local VH data structure, but both are needed to animate and render the scene from the local VH point of view.

## 4    Results

Figure 1(b) and Figure 7 present experimental setups with four users in the same conversation. Two aspects of the results are illustrated: emotionally triggered animations, and a statistical analysis representing increase of events due to NVC.

**Fig. 7.** User-test: (a) visualization of communication areas have been artificially added (Illustrator) in blue for view *Linda*'s (b), green for *Patricia*'s view (c), and yellow for *Joseph*'s view (d), to rendered scenes of the four participants

**Encountered VHs and Memory** – In the participant views of Figure 7 (three pictures on the right) encountered avatars faces are shown with a different rendering: sometimes colored and animated, sometimes black and white and freezed. For instance, in (b) three other VHs have been encountered but only two are currently within the view area, therefore *Patricia* is depicted in black and white. **Relationship between Time, Event, and NVC** – Figures 1(b) and 7 illustrate the effect of NVC with respect to time with corresponding changes of emotional behavior. In the first figure two user points-of-view are shown at initial time ($t_{-1}$ and emotional peek time ($t$). In the second result figure time remains identical but we can see the global view and the different communication range of each involved avatar. **Architecture Testing –** We have tested the computational effect of adding non-verbal events in a 3D-chatting virtual world environment. In terms of computational capability, the entire architecture is running at 60 fps on nowadays classical PCs. We produced 11 tests to compute the additional expected computational cost due to the enriched non-verbal aspect. As illustrated in Figure 8, the increase on the VR-server in input is less than 10 percent. Generation of induced-events (*e.g.* emotional changes), increases output around 70 percent. Two aspect can be concluded: first, the total increase remains small compared to the computer capabilities, and second, the increase factor is not dependant of the number of participants but relative to the user number chatting within each group –which usually is two persons and rarely larger than four. Video demonstrations are also available online for "changes of facial expression" and "test of the general architecture".

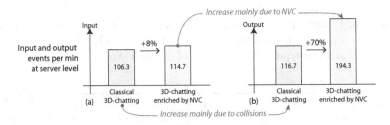

**Fig. 8.** Comparing input and output events occurring at server level between a classical 3D-chatting and a 3D-chatting enriched by NVC

# 5   Conclusion

We have presented a 3D virtual environment conversational architecture enriched with non-verbal communication affecting virtual humans movements. This approach adds a new dimension to animation applicable to virtual worlds as resulting conversations enable to create more natural exchanges. Whereas a companion paper details the emotional model and correlation to emotional animations, this paper focuses on the global event-based architecture and corresponding effect on motion-based NVC. One consequence to this event-based management of emotion is the different aspect of motion that makes VHs to look more natural: change of facial expression, breathing rhythm due to stress level, and full body emotional motions occurring at intense change of emotion. We have also shown that the increase of messages between server and clients due to NVC is not a threat when finding a compromise between visible change of expression and time to react to NVC events. The next phase of this study is a large scale user-test focusing on how users would react in this new way to experience virtual world. This study would also help defining a good parametrization for the management of events.

**Acknowledgements.** The authors wish to thank O. Renault and M. Clavien for their hard work and collaboration in the acting, motion capture, and VH skeleton mapping of *emoMotion*. We thanks J. Llobera, P. Salamin, M. Hopmann, and M. Guitierrez for participating in the multi-user testings. This work was supported by a European Union grant by the 7th Framework Programme, part of the CYBEREMOTIONS Project (Contract 231323).

# References

1. Ahn, J., Gobron, S., Garcia, D., Silvestre, Q., Thalmann, D., Boulic, R.: An NVC Emotional Model for Conversational Virtual Humans in a 3D Chatting Environment. In: Perales, F.J., Fisher, R.B., Moeslund, T.B. (eds.) AMDO 2012. LNCS, vol. 7378, pp. 47–57. Springer, Heidelberg (2012)
2. Becheiraz, P., Thalmann, D.: A model of nonverbal communication and interpersonal relationship between virtual actors. In: Proceedings of Computer Animation 1996, pp. 58–67 (June 1996)
3. Becker, C., Kopp, S., Wachsmuth, I.: Simulating the Emotion Dynamics of a Multimodal Conversational Agent. In: André, E., Dybkjær, L., Minker, W., Heisterkamp, P. (eds.) ADS 2004. LNCS (LNAI), vol. 3068, pp. 154–165. Springer, Heidelberg (2004)
4. Becker, C., Nakasone, A., Prendinger, H., Ishizuka, M., Wachsmuth, I.: Physiologically interactive gaming with the 3d agent max. In: Intl. Workshop on Conversational Informatics, pp. 37–42 (2005)
5. Boellstorff, T.: Coming of Age in Second Life: An Anthropologist Explores the Virtually Human. Princeton University Press (2008)
6. Cassell, J., Vilhjálmsson, H.H., Bickmore, T.: Beat: Behavior expression animation toolkit. In: SIGGRAPH 2001, pp. 477–486 (2001)
7. de Melo, C.M., Zheng, L., Gratch, J.: Expression of Moral Emotions in Cooperating Agents. In: Ruttkay, Z., Kipp, M., Nijholt, A., Vilhjálmsson, H.H. (eds.) IVA 2009. LNCS, vol. 5773, pp. 301–307. Springer, Heidelberg (2009)
8. Ekman, P.: Emotions revealed. Henry Holt and Company, LLC, New York (2004)
9. Gobron, S., Ahn, J., Silvestre, Q., Thalmann, D., Rank, S., Skoron, M., Paltoglou, G., Thelwall, M.: An interdisciplinary vr-architecture for 3d chatting with non-verbal communication. In: EG VE 2011: Proceedings of the Joint Virtual Reality Conference of EuroVR. ACM (September 2011)
10. Hatfield, E., Cacioppo, J.T., Rapson, R.L.: Emotional Contagion. Current Directions in Psychological Science 2(3), 96–99 (1993)
11. Kappas, A., Krämer, N.: Face-to-face communication over the Internet. Cambridge Univ. Press (2011)
12. Kappas, A.: Smile when you read this, whether you like it or not: Conceptual challenges to affect detection. IEEE Transactions on Affective Computing 1(1), 38–41 (2010)
13. Kopp, S., Gesellensetter, L., Krämer, N.C., Wachsmuth, I.: A Conversational Agent as Museum Guide – Design and Evaluation of a Real-World Application. In: Panayiotopoulos, T., Gratch, J., Aylett, R.S., Ballin, D., Olivier, P., Rist, T. (eds.) IVA 2005. LNCS (LNAI), vol. 3661, pp. 329–343. Springer, Heidelberg (2005)
14. Krämer, N.C., Simons, N., Kopp, S.: The Effects of an Embodied Conversational Agent's Nonverbal Behavior on User's Evaluation and Behavioral Mimicry. In: Pelachaud, C., Martin, J.-C., André, E., Chollet, G., Karpouzis, K., Pelé, D. (eds.) IVA 2007. LNCS (LNAI), vol. 4722, pp. 238–251. Springer, Heidelberg (2007)
15. Michael, R., Wagner, J.A.: Second Life: The Official Guide, 2nd edn. Wiley Publishing (2008)
16. Niewiadomski, R., Hyniewska, S.J., Pelachaud, C.: Constraint-based model for synthesis of multimodal sequential expressions of emotions. IEEE Transactions on Affective Computing 2(3), 134–146 (2011)

17. Pelachaud, C.: Studies on gesture expressivity for a virtual agent. Speech Commun. 51(7), 630–639 (2009)
18. Prestonand Frans, S.D., de Waal, B.M.: Empathy: Its ultimate and proximate bases. The Behavioral and Brain Sciences 25(1), 1–20 (2002)
19. Schweitzer, F., Garcia, D.: Frank Schweitzer and David Garcia. An agent-based model of collective emotions in online communities. The European Physical Journal B - Condensed Matter and Complex Systems 77, 533–545 (2010)
20. Weiner, M., Devoe, S., Rubinow, S., Geller, J.: Nonverbal behavior and nonverbal communication. Psychological Review 79, 185–214 (1972)

# Improving Gestural Communication
# in Virtual Characters

María del Puy Carretero[1], Aitor Ardanza[1], Sara García[1],
Helen Díez[1], David Oyarzun[1], and Nuria Ruiz[2]

[1] 3D Animation and Interactive Virtual Environments, Vicomtech,
P. Mikeletegi 57, Donostia-San Sebastián, Spain
[2] Elixir Films S.L., C/ Portuetxe, 23B, 4ª planta, oficina 13-6,
Donostia-San Sebastián, Spain
{mcarretero,aardanza,sgarcia,hdiez,doyarzun}@ivicomtech.org,
nuriarc@elixir-films.com

**Abstract.** Gestural communication is part of non-verbal communication, but it is also a method that deaf people use to communicate with others through sign languages. In this paper, we present the research to improve communication in virtual characters no matter if it is spoken or signed using non-verbal communication. A brief study of hand gestures has been made to obtain some rules to improve natural behaviour in virtual characters. These rules, like the use of beats, are applied in an animation engine that emulates the behaviour of real people. The behaviour of the virtual character can also be modified by other channels such as user's input, so the character's attitude has to be adapted. This paper describes the architecture and main modules of the prototype designed to achieve natural behaviour in virtual characters and present the validation results obtained during the first phase of the development.

**Keywords:** 3D Virtual Character, Natural Behaviour, Communication, Gestures.

## 1 Introduction

Communication through hands is extended and each culture has its own movements. Although there are some gestures that can be considered as universals [1] such as "ok", "stop", "goodbye", "crazy", etc., Birdwhistell [2] concluded that there are no universal gestures, but they are acquired over time influenced by the culture.

Scientific community has established four types of hand gestures [3]:

- Iconics: represent some feature of the accompanying speech.
- Metaphorics: represent an abstract feature concurrently spoken about.
- Deictics: indicate a point in the space.
- Beats: are small formless waves of the hand that occur to emphasize words.

McNeill [4] explains that in some speech contexts about three-quarters of all sentences are accompanied by hand gestures; of these, about 40% are iconic, 40% are beats, and the remaining 20% are divided between deictic and metaphoric gestures.

F.J. Perales, R.B. Fisher, and T.B. Moeslund (Eds.): AMDO 2012, LNCS 7378, pp. 69–81, 2012.
© Springer-Verlag Berlin Heidelberg 2012

These types of gestures accompany verbal communication and their use is to complement the speech. However there is another kind of communication that involves gestures with hands and arms, that is sign language. Thanks to sign languages, deaf people can communicate with others making gestures using their hands and arms but these signs are always accompanied by other non-verbal elements such as facial expressions, pose, etc.

This work presents the research that involves improving gestural communication in virtual characters. There are two main objectives. First, it is to improve natural behaviour in virtual characters thanks to the execution of gestural movements like beats or pointing, as well as other non-verbal elements such as blinking. Secondly, it is to achieve natural transition in the execution of the movements which makes the communication and the behaviour of the virtual character more natural.

Section below summarizes the state of the art of hand gestures. In this section we analyze typical gestures and the moment when they are generally made. Section 3 makes a brief summary about other research related to natural behaviour and methods to achieve it. Section 4 explains the architecture designed to provide natural gestural behaviour to the virtual character. In section 5 two different projects related to improving communication with virtual characters are explained. These projects validate the architecture and one of them has been tested with real users who gave us their opinion. Finally, section 6 shows our conclusions.

## 2    Type of Hand Gestures

In this section a study of hand gestures is presented. As Cassel et. al., [3] explained, there are four types of hand gestures. They are made depending on the purpose of the speaker. However, sometimes they are made unconsciously. Thanks to this study, behaviour rules have been obtained in order to apply them to virtual characters. Thus, natural behaviour in gestural communication is achieved.

### 2.1    Iconic Gestures

McNeill [4] was who named this type of gestures that are characterized by representing something concrete and accompany to what is being said. Other authors [5] had named these gestures as "illustrators" but the definition is the same: they are hand movements that are directly linked with speech and that help to illustrate what is being said verbally.

It seems that iconic gestures represent the shape and/or other physical characteristics of the object or thing that is being spoken [6]. However, some researches expose that the similarity with its referent does not explain totally all the apparitions of iconic gestures [7]. Researches reveal that iconic gestures are influenced by the context [6]. In addition humans are very different from each other. Depending on personal or cultural background, differences in gestures are obvious [8]. That means for example that gestures can be different to represent the same object.

According to McNeill [4] the most important aspect of iconic gestures is the ability to articulate, from the point of view of the orator, which are the most relevant characteristics of the context. McNeill concluded that iconic gestures allow observing the thoughts of the orator because these movements are not forced by rules or standards.

## 2.2   Metaphoric Gestures

Metaphoric gestures are reproduced when a concept is being explained. These gestures are made using three-dimensional space and are used to describe an idea or something specific such as "take hold of an arm" or something more general such as "shake hands". As Cassell [9] explained, the concept metaphoric gestures represent has no physical form; instead the form of the gesture comes from a common metaphor. Cassel gave as an example it can be said "the meeting went on and on" accompanied by a hand indicating rolling motion.

Parrill and Sweetser [10] proposed that even metaphoric gestures have an iconic aspect. This iconic aspect invokes some visual or concrete situation, entity or action, by means of the hand shapes and motions. So it seems that these gestures are similar to iconic gestures. However, the difference is that metaphoric gestures represent a more abstract idea [11].

## 2.3   Deictic Gestures

Deictic gestures accompany to some linguistic elements of pointing. These elements can refer to people such as "you", "he", "she", etc.; to a place like "here", "there", "up", etc.; to time such as "today", "yesterday", "now", etc.

According to Alibali [12] words like "this", "that", etc., need to be accompanied with deictic gestures so they can be interpreted by the interlocutor. Most of the deictic gestures are made with the index finger extended and the rest of the fingers forming a fist. In Table 1 a short list of typical deictic gestures is shown.

**Table 1.** Example of some deictic gestures

| Meaning | Gesture |
|---|---|
| Involve to the interlocutor | Point to interlocutor |
| Involve to oneself | Point to oneself |
| Now/here | One or both index finger pointing down |
| There | Point to somewhere |
| Up/down | Put up/down one arm with the index finger extended |
| To the left/right | Move one arm to left/right |
| Fom up to down / From down to up | Move one arm from up to down / down to up |

Cienki and Müller [13] argued that some uses of abstract deictic could also be considered metaphoric, if the gesture is interpreted as pointing to an event (a new scene) as an object. However as Kobsa et. al., [14] explained deictic gestures not only involves hands and fingers but also other elements such as head, eyes or even pointing with a pencil.

## 2.4   Beats

Beats are short and simple gestures that accompany the rhythm of the discourse, so beats accompany the prosodic peaks of the speech. These gestures are named as beats because they are similar to the movements that conductors make [15].

The function of these gestures is similar to pitch and intonation when speaking. Beats act as markers of the structure of the information associated to the expression [16]. Krahmer and Swerts [17] research shows that there is a connection between the beat gesture and prosody in the production of it as well as in its perception. Thus, it can be said that beats represents the same rhythm than prosody accents.

As Kettebekov [11] explained, these gestures are possibly the most spontaneous and the smallest of the gestures made with hands. According to McNeill [4] the role of beats is to indicate that the narrator is taking the conversation through different states.

## 3     Related Work

Providing natural behaviour to virtual characters is the objective of several research groups. There are different studies about the natural behaviour of virtual characters in diverse applications and cases of study. In most of them, the authors base their research on hand and arm gestures.

For example, with the aim of increasing the success of virtual characters as other method of human-computer interaction, Rieger [18] compiled a list of speech acts to give the message and the state of the system. For example to inform about the status of the system, if a warning message appears, the virtual character has to show importance, if it is busy, shows regrets, if error, shows sorry, etc. In his architecture, Rieger distinguishes between behaviour rules and gesture rules to develop the controller and renderer of the virtual character. The author explains that the behaviour is responsible for the virtual characres mimic, speech, and head-movements; and gesture rules are related to hand movements.

López et. al., [19] established some rules in order to provide realism to a virtual character during the interaction with people in a spoken dialog system. Their objective was to make the virtual character look alive. The experimental case of study was a domotic service where users "called" to home to check the state of their electrical appliance. The strategy followed by the spoken dialog system was designed to deal with some critical states. For example, at the beginning of the dialogue, the virtual character has to look at the camera, smile and wave a hand; when the system starts to speak, the virtual character has to look directly at the user and raise the eyebrows; or when the system gives some explanation to the user, the virtual character has to make beat gestures with the hands.

Bergman and Kopp [20] expose that the speech is also influenced by the gestures. The authors explain that they made some experiments and concluded that when making gestures is allowed, the vocabulary is richer than when gestures are forbidden. They mention the conclusion of Rauscher et. al [21] that prohibiting gestures in cartoon narrations made speech less fluent. In addition in these cases the speaker tends to use more words like "uhm". To conclude, making gestures enriches the language used by people and the communication is more fluent.

Alseid and Rigas [22] studied the user's view of facial expressions and body gestures in e-learning applications. To their experiment they used different expressions (interested, amazed, happy and smiling, neutral and thinking) and eight body gestures categorized into positive (hands clenching – front and back, open palms, pointing, chin stroking and hands steepling) and negative (arms folded and legs grossed). Users evaluated positively body animations. Their results revealed that including specific body gestures in interactive e-learning interfaces could be attractive for users.

In order to improve the transition between two different gestures during the generation of French Sign Language, Efthimiou and Kouroupetroglo [23] use coarticulation parameters to avoid using an intermediate rest posture. In their first version of their technique coarticulation was implemented as a simple interpolation between the last frame of a sequence and the first frame of its following sequence.

The related work shows several authors are researching on improving the natural gestural behaviour of virtual character including body gestures, and researching on developing techniques to make the animation more natural.

Our goal is to provide not only specific gestures in predefined states, but also improve the natural and unpredictable actions of virtual characters. The objective is to establish a randomly but coherent behaviour based in behaviour rules, that is modified by specific gestures depending on the context of the interaction. Besides, these gestures and actions vary depending on the mood of the virtual character. In addition the transition between gestures has to result natural in order to emulate movements of real people. For that purpose it is necessary to develop transition techniques between predefined gestures.

# 4    Architecture

This section explains our platform's global architecture. The main objective is to improve the gestural movements of virtual characters when they communicate with others. Figure 1 shows the modules of the architecture.

The main module is the Animation Engine and it is supplied by the rest of the components of the architecture and it is also in charge of rendering the final appearance and behaviour of the virtual character. This module works influenced by several factors that change the attitude of the virtual character:

- The Cognitive Module takes into account the inputs of the system and it obtains an estimated emotion to modify the behaviour of the virtual character.
- A Markup Language, such as BML (Behaviour Markup Language) [24] or VHML (Virtual Human Markup Language) [25] can be used to indicate some specific movements to the virtual character.
- The TextToSpeech (TTS) module synthesizes text to obtain audio files that form the voice of the virtual character. In addition it obtains a *.pho file that contains the information that is needed to animate the lips according to what text says.
- The Behaviour Rules Database contains some rules of behaviour that are applied randomly but coherently to provide natural behaviour to the virtual character.

## 4.1    Cognitive Module

The Cognitive Module is responsible for estimating the virtual character's emotion depending on the inputs of the system and it is dependent on the logic of the application. That means that it is necessary to know the objectives of the application to be able to predict with which emotion the virtual character has to react to the user's actions.

So, for an interactive system to be capable of generating emotions, it will need to be provided with a module that is automatically capable of generating emotions. The emotions will be the result of a cognitive process that evaluates the events in the environment. There are several emotional models on which this cognitive perspective have been based. Our Cognitive Module implements Roseman Models [26] due to the reasons argued by Ortiz et. al., [27]. This module is able to predict Ekman's emotions.

However, depending on the characteristics of the application it is extensible to adapt this module using another cognitive model which fits better to the objectives of the application. No matter which cognitive model is used, the important result is the estimated emotion with which the virtual character has to react. This emotion has influence on the final animation both facial and corporal.

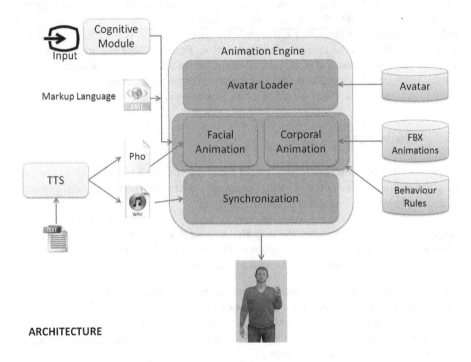

**Fig. 1.** Architecture

## 4.2    TextToSpeech (TTS) Module

The TTS Module uses a commercial synthesizer to obtain the audio file which composes the voice of the virtual character. For our prototypes we use Loquendo TTS that is speech synthesis software available with several voices in different languages, to fully meet the needs of all application environments.

In addition, this module is in charge of obtaining the *.pho file. This file contains the phonemes that are needed to animate the lips of the virtual characters as well as the duration of each phoneme. Thanks to this information, the mouth of the virtual character is animated simulating a real person talking.

## 4.3    Databases

The architecture uses three main databases that feed the animation engine (which will be explained later). Thanks to these databases it is possible to load the virtual character, to apply its behaviour and modify it according to external factors such us user's interaction or behaviour rules that affect the natural behaviour of the virtual character.

- *Avatar database* contains the 3D models that form the physical appearance of the virtual character. A virtual character is created using 3D design software like 3ds Max or Maya. Apart from the physical appearance of the character it is also required that the facial expressions of the virtual character are created in order to apply facial animation techniques as it will be explained in the following section. The structure of each character is stored in an xml file which contains all the 3D models required to load the virtual character and to animate it.
- *FBX animations database* is composed for the pre-defined animations that the virtual character has to execute during its animation. These animations can be obtained thanks to motion capture systems like CyberGlobe II that captures the movements of hand and fingers (http://www.cyberglovesystems.com), or Organic Motion (http://www.organicmotion.com) that captures movements of the whole body. The animations obtained thanks to these systems are applied to the skeleton of each character and stored in the database.
- *Behaviour Rules database* includes some rules to provide virtual characters with natural behaviour. These rules were obtained through the research of several authors as explained in section 2. Most of them are related to hand and arm movements while interacting with others, but they also include rules related to the gaze; for example, looking at the listener when ending a sentence [28], or to the postures, such as changing balance generally caused by fatigue and small variations in body posture due to muscle contractions. These rules pretend to make the virtual character seem more alive and to emulate the behaviour of a real person.

## 4.4    Animation Engine Module

The Animation Engine Module is the main module of the architecture. It is responsible for generating the virtual character's animation as well as to load it. This module is developed using Open Scene Graph (http://www.openscenegraph.org/) and loads the virtual character from the Avatar database. Once the model of the character is loaded, the animation that forms the virtual character's behaviour can be applied. For that purpose there are two different sub-modules: Speech Animation and Behaviour Animation.

The Speech Animation sub-module executes the facial animation when the virtual character speaks. The facial animation is generated using morphing techniques where the key facial expressions considered to make the animation are the Ekman's emotions as well as other expressions such as eyes closed, winks and a neutral face. For this task the phonemes of the speech are needed. As it was explained before, they are given by the *.pho file.

The Behaviour Animation sub-module deals with both the predefined rules for natural behaviour and with the emotion obtained with the cognitive module. The rules are launched automatically but they are executed randomly in order to give impro-vised behaviour as people usually do. The animations of these basic movements are taken from the FBX database and they are applied using inverse kinematics to con-catenate several animations and to obtain realistic movements. The cognitive module changes the behaviour executed by the rules. This module guesses the attitude that the virtual character has to show depending on the inputs of the system. Thus, the speed of the gestures and movements is changed. In addition the character's expression is modified. The face shows the predicted emotion, so it implies more realism to the virtual character.

The natural behaviour of the virtual character can also be modified by other spe-cific movements and gestures. These gestures are provided by the input of the system or by a predefined behaviour in Markup Language files (XML). This may be because it can be needed to execute certain movements at given moments. For example, as it will be explained later, when the virtual character's role is a virtual tutor, the specific movements are given by the real tutor when he/she prepares the course.

The Render module synchronizes the audio (the voice of the virtual character) and the generated animation. The result is a realistic virtual character emulating a real person and his/her natural behaviour while interacting with others.

## 5    Applications That Validate the Architecture

The architecture is being validated in two different projects related with virtual char-acters and natural behaviour in communication with people. In the first one, the main objective is to develop natural behaviour in virtual teachers in order to emulate a real one to improve e-learning courses. The second project improves the behaviour in virtual characters that "speak" Sing Language. These projects are explained in the following sections.

### 5.1    Natural Behaviour in e-Learning

E-learning applications that integrate virtual characters as teachers have been devel-oped during years. However most of these researches are focused on talking heads, or predefined characters that do not have enough realism in their animations and are far from real behaviour.

The objective of our project is to improve the communication between the virtual teacher and students. The virtual teacher has two different tasks: to explain the lessons and to evaluate the students. During the phase of explanation: the virtual character emulates the behaviour of a real teacher giving explanations by speaking and making gestures that help to understand the meaning of the lecture. In addition the virtual teacher makes natural gestures that humans make unconsciously such as beats and others not related to hands, such as blinking.

The gestures that help to understand the meaning of speech are usually associated with words or sentences. It is necessary to know which gestures the virtual character has to reproduce in order to make an analysis of the sentences. That is not an objec-tive of the project, so as a preliminary solution, and as the lessons are pre-edited by real tutors, the course editor indicates which gestures the virtual character has to reproduce while explaining the lesson. For that purpose, we use markup languages oriented to virtual characters like BML (Behaviour Markup Language) or VHML (Virtual Human Markup Language) in order to indicate which gesture goes with which word or sentence. For example, the course editor can select deictic gestures or predefined iconic or metaphoric gestures. These gestures depend on the context so they have to be designed previously.

The gestures that the character has to execute unconsciously, such as blinking or beats, are given by the rules established in the behaviour rules database and executed through the behaviour animation sub-module. However this behaviour can be modified by the markup gestures.

The second phase is the student's evaluation. In this case the natural behaviour is modified depending on the input of the student. The Cognitive Module predicts the emotion that the virtual teacher has to express depending on the student's responses. For example if the student's answers are correct the virtual teacher should be glad and act according to this emotion. In contrast, if the student's answers are wrong, the virtual character gets angry and its behaviour is ruddier. Once the emotion is predicted and it is known if the answer is correct, the character's behaviour is given by the behaviour rules and adapted with the emotion. For example, if the student answers correctly, the virtual character makes gestures with the arms and hands indicating good!, ok!, perfect!, etc. The face shows happiness and the virtual tutor says that the answer is correct and encourages the student to keep up the good work. On the other hand, if the answer is wrong the character makes negation gestures with the arms and hands, the face shows sadness and the virtual tutor replies that the answer is incorrect and advices to concentrate or to revise the lesson.

Fig. 2 shows two different virtual characters' reactions depending on the student's answers. On the left the student answered correctly, so the virtual tutor makes a satisfaction gesture with his arms and his face shows gladness. On the right the student's answer was incorrect so the virtual character rejects the answer and shows a sad expression.

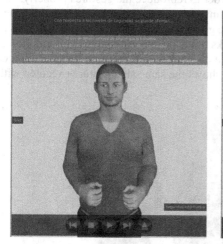 

**Fig. 2.** Different virtual characters' reaction depending on the answer, happy if it is correct (left), sad if it is wrong (right)

## 5.2    Virtual Sign Language Interpreter

The main objective of the second project is to make media services accessible to people with a hearing disability through the use of sign language. For that purpose, a virtual character whose role is to interpret Spanish Sign Language (LSE) is used. What the virtual character has to interpret is given via text, which is translated to LSE and executed by the virtual interpreter. The translation from text to LSE is being developed in a given domain (meteorology) and this will be described in successive papers.

Getting a realistic and natural animation of a signing character in real time is an arduous task. There are two main points to solve. The first point is to ensure that deaf or other hear-disabled people understand the sequence of gestures the virtual character reproduces. To achieve this, a natural and realistic concatenation of gestures is necessary.

The second point is related to a correct interpretation of the gestures. Emotions and mood are reflected by people when they communicate with others. Emotions are noticed by the facial expression; however they also modify the execution of gestures. That means that the same gesture is slightly different depending on how the person feels, for example happy, sad or angry. When someone is happy the movements are a bit quicker, when a person is feeling sad they are a bit slower and when being angry they are more abrupt. So it is necessary to modify the speed of the animation execution. In addition, in Spanish Sign Language (LSE), there are some gestures that are different depending on the mood of the person who signs.

Thanks to the Animation Engine Module, our architecture realizes the animation of the signing character in LSE. The Animation Engine interprets the sequence of gestures that a Text-LSE module obtains from the translation from text to Spanish Sign Language.

The animation engine loads the required gestures from Sign Language Database (FBX database). These gestures are captured previously with a motion capture system and they need to be made by experts in LSE in order to get realistic movements.

The animation engine also loads the virtual interpreter from a database. Avatars have to be designed according to some rules. For example, all the bones and joints of the hands and arms have to be defined in order to reproduce the gestures properly.

The Animation Engine generates the animation corresponding to the sign language translation. This animation is modified by a given emotion that can be given manually or depending on the user's interaction thanks to the cognitive module. This emotion is expressed on the face of the character, but it also has an influence on the execution of the animation changing its speed. Figure 3 shows the same sign gesture executed with different emotions: neutral, angry and sad.

**Fig. 3.** A virtual character signing with different emotions: neutral, angry and sad

In addition the animation engine provides natural behaviour to the virtual interpreter. This means that the character does not just play the necessary gestures, but it also has other movements to improve the communication. Thus it seems that the virtual character is alive. For example, in waiting state (without talking in LSE) it makes movements like a real person does when waiting; while interpreting in sign language, the virtual character acts as a real person moving the head, eyes or body as people do, as well as expressing emotions. That provides realistic behaviour to the virtual interpreter allowing deaf and other hear-disabled people to better understand the information that the virtual interpreter offers.

### 5.3    Evaluation and Results

The virtual tutor application is still under development and has not been evaluated by real users (students and teachers) yet. However we have a first vision of deaf people that have evaluated the virtual interpreter. This not only tests this application, but it also allows us to know if the behaviour of the character seems natural to people. The virtual interpreter was evaluated by one deaf person, by a real interpreter and by a person who knows LSE. They tested the application and made several comments that are summarized as follows:

- Although they understood the sentences interpreted by the virtual character, they suggested that the transition between signs should be smoother.
- The expression of the virtual interpreter has to be more exaggerated because deaf people give importance to this factor. They agree that the emotions can be recognized, but when people use sign language they exaggerate their expression.
- Eyebrows, gaze and shoulders are also important for the correct interpretation of sign language. For example, eyebrows are fundamental to express questions or exclamations. So it is necessary to include some rules to this behaviour.
- The behaviour and attitude during the waiting state is correct. Their opinion was that the virtual character emulates the behaviour or a real person.

In general, the evaluation of deaf people was positive, they appreciate the efforts made to make media services more accessible and their opinion about the result was positive although it was a preliminary development. They mentioned that the behaviour during the waiting state was good emulating the behaviour of real people.

## 6    Conclusions

We have designed and developed an architecture that improves the natural behaviour of virtual characters when they communicate with people. It is focussed on hands and arms but it also includes other aspects such as emotions, blinking, posture, gaze, etc.

For that purpose we have analyzed the common behaviour of people when they communicate with others especially the hands and arms movements. From this behaviour we have obtained some common rules and they have been integrated in the Animation Engine that executes them by default but randomly.

The default behaviour of the virtual character is modified by other specific gestures. In addition the emotion and mood of the character vary the execution of the gestures and the behaviour in the speed of the movements.

The architecture is being tested in two different projects that integrate virtual characters to communicate with people. The first project improves the communication with students in e-Learning applications. The virtual teacher has a natural behaviour and explains the lesson accompanied by gestures that make it easier to understand the concepts. In the second project the virtual character communicates through sign language with deaf people. However the virtual interpreter not only executes the gestures, but he/she also modifies them depending on the mood or emotion. In addition, the virtual character has a default behaviour that improves the realism of the virtual interpreter during the waiting state (without using sign language).

The evaluation was satisfactory. Although the project was in an initial phase, deaf people gave us a good feedback about the result. They suggested to make the transition between gestures a bit smoother and to exaggerate the emotions and expressions because that is something they do when they communicate with others. However they admitted the emotions and the purpose of the character could be recognized.

As future work we plan to improve the way of executing specific gestures. In other words, our objective is to analyze the speech and to obtain the gestures and movements that real people would make in each case. In addition we pretend to extend the basic rules for natural behaviour based on the virtual character's personality. This is because each person has his/her own way of acting so the same idea can be applied to virtual characters.

# References

1. Andersen, M.L., Taylor, H.F.: Sociology: The essentials, 4th edn. Thomson Wadsworth, Beltmon (2007)
2. Birdwhistell, R.L.: El lenguaje de la expresión corporal. Ediciones Gustavo Gili, Spain (1979)
3. Cassell, J., Pelachaud, C., Badler, N., Steedman, M., Achorn, B., Becket, W., Douville, B., Prevost, S., Stone, M.: Animated conversation: Rule-based generation of facial expression, gesture and spoken intonation for multiple conversational agents. In: Computer Graphics. Annual Conf. Series, pp. 413–420. ACM (1994)
4. McNeill, D.: Hand and Mind: What Gestures Reveal about Thought. The University of Chicago Press, USA (1992)
5. Ekman, P., Friesen, W.: The Repertoire of Nonverbal Behavior: Categories, Origins, Usage, and Coding. Semiotica 1, 9–98 (1969)
6. Bergmann, K., Kopp, S.: Modeling the Production of Co-Verbal Iconic Gestures by Learning Bayesian Decision Networks. Applied Artificial Intelligence 24(6), 530–551 (2010)
7. Streeck, J.: Depicting by gesture. Gesture 8(3), 285–301 (2008)
8. Hostetter, A., Alibali, M.: Raise your hand if you're spatial–Relations between verbal and spatial skills and gesture production. Gesture 7(1), 73–95 (2007)
9. Cassell, J.: A Framework For Gesture Generation And Interpretation. In: Cipolla, R., Pentland, A. (eds.) Computer Vision in Human-Machine Interaction. Cambridge University Press (1998)
10. Parrill, F., Sweetser, E.: What we mean by meaning. Gesture 4(2), 197–219 (2004)

11. Kettebekov, S.: Exploiting Prosodic Structuring of Coverbal Gesticulation. In: Proceedings of the ACM International Conference on Multimodal Interfaces, pp. 105–112 (2004)
12. Alibali, M.W., Kita, S., Young, A.J.: Gesture and the process of speech production: We think, therefore we gesture. Language and Cognitive Processes 15(6), 593–613 (2000)
13. Cienki, A., Müller, C.: Metaphor, gesture, and thought. In: Gibbs Jr., R.W. (ed.) The Cambridge Handbook of Metaphor and Thought. Cambridge University Press, Cambridge (2008)
14. Kobsa, A., Allgayer, J., Reddig, C., Reithinger, N., Schmauks, D., Harbusch, K., Wahlster, W.: Combining deictic gestures and natural language for referent identification. In: Proceedings Eleventh COLING, Bonn, Germany, pp. 356–361 (1986)
15. Giorgolo, G.: Space and Time in Our Hands. PhD. Universiteit Utrecht (2010)
16. Pierrehumbert, J., Hirschberg, J.: The meaning of intonational contours in interpretation of discourse. In: Cohen, P., Morgan, J., Pollack, M. (eds.) Intentions in Communication, ch. 14. MIT Press (1990)
17. Krahmer, E., Swerts, M.: The efects of visual beats on prosodic prominence: Acoustic analyses, auditory perception and visual perception. Journal of Memory and Language 57(3), 396–414 (2007)
18. Rieger, T.: Avatar Gestures. Journal of WSCG 2003 11(2), 379–386 (2003)
19. López, B., Hernández, A., Díaz Pardo de Vera, D., Santos de la Cámara, R., Rodríguez, M.C.: ECA gesture strategies for robust SLDS. In: Convention - Communication, Interaction and Social Intelligence on the Symposium on Multimodal Output Generation, Aberdeen, Scotland (2008)
20. Bergmann, K., Kopp, S.: Multimodal content representation for speech and gesture production. In: Theune, M., van der Sluis, I., Bachvarova, Y., André, E. (eds.) Symposium at the AISB Annual Convention: Multimodal Output Generation, Aberdeen, UK, pp. 61–68 (2008)
21. Rauscher, F.H., Krauss, R.M., Chen, Y.: Gesture, speech, and lexical access: The role of lexical movements in speech production. Psychological Science 7, 226–231 (1996)
22. Alseid, M., Rigas, D.: Users' views of facial expressions and body gestures in e-learning interfaces: an empirical evaluation. World Scientific and Engineering Academy and Society, WSEAS (2009)
23. Efthimiou, E., Kouroupetroglou, G. (eds.): Proc. of the 9th International Gesture Workshop, Athens, Greece, May 25-27, 2011, pp. 25–27 (2011)
24. Kopp, S., Krenn, B., Marsella, S., Marshall, A., Pelachaud, C., Pirker, H., Thórisson, K., Vilhjalmsson, H.: Towards a Common Framework for Multimodal Generation in ECAs: The Behavior Markup Language. In: Proceedings of the 6th International (2006)
25. Marriott, A.: VHML – Virtual Human Markup Language. In: Talking Head Technology Workshop, at OzCHI Conference (2001)
26. Roseman, I., Antoniou, A., Jose, P.: Appraisal determinants of emotions: Constructing a more accurate and comprehensive theory. Cognition and Emotion 10 (1996)
27. Ortiz, A., Oyarzun, D., Carretero, M., Posada, J., Linaza, M.T., Garay-Vitoria, N.: Analysing emotional interaction through avatars. A generic architecture. e-Minds: International Journal on Human-Computer Interaction I(5) (March 2009) ISSN: 1697-9613 (print) - 1887-3022 (online)
28. Kendon, A.: Some functions of gaze direction in social interaction. Acta Psychologica 26, 22–63 (1967)

# Multi-view Body Tracking with a Detector-Driven Hierarchical Particle Filter*

Sergio Navarro, Adolfo López-Méndez,
Marcel Alcoverro, and Josep Ramon Casas

Technical University of Catalonia (UPC),
Barcelona, Spain
{adolf.lopez,marcel.alcoverro.vidal,josep.ramon.casas}@upc.edu

**Abstract.** In this paper we present a novel approach to markerless human motion capture that robustly integrates body part detections in multiple views. The proposed method fuses cues from multiple views to enhance the propagation and observation model of particle filtering methods aiming at human motion capture. We particularize our method to improve arm tracking in the publicly available IXMAS dataset. Our experiments show that the proposed method outperforms other state-of-the-art approaches.

**Keywords:** human motion capture, body part detection, multi-view, 3D reconstruction, inverse kinematics.

## 1 Introduction

Human motion capture or, in other words, being able to automatically estimate the human pose and its motion, is a problem that has attracted the interest of the computer vision community in the last decades. Among its wide range of applications, we emphasize its potential for action recognition [1]. Human motion capture has been addressed from several perspectives. One could roughly categorize them into three large fields: monocular approaches, depth-data based approaches and multi-view approaches.

Human motion capture from multiple views is still a challenging problem in realistic scenarios, where a few views are usually available. Some approaches employ a model-based approach in combination with variants of particle filter algorithms in order to efficiently estimate the pose [2][3]. Although achieving an impressive performance on some standard datasets, they usually rely on weak prior models that fail to predict complex motion. For that matter, learning motion models has been proposed as a solution to enrich such prior models [4][5]. The problem with these approaches is the lack of scalability when a large number of motion patterns need to be tracked. Alternatively, one can rely on input video cues in order to improve prior models. This latter approach can be addressed by

---

* This work has been partially supported by the Spanish Ministerio de Ciencia e Innovación, under project TEC2010-18094.

F.J. Perales, R.B. Fisher, and T.B. Moeslund (Eds.): AMDO 2012, LNCS 7378, pp. 82–91, 2012.

detecting body parts on images [6][7]. However, employing image cues and body part detectors is frequently overlooked in multiple view pose estimation due to the difficulty of robustly fusing detections in several views.

In this paper, we propose a novel pose estimation approach that robustly integrates body part detections in multiple views. The method proposed utilizes end-effector detections in order to improve the prior and observation models of a *Layered Particle Filter*. By doing so, we achieve superior scalability in comparison to learning motion models. Our contributions are the following:

- We introduce a method to robustly fuse detections in multiple views into a single 3D position. Our method tackles occlusions and tolerates detection errors in several views.
- We propose a particle propagation model based on Inverse Kinematics which allows to sample pose variables given candidate end-effector detections. The method approximates the reliability of detections by employing the survival rate.
- We propose a *Refinement Layer* that effectively improves the observation model and is able to correct some errors produced by incorrect body part detections.

Our method is evaluated in the publicly available IXMAS dataset [8]. This dataset was designed for action recognition in multiple views, hence we manually annotate ground truth positions for several subjects and actions. As pointed by [1], using 3D information in action recognition from multiple views yields superior performance. For that reason, we believe that improving pose estimation in this dataset, especially without relying on motion models that employ the available action labels, will be of interest for the research community. Since the IXMAS dataset contains several challenging arm motions, we focus our approach towards the improvement of tracking in such cases. Our results show that the proposed method outperforms several state-of-the-art methods for human motion capture.

## 2   Layered Particle Filters

Markerless human motion capture is commonly addressed by means of particle filtering (PF) approaches. Regular PF methods usually suffer from the curse of dimensionality: the state space of human model variables is of high dimensionality, thus the number of required particles usually grows exponentially. This problem has led to a generic set of methods that we term *Layered Particle Filters*, since these methods behave as PFs with a refinement procedure based on layers. A layered filtering implies performing several PF runs (resampling, propagation and likelihood evaluation) the same time instant $t$. The Annealed Particle Filter (APF) [9], Partitioned Sampling (PS) [10] and the Hierarchical Particle Filter (HPF) [3], are *Layered Particle Filters*. That is, one can see these well-known algorithms as instantiations of the *Layered Particle Filter*.

Let us denote $\mathbf{x} = \{x_1, ..., x_h, ..., x_H\}$ the state-space vector and $x_h$ the one-dimensional variables comprising such a vector. Let us define a set of $L$ layers, where the tuplet $\{\mathbf{x}_{t,l}^n, w_{t,l}^n\}$ denotes particles and weights in the $l$-th layer. Assume that $\mathbf{x}_{t,l}^n$ denotes the filtering state of the particles in the layer $l$, thus actually containing all the one-dimensional variables $x_h$. This filtering state generally implies that a subset of pose variables have been filtered up to layer $l$ and that these variables will condition the filtering of a new subset in the $(l+1)$-th layer. Alternatively, the same filtering model allows using all the pose variables in each layer in combination with a layer-specific likelihood function.

*Layered Particle Filters.* Usually tackle the curse of dimensionality by sampling from a distribution that is a *relaxed* version of the posterior. In the case of APF, this relaxation is achieved by applying concepts of simulated annealing, whereas in PS and HPF, this relaxation comes from the fact that one deals with lower-dimensional vectors.

In order to establish a reference method for comparison, in this paper we consider *Layered Particle Filters* employing Gaussian diffusion for particle propagation and silhouette-based observation models. In the absence of a precise motion model, Gaussian diffusion is a common choice in particle filtering algorithms, and it is shown to outperform unsupervised first and second order dynamical models [11]. Similarly, foreground silhouettes in multiple views are often used to approximate the likelihood function:

$$p(\mathbf{z}_t|\mathbf{x}_{t,l}^n) \simeq \tilde{w}(\mathbf{z}_t, \mathbf{x}_{t,l}^n) \propto \mathbf{e}^{-\mathcal{C}(\mathbf{z}_t, \mathbf{x}_{t,l}^n)} \tag{1}$$

where $\mathcal{C}(\mathbf{z}_t, \mathbf{x}_{t,l}^n)$ is the cost computed as the overlap between the projected body model and the silhouette in each view [3]. In this paper we use a surface mesh model articulated through 20 degrees of freedom.

# 3  DD-HPF in Multiple Views

In Layered Particle Filters, the propagation of particles by means of Gaussian diffusion makes the filter blind with respect to evidence. Some research trends focus on tackling such a problem by introducing priors based on trained motion models. This approach, however, has a limited scalability, as one needs to know which motions are performed in the scenario. Hence, it seems more reasonable to resort to image cues related to body parts in order to address the blindness problem. In such a context, partitioned or hierarchical definition of layers emerges as the most efficient approach towards drawing particles, since one can constrain the propagation and filtering to a subset of variables that are related to a particular body part. Interestingly, our preliminary findings with instantiations of Layered Particle Filters revealed that hierarchical layers outperform other state-of-the-art choices in general, and they perform better than APF in the IXMAS dataset. For that matter, we propose the Detection-Driven Hierarchical Particle filter, a novel Layered Particle filter combining hierarchical layers and body part detectors.

## 3.1 Multi-view Body Parts Detection

We present a method for 3D localization of body parts from multiple views. In this work, we focus on body extremities (hands, head and feet), as they are usually easier to detect and provide sufficient information to estimate the pose variables related to a kinematic chain. Our method takes advantage of 3D information to deal with occlusions and visibility issues, hence we can robustly fuse the outcomes of one or several image-based detectors working in different views. To achieve such a goal, we first obtain a set of points on the surface of the human body. Second, we compute the probability of each surface point to be an extremity, using the detections on multiple views. Then, the surface points are filtered using a threshold and clustering technique in order to obtain the most likely extremity locations.

The choice of the image-based detectors affects not only the performance, but how the probabilities in each surface point should be treated. We demonstrate and exemplify the method using a simple yet effective image-based hand detector. Provided that in IXMAS dataset all the subjects have their hands uncovered, we employ the skin detector proposed by Jones and Rehg [12]. Note that this particular choice implies that we cannot distinguish left from right hand and that head is also detected. Hence, and additional classification step is proposed in order to robustly detect 3D hand positions.

**Probability Surface.** To robustly fuse detections in multiple views, we employ a set of points $\mathbf{q}$ with associated normals $\hat{\mathbf{n}}_q$ lying on the surface of the human body. A suitable set $\mathbf{Q}$ comprising such oriented points can be estimated in a two-step fashion by reconstructing a 3D volume and then computing normals on the volume surface. Alternatively, we opt for the method of Salvador et al. [13] that jointly estimates surface points and normals.

Then, we compute the *visibility factor* $\eta_c(\mathbf{q})$, a value representing the visibility of each oriented point $\mathbf{q}$ with respect to the camera $c$:

$$\eta_c(\mathbf{q}) = \begin{cases} -\hat{\mathbf{z}}_c \cdot \hat{\mathbf{n}}_{\mathbf{q}}, & \text{if } \mathbf{q} \text{ is visible} \\ 0, & \text{otherwise} \end{cases} \tag{2}$$

We determine if $\mathbf{q}$ is visible from camera $c$ by means of a standard z-buffering test.

This visibility factor serves to estimate the probability that a surface point $\mathbf{q}$ is representing an extremity:

$$Prob(\mathbf{q}) = \sum_{c=1}^{C} \eta_c(\mathbf{q}) \mathcal{T}(proj_c(\mathbf{q})) \tag{3}$$

where $C$ is the total number of cameras, $proj_c(\mathbf{q}) \in \mathbb{R}^2$ are the pixel coordinates resulting from the projection of the surface point $\mathbf{q}$ in camera $c$, and $\mathcal{T}(proj_c(\mathbf{q}))$ is the probability that the pixel at $proj_c(\mathbf{q})$ is representing an extremity according to an image-based detector. Note that the visibility factor has to be normalized, so $\sum_{c=1}^{C} \eta_c(w) = 1$. We show an example in Figure 1.

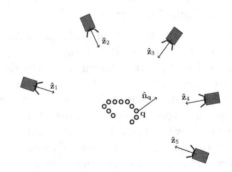

**Fig. 1.** Visibility example for a surface point $\mathbf{q}$ (best viewed in color). The best oriented cameras are green whereas the red cameras have few or null visibility.

Due to the visibility factor, the proposed method effectively handles occlusions and inconsistencies of the visual cones computed directly from detections in multiple views. Moreover, since only the best oriented cameras determine the probabilities of the surface points, our method can infer a 3D extremity location even if it is reliably detected only in a few views. In addition, as the probabilities of surface points are computed from detections inside the silhouettes, all false positives outside them are not taken into account.

**Filtering.** The filtering step aims at estimating candidate 3D locations of the detected extremities and it is analogous to finding relevant modes of the probability distribution lying on the surface manifold $\mathbf{Q}$. We start by computing the subset $\mathbf{Q}'$ of likely surface points:

$$\mathbf{Q}' = \{\ \mathbf{q} \in \mathbf{Q} \mid Prob(\mathbf{q}) \geq \Gamma\ \} \tag{4}$$

where $0 \leq \Gamma \leq 1$ is a threshold.

Then, we cluster the points in $\mathbf{Q}'$ using an efficient method [14] based on a kd-tree representation [15]. The parameters of the clustering method are distance tolerance, $\vartheta_{tol}$, and the minimum and maximum cluster size, $\vartheta_{min}$ and $\vartheta_{max}$, respectively. These parameters are very suitable for our problem, since they can be set by using anthropometric proportions. Finally, cluster centroids are taken as candidates for 3D extremity locations. We illustrate the process in Figure 2.

**Extremes Classification.** In order to determine if any candidate location represents an extremity location, we rely on the pose $\hat{\mathbf{x}}_{t-1}$ estimated on the previous frame. Let us denote $\mathbf{y}'_i = F_i(\hat{\mathbf{x}}_{t-1})$ the position of the end-effector in the $i$-th kinematic chain at previous time instant, where $F_i(.)$ is the Forward Kinematic operator for the chain $i$ [16].

We formulate the classification problem as an optimal assignment problem. Let $\mathbf{D} \in \mathbb{R}^{I \times E}$ be the matrix gathering the distances between the $I$ target end-effectors and the $E$ point candidates, and let $\Upsilon = \{\Upsilon_1, \ldots, \Upsilon_I\}$ denote the vector of maximum distance assignments (each $\Upsilon_i$ models both the expected movement

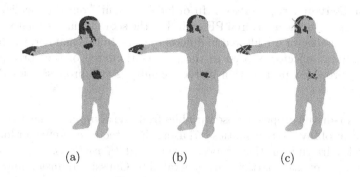

(a)                    (b)                    (c)

**Fig. 2.** Filtering process (best viewed in color). Probability values are represented with the red channel (a) Probability surface. (b) Probability surface after the threshold. (c) Cluster centroids (cyan crosses).

and the size of a specific body part). Assignments are noted as an assignment matrix $\mathbf{P} \in \{0,1\}^{E \times I}$ such that each row contains at most a 1 indicating to which end-effector is the candidate assigned. We consider that an assignment is valid if it exists at least one detected point that satisfies a maximum assignment constraint $\Upsilon_i$. In that case, the problem has a non-trivial solution ($\mathbf{P} \neq \mathbf{0}$) and is formulated as :

$$\min_{\mathbf{P}} \frac{\mathrm{tr}(\mathbf{DP})}{\mathbf{1}_E^T \mathbf{P} \mathbf{1}_I} \tag{5}$$
$$\text{s.t.} \quad \mathrm{diag}(\mathbf{DP}) \preceq \Upsilon$$
$$\text{s.t.} \quad \mathbf{P} \in \{0,1\}^{E \times I} \text{ is a valid assignment matrix}$$

where $\mathrm{tr}(\mathbf{DP})$ denotes the trace of the matrix resulting of the product between distances and assignments, $\mathrm{diag}(\mathbf{DP})$ denotes the vector formed with the diagonal elements of the same matrix, and $\mathbf{1}_I$ is a vector of ones of length $I$. The inequality constraint is formulated as a component-wise inequality between two vectors. Hence, we aim at minimizing the overall distance between candidates and end-effectors while maximizing the number of assignments (subject to the maximum distance constraint). In practice, we solve this problem for head and hands by iteratively assigning pairs with minimum distance until a minimum of Eq. 5 is attained. We experimentally set the left and right hand maximum distances $\Upsilon_1 = \Upsilon_2 = 35cm$ and the head maximum distance to $\Upsilon_3 = 25cm$.

## 3.2  Detector-Driven Hierarchical Particle Filter

In our method, the role of estimated end-effectors within the layered filtering is two-fold. On the one hand, they are used to enhance the particle propagation, thus reducing the blindness of the filter with respect to data. On the other hand, detections are used to enhance the observation model in a *refinement layer*.

**Detector-Driven Propagation.** In order to benefit from the localization of end-effectors we define a Layered PF such that the set of variables related to each particular end-effector are filtered in different layers. In this manner, the position of a certain end-effector is used in the propagation step of the corresponding layer. The proposed propagation method combines two proposals for drawing particles:

1. Detector-driven proposal: pose variables from the appropriate layer are drawn by means of Inverse Kinematics [17] using the detected end-effector locations. Particles drawn from this proposal are termed *IK particles*.
2. Gaussian proposal : particles are generated by Gaussian diffusion in the angle space, in order to account for the uncertainty of having erroneous detections.

The combination of both proposals should consider the error rate of the extremity detections. Instead of estimating such an error rate offline, we propose an online approximation of the detection accuracy by using the *IK survival rate*, i.e., the estimated ratio of IK particles that will be resampled after likelihood evaluation. Whenever this rate is above 0.5, we mutate a small fraction of regular particles into IK particles. On the contrary, when the rate is lower, IK particles are transformed into regular particles. We constrain the algorithm to keep a minimum of 25% of particles of one kind.

**Refinement Layer.** We refine the final pose estimation by introducing the set of end-effector detections, namely $\mathbf{C}_t = \{\mathbf{c}_t^1, .., \mathbf{c}_t^u, ..., \mathbf{c}_t^U\}$, in the likelihood approximation of an additional layer. We add a new cost function taking into account the distance between the observed detections and the model end-effectors. This cost is computed as:

$$\mathcal{D}(\mathbf{C}_t, \mathbf{x}_{t,l}^n) = \frac{1}{U} \sum_{u=1}^{U} \min_i \| \mathbf{c}_t^u - F_i(\mathbf{x}_{t,l}^n) \| \tag{6}$$

and it is introduced the likelihood approximation of Equation 1:

$$\tilde{w}(\mathbf{z}_t, \mathbf{x}_{t,l}^n) \propto \mathbf{e}^{-(\mathcal{C}(\mathbf{z}_t, \mathbf{x}_{t,l}^n) + \kappa \mathcal{D}(\mathbf{C}_t, \mathbf{x}_{t,l}^n))} \tag{7}$$

where $\mathcal{C}(\mathbf{z}_t, \mathbf{x}_{t,l}^n)$ is a silhouettes-based cost function and $\kappa$ is a scaling factor. $\kappa$ is chosen to balance the importance of both cost terms. By using this likelihood approximation, we improve the final pose estimate at each frame, solving mismatches produced by the classification algorithm.

The refinement layer implies a re-weighting of all the particles according to an improved observation model, and does not involve any propagation step, since we do not want to add noise to particles that have been drawn after layered filtering. If no detections are found at time instant $t$, the refinement layer in $t$ is not used.

# 4   Experimental Results

In order to evaluate our method, we conduct several experiments on the IX-MAS dataset [8]. This dataset was recorded for action recognition and hence it does not contain pose ground truth. For this reason, we manually annotate the hands, head and feet of different sequences belonging to 6 different subjects. In particular, we are interested in the evaluation of the performance of our method for actions involving arm movements (i.e crossing arms, hand waving, punching, etc.), so we skip actions not involving relevant arms motion such as walking or turning. Annotations are performed in 1 of every 5 frames[1].

We compare our method with two state-of-the-art *Layered Particle Filters*: the APF and the HPF. In particular, we evaluate our method with (DD HPF$^+$) and without (DD HPF) the refinement layer. In order to perform the comparative, the APF is run with 14 layers and 250 particles per layer, HPF and DD HPF are run using 7 layers and 500 particles per layer, and the DD HPF$^+$ is run with a maximum of 8 layers (7+ refinement layer) and 500 particles per layer (recall that if no detections are found in a frame, the refinement layer is discarded). The 7 layers contain the variables related to torso (and head), left leg, right leg, left shoulder, right shoulder, left elbow and right elbow respectively. Since adding the refinement layer generally implies computing more particle weights, we also provide results for a DD HPF$^+$ using a total of 6 layers (5 + refinement layer) and 500 particles per layer. Using 5 layers implies filtering shoulder and elbow variables of one arm in the same layer.

We compute the mean and standard deviation of the 3D error using all available ground truth data. Results are shown in Table 1.

**Table 1.** Comparative results between the state-of-the-art methods and our proposals. We provide mean 3D error (and standard deviation) in centimeters. Bold figures highlight the result of the best method for each sequence.

| Sequence (Frames) | APF | HPF | DD HPF | DD HPF$^+$ | DD HPF$^+$ (5+1) |
|---|---|---|---|---|---|
| Alba 1 (53-350) | 23.86 (14.79) | 14.38(7.31) | 11.68(5.73) | **10.32(6.02)** | 11.73(7.37) |
| Alba 1 (658-1120) | 17.13 (7.93) | 11.84(6.87) | 10.86(6.03) | **9.37(5.82)** | 10.38(7.96) |
| Chiara 3 (29-292) | 16.05 (7.14) | 13.89(8.12) | 10.87(6.40) | **9.85(4.43)** | 10.08(5.93) |
| Chiara 3 (576-955) | 19.16 (10.16) | 11.29(5.81) | 8.36(5.88) | **6.76(3.22)** | 7.98 (5.89) |
| Julien 1 (47-315) | 18.30 (8.37) | 15.18(7.21) | 13.86(6.85) | 13.30(6.85) | **12.09(7.46)** |
| Julien 1 (596-957) | 26.01 (14.70) | 11.85(6.06) | 9.43(3.63) | 7.87(2.73) | **7.57(3.35)** |
| Daniel 2 (15-306) | 20.13 (10.52) | 16.69(11.41) | 14.24(10.09) | 11.94(8.49) | **11.74 (7.16)** |
| Daniel 2 (631-1119) | 16.92 (8.35) | 10.22(3.74) | 7.29(3.33) | **6.73(2.53)** | 11.00 (8.35) |
| Srikumar 1 (43-368) | 20.06 (10.48) | 15.77(9.84) | **14.20(11.22)** | 14.58(12.14) | 15.59 (16.56) |
| Srikumar 1 (704-1035) | 18.59 (10.23) | 13.60(9.99) | 13.46(8.47) | **10.62(5.59)** | 12.07 (8.87) |
| Amel 1 (51-385) | 20.30 (9.32) | 16.00(8.02) | 16.76(8.47) | **14.40(6.11)** | 15.08 (5.88) |
| Amel 1 (796-1295) | 22.97 (8.05) | 13.07(7.07) | 11.55(5.79) | 11.40(6.90) | **11.35 (5.99)** |

The proposed framework consistently outperforms both the APF and HPF. Apart from reporting a better accuracy in terms of mean error, the standard deviation is consistently reduced, thus reflecting the stability gain and the increased

---

[1] Annotations available at `http://imatge.upc.edu/~marcel/ixmas_data.html`

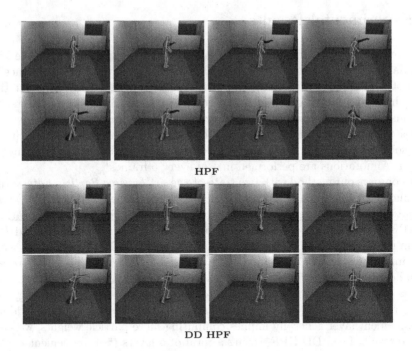

**Fig. 3.** Tracking example of subject 3 "punching"action (set 2) for the HPF and DD HPF using 7 layers and 500 particles per layer for both schemes

robustness in front of tracking failures. Experimental results show the effectiveness of the proposed DD HPF in reducing the blindness of the prior. In Figure 3, we provide a visual example for a fast arm action (action 6) and we compare the outcomes of the best state-of-the-art PF, the HPF, with the DD HPF [2]. As we can see, the HPF gets lost whereas the DD HPF perfectly tracks the arm. The experimental validation also shows the impact of the refinement layer, which is able to filter erroneous particles originated by weaknesses of the silhouette-based observation model and erroneous classifications of extremities. Even when using less particle evaluations, the proposed method outperforms the state-of-the-art approaches.

## 5   Conclusions and Future Work

We have presented a novel method for human motion capture in multi-view setups. Our approach robustly fuses end-effector detections in multiple views to improve both the particle propagation and the observation model. Compared to using learned motion models, our approach is more scalable. We particularize our method to improve arm tracking in several challenging actions of the publicly available IXMAS dataset. The results reported in this paper show the

---

[2] Videos are available at http://imatge.upc.edu/~marcel/ddhpf.html

effectiveness of the proposed method. Future work involves testing our method with several existing detectors as well as research on novel body part detectors.

# References

1. Holte, M.B., Tran, C., Trivedi, M.M., Moeslund, T.B.: Human action recognition using multiple views: a comparative perspective on recent developments. In: ACM Workshop on HGBU. J-HGBU 2011, pp. 47–52. ACM, New York (2011)
2. Gall, J., Rosenhahn, B., Brox, T., Seidel, H.-P.: Optimization and filtering for human motion capture. IJCV 87, 75–92 (2010), doi:10.1007/s11263-008-0173-1
3. Bandouch, J., Beetz, M.: Tracking humans interacting with the environment using efficient hierarchical sampling and layered observation models. In: IEEE Int. Workshop on Human-Computer Interaction (HCI) and ICCV 2009 (2009)
4. Wang, J.M., Fleet, D.J., Hertzmann, A.: Gaussian process dynamical models for human motion. IEEE Transactions on Pattern Analysis and Machine Intelligence 30(2), 283–298 (2008)
5. Gall, J., Yao, A., Van Gool, L.: 2D Action Recognition Serves 3D Human Pose Estimation. In: Daniilidis, K., Maragos, P., Paragios, N. (eds.) ECCV 2010, Part III. LNCS, vol. 6313, pp. 425–438. Springer, Heidelberg (2010)
6. Singh, V.K., Nevatia, R., Huang, C.: Efficient inference with multiple heterogeneous part detectors for human pose estimation. In: Daniilidis, K., Maragos, P., Paragios, N. (eds.) ECCV 2010, Part III. LNCS, vol. 6313, pp. 314–327. Springer, Heidelberg (2010)
7. López-Méndez, A., Alcoverro, M., Pardàs, M., Casas, J.: Real-time upper body tracking with online initialization using a range sensor. In: HCI-ICCV (2011)
8. Inria: The IXMAS Dataset (2006),
   http://4drepository.inrialpes.fr/public/viewgroup/6
9. Deutscher, J., Blake, A., Reid, I.: Articulated body motion capture by annealed particle filtering. In: CVPR, vol. 2, pp. 126–133 (2000)
10. MacCormick, J., Isard, M.: Partitioned Sampling, Articulated Objects, and Interface-Quality Hand Tracking. In: Vernon, D. (ed.) ECCV 2000, Part II. LNCS, vol. 1843, pp. 3–19. Springer, Heidelberg (2000)
11. Bălan, A.O., Sigal, L., Black, M.J.: A quantitative evaluation of video-based 3d person tracking. In: IEEE International Workshop on Visual Surveillance and Performance Evaluation of Tracking and Surveillance, VS-PETS, pp. 349–356 (2005)
12. Jones, M.J., Rehg, J.M.: Statistical Color Models with Application to Skin Detection. In: CVPR, vol. 1, pp. 274–280 (1999)
13. Salvador, J., Suau, X., Casas, J.R.: From silhouettes to 3d points to mesh: towards free viewpoint video. In: Proceedings of the 1st International Workshop on 3D Video Processing, 3DVP 2010, pp. 19–24 (2010)
14. Rusu, R.B.: Semantic 3D Object Maps for Everyday Manipulation in Human Living Environments. PhD thesis, Computer Science department, Technische Universitaet Muenchen, Germany (October 2009)
15. Friedman, J.H., Bentley, J.L., Finkel, R.A.: An algorithm for finding best matches in logarithmic expected time. ACM Trans. Math. Softw. 3, 209–226 (1977)
16. Hauberg, S., Pedersen, K.S.: Predicting articulated human motion from spatial processes. IJCV 94(3), 317–334 (2011)
17. Kallmann, M.: Analytical inverse kinematics with body posture control. Comput. Animat. Virtual Worlds 19(2), 79–91 (2008)

# Real-Time Multi-view Human Motion Tracking Using Particle Swarm Optimization with Resampling

Bogdan Kwolek[3,2], Tomasz Krzeszowski[3,2], André Gagalowicz[1],
Konrad Wojciechowski[2], and Henryk Josinski[2]

[1] INRIA Paris-Rocquencourt, Rocquencourt 78153, France
[2] Polish-Japanese Institute of Information Technology
Koszykowa 86, 02-008 Warszawa, Poland
[3] Rzeszów University of Technology
35-959 Rzeszów, Poland
bkwolek@prz.edu.pl

**Abstract.** In this paper we propose a particle swarm optimization with resampling for marker-less body tracking. The resampling is employed to select a record of the best particles according to the weights of particles making up the swarm. The algorithm better copes with noise and reduces the premature stagnation. Experiments on 4-camera datasets show the robustness and accuracy of our method. It was evaluated on nine sequences using ground truth provided by Vicon. The full body motion tracking was conducted in real-time on two PC nodes, each of them with two multi-core CPUs with hyper-threading, connected by 1 GigE.

## 1 Introduction

In 1995, Dyer et al. [6] in Motion Capture White Paper, which was issued by SGI wrote that "motion capture is one of the hottest topics in computer graphics today". As stated in the mentioned paper, motion capture involves measuring an object's position and orientation in physical space, then recording that information in a computer-usable form. Since then it has been published many survey papers, for example [12][13], and the number of papers grows exponentially.

In the last years many motion capture (also known as MoCap) systems have been developed for gaming and animation [14], sport [1], rehabilitation treatment and medical applications [15][18]. In optical MoCap systems either passive reflective markers or active markers are attached to a performer. The locations of the markers on the suit are designed such that the required body parts (e.g. joints) are covered, and a system of fixed cameras records the position of such markers. In general, existing commercial MoCap systems are only suitable for a well controlled indoor environment. In contrast, marker-less human motion capture consists in capturing human motion without any markers, by operating on image sequences only. The recovery of human body movements from image data without using markers is a very challenging task. The major difficulties are due to large number of degrees of freedom (DOFs) of the human body pose

F.J. Perales, R.B. Fisher, and T.B. Moeslund (Eds.): AMDO 2012, LNCS 7378, pp. 92–101, 2012.
© Springer-Verlag Berlin Heidelberg 2012

that needs to be recovered, large variability in human appearance, noisy image observations, self-occlusion, and complex human motions.

Most previous work on human motion tracking has focused on the use of 3D articulated models of various complexity to recover the position, orientation and joint angles. Such models can be perceived as a kinematic chain, where at least eleven elements correspond to the major body parts. Usually, the 3D geometric model is constructed from truncated cones or cylinders and is used to generate contours, which can be compared with edge contours. A lot of hypothetical body poses is generated, which are projected into image plane to find a configuration of the 3D model, whose projection best fits the image observations.

Particle filters [7] are one of the most popular techniques for body tracking. However, given the high-dimensionality of the models to be tracked, the number of required particles to properly populate the space of possible solutions makes the pose tracking computationally very expensive. Deutscher and Reid [5] developed an annealed particle filter (APF), which adopts an annealing scheme together with the stochastic sampling to achieve better concentration of the particle spread close to the extremum. Additionally, a crossover operation is utilized to achieve improved particle's diversity. Recently, particle swarm optimization (PSO) [9] has been successfully applied to body motion tracking [17]. In PSO each particle follows simple position and velocity update equations. Thanks to interaction between particles a collective behavior arises. It leads to the emergence of global and collective search capabilities, which allow the particles to gravitate towards the global extremum. Human motion tracking can be achieved by a sequence of static PSO-based optimizations, followed by re-diversification of the particles to cover the possible poses in the next time step.

In recent work, John et al. propose a PSO-based hierarchical approach for full body pose tracking [8]. However, the discussed algorithm can have difficulties in escaping from local maxima determined in preceding hierarchical levels. In [10] a parallel PSO algorithm for full body tracking in multi-view image sequences has been proposed. However, the tracking has been done using an ordinary PSO, which has been parallelized and then executed on several multi-core CPUs. In more recent work [11], a PSO algorithm with a pool of best particles has been proposed to achieve better tracking. The pool of candidate best solutions has been obtained through smoothing the objective functions in an annealing scheme and then quantizing them. The better performance has been achieved owing to the ability of the algorithm to deal with observation ambiguities and noise.

Resampling is perhaps the most obvious and simple approach to deal with noise. It is one of the techniques to improve the performance of evolutionary algorithms (EAs) in noisy environment [4]. Motivated by the work mentioned above we elaborated a particle swarm optimization algorithm with resampling to achieve full body tracking in real-time. In contrast to [4], which handles multi-objective problems through mutation operator whose range of action varies over time, our algorithm relies on resampling. During tracking a repository of best particles is selected according to importance weights. One of the contributions of this paper is a parallel particle swarm algorithm with resampling, which allows us to track the full body in real-time using multi-view images.

## 2  Annealed PSO with Resampling

The ordinary PSO algorithm consists of particles representing candidate solutions. Particles move through the solution space, and undergo evaluation according to some fitness function $f()$. The movements of the particles are guided by their own finest known locations in the search-space as well as the entire swarm's best location. While the swarm as a whole gravitates towards the global extremum, the individual particles are capable of ignoring many local optima. The object tracking can be realized by a sequence of static PSO-based optimizations, followed by re-diversification of the particles to cover the possible poses in the next time step. The re-diversification of the particle $i$ can be realized on the basis of normal distribution concentrated around the state estimate determined in the previous frame.

In the ordinary PSO, the convergence of particles towards its attractors is not guaranteed. In order to ensure convergence and to fine-tune the search, Clerc and Kennedy [3] employed a constriction factor $\omega$ in the following form of the formula expressing the $i$-th particle's velocity:

$$v^{i,k+1} = \omega[v^{i,k} + c_1 r_1(p^i - x^{i,k}) + c_2 r_2(g - x^{i,k})] \tag{1}$$

where constants $c_1$ and $c_2$ are responsible for balancing the influence of the individual's knowledge and that of the group, respectively, $r_1$ and $r_2$ stand for uniformly distributed random numbers, $x^i$ denotes position of the $i$-th particle, $p^i$ is the local best position of particle, whereas $g$ is the global best position.

In our approach the value of $\omega$ depends on annealing factor $\alpha$ as follows:

$$\omega = -0.8\alpha + 1.4 \tag{2}$$

where $\alpha = 0.1 + \frac{k}{K+1}$, $k = 0, 1, \ldots, K$, and $K$ is the number of iterations. The annealing factor is also used to smooth the objective function. The larger the iteration number is, the smaller is the smoothing. In consequence, in the last iteration the algorithm utilizes the non-smoothed function. The algorithm termed as annealed PSO with resampling (RAPSO) can be expressed as follows:

1. For each particle $i$
2.    initialize $v_t^{i,0}$
3.    $x_t^{i,0} \sim \mathcal{N}(g_{t-1}, \Sigma_0)$
4.    $p_t^i = x_t^{i,0}$, $f_t^i = f(x_t^{i,0})$
5.    $u_t^i = f_t^i$, $\tilde{u}_t^i = (u_t^i)^{\alpha_0}$
6.    $i^* = \arg\min_i \tilde{u}_t^i$, $g_t = p_t^{i^*}$, $y_t = u_t^{i^*}$
7. For $k = 0, 1, \ldots, K$
8.    update $\omega_\alpha$ on the basis of (2)
9.    For all particles, linearly scale $\tilde{u}_t^i$
10.   For each particle, on the basis of $\tilde{u}_t^i$ compute weight $w_t^i$
11.   Normalize weights $w_t^i$
12.   Draw particles according to importance weights $w_t^i$ and insert them to $G$
13. For each particle $i$

14.  Select a particle from $\{G \cup g_t\}$ and assign it to $g_t^i$

15.  $v_t^{i,k+1} = \omega_\alpha[v_t^{i,k} + c_1 r_1(p_t^i - x_t^{i,k}) + c_2 r_2(g_t^i - x_t^{i,k})]$

16.  $x_t^{i,k+1} = x_t^{i,k} + v_t^{i,k+1}$

17.  $f_t^i = f(x_t^{i,k+1})$

18.  if $f_t^i < u_t^i$ then $p_t^i = x_t^{i,k+1}$, $u_t^i = f_t^i$, $\tilde{u}_t^i = (u_t^i)^{\alpha_k}$

19.  if $f_t^i < y_t$ then $g_t = x_t^{i,k+1}$, $y_t = f_t^i$

The initialization of the algorithm takes place at the beginning of each frame, see lines 1-6 of the pseudo-code. Given the location $g_{t-1}$ of the best particle in time $t - 1$, for each particle $i$ the algorithm determines initial location $x_t^i$ and initial velocity $v_t^i$. Afterwards, best particle locations $p_t^i$ and corresponding fitness values $u_t^i$ are determined. For such fitness values the smoothed values $\tilde{u}_t^i$, the best location $g_t$ and the corresponding best fitness value $y_t$ are calculated. At the beginning of each iteration $k$, the algorithm updates $\omega_\alpha$ and linearly scales $\tilde{u}_t^i$ to range $[0, 1]$. It then calculates the normalized weights $w_t^i$. Finally, a record of best particles $G$ is selected according to importance weights $w_t^i$, see 12th line in the pseudo-code. Each particle selects best particle form such a record, determines its own velocity and location, see lines 14-16 in the pseudo-code. Finally, best locations with the corresponding fitness values are updated.

The fitness score is calculated on the basis of following expression: $f(x) = 1 - (f_1(x)^{w_1} \cdot f_2(x)^{w_2})$, where $w$ denotes weighting coefficients that were determined experimentally. The function $f_1(x)$ reflects the degree of overlap between the extracted body and the projected model's into 2D image. The function $f_2(x)$ reflects the edge distance-based fitness.

The calculation of the objective function is the most consuming operation. Moreover, in multi-view tracking the 3D model is projected and then rendered in each camera's view. Therefore, in our approach the objective function is calculated by OpenMP threads [2], which communicate via the shared memory. The PSO thread has access to the shared memory with the objective function values, which were determined by the local threads as well as the values of the objective functions that were calculated by the cooperating swarm on another cores or computational nodes. We employ asynchronous exchange of the best particle location and its fitness score. In particular, if a sub-swarm, which as the first one finished object tracking in a given frame, it carries out the re-diversification of the particles using its current global best particle, without waiting for the global best optimum determined by the participating sub-swarms. It is worth mentioning that in such circumstances the estimate of the object state is determined using the available global best locations of cooperating sub-swarms.

# 3   Experimental Results

The proposed algorithm was evaluated on several image sequences, which were acquired by four synchronized and calibrated cameras. Each pair of the cameras is approximately perpendicular to the other camera pair. The cameras acquire color images of size $1920 \times 1080$ at 25 fps. In experiments we employed images sub-sampled by 2 in both the $x$ and $y$ directions. A commercial motion capture (MoCap) system from Vicon Nexus was employed to provide the ground truth data. The system uses reflective markers and sixteen cameras to recover the 3D location of such markers. The system is capable of differentiating overlapping markers from each camera's view. The data are delivered with rate of 100 Hz and the synchronization between the MoCap and multi-camera system is achieved using hardware from Vicon Giganet Lab. The location of the cameras and layout of laboratory is depicted in Fig. 1.

**Fig. 1.** Layout of the laboratory with four cameras. The images illustrate the initial model configuration, overlaid on the image in first frame and seen in view 1, 2, 3 and 4.

Our algorithm was tested on a variety of sequences with walking humans, observed from different viewpoints. To provide quantitative evaluation, the pose of walking subject was estimated by our algorithm. On the basis of the pose estimates, the configuration of the 3D model was determined. The model was then overlaid on the images. In each image sequence the same actor performed two walks, consisting in following a virtual line joining two opposite cameras and following a virtual line joining two nonconsecutive laboratory corners. The first subsequence is referred as 'straight', whereas the second one is called 'diagonal'. Figure 2 depicts some results that were obtained in a sequence #1 with a person following a line joining two nonconsecutive laboratory corners. The degree of overlap of the projected 3D model on the performer illustrates the accuracy of the tracking. Focusing on tracking of the torso and the legs, we estimated also the head's pose as well as the pose of both arms. The configuration of the body is parameterized by the position and the orientation of the pelvis in the global coordinate system and the angles between the connected limbs. The human body model consists of eleven rigid body parts, each of which is represented by a truncated cone. The model represents pelvis, upper torso, two upper arms, two lower arms, two thighs, two lower legs and the head, see also Fig. 2.

**Fig. 2.** Articulated 3D human body tracking in four camera setup. Shown are results in frames #0, 20, 40, 60, 80, 100. The left sub-images are seen from view 1, whereas the right ones are seen from view 2.

In Fig. 3 are depicted some results that were obtained in the same image sequence, but with the performer following a virtual line between two opposite cameras. The figure depicts model overlaid on the image from right profile view and the frontal view. The discussed results were obtained by RAPSO algorithm in 20 iterations per frame, consisting of 300 particles.

**Fig. 3.** Articulated 3D human body tracking in four camera setup using frontal and side views. Shown are results in frames #0, 20, 40, 60, 80, 100, 120. Left sub-images are seen from view 1, whereas the right ones are seen from view 2.

The plots in Fig. 4 illustrate the accuracy of motion estimation for some joints. As we can observe the tracking error of both forearms is something smaller in comparison to the remaining limbs. The average error of both knees is about 50 mm, whereas the maximal errors do not exceed 100 mm for the left knee and slightly exceeds 100 mm for the right one. The discussed results were obtained by RAPSO algorithm in 20 iterations and using 300 particles.

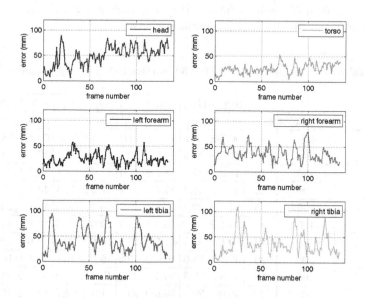

**Fig. 4.** Tracking errors [mm] versus frame number

Figure 5 depicts the distance between ankles, which was registered in sequences P2, P3, and P4. In the sequence P4 the performer walked in the direction to the camera, whereas in sequence P2 and P3 the person moved diagonally. The sequences P2 and P4 depict the best results of the diagonal and the straight walks, respectively, whereas the sequence P3 depicts the poorest result of the diagonal walks. On the basis of the motion estimates the gait cycle is can be detected with good precision.

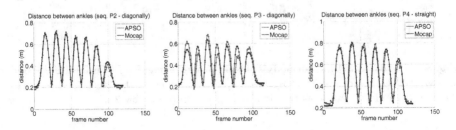

**Fig. 5.** Distance between ankles during walking in sequences P2 (diagonal), P3 (diagonal) and P4 (straight)

In Tab. 1 are presented some quantitative results that were obtained on four image sequences. The errors were calculated using 39 markers. For each frame they were computed as average Euclidean distance between individual markers and the recovered 3D joint locations [16]. For each sequence they were then averaged over ten runs with unlike initializations.

**Table 1.** Average errors for $M = 39$ markers in four image sequences

|  | #particles | it. | Seq. 1 (P1) error [mm] | Seq. 2 (P1) error [mm] | Seq. 3 (P6) error [mm] | Seq. 4 (P6) error [mm] |
|---|---|---|---|---|---|---|
| PSO | 100 | 10 | $50.5 \pm 28.7$ | $56.7 \pm 33.0$ | $56.6 \pm 37.1$ | $54.4 \pm 28.5$ |
|  | 100 | 20 | $45.0 \pm 23.6$ | $49.6 \pm 27.2$ | $46.2 \pm 25.9$ | $47.3 \pm 23.8$ |
|  | 300 | 10 | $45.2 \pm 25.5$ | $48.1 \pm 25.0$ | $47.6 \pm 26.4$ | $48.7 \pm 24.4$ |
|  | 300 | 20 | $41.9 \pm 21.2$ | $45.4 \pm 24.4$ | $41.2 \pm 22.3$ | $43.3 \pm 21.8$ |
| APSO | 100 | 10 | $\mathbf{44.7 \pm 23.8}$ | $51.1 \pm 27.6$ | $\mathbf{46.7 \pm 26.6}$ | $\mathbf{45.7 \pm 23.8}$ |
|  | 100 | 20 | $\mathbf{39.5 \pm 20.2}$ | $46.0 \pm 26.3$ | $\mathbf{40.3 \pm 22.8}$ | $40.8 \pm 20.1$ |
|  | 300 | 10 | $\mathbf{39.6 \pm 19.7}$ | $\mathbf{44.7 \pm 23.8}$ | $40.6 \pm 22.9$ | $\mathbf{39.6 \pm 19.3}$ |
|  | 300 | 20 | $37.0 \pm 18.6$ | $\mathbf{40.4 \pm 19.9}$ | $35.8 \pm 19.6$ | $36.3 \pm 16.6$ |
| RAPSO | 100 | 10 | $46.9 \pm 27.9$ | $\mathbf{50.2 \pm 27.2}$ | $48.8 \pm 28.0$ | $50.9 \pm 26.7$ |
|  | 100 | 20 | $40.0 \pm 20.7$ | $\mathbf{45.6 \pm 23.1}$ | $41.3 \pm 23.7$ | $\mathbf{40.1 \pm 19.6}$ |
|  | 300 | 10 | $40.6 \pm 20.5$ | $45.0 \pm 25.2$ | $43.0 \pm 25.0$ | $40.5 \pm 19.7$ |
|  | 300 | 20 | $\mathbf{36.4 \pm 17.4}$ | $40.4 \pm 20.5$ | $36.2 \pm 20.1$ | $\mathbf{35.3 \pm 15.7}$ |

In Tab. 2 are results illustrating the tracking accuracy of APSO and RAPSO algorithms. For each sequence the bold indicates the best results for the diagonal and the straight walks. As we can observe, both algorithms allow full body tracking with similar accuracy.

**Table 2.** Average errors [mm] for $M = 39$ markers using 300 particles, in 20 iterations

| Person | APSO Straight | APSO Diagonally | RAPSO Straight | RAPSO Diagonally |
|---|---|---|---|---|
| P1 | $37.0 \pm 18.6$ | $\mathbf{40.4 \pm 19.9}$ | $\mathbf{36.4 \pm 17.4}$ | $40.4 \pm 20.5$ |
| P2 | $45.5 \pm 25.8$ | $\mathbf{56.5 \pm 38.2}$ | $\mathbf{44.6 \pm 24.7}$ | $56.9 \pm 38.9$ |
| P3 | $43.4 \pm 23.0$ | $\mathbf{45.8 \pm 17.7}$ | $\mathbf{42.7 \pm 20.8}$ | $46.1 \pm 19.0$ |
| P4 | $\mathbf{43.2 \pm 21.3}$ | $43.1 \pm 19.3$ | $45.0 \pm 23.3$ | $\mathbf{41.9 \pm 18.3}$ |
| P5 | $\mathbf{54.1 \pm 19.3}$ | $52.6 \pm 16.6$ | $54.6 \pm 20.6$ | $53.5 \pm 16.7$ |
| P6 | $\mathbf{35.8 \pm 19.6}$ | $36.3 \pm 16.6$ | $36.2 \pm 20.1$ | $\mathbf{35.3 \pm 15.7}$ |
| P7 | $50.0 \pm 27.3$ | $48.6 \pm 20.5$ | $\mathbf{49.6 \pm 26.3}$ | $\mathbf{47.1 \pm 18.8}$ |
| P8 | $\mathbf{37.8 \pm 25.4}$ | $\mathbf{38.2 \pm 19.4}$ | $38.2 \pm 25.1$ | $38.6 \pm 21.2$ |
| P9 | $\mathbf{45.6 \pm 24.7}$ | $\mathbf{41.7 \pm 21.2}$ | $45.9 \pm 25.3$ | $42.0 \pm 20.7$ |

In Tab. 3 are demonstrated the tracking times, which we achieved for various distributions of the sub-swarms/particles into the computational resources. As we can notice, for the same number of the sub-swarms the computation time is larger on single computer in comparison to a configuration consisting of two nodes connected by 1 GigE network. This means that the time needed for threads scheduling is larger than the time needed for information exchange

**Table 3.** Tracking time [ms] and speed-up for single frame

| #swarms | #particles | #threads PC1 | #threads PC2 | Seq. 1 (P1) time [ms] | Seq. 1 (P1) speed-up |
|---|---|---|---|---|---|
| 1 | 300 | 4 | 0 | 326.7 | - |
| 2 | $2 \times 150$ | 8 | 0 | 175.3 | 1.9 |
| 2 | $2 \times 150$ | 4 | 4 | 172.5 | 1.9 |
| 3 | $3 \times 100$ | 12 | 0 | 147.7 | 2.2 |
| 3 | $3 \times 100$ | 8 | 4 | 123.1 | 2.7 |
| 4 | $4 \times 75$ | 16 | 0 | 125.6 | 2.6 |
| 4 | $4 \times 75$ | 8 | 8 | 88.4 | 3.7 |
| 6 | $6 \times 50$ | 12 | 12 | 79.2 | 4.1 |
| 8 | $8 \times 38$ | 16 | 16 | 65.9 | 5.0 |

in a distributed system. The image processing and analysis takes about 0.2 sec. and it is not included in the times shown in Tab. 3. For the RAPSO algorithm decomposed into two PCs and executing 8 swarms, the motion tracking can be done at about 15 fps. The complete human motion capture system was written in C/C++. The experiments were conducted on two desktop PCs, each equipped with two XEON X5690, 3.46 GHz (6-core) CPUs. The nodes were connected by a TCP/IP 1 GigE (Gigabit Ethernet) local area network. The parallelization of the code was done using OpenMP directives. It is worth noting that on *Lee walk* sequence from Brown University, the processing time of the algorithm proposed in [8], which has been implemented in Matlab, is larger than one hour.

In Tab. 4 are depicted average errors that were obtained on sequence P1 using various number of sub-swarms. As we can observe, the tracking accuracy is far better in comparison to tracking accuracy that was achieved in [10]. The results presented in Tab. 3-4 were achieved on images from sequence P1 sub-sampled by 4 and therefore the tracking accuracy on single computer is worse in comparison to the relevant accuracy shown in Tab. 2.

**Table 4.** Average errors [mm] obtained with various number of sub-swarms

| #swarms | #particles | error [mm] | std. dev. [mm] |
|---------|------------|------------|----------------|
| 1 | 300 | 41.9 | 23.6 |
| 2 | 2 × 150 | 43.0 | 24.2 |
| 3 | 2 × 100 | 44.9 | 25.6 |
| 4 | 4 × 75 | 42.6 | 22.7 |
| 6 | 6 × 50 | 45.4 | 27.3 |
| 8 | 8 × 38 | 50.6 | 35.8 |

## 4   Conclusions

We have proposed a particle swarm optimization with resampling for full body tracking. Owing to resampling the algorithm better copes with noise and reduces premature stagnation. The parallel algorithm, which was executed on two PC nodes with multi-core CPUs allowed us to perform real-time tracking at 15 fps. The accuracy of the algorithm for the real-time full body tracking is better in comparison to recently proposed parallel PSO algorithm. Experimental results on various multi-view sequences of walking subjects demonstrate the effectiveness of the approach.

**Acknowledgment.** This work has been supported by the National Science Centre (NCN) within the research project N N516 483240 and the National Centre for Research and Development (NCBiR) within the project OR00002111.

# References

1. Barris, S., Button, C.: A review of vision-based motion analysis in sport. Sports Medicine 38(12), 1025–1043 (2008)
2. Chapman, B., Jost, G., van der Pas, R., Kuck, D.: Using OpenMP: Portable Shared Memory Parallel Programming. The MIT Press (2007)
3. Clerc, M., Kennedy, J.: The particle swarm - explosion, stability, and convergence in a multidimensional complex space. IEEE Tr. Evolut. Comp. 6(1), 58–73 (2002)
4. Coello, C., Pulido, G., Lechuga, M.: Handling multiple objectives with particle swarm optimization. IEEE Tr. on Evolutionary Computation 8(3), 256–279 (2004)
5. Deutscher, J., Blake, A., Reid, I.: Articulated body motion capture by annealed particle filtering. In: IEEE Int. Conf. on Pattern Recognition, pp. 126–133 (2000)
6. Dyer, S., Martin, J., Zulauf, J.: Motion capture white paper. SGI, ftp://ftp.sgi.com/sgi/A%7CW/jam/mocap/MoCapWP_v2.0.html (accessed March 15, 2012)
7. Isard, M., Blake, A.: CONDENSATION - conditional density propagation for visual tracking. Int. J. of Computer Vision 29, 5–28 (2006)
8. John, V., Trucco, E., Ivekovic, S.: Markerless human articulated tracking using hierarchical particle swarm optimisation. Image Vis. Comput. 28, 1530–1547 (2010)
9. Kennedy, J., Eberhart, R.: Particle swarm optimization. In: Proc. of IEEE Int. Conf. on Neural Networks, pp. 1942–1948. IEEE Press, Piscataway (1995)
10. Kwolek, B., Krzeszowski, T., Wojciechowski, K.: Real-Time Multi-view Human Motion Tracking Using 3D Model and Latency Tolerant Parallel Particle Swarm Optimization. In: Gagalowicz, A., Philips, W. (eds.) MIRAGE 2011. LNCS, vol. 6930, pp. 169–180. Springer, Heidelberg (2011)
11. Kwolek, B., Krzeszowski, T., Wojciechowski, K.: Swarm Intelligence Based Searching Schemes for Articulated 3D Body Motion Tracking. In: Blanc-Talon, J., Kleihorst, R., Philips, W., Popescu, D., Scheunders, P. (eds.) ACIVS 2011. LNCS, vol. 6915, pp. 115–126. Springer, Heidelberg (2011)
12. Moeslund, T.B., Hilton, A., Krüger, V.: A survey of advances in vision-based human motion capture and analysis. CVIU 104(2), 90–126 (2006)
13. Poppe, R.: Vision-based human motion analysis: An overview. Comp. Vision and Image Understanding 108(1-2), 4–18 (2007)
14. Quah, C.K., Koh, M., Ong, A., Seah, H.S., Gagalowicz, A.: Video-based motion capture for measuring human movement. In: Digital Sports for Performance Enhancement and Competitive Evolution: Intelligent Gaming Technologies, pp. 209–228. Information Science Publishing (2009)
15. Saboune, J., Charpillet, F.: Markerless human motion capture for gait analysis. Clinical Orthopaedics and Related Research (2005)
16. Sigal, L., Balan, A., Black, M.: HumanEva: Synchronized video and motion capture dataset and baseline algorithm for evaluation of articulated human motion. Int. Journal of Computer Vision 87, 4–27 (2010)
17. Zhang, X., Hu, W., Wang, X., Kong, Y., Xie, N., Wang, H., Ling, H., Maybank, S.: A swarm intelligence based searching strategy for articulated 3D human body tracking. In: IEEE Workshop on 3D Information Extraction for Video Analysis and Mining in conjuction with CVPR, pp. 45–50. IEEE (2010)
18. Zhou, H., Hu, H.: Human motion tracking for rehabilitation - a survey. Biomedical Signal Proc. and Control 3, 1–18 (2008)

# A Comparative Study of Surface Representations Used in Statistical Human Models

Alexandros Neophytou and Adrian Hilton

Centre for Vision, Speech and Signal Processing, University of Surrey, UK

**Abstract.** This paper presents a quantitative and qualitative analysis of surface representations used in recent statistical models of human shape and pose. Our analysis and comparison framework is twofold. Firstly, we qualitatively examine generated shapes and poses by interpolating points in the shape and pose variation spaces. Secondly, we evaluate the performance of the statistical human models in the context of human shape and pose reconstruction from silhouette. The analysis demonstrates that body shape variation can be controlled with a lower dimensional model using a PCA basis in the Euclidean space. In addition, the Euclidean representation is shown to give more accurate shape estimates than other surface representations in the absence of pose variation. Furthermore, the analysis indicates that shape and pose parametrizations based on translation and rotation invariant representations are not robust for reconstruction from silhouette without pose initialization.

**Keywords:** surface representations, statistical models, human shape and pose.

## 1 Introduction

Over recent years, there have been a number of different approaches proposed for statistical models of human shape and pose. These approaches vary in the choice of surface representation, the parametrization of human body shape and pose space, and the method of statistical analysis. The choice of surface representation is critical, since linear interpolation between points in the shape and pose space must produce physically correct examples without artifacts. Euclidean coordinates are ill-suited for interpolation, since rotations cannot be interpolated, when linearly blending example poses; resulting in artifacts such as shrinking and shearing. The same applies for other linear surface representations such as Laplacian coordinates[18,1,6,14] which are known to produce the same artifacts[4]. This has led to the development of other surface parametrization techniques[6,13,15] where the goal is to encode surfaces irrespective of global positioning and orientation [11]. This introduces intuitive shape similarity metrics, due to translation and rotation invariance. In this paper, we review recent statistical human models with specific emphasis on the surface parametrization and the implications on the statistical analysis of human body shape and pose. We then provide a quantitative and qualitative analysis of linear surface representations with rotation invariant representations.

F.J. Perales, R.B. Fisher, and T.B. Moeslund (Eds.): AMDO 2012, LNCS 7378, pp. 102–113, 2012.

## 2   Statistical Models of Human Body Shape and Pose

Statistical shape modeling has been extensively researched in 3D face analysis from images. From a set of example faces, it is possible to learn a lower dimensional model of the face shape parameters known as "eigenfaces" [5]. Similarly, morphable models can be created that generate realistic human body shapes and poses learnt from a number of examples [16]. In order to perform a meaningful statistical analysis, correspondence between the 3D range scans is required [3,11,2]. The goal is to obtain a set of aligned meshes with corresponding vertex locations while preserving the intrinsic geometric details of the captured surface.

A popular framework for modeling shape and pose variation was developed by Angelov *et al.* [3]where pose and shape models are learnt separately and then combined during reconstruction. The SCAPE model considers pose and shape deformations that align a template model with each mesh in the training set. It is based on a representation that incorporates both non-rigid and articulated deformations. The pose variation model is acquired by embedding an articulated skeleton and learning how the surface deforms relative to a set of joint rotations. Realistic deformation of the surface can be achieved by providing only a few parameters. The SCAPE model considers a single subject in various poses and assumes that learnt non-rigid pose induced deformations may be transferred to other subjects. A separate shape variation model is then learnt using PCA on translation invariant coordinates with the subjects in a template pose. Translation invariance can be achieved either by encoding the surface in terms of its local tangential frames or by considering the Laplacian coordinates of the surface [17,18].

In another framework, Hasler *et al.*[11] proposed a statistical model that combines both shape and pose while avoiding the use of an embedded skeleton. The key contribution of this approach is a rotation invariant surface representation. Relative Rotation Encoding (RRE) is proposed as a rotation and translation invariant mesh representation where the orientation and position of each triangle is expressed relative to those of its neighbors, similar to Kircher and Garland[13]. In this approach, a single PCA basis of shape and pose is learnt. Unlike SCAPE, this model learns shape-dependent pose deformations by considering scans of different individuals in different poses. The downside is that pose and shape cannot be analyzed independently, since the shape and pose components cannot be decoupled. As a result, in order to specify a new pose given a specific shape, linear regression is required to learn how a model deforms given a set of joint angles.

In a more recent approach Hasler *et al.* [10]proposed a bi-linear model where shape and pose deformations can be represented as two consecutive affine transformations on a canonical triangle. Conceptually this framework resembles the SCAPE model where shape and pose deformations are learnt separately and then combined at a later stage. In this case, a skeleton is not required, instead shape-dependent pose deformations are defined as the transformations that align a shape model to a given pose. Two lower dimensional models of body shape and pose parameters are learnt using PCA.

Chen *et al.* [8] proposed a probabilistic generative model based on a Gaussian Process Latent Variable Model (GPLVM). Two separate GPLVMs are used, one for body shape variation and another for pose variation, which are combined to synthesize arbitrary 3D shapes through deformation transfer [7,19]. A GPLVM based model allows the non-linear mapping of the shape and pose data, expressed in Euclidean coordinates, into a low-dimensional manifold where shape and pose deformations can be controlled by a few latent variables. In this framework, similarly to SCAPE, pose variations are learnt using a single subject in different poses. A summary of recent statistical human models is shown in table 1.

**Table 1.** Summary of key components of statistical human models

| Model: | SCAPE[3] | Hasler *et al.*[11] | Hasler *et al.*[10] | Chen *et al.*[8] |
|---|---|---|---|---|
| **Statistical Analysis:** | PCA & Regression | PCA | PCA | GPLVM |
| **Surface Encoding:** | T & Skeleton | R & T | R & T | Euclidean |
| **Pose Training:** | Single Subject | Mult. Subjects | Mult. Subjects | Single Subject |
| **Pose Transfer:** | Skeleton & Regression | Regression | D.-T. | D.-T. |

*Note 1.* D.-T. stands for Deformation Transfer and R,T stands for Rotation and Translation invariance respectively.

## 3    Comparative Framework

This study focuses on the analysis and comparison of the surface representations used in recent statistical human models. We examine first shape-only models produced from the different surface representations, then consider combined models of shape and pose. Our analysis and comparison framework is twofold. Firstly we qualitatively examine generated shapes and poses by interpolating points in the shape and pose variation spaces. Secondly, we evaluate the performance of the different surface representations in the context of human shape and pose reconstruction from silhouette. For the purposes of this study, we restrict the statistical analysis method to a linear approach, namely PCA.

### 3.1   Surface Representations

In this section, we review three surface representations used in recent statistical models of human shape and pose: Euclidean, Laplacian and RRE coordinates.

**Euclidean Representation.** The Euclidean coordinates are expressed with respect to the global position and orientation and are, thus, affected by translation, rotation and scaling.

**Laplacian Representation.** The Laplacian coordinates of a vertex can be defined as a vector, where its magnitude is expressed as the difference of the vertex value and the center of mass of its one-ring neighbors [6]:

$$\triangle f(v_i) = \omega_i \sum_{j=0}^{p} \omega_{ij}(f(v_j) - f(v_i)) \tag{1}$$

where $f : S \rightarrow \mathbb{R}$ is a piecewise linear scalar function defined on a mesh and $i,j$ are incident one-ring neighbors and $\omega_i, \omega_{ij}$ are the normalization weights and edge weights respectively. The Laplacian coordinates are unaffected by translation but not rotation since they are encoded with respect to the orientations of the local neighborhoods.

**Encoding:** The above discretization of the Laplacian operator enforces weights based on the geometric properties of the mesh. This approach is useful for applications where the mesh geometry is always known, such as mesh editing and filtering. For our purposes, we omit the weight information by assuming it is implicitly encoded in the mesh connectivity and therefore, modeled in the PCA basis. The differential coordinates can be obtained using the topological Laplacian:

$$L_{top} = I - D^{-1}A.$$

where $D$ is a diagonal matrix with $D_{ii} = d_i$, $d_i$ being the number of vertices in the neighborhood of vertex $i$ and $A$ is the connectivity matrix of the mesh.

**Decoding:** A mesh can be reconstructed from its differential coordinates using a Poisson surface reconstruction step [6,12]. This approach involves finding the optimal set of vertices that best preserve the geometrical properties of the local areas of the mesh. The Laplacian matrix is by definition translation invariant and, thus, singular [18,17]. Hence, one or more vertices need to be anchored in order to reconstruct the mesh. Therefore, we seek to minimize the energy of the form:

$$E(p') = \sum_{i=1}^{n} \|Lp' - \delta_i\|^2 + \lambda \cdot \sum_{j=1}^{k} \|p'_j - c_j\|^2. \tag{2}$$

where $L$ is the discrete Laplacian operator, $\delta$ are the differential coordinates, and $c_{1..n}$ are the known vertices. The minimum of the energy can be found by solving the system of normal equations: $\mathbf{L}^{\top}\mathbf{L} + \lambda^2\mathbf{I_k} = \mathbf{L}^{\top}\delta + \lambda^2 \cdot c_k$. The known vertices $c_k$ are added to the system as "soft constraints" with a weight value to allow for interpolation.

**Relative Rotation Encoding (RRE) Representation.** RRE is frame-based representation where a mesh is encoded by storing relative transforms between neighboring triangles. Relative transforms are invariant under translation and rotation.

**Encoding:** The first step in encoding the surface is to consider a transformation matrix $U_i$ relative to a rest pose triangle $T_i$, $M = U_iT_i$ where $M$ is matrix containing the vertices of triangle $i$ defined on the mesh. The transformation matrix $U_i$ is equivalent to the connection maps described by Kircher and Garland[13].

By polar decomposition, matrix $U_i$ is split up into a rotation matrix $R_i$ and a remaining stretching deformation matrix $S_i$, hence, $M = R_i S_i T_i$. The matrix $S_i$ is by construction rotation invariant, thus, only a relative encoding of matrix $R_i$ needs to be considered. Relative rotations between pairs of adjacent triangles $i$ and $j$ are computed, one for each neighboring triangle, i.e. $R_{i,j} = R_i R_j^{-1}$. The rotation matrices can be represented as rotation vectors since they are more suited for linear interpolation[11]. The stretching matrix $S_i$ is symmetric, so only the upper-half is stored. The final encoding has 15 degrees of freedom per triangle (6 for in-plane deformation and 3 for each relative rotations).

**Decoding:** In order to reconstruct the mesh, we need to obtain the absolute rotation matrices $R_i$ from the relative rotations $R_{i,j}$ where $j = 1, 2, 3$ of each of the triangles. In order to do so, we can re-arrange the equation $R_{i,j} = R_i R_j^{-1}$ to $R_{i,j} R_j - R_i = 0$. The relationships of adjacent triangles can be inserted into a sparse linear system of equations:

$$\mathbf{MR} = \begin{bmatrix} \cdots & -\mathbf{I} & \cdots & R_{ij} & \cdots \end{bmatrix} \begin{bmatrix} \ldots & R_i & \ldots & R_j & \ldots \end{bmatrix}^\top = 0.$$

The system can be solved in the least square sense by anchoring one or more rotation matrices $R_i$ to guarantee uniqueness: $\mathbf{M}^\top \mathbf{M} + \lambda^2 \mathbf{I_k} = \mathbf{M}^\top \mathbf{R_i} + \lambda^2 \cdot R_k$. The resulting rotation matrices $R_i$ may not be pure rotations and are, hence, factored using polar decomposition to acquire the rotation component matrix. The process described above applies an arbitrary transformation to each triangle effectively, breaking the connectivity of the mesh. The mesh can be reconstructed with a Poisson surface reconstruction step by replacing the topological Laplacian operator with its cotangent discretization[6].

## 3.2 Separate Models of Shape and Pose

Separate models of shape and pose can be constructed by splitting deformations into the two components $S_{jk}$ and $P_{ik}$ respectively [10]:

$$M_{ijk} = P_{ik} S_{jk} T \tag{3}$$

where $M_{ijk}$ is a 3x3 matrix containing the vertices of the $k$th triangle of subject $j$ in pose $i$ and T is a canonical template triangle in the xy-plane. This formulation assumes that all poses are identical and not subject specific. This is not a valid case since for instance, muscle bulging depends on both the pose and the physique of a subject. A shape-dependent pose parameter $P_{ijk}$ can be used instead. By polar decomposition, $P_{ijk} = R_{ijk} D_{ijk}$ and $S_{jk} = R_{jk} D_{jk}$. Equation (3) can be re-written in the form[10]:

$$M_{ijk} = P_{ik} S_{jk} T = R_{jk} R'_{ik} D'_{ik} D_{jk} T \tag{4}$$

where $R'_{ik} = R_{jk}^{-1} R_{ijk} R_{jk}$ and $D'_{ik} = R_{jk}^{-1} D_{ijk} R_{jk}$. Notice, however, how rotation components are re-ordered to restrict deformations $D_{ijk}$ to always act on the xy-plane. This is driven by the fact that scaling and shearing are not rotation invariant. This formulation ensures correct behavior when transferring a pose from one subject to another by generalizing the pose deformation components. The shape parameters $R_{jk}, D_{jk}$ of a subject can be computed as the mean rotation and mean deformation over all poses of the subject in question. Therefore, pose parameters can be calculated by the residual transform: $P_{ik} = M_{ijk}T^+S^+_{ijk}$. For correct pose interpolation, pose transformations need to be encoded using RRE. Alternatively, pose rotations $R'_{ik}$ can be interpolated in a logarithmic space and deformations $D'_{ik}$ stored separately[10].

### 3.3   Human Shape and Pose Reconstruction from Silhouette

Estimating human shape and pose from a single silhouette is a challenging, under constrained problem. To make the problem tractable, prior knowledge of the subject can be used to sufficiently constrain the problem. Low dimensional models of shape and pose parameters can be used to fit a template 3D model to a silhouette through a cost function minimization. The challenge, however, remains in inferring shape and pose parameters from silhouettes without manual intervention. For comparison, we have developed a silhouette fitting framework where the goal is to obtain the 3D mesh model corresponding to a silhouette image using a stochastic optimization algorithm. We opted to use a particle swarm optimization since it is robust and has only a few adjustable parameters. The goal, therefore, is to minimize a silhouette fitting error by stochastically searching the space of permissible human body shapes and poses:

$$E_{Silhouette} = \|I_{target} - I_{estimated}(P, S)\|^2 .  \tag{5}$$

where the estimated silhouette is a function of the pose $P$ and shape $S$ parameters in their respective PCA space. For simplicity and clarity of results, we assume that the camera calibration matrix is known.

## 4   Results and Discussion

This work is based on a database of dense full body 3D scans of 111 subjects aged 17-61, where 57 are male and 54 are female. The mesh models are in vertex correspondence, with each mesh model consisting of 6449 vertices and 12894 faces. All individuals are captured in a standard pose. Other poses, randomly selected from a set of 32 poses may also be included. A shape-only model is constructed using the scans where the subjects are in a standard pose and a shape and pose model is constructed using all scans. For shape-only models rotation and translation invariance is not necessary since all the mesh models appear in the same position and orientation in space. Consequently, the variation of the data exists within small changes in the vertex positions. When modeling pose, however, it is important to capture rigid-invariant shape variations.

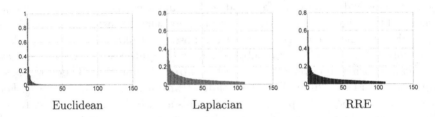

Fig. 1. Eigen values distribution

## 4.1 Shape-Only Models

In order to better understand the attributes and behavior of each parametrization space, we examined the distribution of eigenvalues as well as the variation modes produced by each statistical model. Figure 1 shows graphs of the normalized eigenvalues for each of the PCA basis. The distribution of the eigenvalues defines the energy distribution over the space where shape variation exists in the data set as expressed by each of the parametrization spaces. Higher values indicate the importance of each PCA mode relating to body shape variance. For example, the first PCA mode may represent changes in body shape due to varying height across different individuals. Generally, we are interested in the eigenvalues that account for ≈99% of the total variance. In the Euclidean representation, only the first 20 PCA modes are required. In the other two cases, the shape variation appears to be more evenly spread with the first 90 PCA modes accounting for ≈99% of the total variance. A possible explanation for this difference is that in both cases (Laplacian, RRE) the difference of local frames defined on the mesh geometry is not as distinct as the difference between individual vertices in the global Euclidean representation. Assuming body shape variance is modeled correctly, this would imply that body shape can be controlled with fewer parameters using the Euclidean parametrization.

**Shape from Silhouette.** For testing we split the database into 100 subjects for training and 11 subjects for testing. This process is performed 10 times so that each model is estimated exactly once. This allows us to measure the ground truth error between the estimated shape and the target shape. For shape similarity comparison, three distance metrics are considered based on the Euclidean, Laplacian and RRE spaces. The Euclidean and Laplacian distances are calculated as the average distance between corresponding vertex coordinates. The RRE distance is calculated as the average distance between feature vectors of corresponding triangles. The RRE distance metric is more significant for shape comparison since rigid transformations are not considered. The particle swarm optimization algorithm is initialized with 25 particles and runs for 200 iterations with particle position limits of $\pm 3\sigma$.

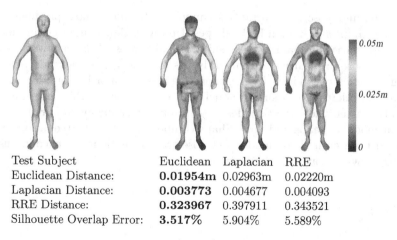

| Test Subject | Euclidean | Laplacian | RRE |
|---|---|---|---|
| Euclidean Distance: | **0.01954m** | 0.02963m | 0.02220m |
| Laplacian Distance: | **0.003773** | 0.004677 | 0.004093 |
| RRE Distance: | **0.323967** | 0.397911 | 0.343521 |
| Silhouette Overlap Error: | **3.517%** | 5.904% | 5.589% |

**Fig. 2.** Shape from silhouette example. Heat maps are calculated with the Euclidean distance metric.

Table 2 shows the average distances based on the three metrics from all the tests for each of the three models. In addition, an average overlap error (%) between the silhouette of the estimated model and the target model is shown. These results indicate that the Euclidean model performs better, both in the case of minimizing the silhouette overlap error and in the case of producing models with smaller distances from the target models. Moreover, the Euclidean model has a less costly error function since it only requires a single matrix multiplication. Figure 2 shows an example of the shape estimation. The results validate the previous observation that a Euclidean model can be used more effectively in an optimization framework since body shape is controlled with fewer parameters. In many cases, the meshes produced by the three shape models have similar shapes; particularly in the outer boundaries of each mesh which is a direct result of the silhouette fitting.

**Table 2.** Shape from Silhouette

| Model: | Euclidean | Laplacian | RRE |
|---|---|---|---|
| Silhouette Overlap Error: | **4.014%** | 5.010% | 6.747% |
| Average Euclidean Distance: | **0.0202m** | 0.0266m | 0.0273m |
| Average Laplacian Distance: | **0.00399** | 0.00428 | 0.00427 |
| Average RRE Distance: | **0.34598** | 0.36998 | 0.36378 |
| Average Time per Estimation: | **83s** | 323s | 1292s |

## 4.2  Shape and Pose Models

Figure 3 illustrates the mean models of shape and pose from each statistical model. The Laplacian and Euclidean representations are ill-suited for modeling both shape and pose since rotations cannot be handled, thus, producing degenerate examples of human body shapes. However, they can effectively model body shape variation making them suitable candidates for a framework where shape and pose are learnt independently. As discussed, pose deformations can be handled effectively either by incorporating a skeleton or by considering pose deformations that align a shape model to a given pose. In this case, we have chosen the latter where the Euclidean and Laplacian shape models are used in a bi-linear model of shape and pose. Shape components $R_{jk}, D_{jk}$ (equation 4) are extracted from each shape model and pose transformations are encoded using RRE to allow for correct interpolation.

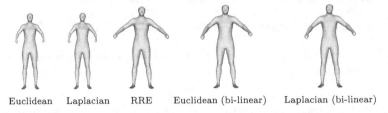

Euclidean    Laplacian    RRE    Euclidean (bi-linear)    Laplacian (bi-linear)

**Fig. 3.** Mean models of shape and pose produced by each representation. Notice how the Euclidean and Laplacian mean models have disproportional human body parts since the representations are not rotation invariant. However, as illustrated in the two rightmost mesh models, the Euclidean and Laplacian shape models can be effectively used in a bi-linear model of shape and pose.

**Shape and Pose from Silhouette.** Typically, shape and pose reconstruction from silhouette frameworks require pose initialization; either by manually placing correspondence points on the silhouette to mark a specific pose[10] or by placing a correctly posed skeleton[9]. In our tests, however, we are interested in how well each model can estimate a specific pose without initialization. We evaluate shape and pose estimation for four models: Euclidean, Laplacian, RRE and a bi-linear model of shape and pose based on the Euclidean shape model. Each model is trained on the full database minus a scan of a subject in a specific pose which is used for testing. This process is repeated once for each of the 32 example poses. Due to the small number of available poses, we retain subjects with the same pose ID. For this set of tests, we have doubled the number of iterations and particles since we are searching for a solution in a much wider space.

The Laplacian and Euclidean models were able to produce good silhouette fits, while generating reasonable approximations to the real solution (table 3). Nonetheless, in most cases the meshes appeared to have shearing and shrinking artifacts, particularly in the area of the arms which is a result of incorrect modeling of pose variation (figure 4). This effect is reflected in the relatively high average RRE distance. The Euclidean and Laplacian models are loosely-constrained since they are not bound by the space of acceptable human body configurations which allows convergence to a solution more freely. On the other hand, the RRE model and the bi-linear model while generating permissible human body

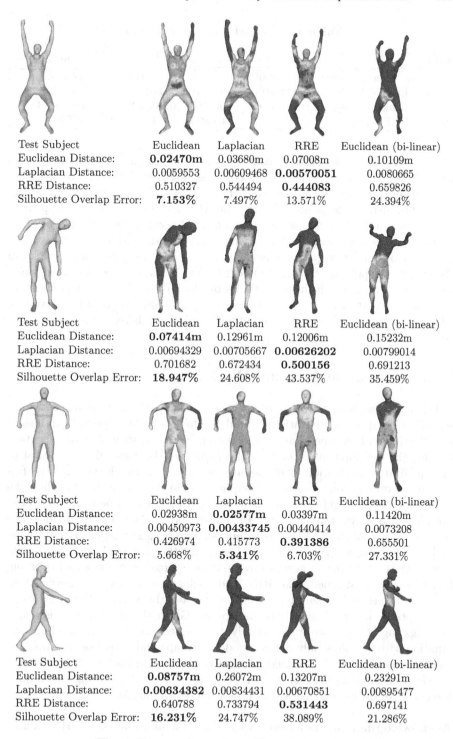

Test Subject | Euclidean | Laplacian | RRE | Euclidean (bi-linear)
Euclidean Distance: | **0.02470m** | 0.03680m | 0.07008m | 0.10109m
Laplacian Distance: | 0.0059553 | 0.00609468 | **0.00570051** | 0.0080665
RRE Distance: | 0.510327 | 0.544494 | **0.444083** | 0.659826
Silhouette Overlap Error: | **7.153%** | 7.497% | 13.571% | 24.394%

Test Subject | Euclidean | Laplacian | RRE | Euclidean (bi-linear)
Euclidean Distance: | **0.07414m** | 0.12961m | 0.12006m | 0.15232m
Laplacian Distance: | 0.00694329 | 0.00705667 | **0.00626202** | 0.00799014
RRE Distance: | 0.701682 | 0.672434 | **0.500156** | 0.691213
Silhouette Overlap Error: | **18.947%** | 24.608% | 43.537% | 35.459%

Test Subject | Euclidean | Laplacian | RRE | Euclidean (bi-linear)
Euclidean Distance: | 0.02938m | **0.02577m** | 0.03397m | 0.11420m
Laplacian Distance: | 0.00450973 | **0.00433745** | 0.00440414 | 0.0073208
RRE Distance: | 0.426974 | 0.415773 | **0.391386** | 0.655501
Silhouette Overlap Error: | 5.668% | **5.341%** | 6.703% | 27.331%

Test Subject | Euclidean | Laplacian | RRE | Euclidean (bi-linear)
Euclidean Distance: | **0.08757m** | 0.26072m | 0.13207m | 0.23291m
Laplacian Distance: | **0.00634382** | 0.00834431 | 0.00670851 | 0.00895477
RRE Distance: | 0.640788 | 0.733794 | **0.531443** | 0.697141
Silhouette Overlap Error: | **16.231%** | 24.747% | 38.089% | 21.286%

**Fig. 4.** Shape and pose from silhouette examples

**Table 3.** Shape and Pose from Silhouette

| Model: | Euclidean | Laplacian | RRE | Euclidean(bi-linear) |
|---|---|---|---|---|
| Silhouette Overlap Error: | **12.560%** | 13.317% | 17.196% | 17.795% |
| Average Euclidean Distance: | **0.06808m** | 0.07917m | 0.08113m | 0.08702m |
| Average Laplacian Distance: | 0.005564 | 0.0058958 | **0.0054262** | 0.0066884 |
| Average RRE Distance: | 0.53393 | 0.55933 | **0.44625** | 0.56900 |

shapes and poses, often failed to converge to a solution; particularly, in the cases where body parts were occluded and pose was not estimated correctly. In other cases, when pose was estimated correctly, shape also converged to a solution; hence, producing good silhouette fits. The RRE and bi-linear models appear to be tightly-constrained decreasing the number of acceptable solutions. In addition, the bi-linear model is split into two correlated spaces which inevitably leads to poorer optimization performance. As mentioned above, generated points in the shape and pose spaces are limited to $\pm 3\sigma$. In many cases, we have found that poses generated within those limits by the RRE and bi-linear models will not always result in a physically correct pose and may also result in artifacts. This occurs since both models attempt to linearize an inherently non-linear pose space.

## 5    Conclusion and Future Work

In this paper, we have provided an analysis and comparison of the surface representations used in recent statistical models. Our goal was to provide an insight into the different parametrization spaces and the reason they play an important role for the development of statistical human models. Through a quantitative and qualitative evaluation of shape-only models, we have shown that the Euclidean representation, despite its simplicity, is in fact more suitable than the Laplacian and RRE representations for estimating body shape from silhouette. We have also shown that both the Euclidean and Laplacian shape models can be used in a framework where pose and shape are learnt separately. A shape and pose from silhouette comparison has shown that the Euclidean and Laplacian models were able to generate reasonable approximates to a real solution; being loosely-constrained. The RRE and bi-linear models were shown not to converge robustly to a solution since they are tightly-constrained to the space of acceptable human body shape and poses. Given this evidence, it is worth investigating in future work how loosely-constrained models can be used in combination with the physically correct models of shape and pose. For instance, the loosely-constrained models could be used to provide an initial estimate to the physically correct models. Furthermore, it may also be interesting to examine the effects of estimating shape and pose from depth images.

**Acknowledgments.** The authors would like to thank *Hasler et al.*[11] for kindly providing the 3D scans database.

# References

1. Alexa, M.: Differential coordinates for local mesh morphing and deformation. The Visual Computer 19(2), 105–114 (2003)
2. Allen, B., Curless, B., Popovic, Z.: The Space of All Body Shapes: Reconstruction and Parameterization from Range Scans. ACM Transactions on Graphics TOG 22(3), 587–594 (2003)
3. Anguelov, D., Srinivasan, P., Koller, D., Thrun, S., Rodgers, J., Davis, J.: SCAPE: shape completion and animation of people. ACM Transactions on Graphics TOG 24(3), 408–416 (2005)
4. Baran, I., Vlasic, D., Grinspun, E., Popović, J.: Semantic deformation transfer. ACM Transactions on Graphics 28(3), 1 (2009)
5. Blanz, V., Vetter, T.: A morphable model for the synthesis of 3D faces. In: Proceedings of the 26th Annual Conference on Computer Graphics and Interactive Techniques SIGGRAPH 1999, vol. 7, pp. 187–194 (1999)
6. Botsch, M., Sorkine, O.: On linear variational surface deformation methods. IEEE Transactions on Visualization and Computer Graphics 14(1), 213–230 (2008)
7. Botsch, M., Sumner, R., Pauly, M., Gross, M.: Deformation transfer for detail-preserving surface editing. In: Vision Modeling Visualization, pp. 357–364. Citeseer (2006)
8. Chen, Y., Kim, T.-K., Cipolla, R.: Inferring 3D Shapes and Deformations from Single Views. In: Daniilidis, K. (ed.) ECCV 2010, Part III. LNCS, vol. 6313, pp. 300–313. Springer, Heidelberg (2010)
9. Guan, P., Weiss, A., Black, M.J.: Estimating Human Shape and Pose from a Single Image. In: Work, ICCV, vol. 2, pp. 1381–1388 (2009)
10. Hasler, N., Ackermann, H., Rosenhahn, B., Thorm, T.: Multilinear Pose and Body Shape Estimation of Dressed Subjects from Image Sets. Image Rochester NY 58(6), 1823–1830 (2010)
11. Hasler, N., Stoll, C., Sunkel, M., Rosenhahn, B., Seidel, H.P.: A Statistical Model of Human Pose and Body Shape. Computer Graphics Forum 28(2), 337–346 (2009)
12. Kazhdan, M., Bolitho, M., Hoppe, H.: Poisson surface reconstruction. In: Proceedings of the Fourth Eurographics Symposium on Geometry Processing, pp. 61–70 (2006)
13. Kircher, S., Garland, M.: Free-form motion processing. ACM Transactions on Graphics 27(2), 1–13 (2008)
14. Lipman, Y., Sorkine, O., Cohen-Or, D., Levin, D., Rossl, C., Seidel, H.P.: Differential coordinates for interactive mesh editing. In: Proceedings Shape Modeling Applications 2004, pp. 181–190 (2004)
15. Lipman, Y., Sorkine, O., Levin, D., Cohen-Or, D.: Linear rotation-invariant coordinates for meshes. ACM Transactions on Graphics 24(3), 479 (2005)
16. Seo, H.: An example-based approach to human body manipulation. Graphical Models 66(1), 1–23 (2004)
17. Sorkine, O.: Differential Representations for Mesh Processing. Computer Graphics Forum 25(4), 789–807 (2006)
18. Sorkine, O., Cohen-Or, D., Lipman, Y., Alexa, M., Rössl, C., Seidel, H.P.: Laplacian surface editing. In: Proceedings of the 2004 Eurographics ACM SIGGRAPH Symposium on Geometry Processing SGP 2004, p. 175 (2004)
19. Sumner, R.W., Popović, J.: Deformation transfer for triangle meshes. ACM Transactions on Graphics 23(3), 399 (2004)

# Combining Skeletal Pose with Local Motion for Human Activity Recognition

Ran Xu[1], Priyanshu Agarwal[2], Suren Kumar[2],
Venkat N. Krovi[2], and Jason J. Corso[1]

[1] Computer Science and Engineering
[2] Mechanical and Aerospace Engineering,
State University of New York at Buffalo, NY, USA
{rxu2,priyansh,surenkum,vkrovi,jcorso}@buffalo.edu

**Abstract.** Recent work in human activity recognition has focused on bottom-up approaches that rely on spatiotemporal features, both dense and sparse. In contrast, articulated motion, which naturally incorporates explicit human action information, has not been heavily studied; a fact likely due to the inherent challenge in modeling and inferring articulated human motion from video. However, recent developments in data-driven human pose estimation have made it plausible. In this paper, we extend these developments with a new middle-level representation called *dynamic pose* that couples the local motion information directly and independently with human skeletal pose, and present an appropriate distance function on the dynamic poses. We demonstrate the representative power of dynamic pose over raw skeletal pose in an activity recognition setting, using simple codebook matching and support vector machines as the classifier. Our results conclusively demonstrate that dynamic pose is a more powerful representation of human action than skeletal pose.

**Keywords:** Human Pose, Activity Recognition, Dynamic Pose.

## 1 Introduction

Bottom-up methods focusing on space-time motion have dominated the activity recognition literature for nearly a decade, e.g., [1–3], and have demonstrated good performance on challenging and realistic data sets like UCF Sports [4]. Although human activity is essentially articulated space-time motion, these methods avoid any need to explicitly model the articulated motion and rather focus on low-level processing to indirectly model the articulated space-time motion. Examples include local space-time interest points (STIP) [1], dense 3D gradient histograms (HOG) [2], and point trajectories [3], among many. More recent efforts have focused on mid-level representations that build on top of these elements, such as Niebles et al. [5] who model the local trajectories of STIP points and Gaidon et al. [6] who learn a time-series kernel to explicitly model repetitive motion in activities. All of these methods have limited transparency from a semantic point-of-view and rely on large amounts of available training data.

Alternatively, it seems reasonable to develop more semantically rich representations, such as those that more explicitly use articulated human models,

F.J. Perales, R.B. Fisher, and T.B. Moeslund (Eds.): AMDO 2012, LNCS 7378, pp. 114–123, 2012.
© Springer-Verlag Berlin Heidelberg 2012

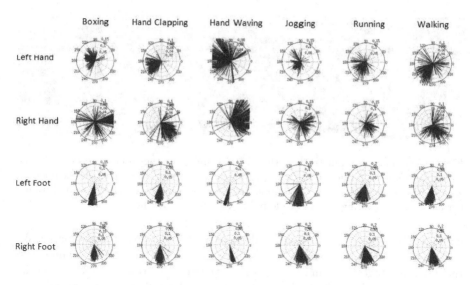

**Fig. 1.** Polar histograms of limb-extrema points in human pose for the six actions in the KTH data set [14]. Note the large similarity for each of the limb-extrema histograms (the rows) across the different actions. These data suggest that pose alone may not be suitable for human activity recognition.

to overcome these issues of transparency and scalability. However, fewer works have directly attempted to use human pose for activity recognition, e.g., [7–9], likely due to the challenging, unsolved nature of the pose estimation problem itself. Recent developments in pose estimation based on data-driven discriminative methods, such as Yang and Ramanan [10] who build a deformable parts model [11] and Bourdev and Malik [12] who learn *poselets* that are tightly coupled in 3D pose-space and local appearance-space, have paved the way for a reinvestigation into the suitability of pose for activity recognition. There has been limited success, yet, in the literature exploiting these better-performing pose estimation methods. Our early experimental evidence implies that pose alone may be insufficient to discriminate some actions. Figure 1, for example, contains polar histograms of limb-extrema for a variety of actions; in many cases the polar histograms across different actions are indistinguishable. Yao et al. [13] also evaluate whether pose estimation helps action recognition by randomly selecting appearance or pose feature in a random forest framework; they found no improvement after combination.

In this paper, we explore a unification of these independent research trends—motion- and pose-based human activity recognition—that addresses the limitations of each separate approach, to some degree. Our main contribution is a new representation called *dynamic pose*. The basic idea is to couple local motion information directly and independently with each *skeletal pose* keypoint. For example, the actions of sitting down in a chair and standing up from the chair are distinct but the set of poses are nearly identical; however, the set of

**Fig. 2.** Dynamic pose illustration: the girl is running to the right. The poses in the second and fourth frames are not very different, but when the joints are augmented with motion information, the distinction between them increases. In the second frame, her arms are expanding and in the fourth, they are contracting.

dynamic poses are indeed distinct and make the two actions distinguishable. We give a visual example of dynamic pose in Figure 2; in this example, we highlight the different stages of running, which have the arms contracting and expanding in one period of the activity giving two separate dynamic poses where only one skeletal pose would be apparent.

We adopt the state of the art pose estimation work of Yang and Ramanan [10] to compute a 13-point *skeletal pose* (i.e., one point for the head, one for the left shoulder, and so on). Then, at each of these 13-points, we compute the motion in a small cube around the point using a histogram of oriented space-time gradients (HoG3D) [2]. We apply the dynamic pose work in an activity recognition setting and propose a novel distance function on the dynamic poses to do so. Our experimental results conclusively demonstrate that dynamic pose outperforms skeletal pose on two benchmarks (UCF Sports [4] and KTH [14]).

**Related Work.** Some methods avoid the need to explicitly compute human pose and yet maintain a rich description of the underlying activity through templates. Exemplary methods along these lines are the space-time shapes [15], local optical-flow templates [16], the Action MACH represent that unifies many example templates into one based on spatiotemporal regularity [4], and the motion-orientation template representation in the action spotting framework [17]. These methods show good performance in some scenarios, but their ability to generalize to arbitrary settings is not clear, largely due to the difficulty in selecting the templates, which is frequently a manual process.

There has been some recent work pushing in the general direction of combining elements of human pose with local motion, but no work we are aware of couples a full skeletal pose with local motion. In contrast, the closest works we are aware of, [18–20], instead use bottom-up part-regions and/or foreground-silhouettes. Tran et al. [18] represent motion of body parts in a sparse quantized polar space as the activity descriptor, but discard the pose/part structure.

Brendel and Todorovic [19] build a codebook jointly on spatial-region appearance features (2D HOG) and motion features tied to these regions. They ultimately use a Viterbi algorithm on the sequence of codebook elements for activity recognition. The key idea is that the shape of the moving region—in this application it is primarily the human torso—will give information about the underlying activity. However, the work does not go far enough as to directly couple the motion information with full human pose and is hence limited in its direct semantic transparency. Lin et al. [20] attend to the moving human and separate the moving human foreground from the background, which they call *shape*. They couple dense motion features in the attended shape region of focus. Actions are then represented as sequences of prototypical shape-motion elements. Our proposed dynamic pose based model clearly differs from these approaches by incorporating local motion directly with full skeletal human pose, leveraging on impressive recent developments in human pose estimation [10].

## 2    Dynamic Pose for Human Activity Recognition

Human pose is the core of our representation for activity recognition. Skeletal pose is represented by 13 joint points, as depicted in the Fig. 3. We use Yang and Ramanan's [10] articulated pose estimation method to extract the initial pose; their method outputs a bounding box for each human parts and we reduce these to the desired 13 joint points.

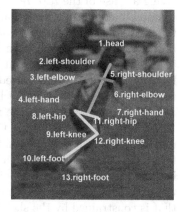

**Fig. 3.** Explanation of the 13 points on the skeletal pose. Section 2.1 explains how the local motion at each of these points is used to enhance the description of the pose for our dynamic pose representation.

We define a local coordinate space for the skeletal pose to allow for scale-invariant inter-pose comparisons. Considering that human action can be represented as pose points' stretch and rotation relative to torso, as well as the whole body movement, we normalize the pose points by eliminating the scale variance and whole body movement. Denote the location of the 13 pose points as $L = \{l_1, ..., l_{13}\}$, in the original image coordinate space $l_i = \{x_i, y_i\}$ (refer to the indices in Fig. 3 to look up specific joint point identities in the following discussion). We anchor the scale-normalization using the extracted head point $(x_1, y_1)$, as we have observed it to be the most stable of the extracted points with the method in use [10]. And, we normalize the spatial scale based on the maximum of the left lower or right lower leg; denote this as $d = \max(\||l_{10} - l_9\||, \||l_{13} - l_{12}\||)$. The scale-normalized skeletal pose $P$ is hence

$$p_i = \left( \frac{x_i - x_1}{d}, \frac{y_i - y_1}{d} \right) . \tag{1}$$

where $i = \{2, \ldots, 13\}$. At last we normalize the 24-dimensional pose vector norm to be 1. In the following sections, we introduce the dynamic pose formulation and then describe how we use dynamic pose for activity recognition.

## 2.1 Dynamic Pose

Although skeletal pose constrains the set of plausible activities a human may be engaging in, our experiments in looking at statistics of joint locations for different activities suggest that pose alone may not be sufficient for good activity recognition (see Figure 1 and Section 3). We hence extend the skeletal pose to incorporate local motion of the joint points, which we expect to add a richness to the pose-based representation for better descriptiveness. For example, jogging and running have similar skeletal poses, but pose with local motion information (e.g. magnitudes of local motion at feet) better encodes their differences.

To capture the local motion information of each skeletal joint point, we compute the histogram of oriented 3D gradients (HoG3D) [2] in the neighborhood around the point. HoG3D has demonstrated strong performance in activity and event classification as it encodes the statistics of local space-time articulation, giving a sense of the *texture* of the motion in the video. The local gradients are computed at multiple spatial and temporal scales in the neighboring vicinity of the joint point and binned according to their orientation and magnitude. Specifically, we define the scales to include $15 - 60$ pixels in each spatial direction and $5 - 20$ frames in time. Ultimately, at each joint-point, the numerous multiscale HoG3D vectors are summarized by a single local motion histogram; a codebook (150 entries) is built over the HoG3D vectors (separately for each joint-point) and then a histogram over the multiscale HoG3D vector-indices is calculated.

We now discuss computing the distance between two dynamic poses. The direct distance of the combined skeletal and local-motion distance is not plausible—for example, one can envision a case where two skeletal poses are quite different, but the local motions of the points are similar. In this contrived case, we expect the two dynamic poses to remain different. In other words, we seek a distance that is constrained by the skeletal pose and incorporates the local motion information only when needed. When two joint points have spatial distance smaller than some threshold, we compute the distance by comparing the histogram of HoG3D descriptor in that joint point; and when the spatial distance is larger than the threshold, we give a maximum distance instead.

Define the threshold that indicates small spatial distance as $\gamma$ and the maximum distance value between the local motion features for a large spatial distance as $\beta$ when we calculate the distance of two skeletal poses $p$ and $q$ (specific values for these parameters are discussed in the experiments). Let $d_i(p, q)$ define some appropriate distance function on joint point $i$ in skeletal poses $p$ and $q$; plausible options are Euclidean distance and cosine distance (since the poses are normalized). At each joint point $i$ for pose $p$, denote the local space-time HoG3D histograms as $h_p(i)$. The distance $D(p, q)$ between two dynamic poses is

$$\delta(i) = \begin{cases} 1 - \min\left(h_p(i), h_q(i)\right) & \text{if } d_i(p, q) < \gamma \\ \beta & \text{if } d_i(p, q) \geq \gamma \end{cases} ,$$

$$D(p, q) = \sum_{i=1}^{12} \delta(i) . \tag{2}$$

We discuss parameter settings in Section 3. The distance function is capable of clustering similar dynamic poses together, and separating different dynamic pose with similar spatial configuration, because the local motion histogram can characterize both joint motion orientation and speed.

## 2.2 Codebook-Based Dynamic Pose for Activity Recognition

To apply our dynamic pose to activity recognition, we use a bag-of-features approach. Incorporating the local motion information with the pose affords this simpler classifier than say a tracking-based one, which may be susceptible to noise in the frame-to-frame pose estimates. For skeletal pose, we construct a k-means codebook of 1000 visual words from the full set of 24-dimensional skeletal pose data. We use a similar technique to generate a 1000 word dynamic pose codebook, using the specified distance function in Eq. (2) instead of the standard Euclidean distance.

For classification we use many one-versus-one histogram intersection kernel SVMs [21]. Given labeled training data $\{(y_i, \mathbf{x_i})\}_{i=1}^{N}$, $x_i \in R^d$, where $d$ is equal to the size of the codebook and $N$ is the number of training data. For vectors $\mathbf{x_1}$ and $\mathbf{x_2}$, the histogram intersection kernel is expressed as:

$$k(\mathbf{x_1}, \mathbf{x_2}) = \sum_{i=1}^{d} \min(x_1(i), x_2(i)) . \tag{3}$$

Since we adopt a one-versus-one strategy, for a classification with $c$ classes, $c(c-1)/2$ SVMs are trained to distinguish the samples of one class from another. Suppose we reduce the multi-class classification to binary classification, with $y_i \in \{-1, +1\}$. We minimize equation (4) in order to find a hyperplane which best separates the data.

$$\tau(\mathbf{w}, \xi) = \frac{1}{2}||\mathbf{w}||^2 + C \sum_{i=i}^{N} \xi_i , \tag{4}$$

subject to:   $y_i((\mathbf{w} \cdot \mathbf{x_i}) + b) \geq 1 - \xi_i$   and   $\xi_i \geq 0 .$ \hfill (5)

where $C > 0$ is the trade-off between regularization and constraint violation. In the dual formulation we maximize:

$$W(\alpha) = \sum_{i=1}^{N} \alpha_i - \frac{1}{2} \sum_{ij} \alpha_i \alpha_j y_i y_j k(\mathbf{x_1}, \mathbf{x_2}) , \tag{6}$$

subject to:   $0 \leq \alpha_i \leq C$   and   $\sum \alpha_i y_i = 0 .$ \hfill (7)

For a given SVM, suppose we have $m$ support vectors $\mathbf{x_l} : l \in 1, 2, ...m$, for each histogram vector $\mathbf{x_i}$, $m$ kernel computations are needed to score it:

$$v(\mathbf{x_i}) = \sum_{l=1}^{m} (\alpha_l y_l k(\mathbf{x_i}, \mathbf{x_l})) . \tag{8}$$

The final classification of a video $\mathbf{x_i}$ is the selected as the positive class in the one-versus-one SVM with the highest score, $v(\mathbf{x_i})$.

**Table 1.** Performance comparison between skeletal pose and dynamic pose on two standard benchmark datasets

| Method | KTH | UCF-Sports |
|--------|-----|------------|
| BoP | 76.39% | 71.33% |
| BoDP | **91.2%** | **81.33%** |

## 3   Experimental Evaluation

We test our algorithm on two benchmarks: KTH [14] and UCF-Sports [4]. The KTH dataset consists of six actions (Boxing, Hand-clapping, Hand-waving, Jogging, Running and Walking) performed about four times each by 25 subjects, for a total of 2396 sequences, including both indoor and outdoor scenes under varying scale. We follow the standard experimental setting described in [14], using person 02, 03, 05, 06, 07, 09, 10 and 22 as testing data and the other 16 people as training data. The UCF Sports dataset consists of ten sports actions (Diving, Golf-Swing, Kicking, Lifting, Riding Horse, Running, Skateboarding, Swing-Bench, Swing-SideAngle and Walk), totally 150 videos in unconstrained environments from wide range of scenes and viewpoints. We apply leave-one-out scheme for training and testing on UCF Sports.

We test using both Bag of Pose (BoP) and our Bag of Dynamic Pose methods (BoDP). As described in Section 2.2, we construct two 1000-dimensional codebooks from 10000 randomly sampled training features of skeletal pose as well as dynamic pose. As for the parameters that we use in the process of training codebook and encoding, we empirically set small distance threshold $\gamma$ as 0.02 and max distance threshold $\beta$ as 1.5. Table 1 summarizes the recognition accuracy of dynamic pose and skeletal pose on both benchmark datasets; the results demonstrate that dynamic pose, as a middle-level representation that incorporate both human pose skeletal and local motion information, is effective to represent articulated human activity.

Fig. 4 shows the visualization of dynamic pose codebook for the KTH dataset (scale-normalized skeletal poses are displayed only for simplicity); the ten samples displayed are the ten codebook centroids with the most support from the data set. We have observed that the first codebook centroid and the 9th one look very similar in the spatial coordinate, so we have inspected the video. We find they are corresponding to the 220th frame of video `person23_handclapping_d4_uncomp.avi` and the 134th frame of video `person25_handclapping_d4_uncomp.avi`. Fig. 5 shows the sequences of frames around the 1st and 9th codebook centroids. It is clear that, although the two canonical poses have great spatial similarity as depicted in the frames with pose skeleton on human, the motion is in the opposite direction. This visualization of codebook echoes our argument that dynamic pose is capable of capturing local motion information, which will definitely contribute to distinguishing different human action; it thus tends to improve classification of different human activities as our experimental evaluation will now show.

**Fig. 4.** The top ten canonical dynamic poses in the learned codebook. The poses are drawn after normalization and without any rendering of the local motion information at each pose point. The number of samples from the training set are given for each example.

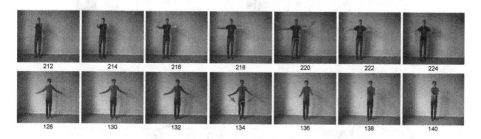

**Fig. 5.** The 1st and 9th dynamic pose codebook centroids visualized in video sequence. The first row corresponds to the 1st centroid: the canonical pose in 220th frame of video person23_handclapping_d4_uncomp.avi, and the second row corresponds to the 9th centroid: the canonical pose in 134th frame of video person25_handclapping_d4_uncomp.avi. The number below the video sequence is frame number, and the arrow indicates the direction of hand clapping.

For the KTH dataset, Fig. 6 shows the confusion matrices of BoP and BoDP, both classified by intersection kernel SVM over 1000 dimensional histograms. BoDP clearly outperforms BoP in every action class. Specifically, with BoP, 14% of jogging is misclassified as walking, whereas with BoDP jogging achieves 100% accuracy; another example is boxing, BoDP reduces 28% misclassification with hand clapping to 11%. These findings indicate that dynamic pose does capture enough articulated local motion information to distinguish spatially similar skeletal poses, e.g., similar feet position distribution among walking and jogging, and similar hand position distribution among boxing and hand-clapping. The overall accuracy increases from 76.4% to 91.2%. BoDP, as a middle level representation of articulated human action, has already achieves results comparable to the state-of-the-art in terms of simple actions.

For UCF-Sports data set, the accuracy of BoP and BoDP are 71.33% and 81.33%, respectively. The confusion matrices in Fig. 7 show that, specifically, the classification result of the action "diving" increased from 71% to 100%, totally distinguish from "riding-horse", "running" and "skating"; and the classification accuracy of "kicking" increases from 70% to 90%, which shows that dynamic pose helps distinguish it from "running", "skating" and "swing-bench". The experiments demonstrate that dynamic pose is also effective in dealing with the complex articulations in UCF Sports.

| | hw | bx | wk | jg | cl | rn | | | hw | bx | wk | jg | cl | rn |
|---|---|---|---|---|---|---|---|---|---|---|---|---|---|---|
| handwaving | 0.89 | 0.03 | 0.06 | 0.03 | 0 | 0 | | handwaving | 1 | 0 | 0 | 0 | 0 | 0 |
| boxing | 0 | 0.64 | 0 | 0.03 | 0.28 | 0.06 | | boxing | 0 | 0.81 | 0 | 0 | 0.11 | 0.08 |
| walking | 0.03 | 0.06 | 0.86 | 0.03 | 0 | 0.03 | | walking | 0.06 | 0 | 0.92 | 0.03 | 0 | 0 |
| jogging | 0 | 0 | 0.14 | 0.83 | 0.03 | 0 | | jogging | 0 | 0 | 0 | 1 | 0 | 0 |
| clapping | 0.03 | 0.25 | 0 | 0 | 0.61 | 0.11 | | clapping | 0 | 0.17 | 0.03 | 0 | 0.78 | 0.03 |
| running | 0 | 0.14 | 0 | 0 | 0.11 | 0.75 | | running | 0 | 0.03 | 0 | 0 | 0 | 0.97 |

**Fig. 6.** Confusion Matrix Comparison over BoP(Left) and BoDP(Right)

| | dv | gf | kk | lf | rd | rn | sk | sb | hs | wk | | | dv | gf | kk | lf | rd | rn | sk | sb | hs | wk |
|---|---|---|---|---|---|---|---|---|---|---|---|---|---|---|---|---|---|---|---|---|---|---|
| diving | 0.71 | 0 | 0 | 0 | 0.14 | 0.07 | 0 | 0.07 | 0 | 0 | | diving | 1 | 0 | 0 | 0 | 0 | 0 | 0 | 0 | 0 | 0 |
| golfing | 0.06 | 0.78 | 0.17 | 0 | 0 | 0 | 0 | 0 | 0 | 0 | | golfing | 0 | 0.83 | 0.06 | 0 | 0 | 0 | 0.11 | 0 | 0 | 0 |
| kicking | 0 | 0.05 | 0.70 | 0 | 0 | 0.10 | 0.10 | 0.05 | 0 | 0 | | kicking | 0 | 0.05 | 0.90 | 0 | 0 | 0.05 | 0 | 0 | 0 | 0 |
| lifting | 0 | 0 | 0 | 0.67 | 0.17 | 0 | 0.17 | 0 | 0 | 0 | | lifting | 0 | 0.17 | 0 | 0.67 | 0 | 0 | 0.17 | 0 | 0 | 0 |
| riding | 0 | 0.08 | 0.08 | 0 | 0.58 | 0.08 | 0 | 0.17 | 0 | 0 | | riding | 0 | 0.08 | 0.08 | 0 | 0.67 | 0.08 | 0.08 | 0 | 0 | 0 |
| running | 0 | 0 | 0.08 | 0 | 0.08 | 0.77 | 0 | 0 | 0 | 0.08 | | running | 0 | 0 | 0.23 | 0 | 0 | 0.62 | 0.08 | 0 | 0 | 0.08 |
| skating | 0.17 | 0.08 | 0.08 | 0 | 0 | 0 | 0.08 | 0 | 0.08 | 0.50 | | skating | 0 | 0.17 | 0.17 | 0 | 0 | 0.08 | 0.33 | 0 | 0.08 | 0.17 |
| swing-bench | 0.05 | 0 | 0 | 0 | 0.05 | 0 | 0 | 0.90 | 0 | 0 | | swing-bench | 0 | 0 | 0 | 0 | 0 | 0 | 0 | 1 | 0 | 0 |
| h-swinging | 0.08 | 0 | 0 | 0 | 0 | 0 | 0.08 | 0 | 0.85 | 0 | | h-swinging | 0 | 0 | 0 | 0 | 0 | 0 | 0.08 | 0 | 0.92 | 0 |
| walking | 0 | 0 | 0.05 | 0 | 0 | 0 | 0.14 | 0 | 0 | 0.82 | | walking | 0 | 0 | 0 | 0 | 0 | 0 | 0.14 | 0 | 0 | 0.86 |

**Fig. 7.** Confusion Matrix Comparison over BoP(Left) and BoDP(Right) on UCF-Sports Dataset

## 4    Conclusion and Future Work

In conclusion, we propose a new middle level representation of articulated human action—dynamic pose—that adds local motion information to skeletal joint points. The basic premise behind dynamic pose is that skeletal pose alone is insufficient for distinguishing certain human actions, those which have similar spatial distributions of limb points over the course of an action. We have implemented our representation in an activity recognition setting using bag of features with kernel intersection SVM as the base classifier. Our experiments conclusively indicate that dynamic pose is a capable middle-level representation of articulated human motion. In the future, we plan to combine our dynamic pose with global context.

**Acknowledgements.** This work was partially supported by the National Science Foundation CAREER grant (IIS-0845282), the Army Research Office (W911NF-11-1-0090), and the DARPA Mind's Eye program (W911NF-10-2-0062).

# References

1. Laptev, I.: On space-time interest points. In: IJCV (2005)
2. Klaser, A., Marszalek, M., Schmid, C.: A spatio-temporal descriptor based on 3d-gradients. In: BMVC (2008)
3. Wang, H., Kläser, A., Schmid, C., Liu, C.L.: Action recognition by dense trajectories. In: CVPR, pp. 3169–3176 (2011)
4. Rodriguez, M.D., Ahmed, J., Shah, M.: Action mach: A spatio-temporal maximum average correlation height filter for action recognition. In: CVPR (2008)
5. Niebles, J.C., Chen, C.-W., Fei-Fei, L.: Modeling Temporal Structure of Decomposable Motion Segments for Activity Classification. In: Daniilidis, K., Maragos, P., Paragios, N. (eds.) ECCV 2010, Part II. LNCS, vol. 6312, pp. 392–405. Springer, Heidelberg (2010)
6. Gaidon, A., Harchaoui, Z., Schmid, C.: A time series kernel for action recognition. In: BMVC (2011)
7. Ali, S., Basharat, A., Shah, M.: Chaotic invariants for human action recognition. In: ICCV (2007)
8. Ramanan, D., Forsyth, D.A.: Automatic annotation of everyday movements. In: NIPS (2003)
9. Shakhnarovich, G., Viola, P., Darrell, T.: Fast Pose Estimation with Parameter-Sensitive Hashing. In: ICCV (2003)
10. Yang, Y., Ramanan, D.: Articulated pose estimation with flexible mixtures-of-parts. In: CVPR (2011)
11. Felzenszwalb, P.F., Girshick, R.B., McAllester, D., Ramanan, D.: Object detection with discriminatively trained part based models. TPAMI 32, 1627–1645 (2010)
12. Bourdev, L., Malik, J.: Poselets: Body part detectors trained using 3d human pose annotations. In: ICCV (2009)
13. Yao, A., Gall, J., Fanelli, G., Gool, L.V.: Does human action recognition benefit from pose estimation? In: BMVC (2011)
14. Schüldt, C., Laptev, I., Caputo, B.: Recognizing human actions: a local SVM approach. In: ICPR (2004)
15. Gorelick, L., Blank, M., Shechtman, E., Irani, M., Basri, R.: Actions as space-time shapes. TPAMI 29(12), 2247–2253 (2007)
16. Essa, I., Pentland, A.: Coding, analysis, interpretation and recognition of facial expressions. TPAMI 19(7), 757–763 (1997)
17. Derpanis, K.G., Sizintsev, M., Cannons, K., Wildes, R.P.: Efficient action spotting based on a spacetime oriented structure representation. In: CVPR (2010)
18. Tran, K.N., Kakadiaris, I.A., Shah, S.K.: Modeling motion of body parts for action recognition. In: BMVC (2011)
19. Brendel, W., Todorovic, S.: Activities as Time Series of Human Postures. In: Daniilidis, K., Maragos, P., Paragios, N. (eds.) ECCV 2010, Part II. LNCS, vol. 6312, pp. 721–734. Springer, Heidelberg (2010)
20. Lin, Z., Jiang, Z., Davis, L.S.: Recognizing actions by shape-motion prototype trees. In: ICCV (2009)
21. Maji, S., Berg, A.C., Malik, J.: Classification using intersection kernel support vector machines is efficient. In: CVPR (2008)

# A New Marker-Less 3D Kinect-Based System for Facial Anthropometric Measurements

Claudio Loconsole[1], Nuno Barbosa[2,3],
Antonio Frisoli[1], and Verónica Costa Orvalho[2,4]

[1] PERCRO Laboratory, Scuola Superiore Sant'Anna
[2] Instituto de Telecomunicações
[3] Faculdade de Engenharia, Universidade do Porto
[4] Faculdade de Ciências, Universidade do Porto
{c.loconsole,a.frisoli}@sssup.it,
nuno.barbosa@fe.up.pt, veronica.orvalho@dcc.fc.up.pt

**Abstract.** Several research fields like forensic and orthodontics, use facial anthropometric distances between a set of pairs of facial standard landmarks. There are tens of attempts to automatize the measurement process using 2D and 3D approaches. However, they still suffer of three main drawbacks: human manual intervention to fix the facial landmarks, physical markers placed on the face and required time for the measurement process.

In this paper, we propose a new marker-less system for automatic facial anthropometric measurements based on Microsoft Kinect and *FaceTracker* API. This new approach overcomes the three measurement drawbacks. We statistically validated the system with respect to the caliper-based manual system, through experimental measurements and one-way ANOVA test comparisons on 36 subjects. The achieved successful percentage in the comparison is equal to 54,5 %.

**Keywords:** facial anthropometry, depth camera, Kinect, measurement error, three-dimensional.

## 1 Introduction

Facial[1] anthropometric measurements are commonly used in the following research fields:

- *forensic and physical anthropology* for finding the characterizing facial anthropometric measurements of populations. The traditional parameters considered in population studies are gender, age and geographical origin [2];
- *orthodontic, maxillofacial and speech researches* for treatment planning, preorthodontic and postorthodontic and/or surgical treatment and evaluation of postoperative swelling [3];

---

[1] According to [1], *"the face is the part of the front of the head between the ears and from the chin to the airline (or where it ought to be if you have lost it!). It includes the forehead, eyes, nose, mouth and chin."*

F.J. Perales, R.B. Fisher, and T.B. Moeslund (Eds.): AMDO 2012, LNCS 7378, pp. 124–133, 2012.

- *syndrome, paralysis and disease* for medical prevention and diagnosis purposes, both in adulthood and in childhood [4];
- *beauty and asymmetry* for investigation, modeling and improvement of the facial beauty [5];
- *face modeling and synthesizing* for Information Communication Technology targets (e.g. teleconference, entertainment, etc.) [6].

Usually, traditional methods of taking facial measurements are dependent on the competences and skills of the operator. In fact, the facial landmarks identification is performed manually by the operator, either by touching or by looking at the facial features. Furthermore, misalignment errors can arise due to the use of the caliper in the measurement of the 3D distances between the selected landmark pairs. Generally, we can identify three main drawbacks in the traditional measurement methods:

1. prerequisite training on live subjects (which can be painstaking);
2. the time-consuming nature of performing multiple direct measurements (especially when we require a large number of measurements);
3. the person to be measured must remain patiently still. For instance, a facial measurement of a child is harder to carry out than of an adult, due to the restlessness of the children.

Some attempts to use 3D data for automating the measurement process were considered in the works by *Kau et al.* [7] in 2005 and by *Hammond et al.* [8] in 2004. They use, respectively, high cost laser scanning and multiple camera systems and are still affected by the drawbacks mentioned above.

A more recent work uses a faster system based on IR cameras [9] that overcomes the cited drawbacks. But it also introduces the dependence on physical markers to be placed on the face to localize landmarks. The use of markers on a subject's face skin is intrusive for the subject itself and still requires human intervention to localize facial landmarks.

In this paper, we propose a new marker-less 3D Kinect-based system for facial anthropometric measurements using a single or multiple frontal shots of a human's face, providing the facial measurements. Our system overcomes the three drawbacks mentioned above, as well as the dependence on physical markers. It also lowers the cost for facial measurement in comparison with the solutions presented in [7] and in [8]. In order to validate the system as an automatic measuring approach, we also conducted an experimental test and statistical comparisons with standard measurement methods on 36 subjects. This research will contribute to all facial anthropometric research laboratories, speeding up and automating the process of facial measurement.

## 2   The Proposed Measurement Method

The system we present provides a set of linear spatial measures that characterize the face of a subject. The measurements are made between pairs of standard

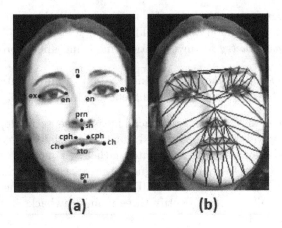

**(a)**          **(b)**

**Fig. 1.** The selected 13 facial landmarks for linear measurements of the face (a). The 66 facial landmarks identified and localized by *FaceTracker* API by *Saragih at al.* on the eye and oral-nasal regions and over the lower face contour (b).

facial landmarks. In Paragraph 2.1, we introduce and motivate the selection of the subset of facial landmarks and corresponding masurements used for our work. In Paragraph 2.2, we present the new system, implemented algorithms and their computational time performances.

### 2.1   Selected Landmarks

*Weinberg et al.* [10] define 28 standard anthropometric facial landmarks and 19 standard linear measurements taken between selected pairs of these 28 landmarks. We use a subset of the *Weinberg et al.* standard landmarks and linear measurements. We selected 13 facial landmarks (see Fig. 1.(a) and Table 1) and 11 euclidean spatial measurements (see Table 1) that cover the eye and oral-nasal regions. Some standard facial landmarks, such as ear landmarks, have been excluded because they can not be correctly identified with frontal camera shots of the face. Other reasons for excluding landmarks are areas covered by hair, like eurion, and those requiring palpation, like gonion.

### 2.2   Description of the System and of the Algorithms

Our system uses a Microsoft Kinect device (http://www.xbox.com/kinect, http://www.primesense.com) that provides visual and depth data, and a processing system. It uses OpenCV (http://opencv.willowgarage.com) OpenNI (http://openni.org) and PCL (http://pointclouds.org) open-source libraries. In order to avoid the use of physical markers or human interventions for landmark identification and localization, we employ a method by *Saragih et al.*. This method is based on constrained local models (CLM), optimized

**Table 1.** List of the selected subset of landmarks among standard anthropometric facial landmarks used by *Weinberg at al.* [10] (left). List of the selected subset of linear measurements between pairs of the selected landmarks (right). L stands for *left*, R stands for *right*.

| No. | Landmark | Description | No. | Linear measurement | Region | Landmarks |
|-----|----------|-------------|-----|--------------------|--------|-----------|
| 1 | n | nasion | 1 | Total facial height | Face | n-gn |
| 2 | gn | gnathion | 2 | Upper facial height | Face | n-sto |
| 3 | sto | stomion | 3 | Lower facial height | Face | sn-gn |
| 4 | sn | subnasale | 4 | Intercantal width | Eye | en-en |
| 5 | en (L) | left endocanthion | 5 | Binocular width | Eye | ex-ex |
| 6 | en (R) | right endocanthion | 6 | Nasal height | Nose | n-sn |
| 7 | ex (L) | left exocanthion | 7 | Nasal projection | Nose | sn-prn |
| 8 | ex (R) | right exocanthion | 8 | Philtrum width | Mouth | cph-cph |
| 9 | prn | pronasale | 9 | Labial fissure width | Mouth | ch-ch |
| 10 | cph (L) | left crista philtri inferior | 10 | Upper lip height | Mouth | sn-sto |
| 11 | cph (R) | right crista philtri inferior | 11 | Upper lip length (L) | Mouth | sn-ch |
| 12 | ch (L) | left chelion | | | | |
| 13 | ch (R) | right chelion | | | | |

through a homoscedastic kernel density estimate (KED) with an isotropic Gaussian kernel [11]. *Saragih et al.* provide a CLM-based C/C++ API for real time generic non-rigid face alignment and tracking called *FaceTracker* (http://web.mac.com/jsaragih/FaceTracker/FaceTracker.html). The *FaceTracker* allows the identification and localization of 66 2D landmarks on the face (see Fig. 1.(b)).

We consider a subset of these 66 2D landmarks composed by 14 points. Twelve out of 14 points are taken directly as seeds for 3D landmarks object of our study (Direct Landmarks: *gn, sto, sn, en (left), en (right), ex (left), ex (right), cph (left), cph (right), ch (left), ch(right), prn*). The other two points are used to calculate, through average operation, the seed of the *n* landmark.

Using an offline preliminary calibration of the Microsoft Kinect, the intrinsic parameters of the Zhang camera model are estimated. Knowing these parameters and the depth data acquired by the Kinect, we can transform a 2D pixel point of the camera image into the corresponding 3D point in the space. So, the corresponding 3D points of the 2D landmarks can be directly calculated. Finally, the distances between selected 3D facial landmark pairs (see Table 1) can be calculated using the distance equation of Euclide. To summarize, we synthetically report the steps followed by our algorithm (see Fig. 2):

1. *Coarse Spatial Filtering*: 2D image (Input no. 1) from Kinect is coarsly filtered using the depth data (Input no. 2) acquired from the IR camera to exclude undesired objects from the image. A black patch is applied to all the image except for the region containing the subject's face;
2. *FaceTracker Processing*: the *FaceTracker* API identifies and localizes 66 2D landmarks on the face;

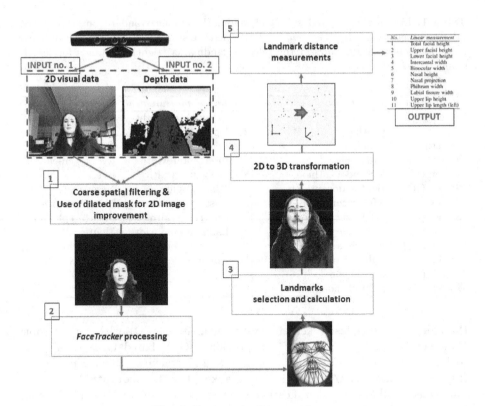

**Fig. 2.** System pipeline overview

3. *Landmark Selection and Calculation*: starting from the 66 localized land-marks, the 13 facial landmarks are selected and calculated;

4. *2D to 3D Transformation*: using the intrinsic parameters of the Kinect cam-era (estimated with a preliminary offline procedure) and the depth data coming from Kinect, it is possibile to transform the 2D landmarks into the corresponding 3D points in the space;

5. *Landmark Distance Measurements*: the euclidean distance between a set of selected pairs of landmarks are calculated in order to extract the linear facial measurements. The output consists of 11 selected linear facial measurement expressed in millimeters.

The computational time for the entire pipeline depends on the *FaceTracker* API status. In particular, if it is the first time that the API is searching for the facial landmarks, the entire pipeline lasts 215 *ms* (average of $10^3$ runs), while if the landmarks are already localized on the face, the pipeline lasts 24 *ms* (average of $10^3$ runs), even if the subject moves the head[2].

---

[2] For pipeline computational time measurements, we use a processing system equipped with an Intel Core i7 CPU at 3.07 GHz, 6 GB RAM and Windows 7 64-bit OS.

# 3  Population and Methodologies

## 3.1  Study Population

The studied population is composed by 36 healthy adults, ranging from 18 to 31 years of age ($\mu = 29.97$ years, SD $= 3.59$ years). There are 29 men and 7 women belonging to four different nationalities. In particular, four males have beard.

## 3.2  Data Collection

In this work, we considered 3 measurement methods (MM): the caliper MM, the Kinect 1 shot MM (*Kinect 1*) and the Kinect 100 shots MM (*Kinect 100*). The caliper measurements are performed by a professional operator. For every method, all 11 measurements reported in Table 1 are taken and registered. This leads to a total of 33 (3x11) facial measurements per person and, so, a total of 1188 (33x36) measurements. The first uses a digital caliper with 0.1 mm resolution and $\pm$ 0.1 mm accuracy. The second and third methods use the proposed marker-less method. In the second method, the 11 facial measurements are taken in one single shot (in 215 *ms*). On the other hand, the third method performs 100 times the same 11 facial measurements and takes, as final measurement results, the average of the measured values. The *Kinect 100* method attemps to statistically improve the precision of Kinect. Additionally, 100 shots required 2,59 seconds ($215 + 99 * 24$ *ms*), so the immobility condition of the measured person is still valid.

The entire data collection procedure for each tested person is composed by four steps. 1. Presentation and explanation of the measurement methods and collection of personal data (age, gender, values of the anthropometric facial measurements). 2. Signing the consent form for the processing of personal data. 3. Manual measurement with the digital caliper of the 11 standard facial measurements. 4. Automatic measurement of the 11 standard facial measurements using the proposed method based on Kinect (see Section 2.2) both according to *Kinect 1* and the *Kinect 100* measurement methods.

# 4  Experimental Results and Discussion

In Figure 3, the resulting mean and Standard Deviation (SD) of the error measurements are reported for each comparison between following method couples: *Kinect 1* and caliper methods; *Kinect 100* and caliper methods; *Kinect 1* and *Kinect 100* methods.

We perform a one-way ANOVA (ANalysis Of VAriance) test (1 degree of freedom and $\alpha = 0.05$) for each of the 11 distance measurements and for each couple of measurement methods, leading to a total of 33 combinations. These tests are performed in order to verify if there are some statistically significant differences between the measurement methods. In fact, the use of one-way ANOVA tests is admissible for our study because each facial measurement method is applied on the same population.

The results of the tests are listed in Table 2, where we synthetically report, also, if the null hypothesis can be considered valid. The validity of the null hypotesis implies that our proposed measurement methods (*Kinect 1* and/or *Kinect 100*) can be considered statistically equal to the caliper method.

Regarding the comparison between *Kinect 1* and *Kinect 100*, it is proved that they are statistically equal for each couple of facial landmarks and that the committed error in the measurement is in line with the precision of the Microsoft Kinect. It is possible to consider our system as a single-shot measurement system that after 215 *ms* provides the facial characterizing distances. In this way, the requirement of substantial immobility of the measured person is completely fulfilled. Therefore, in the following discussion, due to substantial equivalence between *Kinect 1* and *Kinect 100*, we will only compare the *Kinect 1* method to the caliper method.

According to one-way ANOVA tests, the caliper and the *Kinect 1* methods can be considered equivalent for 5 up to 11 distances among facial landmark pairs (see Table. 2): 1. "Upper facial height"; 2. "Nasal height"; 3. "Labial Fissure width"; 4. "Upper lip height"; 5. 11 "Upper facial lenght (left)"; involving the landmarks: *n*; *sto*; *sn*; *ch* left; *ch* right. Each of these landmarks is a common point in more than one of the five aforementioned distances. Therefore, the 5 landmarks are properly identified on the face of the tested people. In addition, the subject's beard does not interfere with the automatic landmark localization for *sto*, *sn*, *chs* landmarks, that are placed in the mouth region.

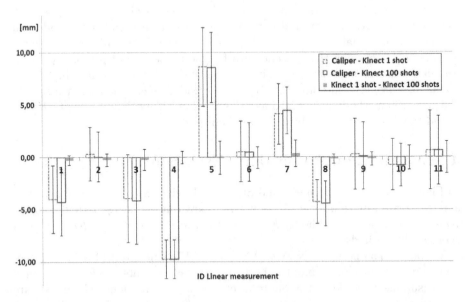

**Fig. 3.** Graph representing the mean and the SD of the measurement error resulting from the comparison between *Kinect 1* and caliper, *Kinect 100* and caliper, and *Kinect 1* and *Kinect 100* methods

**Table 2.** Results of one-way ANOVA tests (DOFs = 1; $\alpha = 0.05$) on different couples of methods: *Kinect 1* and caliper, *Kinect 100* and caliper, and *Kinect 1* and *Kinect 100* methods

| Measurement error | | Caliper - *Kinect 1* [mm] | | | Caliper - *Kinect 100* [mm] | | | *Kinect 1 - Kinect 100* [mm] | | | Null hypothesis valid | |
|---|---|---|---|---|---|---|---|---|---|---|---|---|
| No. | Landmarks | $F$ | $\rho$ | $F_{crit}$ | $F$ | $\rho$ | $F_{crit}$ | $F$ | $\rho$ | $F_{crit}$ | Yes | No |
| 1 | n-gn | 5,272 | 0,025 | 3,978 | 6,079 | 0,016 | 3,978 | 0,029 | 0,865 | 3,978 | | x |
| 2 | n-sto | 0,063 | 0,803 | 3,978 | 0,001 | 0,977 | 3,978 | 0,052 | 0,820 | 3,978 | x | |
| 3 | sn-gn | 8,815 | 0,004 | 3,978 | 10,368 | 0,002 | 3,978 | 0,037 | 0,848 | 3,978 | | x |
| 4 | en-en | 256,504 | 0,000 | 3,978 | 258,285 | 0,000 | 3,978 | 0,000 | 0,985 | 3,978 | | x |
| 5 | ex-ex | 42,543 | 0,000 | 3,978 | 43,796 | 0,000 | 3,978 | 0,003 | 0,957 | 3,978 | | x |
| 6 | n-sn | 0,259 | 0,612 | 3,978 | 0,204 | 0,653 | 3,978 | 0,004 | 0,952 | 3,978 | x | |
| 7 | sn-prn | 46,204 | 0,000 | 3,978 | 80,559 | 0,000 | 3,978 | 0,286 | 0,594 | 3,978 | | x |
| 8 | cph-cph | 113,627 | 0,000 | 3,978 | 128,623 | 0,000 | 3,978 | 0,354 | 0,554 | 3,978 | | x |
| 9 | ch-ch | 0,121 | 0,729 | 3,978 | 0,015 | 0,904 | 3,978 | 0,046 | 0,830 | 3,978 | x | |
| 10 | sn-sto | 1,424 | 0,237 | 3,978 | 1,820 | 0,182 | 3,978 | 0,012 | 0,913 | 3,978 | x | |
| 11 | sn-ch | 0,639 | 0,427 | 3,978 | 0,689 | 0,409 | 3,978 | 0,002 | 0,965 | 3,978 | x | |

Regarding the other landmark distances that have not passed the one-way ANOVA tests (distances: "Total facial height", "Lower facial height", "Intercantal width", "Binocular width", "Nasal projection" and "Philtrum width"), we can attribute this errors to a localization displacement of the facial landmarks: *gn, exs, ens, prn* and *cphs*. Indeed, these errors can not be attributed to Kinect measurements, since it has achieved good results with the distance measurements mentioned above.

The motivations for the committed errors in landmark localization are:

1. for *gn* landmark, it is necessary to palpate the chin in order to feel the bone, especially if we consider that: 1. the part between the chin and the throat is not always planar; 2. under the chin there is usually an accumulation of fat that can visually provide wrong position of the chin itself.
2. for *ex (left) and ex (right)* landmarks, the capacity of the *FaceTracker* to unproperly localize the exocanthion. In fact, the *FaceTracker* places the exocanthions over the most external points of the eyes where the eyelids touch. This leads to an underestimation of the "Binocular width" (the distance error is always positive) and to a doubled distance error (both for the left and for the right side). This diverted landmark localization can be solved through a further computer vision elaboration of the picture in the area around the exocanthion identified by the *FaceTracker* algorithm;
3. for *en (left) and en (right)* landmarks, the capacity of the *FaceTracker* to unproperly localize the endocanthion. In fact, the *FaceTracker* places the endocanthions over the eye caruncles. This leads to an overestimation of the "Intercantal width" (the distance error is always negative) and to a doubled distance error (both for the left and for the right side). Moreover, through

a further one-way ANOVA test, we prove ($F = -3E - 14$, $\rho << 0,001$ and $F_{crit} = 3,978$) that the committed error for the "Intercantal width" is systematic and equal to 9, 76 $mm$. The resulting localization displacement can be solved through a further computer vision elaboration of the picture in the area around the caruncles identified by the *FaceTracker* algorithm;

4. for *prn* landmark, the non-use of the *FaceTracker* of the 3D information for the nose. A further improvement can be to consider as correct *prn* landmark, the point belonging to a small picture area centered into the identified *prn*, but nearest to Kinect (considering the facial plane perpendicular to the Kinect);

5. for *cph (left) and cph (right)* landmarks, the numerosity of different shapes and colors of lips and the colors of the skin around the lips. Even in the measurements taken with the caliper, the cph landmarks were most of the times difficult to localize, especially when: 1. the *cphs* did not have a pointed shape; 2. the upper part of the lip and the skin had the same color. Additionally, through a further one-way ANOVA test, we rejected the hypothesis according to the error is due to beard.

In order to improve the proposed method, an enhancement of the *FaceTracker* API is required. It can be done applying further computer vision algorithms (such as those involving Laplacian and gradient filters) and using 3D information from the Kinect. This can lead to solve the localization landmark displacements.

Finally, only by using the caliper measurements, we have statistically rejected the hypotesis reported in many works of the literature that states the equivalence of the following equations: $dist_{n-gn} = dist_{n-sn} + dist_{sn-gn} \Leftrightarrow Total facial height = Nasal height + Lower facial height$.

Measurement error statistics ($\mu = -4.28$, $SD = 3.58$, $F = 5,226$, $\rho = 0,025$ and $F_{crit} = 3,978$) show that the group *n-gn* and the group (*n-sn* + *sn-gn*) are significantly different.

# 5    Conclusion and Future Works

In this paper we introduced and discussed a new marker-less 3D Kinect-based system for facial anthropometric measurements. It allows to overcome the main drawbacks which characterize the existing facial measurement solutions. Commonly used solutions require an high professional human intervention to correctly localize the facial landmarks. Moreover, in some cases, it is expected to fix the markers on the subject's face, leading to an increase of the degree of intrusiveness of the measurement system.

Furthermore, our adopted approach allows to keep the cost of the system low and to perform the measurement process in 215 $ms$, avoiding any potential error due to head movements. The experimental part revealed a successful percentage of our method for 54,5 % of the total measured distances with respect to the caliper-based manual system (considering the systematic error committed on "Intercantal width"). The increase of the performances, as well as the decrease of magnitude and variance of the measurement errors are the aim of future works.

Considering the causes of the landmark localization displacements presented in Section 4, we want to improve the automatic localization of the facial landmarks and speed up the pipeline process with a GPU version of the algorithm.

**Acknowledgments.** This work is partially supported by Instituto de Tele-comunicações, Fundação para a Ciência e Tecnologia (SFRH/BD/69878/2010, SFRH/BD/33974/2009), VERE project (ref: 257695), LIFEisGAME project (ref: UTA-Est/MAI/0009/2009) and Golem project (ref.251415, FP7-PEOPLE-2009-IAPP). Special Thanks go to Jacqueline Fernandes for helping with the editing of the article.

# References

1. Sinnatamby, C.: Last's anatomy. Regional and Applied 10 (1999)
2. Choe, K., Sclafani, A., Litner, J., Yu, G., Romo, T.: The korean american woman's face. Archives of Facial Plastic Surgery 6(4), 244 (2004)
3. Bianchini, E.M.G.: Avaliaçao fonoaudiológica da motricidade oral-disturbios mio-funcionais orafaciais ou situações adaptativas; Speech-pathologist evaluation-orofacial myofunctional disorders or compensatory situation. Rev. Dent. Press Ortodon. Ortop. Maxilar 6(3), 73–82 (2001)
4. Ward, R., Jamison, P., Allanson, J.: Quantitative approach to identifying abnormal variation in the human face exemplified by a study of 278 individuals with five craniofacial syndromes. American Journal of Medical Genetics 91(1), 8–17 (2000)
5. Porter, J., Olson, K.: Anthropometric facial analysis of the african american woman. Archives of Facial Plastic Surgery 3(3), 191 (2001)
6. DeCarlo, D., Metaxas, D., Stone, M.: An anthropometric face model using vari-ational techniques. In: Proceedings of the 25th Annual Conference on Computer Graphics and Interactive Techniques, pp. 67–74. ACM (1998)
7. Kau, C., Richmond, S., Zhurov, A., Knox, J., Chestnutt, I., Hartles, F., Playle, R.: Reliability of measuring facial morphology with a 3-dimensional laser scanning system. American Journal of Orthodontics and Dentofacial Orthopedics 128(4), 424–430 (2005)
8. Hammond, P., Hutton, T., Allanson, J., Campbell, L., Hennekam, R., Holden, S., Patton, M., Shaw, A., Temple, I., Trotter, M.: 3d analysis of facial morphology. American Journal of Medical Genetics Part A 126(4), 339–348 (2004)
9. Schimmel, M., Christou, P., Houstis, O., Herrmann, F., Kiliaridis, S., Müller, F.: Distances between facial landmarks can be measured accurately with a new digital 3-dimensional video system. American Journal of Orthodontics and Dentofacial Orthopedics 137(5), 580–e1 (2010)
10. Weinberg, S., Scott, N., Neiswanger, K., Brandon, C., Marazita, M.: Digital three-dimensional photogrammetry: evaluation of anthropometric precision and accuracy using a genex 3d camera system. The Cleft Palate-Craniofacial Journal 41(5), 507–518 (2004)
11. Saragih J., Lucey S., Cohn J.: Deformable model fitting by regularized landmark mean-shift. International Journal of Computer Vision, 1–16 (2011)

# Automatic Detection of Unconscious Reactions to Illuminance Changes in Illumination

Kensuke Kitamura[1], Noriko Takemura[1], Yoshio Iwai[2], and Kosuke Sato[1]

[1] Graduate School of Engineering Science, Osaka University
Machikaneyama 1-3, Toyonaka, 560-8531 Osaka, Japan
{kitamura,takemura}@sens.sys.es.osaka-u.ac.jp, sato@sys.es.osaka-u.ac.jp
[2] Graduate School of Engineering, Tottori University
Koyamachominami 4-101, Tottori, 680-8552 Tottori, Japan
iwai@ike.tottori-u.ac.jp
http://www-sens.sys.es.osaka-u.ac.jp/

**Abstract.** In this study, we investigated expressive facial reactions in response to changes in the visual environment and their automatic extraction from sensors, in order to construct a comfortable level of illumination in personal living spaces. We conducted an experiment that showed that expressive facial reactions occur when illumination in the visual environment changes. We captured facial images and manually classified them as expressing or not expressing discomfort. We then conducted a second experiment that showed that automatic image processing can be used to extract and identify these expressive facial reactions. We extracted facial features and used a support vector machine to learn the classification in this experiment.

**Keywords:** expressive facial reaction, light environment, ambient sensing, image processing, automatic feature extraction, sensor networks, human-computer interaction.

## 1 Introduction

In recent years, much research has been conducted in the field of ambient intelligence (AmI). AmI aims to construct intelligent environments[1]. In AmI, computers are embedded in the environment to autonomously analyze information about users and automatically provide flexible and intelligent adjustments to the environment on the basis of each user's psychological state and situation. AmI includes many specialized fields such as artificial intelligence, robotics, sensor network systems, and human-computer interaction.

Within this context, the goal of our research is to construct an autonomous system that controls illumination in a room through ambient sensing to detect an individual's comfort or discomfort. We focus on the indoor environment because of the following reasons. First, most commonly used light controllers are designed for manual operation by a single user based on the user's intentions and not for automatic change of the lighting. Second, the comfort level of lighting in the

F.J. Perales, R.B. Fisher, and T.B. Moeslund (Eds.): AMDO 2012, LNCS 7378, pp. 134–143, 2012.
© Springer-Verlag Berlin Heidelberg 2012

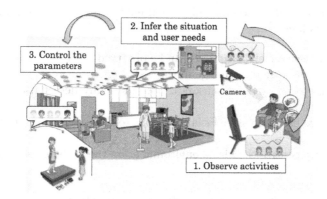

**Fig. 1.** Proposed system configuration

visual environment depends on individual users' feelings and specific situations. In particular, in the architectural research field, numerous conventional methods focus on controls for maintaining a uniform visual environment without noise. As explained in [2], this approach is optimal from the average viewpoint, but it is not optimal for each individual.

In this study, we investigate camera-captured unconscious expressive reactions facial expressions, eye direction, and other facial gestures [3] that reveal an individual's psychological state when there are changes in the visual environment illumination. Figure 1 shows a conceptual diagram of our proposed system. If this system can correctly estimate a user's psychological state on the basis of expressive reactions, it can provide a comfortable visual environment for users.

One of the main goals of affective computing is to automatically recognize users' psychological states [4], and numerous methods exist for determining these states on the basis of users' actions and physiological cues [5]. In particular, useful information about a user's psychological state can be obtained from facial expressions and subordinate actions [3]. Moreover, a significant amount of research in the past two decades has focused on facial expression recognition [6].

Active appearance models [7][8] as well as hidden Markov models [9] are often used for facial expression recognition. However, many methods for recognizing facial expressions use facial images with intentional expressions and do not consider facial images with unconscious expressions of a subject. Facial image databases can be obtained from various sources such as universities and laboratories. However, these databases are inadequate for our purpose because we are investigating unconscious facial expressions caused by changes in illumination.

## 1.1 Problems Addressed

Unconscious facial expressions such as those caused by illumination changes have not been investigated in most facial expression recognition studies. Many problems must be addressed so that unconscious facial expressions can be used as a basis for providing comfortable visual environments. These problems can be classified as follows:

1. What expressive facial reactions can be observed when a person experiences discomfort because of a change in the visual environment?
2. How can we use ambient sensors to automatically detect users' expressive facial reactions?
3. How can we use expressive facial reactions to determine users' psychological states?
4. How can we control the visual environment on the basis of users' psychological states?

In this study, we conduct two experiments and analyze their results to address the first and second problems. There are two types of environmental comforts: the first type reflects the absence of bodily stimulation and the second involves the actual feeling of comfort. In our problem domain, the former occurs when there is no glare or flickering in the lighting and the visual environment is maintained at an appropriate level of illumination. The latter occurs when the visual environment has a lower level of illumination, for example, that provided by antique lights. In our research, we focus on the former requirements because they should be met before any attempt is made to address the latter requirement.

## 2    Extraction of Expressive Facial Reactions

In this section, we address our first problem: What facial reactions can be observed when a person experiences discomfort because of a change in the visual environment? We conducted an experiment with 51 subjects to investigate their observable facial reactions to changes in the visual environment. The purpose of this experiment was to gain an understanding of unconscious reactions to discomfort caused by the visual environment, so that these reactions can be used to trigger illumination control.

### 2.1    Experimental Method

In this experiment, each subject was asked to perform two tasks and was exposed to various changes in illumination. The subjects' reactions were recorded by a camera. The tasks performed in the experiment were (1) silently reading an essay on a laptop computer screen and (2) declaring discomfort resulting from changes in illumination. The subjects declared discomfort caused by a change in illumination by pressing a foot switch (hereafter referred to as "declared"). The time of each depression of the foot switch was logged during the experiment. The subject was instructed to release the foot switch when the subject did not feel discomfort (hereafter referred to as "not declared"). The camera used in the experiment was built into the laptop computer and was concealed from the subject in order to eliminate possible effects caused by the monitoring. Examples of

**Table 1.** Subjects for the first experiment

| age | 20 | 30 | 40 | 50 | total |
|---|---|---|---|---|---|
| male | 19 | 5 | 3 | 4 | 31 |
| female | 14 | 3 | 2 | 1 | 20 |

**Fig. 2.** Experimental room

**Fig. 3.** Configuration of the room

discomfort states were described to the subjects, including "dark illumination," "bright illumination," "blinding illumination," "difficulty to view the monitor," "an unpleasant atmosphere," and "extremely uncomfortable illumination." All subjects were asked to moderate conversation with other subjects during the experiment. We conducted three tests: training, trial 1, and trial 2 of durations 2.5 min, 19 min, and 11 min, respectively. In the following section, we analyze the results of trials 1 and 2.

**Subjects.**

Fifty-one subjects (31 male, 20 female) from the age groups shown in Table 1 participated in this experiment.

**Experimental Setting.**

Figure 2 shows the room used for the experiments, and Fig. 3 shows the configuration of the room. The room has four ceiling panel lights and a spurious window. The light from the spurious window simulates ambient sunlight. The lighting parameters in the experimental room are remotely online controlled by a PC. We use 32 patterns as a configuration of luminance, illuminance and color temperature. We simultaneously use three seats ((1), (2), and (3) in Fig. 3) in front of the window.

## 2.2 Experimental Results and Discussion

We manually extracted unconscious reactions to discomfort from the data collected during the experiments. Figure 4 shows an example of an unconscious reaction, and Fig. 5 shows the percentage of each type of unconscious reaction. There were 62 unconscious reactions, and we extracted expressive facial

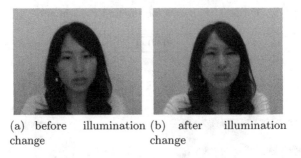

(a) before illumination (b) after illumination
change change

**Fig. 4.** Example of an unconscious reaction

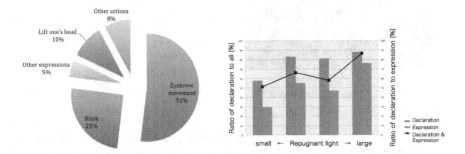

**Fig. 5.** Percentages of unconscious reactions

**Fig. 6.** Percentages of declarations and unconscious reactions

reactions (expressive reactions), eye direction, gestures, and posture. They were conducted by one of us in order to eliminate the possibility of interobserver correlation. In the case of extracting expressive reactions, we used Facial Action Coding System (FACS) devised by Paul Ekman[10], for example, we used the following 4 Action Units (AU) "Eyebrow movement": Inner Brow Raiser (AU: 1), Brow Lowerer (AU: 4), Nose Wrinkler (AU: 9) and Squint (AU: 44) . Figure 5 shows that expressive facial reactions constituted 82% of the total reactions, and there were many illumination changes that involved the eye regions such as "Eyebrow movement" and "Blink." Figure 6 shows the ratios of the number of declarations to the total number of subjects and those of the number of reactions during illumination changes to the total reactions during the experiments. The figure indicates that some kind of reaction to changes in the illumination was observed in more than half of the subjects. In particular, expressive reactions were observed for 86% of the subjects for a significant change in illumination. From these results, it is clear that there are unconscious reactions to discomfort situations that can be generalized for a relatively large percentage of the subjects and that these expressive reactions can be used to trigger illumination control. In the next section, we focus on automatic recognition of expressive reactions, particularly recognition of changes in the region of the eyes.

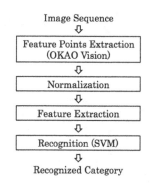

Image Sequence
⇩
Feature Points Extraction
(OKAO Vision)
⇩
Normalization
⇩
Feature Extraction
⇩
Recognition (SVM)
⇩
Recognized Category

**Fig. 7.** Flowchart of the recognition process

**Fig. 8.** Facial featurepoints

**Fig. 9.** Distances used in the feature vector for recognition

## 3    Automatic Recognition of Expressive Reactions

In this section, we address the second problem: How can we use ambient sensors to automatically detect expressive facial reactions? We conducted an experiment involving four subjects to evaluate the adequacy of our manual extraction of unconscious expressive reactions to discomfort for use in automatically detecting discomfort.

### 3.1    Recognition Method

Figure 7 shows a flowchart of the recognition process. Facial feature points for the four subjects were extracted from an input image and then the positions of the facial feature points were normalized and adjusted by affine transformation. A feature vector for discomfort recognition was calculated from the extracted facial feature points and was used as an input vector for a two-class comfort-discomfort support vector machine (SVM). We used the dataset from trial 1 as training data and that from trial 2 as verification data.

**Extraction of Facial Feature Points.** Facial feature points were extracted from each data frame using OKAO Vision (Windows version: OkaoG52 Ver. 47.5, R242) developed by Omron Co., Ltd. A total of 87 facial feature points were extracted, as shown in Fig. 8, with each facial feature point represented by its two-dimensional coordinates in the image.

**Normalization of Facial Feature Points.** It was necessary to normalize the facial feature points in all frames in order to correctly determine the displacement of facial feature points. This is because the positions and orientations of the subjects' faces were not fixed. All facial feature points were normalized by affine transformation calculated with three facial feature points (the blue points in Fig. 8): the two inside corner points of the eyes and the bottom point of the nose.

**Table 2.** Subjects for the second experiment

| subjects | sex | age |
|----------|--------|-----|
| subject A | male | 30 |
| subject B | female | 50 |
| subject C | male | 50 |
| subject D | female | 30 |
| subject E | female | 20 |
| subject F | female | 20 |

**Table 3.** Recognition experiments

| experiment no. | learning data | recognition data |
|----------------|----------------|------------------|
| 1 | except subject A | subject A |
| 2 | except subject B | subject B |
| 3 | except subject C | subject C |
| 4 | except subject D | subject D |
| 5 | except subject E | subject E |
| 6 | except subject F | subject F |

**Calculation of the Feature Vector.** Based on the results in the previous section, we used the following features for automatic expressive reaction recognition:

- the degrees of openness of the left and right eyes,
- the distance between each eyebrow and the corner point of the corresponding eye, and
- the distance between eyebrows.

The arrows in Fig. 9 indicate the facial feature points used to determine the degree of eye openness, the distance between eyes and eyebrows, and the distance between eyebrows.

**Learning Expressive Reactions.** Datasets for subjects who displayed a high frequency of "Eyebrow movement" in the previous experiment were used for the recognition of expressive reactions. Using the data for each subject that were manually classified into frames with and without expressive reactions, an SVM with a polynomial kernel constructed models of subjects expressive reactions. The number of frames in the training data for each subject was approximately 7000.

**Experimental Setting.** We conducted recognition experiments for the expressive reactions of six subjects (A, B, C, D, E, and F) using Leave-one-out cross-validation (LOOCV). The subjects are shown in Table 2.

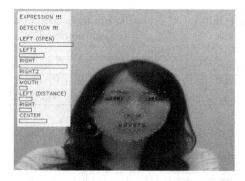

**Fig. 10.** Monitor display during the experiment

**Table 4.** Recognition result 1
(recognition for A)

|  | true value P | true value N |
|---|---|---|
| recognition P | [TP] 78.23% | [FP]  6.81% |
| recognition N | [FN] 21.77% | [TN] 93.19% |

**Table 5.** Recognition result 2
(recognition for B)

|  | true value P | true value N |
|---|---|---|
| recognition P | [TP] 95.80% | [FP]  14.66% |
| recognition N | [FN] 4.20% | [TN] 85.34% |

**Table 6.** Recognition result 3
(recognition for C)

|  | true value P | true value N |
|---|---|---|
| recognition P | [TP] 91.76% | [FP]  99.30% |
| recognition N | [FN] 8.24% | [TN] 0.70% |

**Table 7.** Recognition result 4
(recognition for D)

|  | true value P | true value N |
|---|---|---|
| recognition P | [TP] 67.31% | [FP]  4.29% |
| recognition N | [FN] 32.69% | [TN] 95.71% |

## 3.2  Experimental Results and Discussion

Figure 10 shows the monitor display during the experiment. White circles denote facial feature points fitted onto the subject's facial image, and the bars shown on the left side of the monitor denote each element of the feature vector. If the image was taken at a moment that was "declared" by the subject, "EXPRESSION!!!" is displayed in the upper left corner of the monitor. If the image is recognized as a frame with an expressive reaction, "DETECTION!!!" is displayed.

The experimental results shown in Table 3 are summarized in Tables 4 -9 , which show the percentages of true positive (TP), false positive (FP), true negative (TN), and false negative (FN) recognitions. Table 9 shows a high percentage of FP recognitions. This might be attributable to C's habit of narrowing his eyes during silent reading. Therefore, his facial expressions when he did not feel discomfort might have been perceived as discomfort. As a result, it was difficult to accurately and manually classify the dataset for C into frames with and without expressive reactions. Thus, the averaged percentages calculated for each learning model exclude the results for C; these are shown in Table 10. This table shows that our proposed method was effective except in the special case of C.

**Table 8.** Recognition result 5
(recognition for E)

**Table 9.** Recognition result 6
(recognition for F)

|  | true value P | true value N |
|---|---|---|
| recognition P | [TP] 73.41% | [FP]   15.20% |
| recognition N | [FN] 26.59% | [TN] 84.80% |

|  | true value P | true value N |
|---|---|---|
| recognition P | [TP] 87.69% | [FP]   31.64% |
| recognition N | [FN] 12.31% | [TN] 68.36% |

**Table 10.** Averaged recognition ratios

|  | true value P | true value N |
|---|---|---|
| recognition P | [TP] 80.49% | [FP]   14.52% |
| recognition N | [FN] 19.51% | [TN] 85.48% |

# 4  Conclusion

In this paper, we proposed an autonomous system that controls illumination in a room using ambient sensing to judge user comfort. We conducted two experiments. Expressive reactions to uncomfortable environments were clearly observed in our first experiment, and these can be used as triggers for the system to control illumination. The results of our second experiment show that our recognition method, which used an SVM, based on facial feature points around the eyes revealed a high discomfort recognition rate in five out of six subjects. Furthermore, we explained why one subject was a special case.

In our future work, we will classify subjects according to the type of their expressive reactions and will develop a model for each type of expression. We anticipate that recognizing subjects' expressions through models of each expression type will improve the recognition rate. In addition, taking into account that discomfort is not a binary problem, we will separate them into several classes.

# References

1. Nakashima, H., Aghajan, H., Augusto, J.C.: Handbook of Ambient Intelligence and Smart Environments. Springer (2010)
2. Miki, M., Hiroyasu, T., Imazato, K.: Proposal for an intelligence lighting system and verification of control method effectiveness. In: Proc. IEEE CIS, vol. 1, pp. 520–525 (2004)
3. Kurokawa, T.: Nonverbal Interface. Ohmsha (1994) (in Japanese)
4. Pical, R.W.: Affective Computing. The MIT Press, MA
5. Zeng, Z., Pantic, M., Roisman, G.I., Huang, T.S.: A survey of affect recognition methods: Audio, visual and spontaneous expressions. In: Proceedings of the 9th International Conference on Multimodai Interfaces, pp. 126–133. ACM, NY (2007)
6. Akamatsu, S.: Recent Research on Face Recognition by Computer. The Journal of the Institute of Electronics, Information and Communication Engineers 80(3), 257–266 (1997)
7. Cootes, T.F., Edwards, G.J., Taylor, C.J.: Active appearance models. In: Proc. of the 5th European Conference on Computer Vision, vol. 2, pp. 484–498 (1998)

8. Matthews, I., Baker, S.: Active Appearnce Models Revisited. International Journal of Computer Vision 60(2), 135–164 (2004)
9. Otsuka, T., Ohya, J.: Recognizing abruptly changing facial expressions from time-sequential face images. In: Proceedings of the IEEE Computer Society Conference on Computer Vision and Pattern Recognition, pp. 808–813 (1998)
10. Ekman, P., Friesen, W.: Facial Action Coding System: A Technique for the Measurement of Facial Movement. Consulting Psychologist Press, Palo Alto (1998)
11. Black, M.J., Yacoob, Y.: Recognition facial expressions in image sequences using local parameterized models of image motion. International Journal of Computer Vision 25(1), 23–48 (1997)

# Deformation Measurement
# of a Human Chest Experiencing Global Motion

Stuart Bennett and Joan Lasenby

Signal Processing and Communications Laboratory,
Cambridge University Engineering Department, Cambridge, CB2 1PZ, UK
{sb476,jl221}@cam.ac.uk

**Abstract.** Current state-of-the-art techniques for determination of the
change in volume of human chests, used in lung-function measurement,
calculate the volume bounded by a reconstructed chest surface and its
projection on to an approximately parallel static plane over a series of
time instants. This method works well so long as the subject does not
move globally relative to the reconstructed surface's co-ordinate system.
In practice this means the subject has to be braced, which restricts the
technique's use. We present here a method to compensate for global motion of the subject, allowing accurate measurement while free-standing,
and also while undergoing intentional motion.

**Keywords:** Motion compensation, deformable objects, structured light
surface reconstruction, volume measurement.

## 1   Introduction

Medicinally, it is of great interest to be able to measure respiratory performance,
both as a diagnostic tool and for monitoring purposes. The established solution,
using a common pressure-differential based flow meter (spirometer) has a number
of deficiencies: in use they are too invasive to be used with young and frail
patients, are unsuitable for long term monitoring, and provide blended data
only offering a single measurement for the whole lung system. Further barriers
are present in veterinary use, where animals must typically be intubated prior
to spirometry.

Previous works by de Boer et al. [3] and Bennett [2] have developed a structured light-based system which measures dynamic surface deformation of the
subject's chest over time to provide both volumetric measurement or "plethysmography" (from which flow may be derived) and comparative regional measurement. A structured light system is well-suited to the application, being cheap,
compact and able to provide accurate data in real-time. Importantly, no physical contact with the patient is required in Structured Light Plethysmography
(SLP). The overall volume results are comparable to those gained via spirometry,
as found by Brand et al. [4] and Lau et al. [6].

As described in [3], the existing system calculates a plane (the "work bench")
approximately parallel with the mean pose of the reconstructed chest surface.

F.J. Perales, R.B. Fisher, and T.B. Moeslund (Eds.): AMDO 2012, LNCS 7378, pp. 144–152, 2012.

The projection of the surface onto this plane forms a volume, and the change in this volume over time is found by application of Gauss' theorem. Since the world co-ordinate system is relative to the position of the cameras recording the scene, any extraneous motion made by the subject causes the chest volume measurement to be distorted, and indeed overwhelmed, by the components of motion perpendicular to this work bench.

An alternative method, Optoelectronic Plethysmography (OEP) [1] [5], avoids this problem by placing many markers all over the subject and finding (and subtracting) gross motion using regions of the upper body whose motion is independent of breathing. Compared to regular SLP however this technology has limited clinical use, as the motion capture hardware is expensive, non-portable, and the placement of markers (commonly 89) requires significant patient contact and is impractically time-consuming.

In this paper we present a two stage process to remove global motion components and retrieve the underlying respiratory signal. The next section describes a method to determine the position and pose of the subject relative to the camera co-ordinate system over time, and then compensate for these motion elements. Section 3 describes the adoption of a consistent subject-relative co-ordinate system permitting the tracking and measurement of a consistent volume of the chest. Later sections present some results, directions for future research, and conclusions on the use of this process.

## 2 Motion Compensation

In order to remove the global motion, it must first be accurately measured. Initial experiments attempted to derive these data from the frontal chest surface reconstruction, but the whole surface undergoes significant deformation during breathing, such that an accurate measurement of the torso's motion cannot be easily obtained. The surface of the back however exhibits little deformation during normal breathing. A PhaseSpace IMPULSE [7] active marker motion capture system allows positions to be recorded to sub-millimetre accuracy, and by placing three such markers on the subject's back a plane may be defined whose motion tracks that of the back.

Although this appears a similar approach to the OEP system, we need just 3 markers (rather than 89) as the frontal surface is still observed using inexpensive portable SLP. We also anticipate a system obtaining the back motion without requiring a marker-based motion capture system in a later section.

When tracking the back we make two key assumptions:

- There is no significant deformation of the back during motion.
- The motion of the back describes that of the torso as a whole.

These assumptions together, for the purpose of the application, are equivalent to assuming the torso motion is rigid-body. As will be shown subsequently in the results section this is a legitimate assumption for a variety of motions.

The SLP camera system and the marker-based motion capture system must be co-calibrated, such that a transformation comprising a rotation and translation between the two systems may be calculated. This is achieved by observing three or more active-markers with the camera system, reconstructing their positions in 3D ($\mathbf{Q}$), then using Procrustes methods to determine the relationship with the matched marker positions as recorded by the motion capture system ($\mathbf{P}$). In the subsequent explanation points are represented as row vectors.

First the centroid of each set is translated to the origin, then the camera system set is scaled to the motion capture system set:

$$P'_i = P_i - \bar{P} \tag{1}$$

$$s = \sqrt{\frac{\sum_{i=0}^{2} \sum_{j=1}^{3} P'^{\,2}_{ij}}{\sum_{i=0}^{2} \sum_{j=1}^{3} (Q_i - \bar{Q})_j^{\,2}}} \tag{2}$$

$$Q'_i = (Q_i - \bar{Q}) \times s \tag{3}$$

where $\bar{P}$ and $\bar{Q}$ are the centroids of sets $\mathbf{P}$ and $\mathbf{Q}$ respectively, $s$ is a scale factor, and $i$ and $j$ index the matched points and dimensions. The rotation $R$ between $\mathbf{P}'$ and $\mathbf{Q}'$ is found using the singular value decomposition $\mathbf{P}'^T \mathbf{Q}' = U \Sigma V^T$, so

$$R = UV^T. \tag{4}$$

Controlling a motion capture marker such that it only operates when the SLP system is recording permits post-process synchronization of the two systems, allowing position data ($\mathbf{D}$) of the back-markers of the motion capture system to be known at each corresponding time instant of SLP reconstruction. Applying the co-calibrated transformation, the back-markers may first be transformed into the same co-ordinate system as the SLP surface vertices by $D'_i = ((D_i - \bar{P})R) + \bar{Q}$, before the composite rotation of the back-plane relative to an origin-centred, axis-aligned frame is constructed using orthonormalized vectors describing the back-plane as columns ($R'$). The translation to move the rotated back-plane to the origin is also found as the centroid of this plane:

$$\overline{D''} = \frac{1}{3} \sum_{i=0}^{2} D'_i R'. \tag{5}$$

This rotation and translation, along with the previously found scale factor, are then applied to each of the SLP surface vertices $S_i$

$$S'_i = S_i R' s - \overline{D''}. \tag{6}$$

The resultant surface is therefore approximately axis-aligned (since the back is approximately parallel with the front of the chest) and approximately centred on the origin in the $x$ and $y$ directions but displaced by the subject's depth from the origin in the $z$ direction.

# 3   Consistent Volume Measurement

While it is possible to perform the volume calculations described in [3] at this stage, the result lacks consistency: the vertices of the surface mesh arose from the projected pattern which is static relative to the SLP cameras, and hence will be *sliding* over the subject as they move. *In extremis*, where for example the subject was jumping, a vertex initially projected on the rib-cage would during the jump be projected on the abdomen. Should the projected grid only cover the required area of the chest initially, parts of the required area will cease to be covered during motion. Should the grid cover a larger area other irrelevant body areas would be measured.

The same problem affects even small motions: for a projected vertex that the cameras observe to be on the edge of the chest a small sideways motion will result in a significant depth change for the marker. With the relatively coarse projected grid (say the pattern incident on the subject has squares of side 20mm) this will cause an appreciable change in the volume measured.

This complication is of course avoided in OEP, where the body-mounted markers do not *slide*, but using the following method the difficulty is elegantly overcome regardless:

The solution to the inconsistency of not measuring the same places on the subject's surface from frame to frame is straightforward, since the co-ordinate system is now subject-relative. We form a Delaunay triangulation of the reconstructed 3D surface points and form a smooth cubic surface over this triangulation. A new regular mesh is defined in $x$ and $y$ in subject-relative co-ordinates, and the $z$ co-ordinates at each mesh vertex are found by sampling from the smooth continuous surface at the appropriate $x$ and $y$ co-ordinates, thereby gaining a temporally consistent chest surface. This interpolation is performed afresh for each frame, but the $x$ and $y$ components of the vertices of the resampled grid remain constant. A sketch depicting the relationships of the various grids is given in Fig. 1.

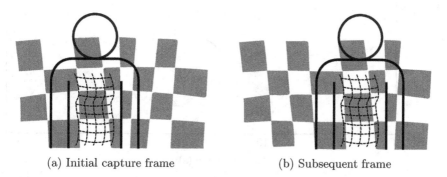

(a) Initial capture frame            (b) Subsequent frame

**Fig. 1.** Between (a) and (b) the subject moves to their left, causing the projected grid (grey quadrilaterals) to slide across their chest. The mesh used in volume calculations (dashed lines) stays anchored to the subject.

Each frame's resampled surface may then be projected back to a newly defined work bench (trivially the plane $z = 0$), and volume calculations proceed as before.

To avoid having discontinuities in the volume measurement, due to parts of the contributing resampled area becoming undefined, only the chest area with (resampled) points available in *all* frames may be used. It is therefore vital that the projected grid initially extends beyond the subject, so that grid points are still observable on the chest surface during motion, otherwise the surface from which to interpolate and resample is undefined.

## 4   Results

Without motion compensation it has previously been found that breathing can be accurately measured for a subject sitting rigidly. In Fig. 2 the first 12 seconds have the seated subject immobile, while motion is introduced subsequently. It may be seen that the non-compensated plot (green dashed line) matches well with the spirometry (red dotted line) initially, and the motion compensated plot (blue solid line) is no worse than that without compensation. In this figure, and all of those following, the spirometry trace's amplitude has been scaled to that of the SLP system, since they are in general related by a subject-dependent factor.

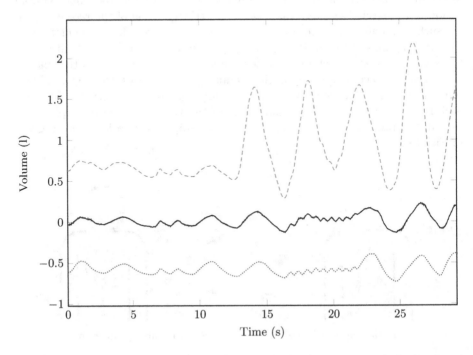

**Fig. 2.** Comparison of measured lung volumes using no compensation (- -), the above process (—), and conventional spirometry (· · ·) on an initially nominally motionless seated subject

When motion is introduced the breathing signal is not obvious from the non-compensated plot, while the volume calculated from the motion compensated surface continues to follow the spirometry plot well (small differences are permissible, owing to spirometry being a proxy for lung volume by measuring air-flow at the mouth, and SLP a proxy by measuring overall chest volume).

To accurately measure the breathing of a standing subject they must be braced against a support to remove unintentional sway, when no motion compensation is employed. In Fig. 3 we see the case of a freestanding person trying to be immobile while breathing regularly. The volume trace gained without motion compensation is shown by the green dashed line, and in the red dotted line we see the simultaneous integrated spirometry data. Significant differences in shape are immediately apparent, both in the shape of individual inhalation and exhalation cycles, and in the relative amplitudes of consecutive cycles. The solid blue line, gained by the process described in the previous sections is very similar to the spirometry.

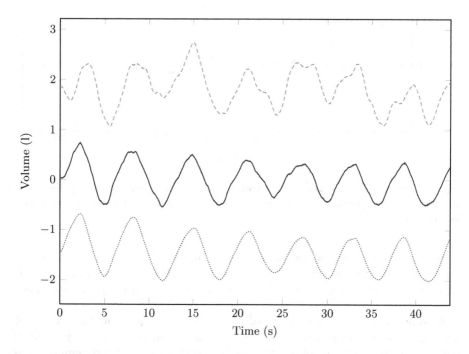

**Fig. 3.** Comparison of measured lung volumes using no compensation (- -), the above process (—), and conventional spirometry (⋯) on a nominally motionless standing subject

Finally, in Fig. 4 we see the process' performance for a standing subject making large rocking motions while breathing irregularly. Clearly without compensation the SLP volume is a very poor measure of lung function, but the plot is included to be indicative of the amplitude and timing of the motion. The motion compensated SLP volume follows the spirometry reasonably well, though differences are inevitable since during intentionally irregular breathing the chest surface need not necessarily follow the airway flow exactly.

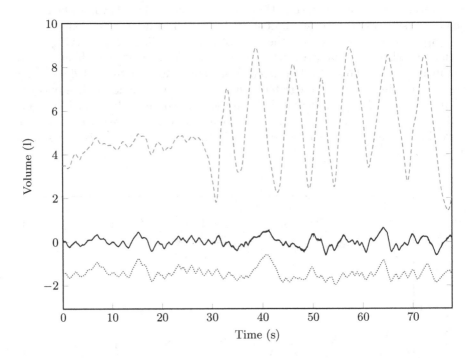

**Fig. 4.** Comparison of measured lung volumes using no compensation (- -), the above process (—), and conventional spirometry (· · ·) on a standing subject adopting a rocking motion

Since the motion compensation method has produced similar volume traces to those gained by spirometry in all three cases described above we may conclude there to be justification for the rigid-body motion assumption previously made in Section 2.

Rigorous quantitative evaluation of the three datasets presented above is challenging for a number of reasons. Some motion due to breathing may occur in parts of the chest surface not included in the reconstruction; this is manifested as "lost" volume and phase discrepancies versus spirometry. Spirometry is known to be inexact, with notable difficulties in calibration of the pressure transducer and avoiding drift when integrating flow to get volume measurements. These effects make acquisition of ground truth data impractical. Nevertheless, we present some indicative measures of the precision of the method, which may be viewed practically as forming an upper bound.

Segmenting the data on each inhalation/exhalation's volumetric zero crossing, we calculate the ratio of the peak volume found using SLP to that found using spirometry. Due to the spirometric scaling stated previously the mean of these ratios is expected to be approximately one. The standard deviation of the ratios is also calculated; a small deviation signifies close similarity between the measurements.

For the data in Fig. 2 we may consider the stationary and moving regimes separately. When the subject is still the ratio mean ($\mu$) is 0.99, with the standard deviation ($\sigma$) being 0.084, for the compensated trace. The non-compensated SLP data for this period has $\mu = 1.08$ and $\sigma = 1.2$. Clearly the compensated data shows less variance against spirometry even without motion. Over the movement period the compensated $\mu$ is 1.04 while $\sigma$ rises to 0.80. Compared against the non-compensated data however ($\mu = 1.75$, $\sigma = 7.0$) a significant improvement is still apparent.

Taking the data shown in Fig. 3 the compensated ratio mean is 0.97 and the standard deviation 0.031, indicating a very close similarity. The non-compensated measurements are much worse, with $\mu = 1.02$ and $\sigma = 0.26$.

Application of these metrics to the data of Fig. 4 gives $\mu = 0.98$, $\sigma = 0.16$ for the compensated method over the static period, compared with $\mu = 0.76$, $\sigma = 1.03$ uncompensated. During the rocking motion these increase to $\mu = 1.05$, $\sigma = 0.43$ and $\mu = 1.10$, $\sigma = 7.0$ respectively. The same pattern of improvement due to the compensation technique may be seen, even though the breathing is rapid and shallow – behaviour prone to reduce the agreement between spirometry and SLP measurements.

## 5   Future

Given the success of compensating for the body motion by measuring back position, and the utility of non-braced lung-function measurement, it is clinically desirable to be able to achieve such results with a system of similar manoeuvrability and cost to the front-only SLP system. The PhaseSpace motion capture system costs an order of magnitude more than the SLP system, and is not easily moved. An obvious avenue of research is to determine the effectiveness of using a second structured light system to record the subject's back, and to use this surface to perform motion compensation.

A simple utilization of the surface would be to robustly reduce it to a moving plane, and proceed as with the PhaseSpace derived plane. A more complicated case would involve using Procrustes methods to estimate interframe spacial transformations of the surface as a whole.

## 6   Conclusions

In this paper we have described a conceptually simple process to negate the dominant effects of rigid-body motion imposed on externally measured change in chest volume. The process has been applied to a variety of plausible real-world scenarios in which structured light-based lung function measurement has not previously been applicable, and our results indicate that measurements comparable to those derived through spirometry may be achieved.

We have determined the validity of employing the motion of the subject's back as a reliable indicator of global torso motion, and found that common motions involve little back deformation. Combining these observations with a subject-relative frame of reference permits consistent volumetric calculation of the subject's chest, even as the body as a whole moves relative to the system measuring its surface.

# References

1. Aliverti, A., Pedotti, A.: Opto-electronic plethysmography. Monaldi Archives for Chest Disease 59(1), 12–16 (2003),
   http://archest.fsm.it/pne/pdf/59/1/pne59-1_06aliverti.pdf
2. Bennett, S.: Chess-board pattern tracking. Tech. Rep. CUED/F-INFENG/TR.672, Signal Processing and Communications Laboratory, CUED (2011),
   http://www-sigproc.eng.cam.ac.uk/~sb476/publications/tracker_writeup.pdf
3. de Boer, W., Lasenby, J., Cameron, J., Wareham, R., Ahmad, S., Roach, C., Hills, W., Iles, R.: SLP: A zero-contact non-invasive method for pulmonary function testing. In: Proceedings of the British Machine Vision Conference, pp. 85:1–85:12. BMVA Press (2010),
   http://www.bmva.org/bmvc/2010/conference/paper85/paper85.pdf
4. Brand, D.H., Lau, E., Usher-Smith, J.A., Wareham, R., Cameron, J., Bridge, P., Hills, W., Roberts, G., Lasenby, J., Iles, R.: Measurement of tidal breathing: a comparison of structured light plethysmography with pneumatachography. Thorax 64, A52 (2009),
   http://thorax.bmj.com/content/64/Suppl_4/A51.full
5. BTS Bioengineering: OEP - optoelectronic plethysmography,
   http://www.optoelectronic-plethysmography.com/
6. Lau, E., Brand, D.H., Usher-Smith, J.A., Wareham, R., Cameron, J., Bridge, P., Hills, W., Roberts, G., Lasenby, J., Iles, R.: Comparison of forced expiratory volumes measured with structured light plethysmography and pneumatach spirometry. Thorax 64, A52 (2009),
   http://thorax.bmj.com/content/64/Suppl_4/A51.full
7. PhaseSpace Inc.: IMPULSE motion capture solution,
   http://www.phasespace.com/impulse_motion_capture.html

# Automatic Estimation of Movement Statistics of People

Thomas Jensen, Henrik Rasmussen, and Thomas B. Moeslund

Visual Analysis of People Lab, Aalborg University, Denmark

**Abstract.** Automatic analysis of how people move about in a particular environment has a number of potential applications. However, no system has so far been able to do detection and tracking robustly. Instead, trajectories are often broken into tracklets. The key idea behind this paper is based around the notion that people need not be detected and tracked perfectly in order to derive useful movement statistics for a particular scene. Tracklets will suffice. To this end we build a tracking framework based on a HoG detector and an appearance-based particle filter. The detector is optimized by learning a scene model allowing for a speedup of the process together with a significantly reduced false positive rate. The developed system is applied in two different scenarios where it is shown that useful statistics can indeed be extracted.

## 1 Introduction

Algorithms that can automatically analyze how people move about have a number of interesting applications. In the research community, the most wellknown is perhaps surveillance applications for the purpose of crime fighting and terror prevention. But a number of other relevant applications also exist where the goal is to determine how people move around in a particular environment. This could be to understand the usage of urban spaces like squares [1] or entire cities [2]. Another emerging application domain where automatic analysis of peoples' whereabout is of great interest is in the retail and commercial industries, for example to understand the attractiveness of a particular shop display. This paper deals with exactly this, namely to construct a system that automatically generates statistics of peoples' whereabouts.

Different approaches can be taken to extract movement information about people. Examples include analysis of license plates (where do people drive) and analysis of signals from smartphones like GPS, Blue-tooth and WiFi. Such approaches have obvious limitations and an interesting alternative is therefore to apply video cameras since these are already installed in many environments. A massive amount of research has been conducted dealing with automatic video analysis of the movement of people in general and in tracking in particular [3]. One of the fundamental problems is that the environment and illumination changes significantly affect the detections. Another problem is that people occlude each other partially or completely. State of the art methods try to handles these situations by online updating appearance models of individuals [4,5] or by including environmental and/or social models of how people behave during partial and total occlusion [6,7]. No system has, however, so far presented a generic tracking solution.

F.J. Perales, R.B. Fisher, and T.B. Moeslund (Eds.): AMDO 2012, LNCS 7378, pp. 153–162, 2012.

The key idea behind this paper is based around the notion that people need not be detected and tracked perfectly in order to derive useful movement statistics for a particular scene. A number of tracklets (short and reliable trajectories) will suffice. To this end we adapt, what we believe to be, the most robust people tracker [8], and improve it by incorporating scene context. The paper is organized as follows. In section 2 we describe our tracking framework. In section 3 we describe how scene context is automatically learned and incorporated. Section 4 deals with the generation of movement statistics and how to visualize such information. The suggested method is evaluated in section 5, before section 6 concludes the paper.

## 2   Tracking

The purpose of this block is to extract trajectories of people passing through the scene. The tracking framework for doing so consists of three parts; a detection part, a data association part and lastly a trajectory updating part. Below each part is described separately.

### 2.1   Detection

We apply the sliding window approach of [9]. The basic idea is to represent a human by edges that are modeled using a number of histograms each containing the local orientation of pixel gradients (HoG). An SVM classifier is then trained to separate image patches containing a person and image patches not containing a person. Each new input image is divided into a number of image patches of different positions and sizes and the gradient information is extracted. Each image patch is now labeled person or non-person using the SVM. Moreover an uncertainty measure is estimated. This approach works well as long as a good contrast between a person and the background is present, but gradually fails as the contrast decreases.

### 2.2   Data Association

The purpose of this part is to associate the detections with the current persons being tracked - each denoted a *tracker*. To this end a matching-score is needed. The scoring function is defined as:

$$S(tr, d) = g(tr, d) \cdot (c_{tr}(d) + \alpha \cdot D(tr, d)) \tag{1}$$

where $tr$ is a tracker, $d$ is a detection, $g(tr, d)$ is a gating function, $c_{tr}(d)$ is an appearance parameter, $\alpha$ is a weight factor, and $D(tr, d)$ is a distance function. The gating function expresses the motion and size similarity of the tracker with respect to a detection. For calculating the appearance parameter, $c_{tr}(d)$ the detection is classified by a classifier that has been learned online for each tracker. The classifier is a strong classifier combined by a number of weak classifiers in an AdaBoost framework. We apply an online boosting based feature selection framework suggested in [10]. The raw output from the classification of a detection is an expression for the similarity in appearance between the detection and the tracker, which the classifier belongs to. This raw output is used in the scoring function. The distance parameter, $D(tr, d)$ is not only calculated from the center of the tracker to the center of the detection. Since the tracker makes use of a particle filter (see below) for estimating the target position, all the particles can be seen as hypotheses for the position of a target at a given time step. All these hypotheses are included in the distance parameter by defining the distance to be the sum of distances between all particles and the detection. All distances are evaluated on a Gaussian distribution.

After having calculated the scoring function for all pairs of detections and trackers, a greedy search associates the detection/tracker pair with the highest score - if it exceeds a threshold. The associated detection and tracker are removed from the search, and the search for the highest score is performed again. This is repeated until all tracker/detections pairs are associated or until no one has a score higher than the threshold. A tracker is initialized, when a non-associated detection overlaps another non-associated detection in a few previous frames. Similarly, when a tracker has no detections in a number of consecutive frames it is deleted.

## 2.3 Updating the Trackers

A particle filter, with a first order linear motion model, is initiated for each tracker. The weight for each particle is updated like this:

$$w_{tr,p} = \underbrace{\beta \cdot \mathcal{I}(tr) \cdot p_{\mathcal{N}}(p - d^*)}_{\text{detection}} + \underbrace{\gamma \cdot d_c(p) \cdot p_o(tr)}_{\text{detector confidence}} + \underbrace{\eta \cdot c_{tr}(p)}_{\text{classifier}} \qquad (2)$$

where $w_{tr,p}$ is the weight for particle $p$ from tracker $tr$ and $d^*$ is the detection associated with $tr$. $\beta$, $\gamma$ and $\eta$ are weight factors. $\mathcal{I}(tr)$ is an indicator function. It returns 1 if the tracker $tr$ has an associated detection, and 0 otherwise. Thus, the detection term is only included in the calculation of the particle weight if the tracker has a detection. In that case, the detection term evaluates the distance between a particle and the associated detection on a zero-mean normal distribution, $p_{\mathcal{N}}(\cdot)$. In the last term $c_{tr}(p)$ is the tracker-specific classifier evaluated for $p$.

The detector confidence term combines the detector confidence density $d_c(p)$ at the position of the particle with an inter-object occlusion reasoning expression, $p_o(tr)$, for $tr$. The detector confidence density corresponds to the raw SVM output from the detector, see section 2.1. In certain cases, background structures can cause the detector confidence density to produce values that are too high, making it unreliable. To increase the reliability of the detector confidence density, inter-object occlusion reasoning is performed by the $p_o(tr)$ function. The rationale behind the inter-object occlusion is that if a tracker has no detection, and no other trackers are close, the detector confidence density should be 0, as it is influenced by background structures otherwise. If a tracker has an associated detection, the detector confidence density is caused by foreground structure. In the case where a tracker has no associated detection, but is close to another tracker that has an association, the detector confidence density is most likely caused by the foreground and not the background. This could happen in a situation, where only one of the trackers was detected due to occlusion. Therefore, $p_o(tr)$ increases the detector confidence density as a tracker gets closer to another tracker. The inter-object reasoning function, $p_o(tr)$ is expressed in Equation 3.

$$p_o(tr) = \begin{cases} 1 & \text{if } \mathcal{I}(tr) = 1 \\ \max_{tr':\mathcal{I}(tr')=1} p_{\mathcal{N}}(tr - tr') & \text{else if } \exists \mathcal{I}(tr') = 1 \\ 0 & \text{otherwise.} \end{cases} \tag{3}$$

where $tr$ is the tracker for which the function is evaluated, $tr'$ is the closest tracker close to $tr$ and $\mathcal{I}(tr)$ is a function that indicates, whether $tr$ has an associated detection.

A weighted mean of the particles for each tracker is used to update the position in each frame. Concatenating these and lowpass filtering them, in theory results in a trajectory for each person passing through the scene. In reality the trajectories are sometimes broken due to missing detections resulting in a number tracklets rather than complete trajectories, see figure 1. For more details and parameter settings see [11].

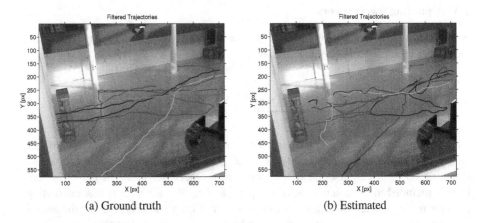

(a) Ground truth                              (b) Estimated

**Fig. 1.** The ground truth and estimated trajectories in a sequence with ten people

## 3    Scene Estimation

Since a camera makes use of perspective projection, the height of a person varies as the distance between the camera and the person changes. Consequently, the human detector (described in Section 2.1) must search for people of different sizes in all areas of the image. The consequence of this is twofold. Firstly, a computational extensive search-space and secondly, a high number of false positives. We address this challenge by introducing an automatic obtained model that expresses the average height of people as a function of image coordinates $(u, v)$. We assume that people are walking on a flat surface and seek a scale factor describing the relationship between the pixel height of the detected person in an image and the pixel height of the persons in the data used for training the human detector. Thus, the scene model must estimate the human scale factor given an image coordinate. The scale factor is defined as:

$$s = \frac{h_p}{ht_p} \tag{4}$$

where $h_p$ is the pixel height of the person and $ht_p$ is the height of the persons in the human detector training data.

## 3.1   Scene Model

The relationship between image coordinates and the human scale factors in two different datasets is analyzed. Image coordinates and heights of persons in the frames are annotated manually in various frames from the datasets. The result of this experiment is shown in Figure 2.

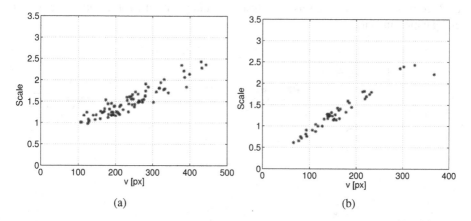

(a)                                    (b)

**Fig. 2.** The results of the experiment showing the relationship between $s$ and $v_b$ performed on two different datasets. The $u$-axes are omitted, and thus the data is projected from 3D to 2D, which causes the points to appear more spread.

The figures show a linear relationship between the image coordinates and the human scale factor. Therefore it is chosen to use a linear scene model as expressed below:

$$s(x, y) = a \cdot x + b \cdot y + c \tag{5}$$

where $a$, $b$ and $c$ are the model parameters that are to be estimated. When detecting people in a shopping mall there will be a variance in the heights of people at the same image coordinates. Thus, this must be incorporated in the scene model. This is done by introducing two margin planes that are achieved by offsetting the estimated plane positively and negatively by a scale margin along the scale axis. This makes the scene model more robust towards the variance of the heights of people. The margin planes are defined as $s(x, y) \pm m$. When the parameters have been estimated, the human detector only needs to search for persons of scales within these two planes, thus reducing the computational complexity and reducing the number of false positives.

## 3.2   Scene Model Estimation

For estimating the parameters of the linear scene model, $s(x, y)$, a linear regression is used. The data used for this consists of high confidence detections from the human detector. The confidence of a detection is measured on the raw output from the SVM classifier. The higher the output, the higher resemblance between the detection and the training data used for the SVM classifier.

To cope with outliers the plane is estimated in two passes. In the first pass, outliers are removed, and in the second, the plane is estimated. This is done to estimate a plane that models the actual human scale more accurately. Outliers are removed by estimating the best fitting plane from all elements in the data. The upper and a lower margin planes are then used to filter out the outliers and the data points inside the margin planes are used to estimate the final scene model.

In Figure 3 the output from the human detector achieved by using an SVM threshold of 2 from two different datasets are illustrated along with the estimated scene model and the margin planes.

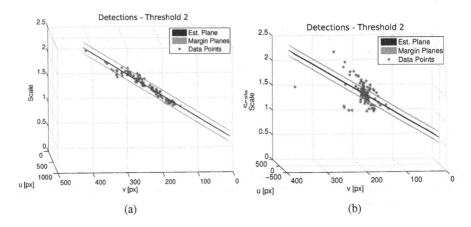

(a)                                              (b)

**Fig. 3.** Output from the human detector with an SVM threshold of 2. Tested on two different datasets.

For determining the margin, $m$ for the upper and lower margin planes used at run-time, an experiment is conducted where the margin is varied from 0.1 to 1. The false positives and recognition rates are counted for each margin. This is illustrated in Figure 4. The figure shows that a scale margin of 0.3 produces a low number of false positives and a high recognition rate for both datasets. Therefore, this value has been chosen for the detector. Armed with these findings, the scene parameters for the human detector can be estimated automatically in new scenarios. In our two test scenarios, see section 5, the processing time and false positive rates were reduced with a factor 1.6 and 12, respectively, after introducing the scene knowledge.

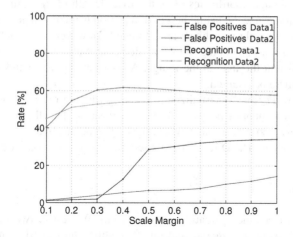

**Fig. 4.** Performance of the human detector in terms of Recognition Rate and False Positives as a result of varying scale margins. Tested on two different datasets.

# 4   Statistics and Visualization

This section describes the visualization part of our algorithm, i.e. it describes which statistics we choose to extract from the trajectories and how we visualize these.

After a preprocessing step, where the noise in the output from the Multi-Human Tracker is reduced, a number of statistics are extracted. For this, we divide the image into a grid, where most of the statistics are generated independently for each bin. The statistics that we have chosen are listed below[1]:

**Person Position:**  The number of persons walking through each bin.
**Dwell Analysis:**  Where persons tend to dwell. That is, areas within the image where people tend to slow down.
**Direction:**  The mean directions of people passing through each bin.
**Number of Persons:**  A curve showing the number of persons in the scene as a function of time.
**Speed:**  The average speed of persons.

As the size of a person varies throughout the image, the raw pixel speed of a person will be inconsistent. To overcome this, we define the speed by:

$$speed \equiv ||P_{s_i} - P_{s_{i-1}}|| \tag{6}$$

where $P_{s_i}, P_{s_{i-1}}$ are scaled scene coordinates of a person in frame $i$ and $i-1$, respectively. The scaled scene coordinates, $P_{s_i}$ and $P_{s_{i-1}}$ are defined by:

$$P_{s_x} \equiv \frac{u}{s} \qquad P_{s_y} \equiv \frac{v}{s} \qquad P_{s_z} \equiv -\frac{f}{s} \tag{7}$$

---

[1] The statistics are chosen in collaborating with a manager of a local shopping mall.

where $(u, v)$ are image coordinates, $f$ is the focal length of the camera and $s$ is the human scale factor. Since the actual height of a person is unknown here, one might use the average person height to achieve an estimated. However, we choose to omit this constant. This way of calculating the speed does not yield an exact speed, but rather one that is consistent throughout the image. A constant framerate and a known focal length of the camera is assumed.

The Number of Persons is visualized as a curve, which provides temporal information about the movement of people. The Person Position, Dwell Analysis and Speed statistics are visualized as heatmaps, where the bins of the heatmaps are color coded by their respective values. The Direction statistics are visualized as vector maps.

## 5   Evaluation

This section describes the evaluation of our system. We test in two scenarios; a lab scenario with an average framerate and image quality. The second scenario is from a real surveillance camera in a shopping mall. Here the resolution and the image quality are significantly lower. We perform qualitative and quantitative tests for both scenarios.

In the qualitative assessment we observed the videos and compared them visually with the estimated statistics and found high similarity. For a more fine grained analysis, we manually annotated a few representative sequences and manually compared them, examples can be seen in figure 5. Moreover we annotated the statistics manually and calculated the errors for our two scenarios, see table 1.

**Table 1.** Quantitative results for two different scenarios. All percentages have been calculated using the Symmetric Mean Absolute Percentage Error [12].

| Statistic | Mall error | Lab error | Requirements |
|---|---|---|---|
| Position. | 0.0725 | 0.0542 | 0.1 |
| Speed. | 5.71 % | 5.40% | 15% |
| Dwell. | 0.0050 | 0.0033 | 0.1 |
| Mean Directions; angle. | 4.54° | 5.23° | 10° |
| Mean Directions; magnitude. | 5.09% | 4.68% | 15% |
| Number of Persons. | 1.1933 | 0.5714 | 1.5 |

## 6   Discussion

Tracking is still an unsolved problem. It has been shown to work in specific scenarios, but no general solution exist. We have in this work applied a modified version of a state-of-the-art tracker, and still, it was only able to track with a precision around 50% (according to the MOTA protocol [8,13]). One of the points of this paper has therefore been to document that even partial tracking can be useful in applications where the overall whereabouts of people are in question. We may not be able to track all people through the entire scene, but we can track most people for a shorter of longer period - tracklets. This allows for estimation of useful statistics as seen in this paper.

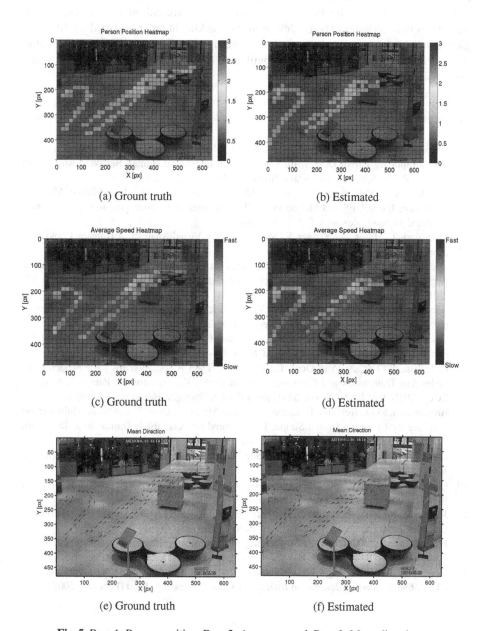

(a) Grount truth

(b) Estimated

(c) Ground truth

(d) Estimated

(e) Ground truth

(f) Estimated

**Fig. 5.** Row 1: Person position. Row 2: Average speed. Row 3: Mean direction.

One obvious question is whether the results in table 1 are useful for example for the retail industry. To this end we have consulted a manager of a local shopping mall to assess the precisions of the statistics for them to be useful. The outcome is listed and the last column in table 1. This indicates that our statistics are indeed useful. Future work within this field includes a) better detection and tracking in order to also allow for more global statistics and b) speed up of all processes in case they are to be implemented in real-world scenarios where one server will have to process video streams from many cameras.

# References

1. Poulsen, E., Andersen, H., Gade, R., Jensen, O., Moeslund, T.: Using Human Motion Intensity as Input for Urban Design. In: Workshop on Interactive Human Behavior Analysis in Open or Public Spaces, Amsterdam, Holland (2011)
2. Christensen, P., Mikkelsen, M.R., Alexander, T., Nielsen, S., Harder, H.: Children, Mobility and Space: Using GPS and Mobile Phone Technologies in Ethnographic Research. Journal of Mixed Methods Research 5, 227–246 (2011)
3. Moeslund, T., Hilton, A., Kruger, V., Sigal, L. (eds.): Visual Analysis of Humans Looking at people. Springer (2011)
4. Kuo, C.H., Huang, C., Nevatia, R.: Multi-target tracking by Online Learned Discriminative Appearance Models. In: Computer Vision and Pattern Recognition, San Francisco, CA, USA (2010)
5. Babenko, B., Yang, M.H., Belongie, S.: Visual tracking with online Multiple Instance Learning. In: Computer Vision and Pattern Recognition (2009)
6. Moore, B., Ali, S., Mehran, R., Shah, M.: Visual Crowd Surveillance through a Hydrodynamics Lens. Communications of the ACM 54, 64–73 (2011)
7. Pellegrini, S., Ess, A., Van Gool, L.: Improving Data Association by Joint Modeling of Pedestrian Trajectories and Groupings. In: Daniilidis, K., Maragos, P., Paragios, N. (eds.) ECCV 2010, Part I. LNCS, vol. 6311, pp. 452–465. Springer, Heidelberg (2010)
8. Breitenstein, M.D., Reichlin, F., Leibe, B., Koller-Meier, E., Gool, L.V.: Online Multi-Person Tracking-by-Detection from a Single, Uncalibrated Camera. IEEE Transactions on Pattern Analysis and Machine Intelligence (in press)
9. Dalal, N., Triggs, B.: Histograms of Oriented Gradients for Human Detection. In: Computer Vision and Pattern Recognition (2005)
10. Grabner, H., Bischof, H.: Online Boosting and Vision. In: Computer Vision and Pattern Recognition, New York, NY, USA (2006)
11. Jensen, T., Rasmussen, H.: Automatic Estimation of Statistics on the Movement of People in Complex Indoor Scenes. Master's thesis. Aalborg University (2011)
12. Flores, B.E.: A Pragmatic View of Accuracy Measurement in Forecasting. Omega 14, 93–98 (1986)
13. Bernardin, K., Stiefelhagen, R.: Evaluating multiple object tracking performance: The CLEAR MOT metrics. Journal on Image and Video Processing, 1–10 (February 2008)

# Granular Material Deposition
# for Simulation and Texturing

Seth Holladay and Parris Egbert

Brigham Young University, Computer Science Department
{seth_holladay,egbert}@byu.edu

**Abstract.** Dry granular materials are commonly needed in visual effects. To simulate a material involving individual grains, every granule must first be settled into place by running a pre-simulation. This pre-simulation can take minutes or hours, and the resulting look can be difficult to control. We introduce a faster, more directable method for depositing particles. We scatter granules in the desired area, guaranteeing that they are interpenetrating, then push them apart by means of penetration resolution such that they are in contact but not overlapping. This results in a natural, aperiodic layout of granules that mimics settled granular materials with little cost to production time. We also introduce particle shaders, a method for generating granular detail at render time.

## 1 Introduction

*Granular materials* are a unique yet ubiquitous type of matter that are a part of our every day lives. These particulate substances cover landscapes from sandy beaches and deserts to dirt roads. They are an integral part of our lives from foods such as wheat to building the roads we drive on. This naturally means that granular materials will show up in the images and films we create.

Granular simulations need to reproduce the particulate detail and complex behavior of granular materials, which is difficult. Granules pack together *aperiodically* (Figure 1), creating a random pattern with small pockets of space that form a heterogeneous density. Computationally simulating every single granule will realistically reproduce this behavior, but is prohibitively expensive [8]. To set up these discrete granular simulations, granules must be settled correctly into their initial positions. This requires a pre-simulation that populates the granules in place, piled in a natural, aperiodic pattern. However, there can be thousands of particles, so running such pre-simulations can take significant time. It can also be difficult to art direct the shape in which they settle.

We present a fast *deposition* method, initializing granule positions for simulations, resulting in a natural aperiodic, overlapping distribution of individual granules. Our method scatters granules within an artist-defined volume such that some overlap is *guaranteed*. We then run a contact resolution step to push them apart. This allows arbitrarily-shaped granules to closely pack together as granular materials do. We also introduce *particle shaders*, a method for populating granular detail onto surfaces at render time to give them the appearance of granular materials. Our process saves production time and is directable.

F.J. Perales, R.B. Fisher, and T.B. Moeslund (Eds.): AMDO 2012, LNCS 7378, pp. 163–172, 2012.
© Springer-Verlag Berlin Heidelberg 2012

## 2    Related Work

The complex behavior of granules has been reproduced computationally. *Discrete element methods* (DEM) were introduced by Cundall [9] as a numerical method for simulating numerous rigid objects, applied to granular materials by Cundall and Strack [8]. Bell, et al. [4] optimized DEM using a soft-sphere method.

DEMs use *rigid body dynamics* (RBD), which compute the physics of complex-shaped rigid objects [13] [15]. They handle three main situations. First, a *collision* pass calculates whether each pair of moving objects collide and how collisions affect their momentum. Second, the *contact* phase finds all pairs of static objects resting against each other and prevents them from sinking into each other. Finally, *penetration resolution*, or similarly *shock propagation* [13], pushes apart any interpenetrating pairs of objects so that they are just touching.

Granular materials have unique properties that DEMs model accurately [12]. For example, granules are too large to be affected by electrostatic forces [6], unlike fluids and fine powders, so friction determines internal granular structure [22]. This friction causes *bridging* [19], small supporting arches of granules throughout the mass (Figure 1a). Due to bridging, granular materials heterogeneous *packing densities*, the ratio of space inhabited by granules to the entire filled volume. This is called a random close packing, "random" because the distribution of the particles is *aperiodic* (Figure 1b), forming no regular patterns in their packing. It has been experimentally verified that the maximum random packing density (volume-space ratio) for spherical granules is ~0.64 [5]. On the other hand, spheres populated on a regular, periodic grid (Figure 1c) have a packing density of 0.74. We want to closely reproduce natural aperiodic and bridging patterns. We will use the term *stable packing* to refer to packed granules that have a distribution similar to but not as dense as random close packing.

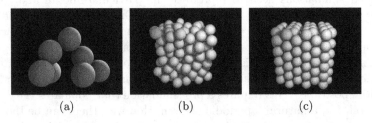

(a)                          (b)                          (c)

**Fig. 1.** a) Friction between granules can form arches, or "bridges". b) An aperiodic distribution of granules, mimicking how granules settle in nature. b) A regular distribution of granules has a synthetic look.

There are various approaches in the literature for setting up particle simulations. One approach is to settle particles into place using DEM [1]. Barabási [3] deposits granules one at a time to get a proper packing. Hsu and Keyser [14] make piling objects more efficient by constraining it to a desired angle of rest. Mehta and Barker [20] present a non-sequential restructuring algorithm that iteratively shifts and relaxes the grains until settled. These iterative methods mimic nature well and handle complex-shaped granules, but they are often time intensive and do not provide fine control of the resulting shape.

Constructive techniques can be faster than simulation, but they only handle simple shapes such as disks [11] [2] or must follow a periodic grid [3]. Poisson distribution [17] places spheres randomly while enforcing a minimum distance between the particles but does not guarantee contact. Constructive methods are difficult to extend to three dimensions and do not handle arbitrary shapes.

Granular substances with irregularly shaped particles present an even more difficult problem. Legakis, et al. [18] take a pre-existing generated texture and line it up with a mesh in 3D space. Miyata [21] generates intricately-fitting tile patterns by subdividing a regular grid then adjusting its vertices to fit. Peytavie, et al. [23] stack rocks using corner cube grids then erode them to fit together. These iterations are too time consuming for large granular materials. Where these methods place the texture then adjust the shapes to fit, we instead want to create the granules then adjust their position to fit.

From a texturing standpoint, granular detail is often excluded from granular surfaces [24]. Fearing [10] refines a displaced surface grid, and Kimmel et al. [16] simulate the appearance of sand from a distance, but these do not have the detail of visibly overlapping particles up close. Surfaces generally lack granular detail unless they are part of a full granular simulation [1].

## 3   Granule Deposition

We present a granule deposition process that iterates quickly and whose shape is easily art-directed. This process scatters interpenetrating granules in a user-defined volume then pushes them apart into a stable packing.

### 3.1   Scattering Granules

In order to correctly deposit the granules, we first need to determine where the granules will be scattered. To do this, an artist builds a closed mesh, $M$, which represents the desired outer boundary of the granules (Figure 2a). If the user wants to leave part of the volume hollow, they also model an interior boundary mesh, $M_{interior}$, that will be subtracted from $M$ (Figure 2a). We define the volume $V$ as $M - M_{interior}$, the volume enclosed by $M$ but excluding $M_{interior}$ (Figure 2b). This provides artistic control that is difficult to achieve with traditional deposition methods.

To generate a stable packing of granules, given $V$, we first generate a density field $D$ that fills $V$ (Figure 2c) and has varying density $\rho_D$. We next generate a random scattering of points, $P$, inside $D$ (Figure 2d). Our scatter density, $\rho_P$, or the number of scattered points per unit volume, is relative to the volume of a single granule, $V_{granule}$, resulting in the following formula:

$$\rho_P = \frac{\rho_D}{V_{granule}} \qquad (1)$$

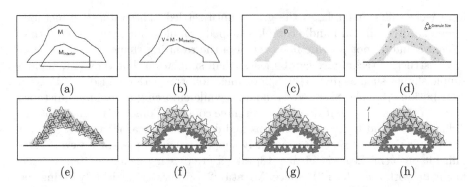

**Fig. 2.** A 2D cutout of our granule deposition process. a) The artist builds a mesh, $M$. Optionally, they can build $M_{interior}$, where b) granules will be excluded from $M$. c) $V$ is filled with density $D$. d) Points in $P$ are scattered, their density based on $D$. e) Granules are placed at each point in $P$. Note the overlapping. f) Granule penetrations are resolved. Static granules (red) constrained to $M_{interior}$. g) Granules outside of $D$ are deleted. h) Gravity settles remaining granules.

where $0 \ll \rho_D \leq 0.64$ equals the desired stable packing density. Our scattering algorithm is a simple "dart throwing" method, randomly placing points in $D$, though a Poisson scattering [17] could get even more accurate results.

Each voxel, $D_{uvw}$, in this density field is assigned its own density, $\rho_{D_{uvw}} \cdot \rho_{P_{xyz}}$ is the local density of points in $P$ at position $(x, y, z)$, based on the closest $\rho_{D_{uvw}}$. Given Equation 1, at any given position $(x, y, z)$, the scatter density is

$$\rho_{P_{xyz}} = \frac{\rho_{D_{uvw}}}{V_{granule}} \qquad (2)$$

The scattered points are then instanced with granules, $G$ (Figure 2e), filling $V$. $\rho_P$ must be high enough that enough granules penetrate each other so that the resolution step works. To make certain that a high enough percentage of granules overlap, we can adjust $\rho_{D_{uvw}}$ by a small amount:

$$\rho_{P_{xyz}} = \frac{\rho_{D_{uvw}} + \epsilon\left(1 - \rho_{D_{uvw}}\right)}{V_{granule}} \qquad (3)$$

where $0 < \epsilon \ll 1$ is the desired percentage of overlap.

If our granules have elongated or flattened shapes, we want our granules to settle anisotropically, or fit together along their flatter sides as in [23]. For such a fit, we orient the initial particles $P$ with the normals of $M$ or $M_{interior}$.

## 3.2   Resolving Penetrations

Next, we run the *penetration resolution* step. This iteratively resolves all penetrations in $G$ by running just the penetration resolve step of a rigid body simulation. For details on resolving rigid body penetrations, see [13].

The penetration resolution iteratively pushes apart all interpenetrating pairs of granules, translating and rotating them to be exactly adjacent. Their velocities are not affected in this step. If an iteration causes another intersection, the next iteration pushes it apart, percolating outward into the empty space outside M until all penetration constraints are resolved. With enough iterations, this results in non-intersecting granules, $G_{resolved}$, that are in contact with their neighbors. All points in $P$ are now at new positions $P_{resolved}$ (Figure 2f).

If $M_{interior}$ is included in the computation of $V$, we scatter granules $G_{static}$ along the surface of $M_{interior}$, make them static by locking them to the surface, and include them in the penetration resolution. In the resolution step, they push the granules in $G$ outward from $M_{interior}$. Then, in the follow-up simulation, $G_{static}$ will support $G_{resolved}$ better than $M_{interior}$ would alone.

The forced overlapping of granules in $G$ is a key contribution of our process, as it gives us the tight packing we need. It also makes for interesting granular positioning as they move and rotate to resolve the penetrations. It gets us very close to an aperiodic, stable packing for any shape of granule within an art-directed volume. It is also faster than running a full DEM simulation since it does not require any collision or contact computations.

Once the penetrations are resolved, we could easily stop here, freezing the granules in place. However, if the follow simulation cannot let the deposited particles fall outside of $V$ or if the granules must be completely settled and not frozen, we continue on with Sections 3.3 and 3.4.

### 3.3   Deleting Out-of-Bound Granules

Next, since the granules were pushed outward, $P_{resolved}$ inhabits more space than $V$. We update $P_{resolved}$ by getting rid of all points in $P_{resolved}$ that lie outside of $D$ (Figure 2g), only keeping the points within $D$.

$$P_{resolved} = P_{resolved} \bigcap D \qquad (4)$$

The percentage of deleted granules will be small, due to Equation 3. If $\rho_{D_{uvw}}$ is close to the close packing density, that percentage will be low.

### 3.4   Settling Granules

Finally, we can optionally run a single rigid body simulation with gravity [15] to settle any loose granules into place (Figure 2h). This step resolves both collisions and contacts, ensuring that the granules are stablized by gravity. We have minimized the number of these simulation steps by getting the majority of granules into place with our penetration resolution step.

## 4   Particle Shaders

We use our particle deposition method to create *particle shaders*, particulate detail applied to a surface at render time. The advantage to making our granule deposition into a render-time shader is that it can be optimized to only generate granules inside the camera's frustum. Granules generated on previous frames can be reused if they remain in frame. We compute the contact resolution for these particles in the CPU, as detailed in Section 3, though the speed benefit of our method could be fully realized if extended to the GPU.

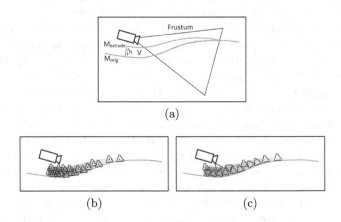

(a)

(b)                              (c)

**Fig. 3.** a) In particle shaders, the extruded surface determines $V$, $h$ based on distance from the camera. b) Granules are scattered in $D$, less dense further from the camera. e) Penetrations are resolved, and granules outside $D$ are deleted.

## 4.1    Scattering Shader Particles

Given a surface mesh, $M_{orig}$, (Figure 3) we extrude $M_{orig}$ outward along the normals by a user-defined height, $h$, to generate a second surface, $M_{extrude}$. $M_{extrude} - M_{orig}$ isolates $V$, the volume sandwiched between $M_{orig}$ and $M_{extrude}$.

We optimize our particle shader at render-time by limiting the area of $M_{extrude}$ (Figure 3a). We generate only granules within the camera frustum's camera-aligned bounding box, extruding only points within that bounding box.

$$h = \begin{cases} h & \text{if inside frustum bounding box} \\ 0 & \text{otherwise} \end{cases} \qquad (5)$$

This limits $M_{extrude}$ to the camera view, thus optimizing $D$.

We also optimize by applying level of detail (LOD). We adjust the extrude height, $h$, (Figure 3a) as well as the density of the $D$ (Figure 3b) based on distance from the camera. The farther away from the camera, the less we extrude:

$$h = h \left( \frac{maxdist - curdist}{maxdist} \right) \qquad (6)$$

where $maxdist$ is the distance from the camera at which $h$ should go to zero.

We generate $D$ then scale the density $\rho_{D_{uvw}}$ based on each voxel's distance from the camera, lower densities being farther away:

$$\rho_{D_{uvw}} = \rho_{D_{uvw}} \left( \frac{maxdist - dist_{uvw}}{maxdist} \right) \tag{7}$$

where $dist_{uvw}$ is the distance of voxel $D_{uvw}$ from the camera, and $maxdist$ is the distance from the camera at which the density goes to zero. We then scatter points in $P$ based on $\rho_D$ then generate $G$ (Figure 3b).

### 4.2   Penetration Resolution

We next run the penetration resolution pass. We include $M_{orig}$ in the penetration resolution of $G$ to avoid surface penetration. After the penetration resolution pass, we can either delete granules outside of $D$, resulting in Figure 3c, or else skip the deletion step, allowing the granules to form a more jagged surface.

## 5   Results

We compare our granular deposition method with a more "traditional" method of simulating objects to fall into place. In our tests, we fill a sandbox with sand. We then run our results with the Bullet Physics solver [7].

In our first case, we built a fairly flat sand surface (Figure 4). In the traditional simulation, we set up a grid of granules and let them fall and settle (Figure 5). 6068 granules took 7 minutes 54 seconds in 20 frames to settle the granules.

Using our method, we started with the surface $M$ in Figure 4a and scattered with density $\rho = 0.52$, causing an overlap of 1.5% of the granules. The penetration resolution step took an average of 43 seconds to resolve 6938 granules (Table 1), resulting in under 0.01% overlap and $\rho_{result} = 0.51$. It pushed 392 granules out of bounds, so we only had to delete 5.6% of the granules in the deletion step. The resolved distribution is aperiodic (Figure 4c), even though granules were initially scattered with the same orientation. Settling the granules took 20 time steps and 3 minutes 19 seconds. Thus, our penetration step was not only a faster method to distribute the granules, it also made the settling step twice as fast.

**Table 1.** Results of two test cases shows the significant speed improvement of penetration resolution over the traditional method of settling granules. Case two simulates in less time since less granules were involved due to $M_{interior}$.

|  | Traditional | Penetration resolution (PR) | Settling after PR |
|---|---|---|---|
| Case 1 | 7 min 54 sec (20 frames) | 43 sec | 3 min 19 sec (10 frames) |
| Case 2 | 3 min 44 sec (50 frames) | 29 sec | 3 min 18 sec (50 frames) |

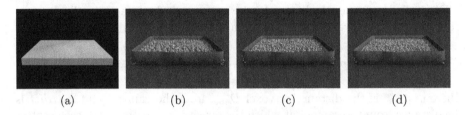

**Fig. 4.** Case 1 with our method. a) Surface mesh $M$. b) Intersecting sand. c) Penetration resolution expands the pile. d) Granules outside of $V$ are deleted.

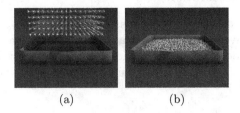

**Fig. 5.** Case 1 with the traditional method

For our next test case, we built a surface $M$ with a more interesting shape and cut out $M_{interior}$ (Figure 6). Note the direct control over the shape of our resulting pile, comparing Figures 6a and 6c. This simulation took 29.5 seconds to resolve the penetrations. It then took 50 frames in the settling stage, running for an additional 3 minutes 18 seconds. This is because $M$ exceeds the angle of rest for our granules, so they avalanche down in the settling stage. Nevertheless, comparing this with the traditional method (Figure 7), our method still retains the desired shape better. The traditional method simulated on top of our mesh $M_{interior}$ and took 3 minutes 44 seconds to simulate in 50 frames.

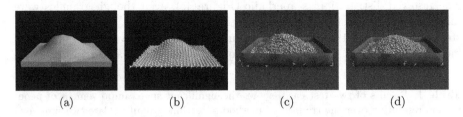

**Fig. 6.** Case 2 with our method. a) $M$ is quickly modeled. b) $M_{interior}$. c) Granules are deposited and penetrations resolved. d) After settling, supported by $M_{interior}$.

Finally, our particle shader (Figure 9) properly extrudes and scatters granules close to the camera. The penetration resolution took 1 minute 3 seconds. This faster result is due to the fact that we only have to resolve penetrations closer to the camera where overlapping occurs (see Figure 3b).

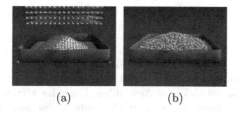

**Fig. 7.** Case 2 traditional method is a) falling onto an interestingly shaped surface, but b) the shape is lost

**Fig. 8.** These almond shapes were aligned with the surface normals before contact resolution before penetration resolution

**Fig. 9.** a) A render showing the results of our particle shader. b) The displaced portion of the surface (white) only falls within the frustum bounding box. c) A top view shows the fall off of the particle density.

## 6  Conclusion

Our method takes a new approach to generating granules quickly to fill an artist-defined area in preparation for simulations by using penetration resolution. It avoids drawn out, complex pre-simulations with easy, intuitive artist setup, and it is easy to simulate. It is flexible enough to use complex-shaped granules in a 3D environment. With increasing computation speeds and the rising practicality of rendering granular detail, the direction we are taking will help make granular detail more accessible and artist friendly.

# References

1. Ammann, C., Bloom, D., Cohen, J., Courte, J., Flores, L., Hasegawa, S., Kalaitzidis, N., Tornberg, T., Treweek, L., Winter, B., Yang, C.: The Birth of Sandman. In: ACM SIGGRAPH 2007 Sketches (2007)
2. Bagi, K.: An Algorithm to Generate Random Dense Arrangements for Discrete Element Simulations of Granular Assemblies. Granular Matter 7, 31–43 (2005)
3. Albert-Lászlá, B., Harry, E.: Fractal Concepts in Surface Growth, pp. 77–86. Cambridge University Press (1995)
4. Bell, N., Yu, Y., Mucha, P.: Particle-based Simulation of Granular Materials. In: ACM SIGGRAPH/Eurographics Symp. on Computer Animation, pp. 28–55 (2005)
5. Berryman, J.: Random Close Packing of Hard Spheres and Disks. Physical Review A 27, 1053–1061 (1983)
6. Bertrand, F., Leclaire, L., Levecque, G.: DEM-based models for the mixing of granular materials. Chemical Engineering Science 60, 2517–2531 (2005)
7. Coumans, E.: Bullet Physics Library (2005), http://bulletphysics.org/wordpress
8. Cundall, P., Strack, O.: A Discrete Numerical Model for Granular Assemblies. Geotechnique 29, 47–65 (1979)
9. Cundall, P.: A Computer Model for Simulating Progressive Large Scale Movements in Blocky Rock Systems. In: Symp. of the Intl. Soc. of Rock Mechanics (1971)
10. Fearing, P.: Computer modelling of fallen snow. Computer Graphics and Interactive Techniques 27, 37–46 (2000)
11. Feng, Y.: Filling Domains with Disks: An Advancing Front Approach. International Journal for Numerical Methods in Engineering 56, 699–713 (2003)
12. Geng, Y., Yu, H., McDowell, G.: Simulation of Granular Material Behaviour Using DEM. Procedia Earth and Planetary Science, 598–605 (2009)
13. Guendelman, E., Bridson, R., Fedkiw, R.: Nonconvex Rigid Bodies with Stacking. In: SIGGRAPH 2003 (2003)
14. Hsu, S., Keyser, J.: Piles of Objects. ACM SIGGRAPH Asia, 155:1–155:6 (2010)
15. Kaufman, D., Edmunds, T., Pai, D.: Fast Frictional Dynamics for Rigid Bodies. ACM Transactions on Graphics 24, 946–956 (2005)
16. Kimmel, B., Baranoski, G.: Simulating the Appearance of Sandy Landscapes. Computers and Graphics 34, 441–448 (2010)
17. Lagae, A., Dutré, P.: Poisson Sphere Distributions. In: Vision, Modeling and Visualization, pp. 373–379 (2006)
18. Legakis, J., Dorsey, J., Gortler, S.: Feature-based Cellular Texturing for Architectural Models. In: SIGGRAPH 2001 (2001)
19. Mehta, A., Luck, J., Berg, J., Barker, G.: Competition and Cooperation: Aspects of Dynamics in Sandpiles. Journal of Physics: Condensed Matter 17 (2005)
20. Mehta, A., Barker, G.: Vibrated Powders: A Microscopic Approach. Phys. Rev. Letters 67, 394–397 (1991)
21. Kazunori, M.: A Method of Generating Stone Wall Patterns. Computer Graphics 24, 387–394 (1990)
22. Panaitescu, A., Kudrolli, A.: Spatial distribution functions of random packed granular spheres obtained by direct particle imaging. Phys. Rev. E 81 (2010)
23. Peytavie, A., Galin, E., Grosjean, J., Merillou, S.: Procedural Generation of Rock Piles using Aperiodic Tiling. Pacific Graphics 28 (2009)
24. Sumner, R., O'brien, J., Hodgins, J.: Animating Sand, Mud and Snow. Computer Graphics Forum 18, 17–26 (1999)

# Fast 3D Structure From Motion with Missing Points from Registration of Partial Reconstructions

Nader Mahmoud[1,2], Stephane A. Nicolau[1], Arabi Keshk[2],
Mostafa A. Ahmad[2], Luc Soler[1], and Jacques Marescaux[1]

[1] IRCAD (Institut de Recherche contre les Cancers de l'Appareil Digestif), France
[2] Department of Computer Science, Faculty of Computers and Information,
Menofia University, Egypt

**Abstract.** Structure From Motion (SFM) technique is usually used for camera motion recovery and 3D shape estimation. But the major problem with SFM is the occlusion of feature points which lead to hallucinate them, and thus increase the computation time. In this paper, we propose a method for a 3D shape reconstruction from a video sequence based on registering multiple partial reconstructions (patches). The proposed method avoids relying on hallucination step, which means a reduction of computation time. A realistic 3D textured shape is provided using a texture mapping pipeline based on the recovered motion of the camera. Experimental results on both synthetic and real images show that the proposed method is more than 200 times (on average) faster than the classical SFM methods which need to hallucinate the occluded points.

**Keywords:** 3D Reconstruction, SFM, Feature Tracking.

## 1 Introduction and Related Work

SFM refers to the problem of recovering the camera motion parameters and 3D shape from a series of frames captured by calibrated or un-calibrated moving cameras. SFM has been one of the widest researched problems in computer vision for many decades, and many techniques have been proposed to address issues embedded in the SFM implementation. In general, SFM techniques fall in two categories : batch/off-line techniques [1],[2] which can be launched after all 2D coordinates data have been gathered from all frames, and Real-Time techniques which create an initial estimation of the shape and try to refine it as new frames are incorporated. The major advantage of the batch techniques is that it can provide an accurate estimation of shape and motion of the camera, whilst the major drawback is that it usually takes long computation time to provide an initial estimation of the shape. Indeed, in case of highly occluded data, it is necessary to estimate all the 2D coordinates of the occluded points to fill the measurement matrix (which contains all the 2D coordinates of the points in all images) before we can apply the SFM algorithm. This process,

F.J. Perales, R.B. Fisher, and T.B. Moeslund (Eds.): AMDO 2012, LNCS 7378, pp. 173–183, 2012.
© Springer-Verlag Berlin Heidelberg 2012

called occlusion handling, usually takes a long time. The next step of the batch techniques is usually a refinement using Bundle Adjustment, which is a process to find the optimal set of 3D shape and camera positions that minimizes reprojection error. It can be computationally expensive or stuck in local minima if the initial estimation is not good enough, and thus inappropriate for on-line/real-time applications. Accurate and quick initialization for Bundle Adjustment step is still an open problem.

There have been several efforts to use SFM with real time applications such as vision sensors mounted on a moving robotic vehicle. In [3], Schweighofer and Pinz formulated the problem of recovering shape and motion as a cost function, which they try to optimize. Using this cost function, the structure and the translation part of the motion can be estimated in a closed form, then the rotation part of the motion is optimized using the recovered structure and translation. But the time complexity will increase as a new frame is incorporated because the rotation of all the previous frames will be optimized as well as the one, which has been added recently. In [4], Schweighofer et. al. tried to tackle the problem of increasing time complexity as frames are incorporated by dividing the frames into two sets : frames which 3D position stay constant "Fc" and frames which 3D position are optimized "Fo". When a new frame is encountered, it will be added to "Fo" set and frames from "Fo" which 3D position are no longer varying after optimization will be removed. Therefore, the optimization process is performed on a small set of frames. In fact, this approach raises a question: what would be the result if some frames in "Fc" set are not well estimated? If some points are not well reconstructed from the frames in "Fc" set, they might propagate errors with the following frames in "Fo" set.

In [5], Mouragnon et. al. proposed a method based on epipolar geometry and triangulation to reconstruct the 3D points. From a video sequence, *key frames* will be chosen to give an initial estimation of the 3D points and local bundle adjustment will be used to refine the initial estimation as a new *key frame* arrive. In fact, to get a better estimation of a 3D point, the baseline between the two *key frames* should be sufficiently large, thus the selection of the *key frames* has a great effect on how close or far we are from the correct estimation. In addition, the use of more than two views whenever possible makes the 3D points estimation more stable than estimation obtained by using just two views. Other approaches [6],[7] use Kalman filters or extended Kalman filters to gradually improve structure and motion estimation using multi-image reconstruction methods. However, such filters are known to provide less accurate results than Bundle Adjustment approach[5].

**Time Complexity vs. Accuracy.** A lot of algorithms try to provide an estimation in less time, which usually reduces the accuracy. It is well known that batch techniques provide much better accuracy than Real-Time techniques, but they require a longer computation time in case of highly occluded data. That is why it is a good choice for off-line application if we care about the accuracy only. In this paper, we propose a method to use the batch technique with a low computation time for applications involving many occluded points during the camera motion. Indeed, our method does not need to hallucinate the occluded points which usually takes very long time.

The remaining of the paper is organized as follows. An overview of the proposed method is presented in Sec. 2. In Sec. 3, the SFM technique and our sub-matrix selection method to reconstruct several patches are described in detail. In Sec. 4, we show how we select texture samples from all available images to provide a proper texture of the surface. Finally, we present in Sec. 5 the experimental results with synthetic and real data and show the great benefit of our approach.

## 2   Method Overview

We follow several steps to get a 3D textured shape (cf. Fig. 1). Like any 3D reconstruction algorithm we begin with **detection and tracking** of feature points: we assume an algorithm provides us 2D coordinates of features followed along frames. During the camera movement, 2D pixel coordinates are recorded for all points that are currently tracked in the video. Points going out of the camera field of view are no longer tracked and new points are detected in regions appearing in the field of view. Therefore, the whole camera field of view always contains tracked features. The input to the **factorization method** is a measurement matrix, containing 2D image positions of feature points over several frames. Typically, this matrix will be highly occluded due to the panoramic camera movement. There are many solutions to handle the problem of features occlusion [1],[8]. As a matter of fact, it is well-known that we do not need all the 2D coordinates of the feature points in all images in order to reconstruct its 3D coordinates. Consequently, we **choose all the filled sub-matrices** from the measurement matrix and apply the factorization algorithm to each sub-matrix to get a partial reconstruction for each point set, which we call patch. The common 3D points between each two consecutive patches can be used to **compute the transformation matrix** (rotation and translation) between these patches.

**Fig. 1.** General overview of our approach to recover textured mesh from camera motion and feature tracking

Using all transformation matrices we put all patches in the first patch coordinate system to get one final shape matrix. We can do the same process for the camera motion matrix of each sub-matrix. Any triangulation algorithm (eg: 2D delaunay and 3D delaunay) can then be used to acquire the wireframe of all 3D points, which have been reconstructed. Sometimes the triangulation algorithms will not provide a consistent result, because there will be many different triangulation possibilities. A consistent 3D triangulation is provided based on the 2D triangulation from the image set. Finally, acquiring a textured surface using one image is not a big issue, but we have more than one image. In this case, we have to choose **the best image for each triangle** based on the information from the SFM method. Once we have determined the best image for each triangle, we can directly map the texture to get a realistic 3D textured surface.

## 3    Sub-matrix Selection for Fast Surface Reconstruction

In this section, we will firstly recall the factorization method of Tomasi and Kanade [1] which allows recovering shape and motion under orthographic projection model. Poleman and Kanade [9] have extended the factorization method to include scaled-orthographic projection as well as para-perspective projection. Christy and Horaud [10] further extend the work of Poleman and Kanade to work with perspective projection in an iterative manner. In all cases, the input of the factorization method is a measurement matrix W, containing 2D coordinates of the feature points in several images. Assuming there are P feature points over F frames, let $(X_{fp}, Y_{fp})$ be the image position of $p^{th}$ feature in frame $f$ , W is a 2F × P matrix, such that:

$$
W = \begin{bmatrix} x_{11} & \cdots & x_{1P} \\ \vdots & & \vdots \\ x_{F1} & \cdots & x_{FP} \\ y_{11} & \cdots & y_{1P} \\ \vdots & & \vdots \\ y_{F1} & \cdots & y_{FP} \end{bmatrix} = \underbrace{\begin{bmatrix} S_1 \\ \vdots \\ S_P \end{bmatrix}}_{S} \underbrace{\begin{bmatrix} M_1 & \cdots & M_{2F} \end{bmatrix}}_{M}
$$

where S is P × 3 matrix and M contains 3 × 2F camera motion matrix.

Using the singular value decomposition (SVD) and the Rank Theorem [1] an estimation $\hat{S}$ and $\hat{M}$ of **S** and **M** can be recovered up to an affine transformation. Using some metric constraints, we can compute the true shape and motion matrices up to a scale factor. In fact, we can not directly apply the factorization method to the measurement matrix of the 2D images points, because of the occlusion. Fig. 2a shows an example of an occluded matrix. Tomasi and Kanade [1] proposed the following method for handling the occlusion of many points. They begin by searching for the largest filled sub-matrix and apply the factorization method to recover the 3D coordinates of these points and the corresponding camera motions, and they estimate all the missing entries iteratively by re-projecting the recovered 3D points. Each time they add either one row or one column to the initial filled sub-matrix and apply the factorization again, and so on.

There are some other works to handle the occlusion without searching for the initial filled sub-matrix [8], but in all cases it is computationally expensive to recover all missing points before applying the factorization method. Since, we do not need all the 2D coordinates of the feature points in all images to estimate their 3D coordinates, we propose to search for all filled sub-matrices in the measurement matrix and apply the factorization method to each sub-matrix to get a set of partial reconstructions. However, in order to perform this step, we need to re-organize the measurement matrix in a shape which makes the search easier and faster.

### 3.1  Matrix Re-organization

Typically, the occluded measurement matrix will consists of a lot of stairs, as shown in Fig. 2a, where each stair represents the appearance of new feature points starting from the current frame. We can consider the coordinates of each point set appearing in the same stair as a sub-matrix and sort each sub-matrix in ascending order (the shortest column first) as shown in Fig. 2b.

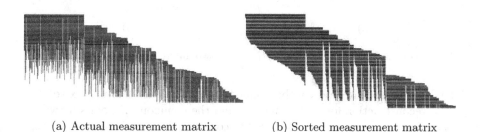

(a) Actual measurement matrix          (b) Sorted measurement matrix

**Fig. 2.** Matrix re-arrangement (shaded entries are known image coordinates)

### 3.2  Selection of Sub-matrices

We consider each point set appearing at the same stair as a patch, which we will try to reconstruct. Fig. 3a shows a zoomed part of the sorted measurement matrix. After we have computed the stair index of each point set (Fig. 3a shows two patches, one is bounded in blue and the other one in red), we can extract from the original measurement matrix the blue sub-matrix which starts from the row index of the stair until the end of the first column (the shortest column), as the first patch. For the second patch (point set bounded in red) we need to include all the points bounded in green (common points between first and second patches) in order to compute the transformation matrix between the two patches. In fact, we need three common points only between each two consecutive patches, but the transformation matrix estimation is more accurate if we include more points in the estimation. In this case, after we have determined the number of rows in the second sub-matrix (based on the column length of the first column in this patch), we include as much common points as possible (cf. Fig. 3a points bounded in green). Thus, we should extract the sub-matrix which starts from the column=60 to column=120. Fig. 3b shows another example of a measurement matrix: in this case the column length of the first point in the current patch (points bounded in red) is long (row=70) and the number of common points is less than 3. In this case, we will reduce the number of rows of the sub-matrix so that we can include at least 3 common points (points bounded in green) thus, the index of the last row of the current sub-matrix will be 60 instead of 70, Fig. 3b.

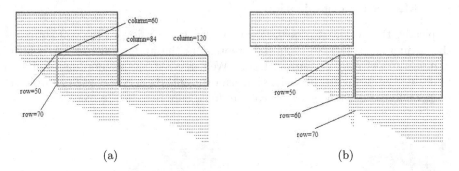

(a)                                                           (b)

**Fig. 3.** Two examples of sub-matrix selection from two different measurement matrices

The factorization method can be applied directly to each sub-matrix to get a partial reconstruction for each point set, and the common 3D points between each two consecutive patches can be used to compute the transformation matrix (translation and rotation) using 3D/3D point registration [11].

## 4    Texture Pipeline

### 4.1    Triangulation

After the reconstruction of the 3D points, there are many possible 3D triangulations depending on the chosen method, each of them providing a different shape. In order to get a consistent triangulation of the 3D points, we can use information from the images. Thus, we recorded the 2D points coordinates of the first frame (frame A) in the first patch (point set bounded in blue in Fig. 3a) and 2D points coordinates of the first frame (frame B) in the second patch (point set bounded in green and red). A 2D/2D registration using the common points (bounded in green) is performed to register frame B in frame A. We iterate this process for each patch and finally register in a common frame all first frames of each patch (in fact, we do a kind of naive mosaicing). 2D Delaunay triangulation algorithm is then used to mesh the 2D points. Since each 2D point in the image corresponds to a 3D point, the mesh relationship of the 3D points correspond to the mesh relationship of the 2D points, as shown in Fig. 4.

**Fig. 4.** Left (a): Green markers have been stuck on a phantom and tracked on a video sequences. Middle (b): 2D Wireframe from 2D Delaunay. Right (c): Resulting 3D wireframe from mesh relationship provided by 2D Delaunay.

## 4.2   Texture Mapping

Once all 3D points are triangulated, the resulting mesh is textured with images taken from the video sequence to create a realistic representation of the shape. We propose to texture each triangle with the most orthogonal image to the considered triangle. The normal vector of each triangle is computed (Fig. 4 (c) normal vectors indicated in green) as well as the normal vector of each image using the recovered camera motion. Once both of the two normal vectors are obtained we can choose the image which has the smallest angle with the normal vector of the considered triangle. Fig. 5 shows the selection of the texture for each triangle from the most orthogonal images to this triangle.

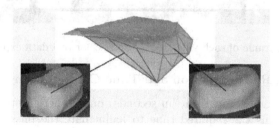

**Fig. 5.** Textures of red (resp. green) triangle are mapped from left (right) image

It is worthy noting that this technique will result in too much textures and thus too much seams. Additional problems would happen due to surface bumping and irregularities, which will be part of our future work.

## 5   Results

The proposed method has been validated with synthetic and real data.

### 5.1   Experiment Set Up

**Synthetic Data.** We have used synthetic data with a known ground truth to test the reconstruction of 3D points using a set of patches. 3D points are randomly generated within a $100 \times 100$ cube and orthographic projections of these points are computed on a set of planes in random direction. After creating the measurement matrix using the 2D coordinates of the projected points, we simulated the occluded measurement matrix by randomly removing some 2D points. To evaluate our method, we report the accuracy and computation time for our method and the standard method proposed in [1], with a number of points and frames varying in the range [10 , 1000].

**Real Data.** Several videos of different shapes have been used. Shi-Tomasi method [12] has been used to extract features from the video and Lucas-Kanade [13] to track them along frames. Fig. 6 displays the first frame of each video sequence. In the first experiment, we used a video of a glass [1280x720 pixels] with some marked points. In such case, we will have many occluded points because of the high curvature of the glass. In the second experiment, we used 267 images from an endoscopic video of a pig colon [1920x1080 pixels]. Finally, we used 391 frames from a facial video [1280x720 pixels]. Tab.2 shows the number of points detected at the beginning, number of points which have been added during the movement, and the total number of frames for each video sequence.

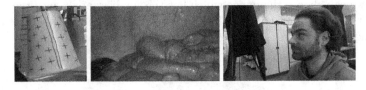

**Fig. 6.** First frame of each video sequence used for real data experiments

## 5.2   Results of Reconstruction and Time Computation

Tab.1 shows the time comparison (in seconds) on synthetic data. The bottom of each cell contains the required time to hallucinate the missing points and reconstruct all 3D points using standard method in [1], and the top of each cell contains the required time by our proposed method. The accuracy of both methods is measured according to the Root Mean Square Error (RMS) between the original generated points and the reconstructed points. Both methods provide accuracy with $10^{-7}$ m.m of error.

As shown from Tab.1, the difference in computation time dramatically increases as the number of points and frames is increased. One can see that our method based on patch registration is on average 200 times faster than the standard method. The gain of our method comes from measurement matrix shape, since the more occluded points it contains, the faster the reconstruction will be in comparison with standard method. More generally, for a fixed number of points, the gain of our method is increases quadratically with the number of frames because we do not need to hallucinate all the missing points in all frames. We also evaluated the influence of noise on the accuracy. We added a Gaussian noise with a standard deviation of 1.0 pixel to the projected 2D points and report no significant accuracy difference between both methods (less than 2%).

**Table 1.** Time comparison (in seconds) between the proposed method and the method in [1] on synthetic data in case of no noise is present

| Points<br>Frames | 100 | 200 | 300 | 400 | 500 |
|---|---|---|---|---|---|
| 100 | 0.035<br>3 | 0.146<br>10 | 0.35<br>17 | 0.69<br>25 | 1.27<br>34 |
| 200 | 0.05<br>13 | 0.21<br>47 | 0.475<br>93 | 0.967<br>141 | 1.64<br>181 |
| 300 | 0.059<br>27 | 0.231<br>102 | 0.558<br>221 | 1.133<br>354 | 1.99<br>529 |
| 400 | 0.077<br>47 | 0.261<br>175 | 0.651<br>390 | 1.292<br>673 | 2.2<br>1017 |
| 500 | 0.084<br>69 | 0.296<br>265 | 0.733<br>600 | 1.44<br>1060 | 2.4<br>1632 |

Tab.2 shows the time comparison (in seconds) for 3D point reconstruction from real video sequence between the proposed method and the method involving hallucination of occluded points [1].

**Table 2.** Time comparison (in seconds) on real data

|  | Initial<br>point Nb. | New points | Total Nb. of<br>frames | Comp. Time<br>of our method | Comp. Time<br>of standard method |
|---|---|---|---|---|---|
| glass | 9 | 44 | 484 | 0.04 | 25 |
| facial | 22 | 20 | 391 | 0.02 | 12 |
| colon | 168 | 173 | 267 | 0.73 | 297 |

Fig. 7 shows the reconstructed 3D textured shapes for three video sequences from different viewpoints.

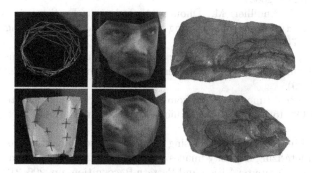

**Fig. 7.** Experimental results. Each column of images illustrate the result of each video sequence from different viewpoints.

Additional experiments on well known real data are still needed to assess the accuracy difference between both methods. However, we are confident that our method can provide at least the same accuracy than standard method since hallucinated points propagate uncertainty in the measurement matrix, whereas these hallucinated points are considered with same confidence than observed points, which is a wrong assumption.

## 6   Conclusion and Future Work

In this paper, we proposed a method to reduce the computation time of SFM with occluded data, based on the registration of multiple partial reconstructions (patches). Experimental results on synthetic and real data show that our method is 200 to 600 times (on average) faster than the method which hallucinates the occluded points (depending on the camera movement). The accuracy of our method has also been evaluated on synthetic data and the results show that both methods seems to operate at the same accuracy level. Moreover, the texture mapping pipeline may be extended to use planar homography on sequence of images, which will be used in texture mapping to reduce the perspective distortion.

## References

1. Tomasi, Kanade, T.: Shape and Motion from Image Streams Under Orthography: A Factorizaltion Method. International Journal of Computer Vision 9(2), 137–154 (1992)
2. Wu, C., Sun, Y., Chang, C.: Three-dimensional modeling from endoscopic video using geometric constraints via feature poisitioning. IEEE Trans. on Biomedical Engineering 54(7) (2007)
3. Schweighofer, G., Pinz, A.: Fast and Globally Convergent Structure and Motion Estimation for General Camera Models. In: Proceedings of British Machine Vision Conference, vol. 1, pp. 147–156 (2006)
4. Schweighofer, G., Segvic, S., Pinz, A.: Online/Realtime Structure and Motion for General Camera Models. In: IEEE Workshop on Applications of Computer Vision, pp. 1–6 (January 2008)
5. Mouragnon, E., Lhuillier, M., Dhome, M., Dekeyser, F., Sayd, P.: Generic and real-time structure from motion using local bundle adjustment. Image and Vision Computing 27(8), 1178–1193 (2009)
6. Matthies, L., Kanade, T., Szeliski, R.: Kalman filter-based algorithms for estimating depth from image sequences. International Journal of Computer Vision 3(3), 209–238 (1989)
7. Mazzon, R.: Real-time structure from motion for monocular and stereo cameras. In: MELECON 15th IEEE Mediterranean Electrotechnical Conference, pp. 498–503 (April 2010)
8. Jacobs, D.: Linear fitting with missing data: applications to structure-from-motion and to characterizing intensity images. In: Proceedings of IEEE Computer Society Conference on Computer Vision and Pattern Recognition, pp. 206–212 (June 1997)
9. Poelman, C.J., Kanade, T.: A paraperspective factorization method for shape and motion recovery. IEEE Transactions on Pattern Analysis and Machine Intelligence 19(3), 206–218 (1997)

10. Christy, S., Horaud, R.: Euclidean shape and motion from multiple perspective views by affine iterations. IEEE Transactions on Pattern Analysis and Machine Intelligence 18(11), 1098–1104 (1996)
11. Arun, K.S., Huang, T.S., Blostein, S.D.: Least-Squares Fitting of Two 3D Point Sets. IEEE Transactions on Pattern Analysis and Machine Intelligence 9(5), 698–700 (1987)
12. Jianbo, S., Tomasi, C.: Good features to track. In: Proceedings of IEEE Computer Society Conference on Computer Vision and Pattern Recognition, pp. 593–600 (June 1994)
13. Lucas, B.D., Kanade, T.: An iterative image registration technique with an application to stereo vision. In: Proceedings of Imaging Understanding Workshop, pp. 121–130 (1981)

# Evaluation of the Reproducibility
# of Non-verbal Facial Animations

Xiangyang Ju[1,2], Balvinder Khambay[1], Emer O'Leary[1],
Thamer Al-Anezi[1], and Ashraf Ayoub[1]

[1] Biotechnology & Craniofacial Sciences Research Group,
Glasgow University Dental Hospital & School, MVLS College,
Univeristy of Glasgow, Glasgow, UK
[2] Medical Device Unit, NHS Greater Glasgow and Clyde, Glasgow, UK
Xiangyang.Ju@glasgow.ac.uk

**Abstract.** Facial functional impairments develop from a variety of causes. In order to quantify the impairments of animations, the reproducibility of facial animations was investigated. In this paper, non-verbal facial animations of maximal smile, check puff and lip purse were captured by a video stereo photogrammetry system; and anatomical facial landmarks were tracked automatically. The same facial animations of the same persons were captured twice in an interval of 15 minutes for comparison. The set of landmarks was spatially-temporally aligned and the magnitude, speed of reaching the animation peaks and the similarity of the dynamic movements between the first and second captures were calculated. The statistical analysis revealed that the maximal smile was more reproducible than the other two expressions.

**Keywords:** facial animation reproducibility, landmark tracking, facial functional impairments.

## 1   Introduction

Facial appearance has a major impact on how we are perceived in society and how others perceive us. However, interaction of individuals with facial functional impairments may be different. Functional impairments may be caused by facial nerve paralysis, cleft lip and palate, facial trauma or facial scarring. Many individuals may seek help to have corrective and reconstructive surgery to correct the underlying deformities and functional impairments. Evaluation and quantification of facial muscle movements is becoming particularly important to aid in the diagnosis, treatment planning and to improve the outcome assessment for the individuals with facial functional impairments. Therefore, a reliable method is required to record the facial morphology and accurately measures the animation.

   Three dimensional imaging techniques have been applied to measure facial shapes and characterize the underlying morphology. The suitability of using 3D photographs supported by three-dimensional software for measuring the facial soft tissue morphology was investigated, and proved accurate when the results were compared with the data

F.J. Perales, R.B. Fisher, and T.B. Moeslund (Eds.): AMDO 2012, LNCS 7378, pp. 184–193, 2012.

obtained by electromagnetic direct digitization [1]. Stereophotogrammetry systems have been used to imaging the facial region and demonstrated an accuracy within 0.5mm [2, 3]. Weinberg et al [4] assessed the precision and accuracy of facial measurements obtained from digital 3D images. The authors concluded that the digital 3D photogrammetry was sufficiently precise and accurate for analysis. Khambay et al [5] assessed the accuracy and reproducibility of a stereophotogrammety system and found that overall errors in landmarks' digitization were within 0.21mm and the reproducibility was within 0.13mm. Wong et al [6] compared the validity and reliability of 3D digital photogrammetry with direct anthropometry. The study confirmed the reproducibility of 3D recording of the face at rest position. Three dimensional laser scanners have been applied to capture facial morphology [7-9]. Laser scanning systems did not measure the facial animation in dynamic motion which is one of the main drawbacks of the method.

Recently, quantification of facial animation has been achieved using 3D motion capture system [10, 11]. A video based motion capture system was used to analyze lip movements. The results showed that the accuracy of the system was within the range of 0.53mm to 0.73mm. Popat et al [12] also conducted a cross-sectional study and succeeded in constructing 3D templates of average lip movement.

Despite the advanced technique to measure facial animation, there is still insufficient information on the dynamics of facial animation. One of the major obstacles of studying facial animations is the number of anatomical landmarks which have to be digitized to study the dynamics of shape change throughout the course of muscle movements and its associated animation. Direct labeling of anatomical landmarks on the face before capture has been reported [13]. However, the method is impractical for daily use and inconvenient for the patients. On the other hand digitizing facial landmarks on 3D digital models is time consuming and not suitable for routine clinical use especially with real time recording in which 60 3D frames are captured per second. It would be almost impossible to digitize all facial landmarks of each one of these frames of a facial animation sequence.

Automatic tracking software has always been an objective for our research team to overcome the technical difficulties of manual digitization of thousands of anatomical landmarks to track facial animation. Automatic tracking software was developed [14] which promises to be a reliable and fast tracking method of anatomical facial landmarks identification.

The reproducibility of verbal and non-verbal facial expressions were investigated [15]. Principal component analysis was used to analyze the dynamics of lip movement of individual facial expressions [16]. The modes of variations (MOV) described the differences in the pattern and dynamics of facial expressions. It was concluded that verbal facial expressions were more reproducible than the nonverbal smile expressions [15].

The main objective of our research group is the diagnosis of the facial functional impairments of our patients. Therefore, the assessments of verbal facial expressions are not adequate for this purpose. Non-verbal facial expressions of maximum smile, check puff and lip purse were selected for our study. It was our target to investigate the reproducibility of individual anatomical facial landmarks of particular expressions instead of analyzing the MOV. The rational of this study was that the movements of individual anatomical landmarks would provide direct information on the underlying muscle activities and related nerve impairments.

In this paper, three non-verbal facial expressions were investigated. The parameters of quantifying facial expression animations were explored and statistically analyzed. The reproducibility of three non-verbal animations was evaluated.

## 2    Video Stereo Photogrammetry System

The system (Figure 1) consisted of two grey scale camera (Model avA 1600-65km/kc. Resolution 1600x1200 pixels, Kodak sensor model KAI-02050. Basler, Germany), one colour camera functioned at 60 frames per second, and a lighting system (Model DIV-401-DIVALITE, KINO FLO Corporation, USA). The 4D capture system was connected to a personal computer (Win 7 professional, Intel core i7 CPU – 3.07 GHz). The system used a combination of passive stereo photogrammetry to recover a sequence of 3D models from a stereo pair of synchronized video streams and dense optical flow tracking to track every pixel from one image frame to frame through the video streams with sub-pixel precision [14]. This allowed a landmark to be placed on the surface of the first 3D model in the sequence, then projected to an image location in the first stereo pair of images. The optical flow tracking information was then used to locate automatically the same point in the second stereo pair of images, which was then projected onto the surface of the second 3D model, and so on for subsequent frames. Study on the validation of the facial landmark tracking software discovered that the automatic landmark tracking provide reasonable landmark tracking accuracy (mean error of 0.55mm, 87% of errors less than 1mm; 95% less than 2mm) which can be used for evaluating the dynamics of facial animations that may take up to 3 seconds.

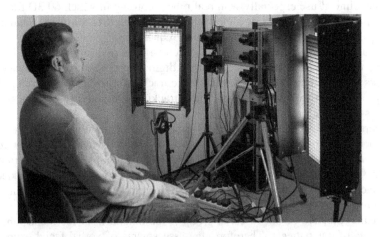

**Fig. 1.** Video Stereo Photogrammetry System

## 3    Recording Facial Animations

After obtaining the appropriate approval from the local ethics committee the study was carried out on 16 females and 16 males of an age ranged from 18-35 years.

Subjects were given verbal and written explanations of the purpose of the project and the details of their involvement. The subjects did not have a history of facial deformity or previous corrective surgery.

Twenty three facial points (Figure 2) were marked on each subject's face [17, 18] by the same operator using a 0.5 mm non-permanent coloured ink (Staelier, Germany) before capturing  facial animations. The pre-labelled ink marking was used to minimise the human errors of landmark digitisation of the 3D digital models. The operator demonstrated *maximal smile, check puff, lip purse* and rest position in front of each participant and trained each participant for 5 minutes before the capturinge started. The participants were asked to keep in rest position following a standardized protocol [19]. They were instructed  to perform maximal smile, check puff and lip purse in the front of the imaging system to capture the facial animations.

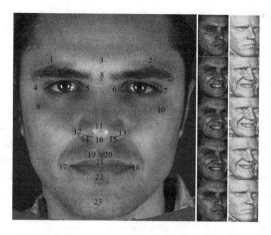

**Fig. 2.** 23 anatomical facial landmarks and five key frames of the maximum smile in textured and shaded models (yellow landmarks can be seen on these models)

For all image sequence captures, the participants were seated on a chair directly in front of the imaging system in an upright and comfortable position.  To standardize image capture, participants were shown photographic cue cards which illustrated each of the expressions. At the beginning of capture sessions, each facial animation was practiced 5 times to ensure that the individual participant understood the instructions. For each image capture, the participants were asked to keep their eyes open and remain steady during the image capture. A distance of 95cm was measured using a measuring tape from the cameras to the particpant's cheek.  A second operator checked the length before each capture.  The lighting system was set to maximum power before the image capture started.

It took 3 seconds to capture each facial animation at a rate of 60 frames per second. Each capture began at the rest position and over 2 seconds the maximal animation was recorded then the face returned  to the rest position.  The images were reviewed immediately after the capture to ensure absence of acquisition errors including image blurring and artefacts. The images were saved for future processing. The participants were invited back after 15 minutes to record the same expressions following the same protocol of the first capture. Each 3D image sequence of each facial animation was imported into the landmark tracking software and the 23 facial pre-labelled landmarks of the first frame were digitized directly on the computer screen. The landmarks of all consecutive frames were automatically tracked guided by the coordinates of the 23 landmarks manually digitized on the first frame of each animation sequence. We validated that the manual landmark digitization error was less than 0.2mm by repeated digitisation of the facial landmarks of randomly selected 10 cases.

## 4 Reproducibility Study of the Facial Animations

After the facial landmarks were automatically tracked, the motion curves which described the dynamics of movements of the landmarks throughout the course of animation were produced. The findings were compared between the first capture and the second capture of each of the three animations. The motion curves were compared between the frame when the expression started to change from the rest face gesture (animation start) and the frame when the expression reached its maximal gesture (animation peak) (figure 3). These two frames were selected by the operator who observed the motion videos. The *magnitude* of individual facial landmark displacement was defined by the distance of the landmark position at the frame of the "animation start" and that at the frame of the "animation peak". *Speed* of the landmark to reach the "animation peak" was calculated by dividing the magnitude by the time $t$ from the start frame to the peak frame.

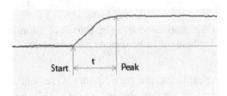

**Fig. 3.** Illustration of motion curve and the start and peak animation frames

*Similarity* of the individual landmark dynamic movements between the first and the second captures of the same animation was calculated after they were spatially and temporally aligned. After the alignment, the normalized geometric distance $d$ between the 3D motion curves was calculated and the similarity between the landmark motion curves of the first and the second captures of the same animations was equal to $1.0/(1.0+d)$. Three steps were taken to align the motion curves: a) Individual head movement elimination; b) Spatial motion alignment; and c) Temporal motion curve alignment.

## 4.1    Head Movement Elimination

Although the participants were asked to stay steady during the capturing, there were slight head movements. The head movements were eliminated by aligning the repeated animations on a stable subset of the facial landmarks which were identified on the first frame of the animation.

## 4.2    Spatial Motion Alignment

Since the individual expressions were captured at different time, the coordinates of landmarks have to be transferred into a universal coordinate sytem for comparison. The coordinates of the first capture was treated as the universal (reference) for alignment and comparisons. The second time captured motion curves were transfer to the 3D coordinates of the first capture. The 3D coordinate transformation was calculated from the corresponding stable landmarks of the two sequences of repeated animations at the frames of the "animation start"; and the 3D coordinate transformation was applied to all the landmarks of all frames of the same animations of the second captures.

## 4.3    Temporal Motion Curve Alignment

Since the expressions can be performed at different speeds that the motion curves have to be temporal aligned. Benedikt et al [16] compared the various techniques such as Frechet distance, correlation coefficients, Dynamic Time Warping (DTW), continuous DTW, weighted DTW and hidden Markov models. DTW showed comparable performance. Therefore, in this study DTW was applied to the two set of cohort motion curves of all landmarks rather than individual motion curves by calculating the DTW distance matrix from sum of distances of all landmarks between the frames of the sequences of facial animations, so that the animations were temporally aligned. This type of DTW was refeered to as eDTW. Following the application of eDTW for temporal alignment of the motion curves of first and second captures, the similarities between motion curves of individual landmarks of the same repeated animations were calculated.

# 5    Results and Discussion

Figure 4 (left) shows the landmark motions in 3D, the blue points represent the motions before the elimination of head movement and the red points after its elimination. The elimination of head movement was based on the landmarks Endocanthion (5, 6) and Pronasale (11). The selection of the landmarks of 5, 6 and 11 was due to the minimal facial soft tissue displacements at these points during the three facial animations captured in the study. After the head movement elimination, the landmarks 5, 6 and 11 should be located in a constant coordinate system for all frames, however, there were residual errors in their individual coordinates, with standard deviation errors of less than 0.5mm. Figure 4 (right) showed the landmarks motions of the first and second captures after the spatial alignment based on the landmarks 5, 6, 11 at their frames of "animation start".

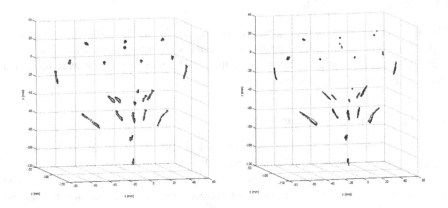

**Fig. 4.** (Left) landmarks motions of one animation (maximum smile) before (blue) and after (red) head movement elimination; and (right) landmarks motions spatial alignment of the first and second captures based on the landmarks 5, 6, 11 at their start frames of the animation

After the mathematical elimination of head movement and spatial alignment, the motion curves describing the dynamics of facial animations were temporally aligned by the eDTW algorithm between the frame of the "animation start" and the frame of the "animation peak". The student $t$-test has been applied to the *magnitudes* and *speeds* of all landmarks except landmarks 12 and 13 which were excluded from analysis because their 3D data was compromised as a result of object occlusion during capture. Figure 5 shows the boxplots of the magnitudes of the landmarks' movements comparing the values of the first and second captures of the three animations. The two sample student $t$-test on individual landmarks' movements resulted in all $p$-values being larger than *0.05*, there were no significant differences in magnitudes of the individual landmarks movement/displacement between the first capture and second capture for the maximal smile animation. The same results were noted for the lip purse animation. For the check puff animation, there were significant differences between the first and second capture regarding the magnitudes of movements of landmarks 1, 3 and 7; there were no significant differences in the rest of landmarks. Figure 6 showed the boxplots of the speeds of the landmarks' movement during animation comparing the values of the first and second captures of the three expressions. The two sample student $t$-test of the differences of individual landmarks' speeds in the repeated animations resulted in all $p$-values were larger than *0.05*, there were no significant differences in speeds of the individual landmarks between the first capture and second capture for the maximal smile animation. The same results were noted in the lip purse animation. For the check puff animation, there were significant differences between the repeated animations in speeds at the landmark 1, 3 and 7; the there were no significant differences in the rest of landmarks.

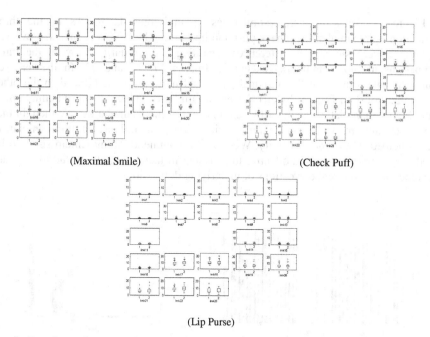

(Maximal Smile)                    (Check Puff)

(Lip Purse)

**Fig. 5.** Boxplots of magnitudes of landmarks' movements in two captures of the three expressions (landmarks 12 and 13 were excluded)

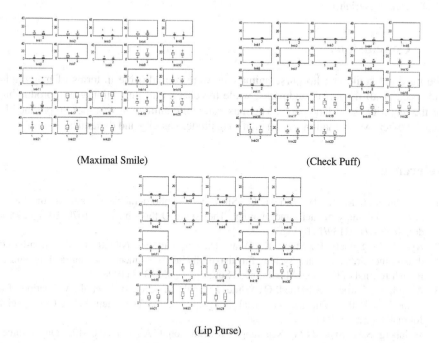

(Maximal Smile)                    (Check Puff)

(Lip Purse)

**Fig. 6.** Boxplots of speeds of landmarks' movements in two captures of the three expressions (landmarks 12 and 13 were excluded)

Figure 7 shows the mean similarities of individual landmarks of the three animations - maximal smile, check puff and lip purse. The ANOVA analysis revealed that there were significant differences regarding the similarity between the three animations at most landmarks except landmarks 17, 18 and 22. In the term of similarity, we found that the maximal smile had more reproducibility than the other two animations. In Figure 7 (left) the mean similarity values of the maximal smile were higher than that of the other two expressions at most landmarks. We thought that the participants might be more familiar with maximum smile as a routine animation which helped in its reproducibility. We would recommend the maximum smile to be used clinically to assess and quantify impairment in facial animations and to measure the outcome of surgical corrections of underlying deformities.

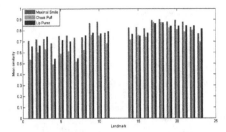 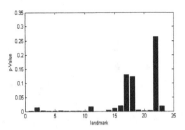

**Fig. 7.** Mean similarities of individual landmarks of the three expressions (left) and $p$-values of ANOVA analysis (right)

## 6     Conclusions

The maximal smile and lip purse animations were reproducible in terms of magnitude and speed at all the facial landmarks; while the check puff animation was reproducible for the majority facial landmarks. The maximal smile animation was more reproducible than the other two animations in terms of magnitude, velocity and dynamics.

## References

1. De Menezes, Rosati, R., Allievi, C., Sfora, C.: A photographic system for the three-dimensional study of facial morphology. The Angle Orthodontist 79, 1070–1077 (2009), doi:10.2319/10.2139/111008-570
2. Ayoud, A., Siebert, P., Moos, K., Wray, D., Urquhart, C., Niblett, T.: A vision-based three-dimensional capture system for maxillofacial assessment and surgical planning. British Journal of Oral and Maxillofacial Surgery 36, 353–357 (1998)
3. Ayoud, A., Garrahy, A., Hood, C., White, J., Bock, M., Siebert, J., et al.: Validation of a vision-based, three-dimensional facial imaging system. The Cleft Palate-Craniofacial Journal 40, 523–540 (2003)
4. Weinberg, S.M., Scott, N.M., Neiswanger, K., Brandon, C.A., Marazita, M.L.: Digital three-dimensional photogrammetry: evaluation of anthropometric precision and accuracy using a Genex 3D camera system. The Cleft Palate-Craniofacial Journal 41, 507–518 (2004)

5. Khambay, B., Nairn, N., Bell, A., Miller, J., Bowman, A., Ayoub, A.: Validation and reproducibility of a high-resolution three-dimensional facial imaging system. British Journal of Oral and Maxillofacial Surgery 46, 27–32 (2008), doi:10.1016/j.bjoms.2007.04.017

6. Wong, J.Y., Oh, A.K., Ohta, E., Hunt, A.T., Rogers, G.F., Mulliken, J.B., et al.: Validity and reliability of craniofacial anthropometric measurement of 3D digital photogrammetric images. The Cleft Palate-Craniofacial Journal 45, 232–239 (2008), doi:10.1597/06-175.1

7. Kau, C.H., Richmond, S., Zhurov, A.I., Knox, J., Chestnutt, I., Hartles, F., et al.: Reliability of measuring facial morphology with a 3-dimensional laser scanning system. American Journal of Orthodontics and Dentofacial Orthopedics 128, 424–430 (2005), doi:10.1016/j.ajodo.2004.06.37

8. Ma, L., Xu, T., Lin, J.: Validation of a three-dimensional facial scanning system based on structured light techniques. Computer Methods and Programs in Biomedicine 94, 290–298 (2009), doi:10.106/j.cmpb.2009.01.010

9. Toma, A., Zhurov, A., Playle, R., Ong, E., Richmond, S.: Reproducibility of facial soft tissue landmarks on 3D laser-scanned facial images. Orthodontics & Craniofacial Research 12, 33–42 (2009)

10. Mishima, K., Yamada, T., Ohura, A., Sugahara, T.: Production of a range image for facial motion analysis: a method for analyzing lip motion. Computerized Medical Imaging and Graphics 30, 53–59 (2006), doi:10.1016/j.compmedimag.2005.11.002

11. Mishima, K., Yamada, T., Matsumura, T., Moritani, N.: Analysis of lip motion using principal component analyses. Journal of Cranio-Maxillofacial Surgery 39, 232–236 (2010), doi:10.1016/j.jcms.2010.04.006

12. Popat, H., Richmond, S., Marshall, D., Rosin, P.L.: Facial Movement in 3 Dimensions: Average Templates of Lip Movement in adults. Otolaryngol Head Neck Surg. 145, 24–29 (2011), doi:10.1177/0194599811401701

13. Trotman, C.: Faces in 4 dimension: Why do we care, and why the fourth dimension. American Jornal of Orthodontics and Dentofacial Orthopedics 140, 895–899 (2011), doi:10.1016/j.jodo.2011.07.014

14. Urquhart, C.W., Green, D.S., Borland, E.D.: 4D Capture using Passive Stereo Photogrammetry. In: CVMP 2006, November 29-30, p. 196 (2006)

15. Popat, H., Henley, E., Richmond, S., Benedikt, L., Marshall, D., Rosin, P.: A Comparison of the Reproducibility of Verbal and Nonverbal Facial Gestures Using Three-dimensional Motion Analysis. Otolaryngology-Head and Neck Surgery 142, 867–872 (2010)

16. Benedikt, L., Kajic, V., Cosker, D., Rosin, P.L., Marshall, D.: Facial Dynamics in Biometric Identification. In: BMVC 2008 (2008), doi:10.5244/C.22.107

17. Farkas, L.G.: Photogrammetry of the face. Anthropometry of the Head and Face, 79–88 (1994)

18. Hajeer, M.Y., Ayoub, A.F., Millett, D., Bock, M., Siebert, J.: Three-dimensional imaging in orthognathic surgery: the clinical application of a new method. The International Journal of Adult Orthodontics and Orthognathic Surgery 17, 318–330 (2002)

19. Zachrisson, B.U.: Esthetic factors involved in anterior tooth display and the smile: vertical dimension. Journal of Clinical Orthodontics 32, 432–445 (1998)

# Continuous Level of Detail for Large Scale Rendering of 3D Animated Polygonal Models

Francisco Ramos, Oscar Ripolles, and Miguel Chover

Institute of New Imaging Technologies
Universitat Jaume I
Av. Vicent Sos Baynat s/n, Castellón, Spain
{Francisco.Ramos,chover}@uji.es, oripolles@ai2.upv.es

**Abstract.** Current simulation applications are mainly focused on the efficient management of scenarios with static objects. However, managing dynamic objects, such as animated characters, is very different and requires more specific processing methods which tend to have a high computational cost. Recent advances in graphics hardware offer more ways to improve the performance of these scenes. In this paper, we introduce a new method for rendering large crowds of animated characters at interactive frame rates. Our method is a fully-GPU hybrid combination of mesh instancing, continuous level of detail and hardware palette skinning. Thus, we take advantage of mesh instancing to render multiple instances of a given mesh belonging to a continuous level of detail model, avoiding the typical popping artifacts existing on previous approaches. We finally obtained a low storage cost, performance improvements when applying level of detail and mesh instancing techniques and, moreover, a minimization of the overhead produced by animating.

**Keywords:** crowd models, GPU, level of detail, animated character.

## 1 Introduction

Nowadays, simulation applications such as video games require more and more realism in the 3D scenes they represent. However, despite the increasing power of graphics hardware, there exists a bandwidth bottleneck between applications and graphics hardware in such a way that real-time rendering becomes an expensive task that limits the size of the geometric objects that can be processed, thus affecting the realism of the scene. These limitations are even worse in those scenes containing dynamic objects, such as animated characters, as the computational cost of the behavioural management of these dynamic objects tends to be a very time-consuming task. This is the reason why rendering articulated characters has usually been limited by using few characters, by selecting low-detailed meshes or by resorting to impostors or poor animation. Thus, at present time, reducing the number of calculations and polygons sent to the graphics hardware to achieve interactive rates in scenes with multiple animated characters is still a challenge.

The capabilities of recent graphics hardware have led to great improvements in rendering, and animated characters can also be favoured when they are rendered

F.J. Perales, R.B. Fisher, and T.B. Moeslund (Eds.): AMDO 2012, LNCS 7378, pp. 194–203, 2012.

directly in the programmable pipeline. With the current architecture of GPUs, it is possible to use GPU-friendly level of detail techniques and perform skinning in the GPU in order to generate animations, which would greatly increase performance. This increase could be greater if instancing was applied.

Regarding multiresolution modeling, it becomes essential in crowded scenarios as a large number of characters will be rendered at different distances from the viewer. In this sense, geometry management becomes fundamental to achieve a balance between visual accuracy and the amount of time required for geometry processing. It is possible to use discrete solutions, which contain a fixed and small set of approximations, or continuous models, which offer a continuous spectrum of approximations. In the literature, most approaches that manage dynamic objects use discrete models, which entail some limitations as these models present some artifacts when switching among the different approximations and also a high storage cost. In contrast, continuous level of detail offers a better granularity avoiding popping effects while offering a better storage cost as information is not duplicated.

From a different perspective, performing skinning in the GPU boosts the performance of the 3D applications. Instead of storing the animation frames in shader constants, hardware palette skinning offers a nice codification of all the animation information on a texture. This technique permits using the same skinning information for many meshes which can be in different frames within the animation.

In general, rendering of a 3D scene composed of polygonal objects involves drawing these objects by calling some *draw* functions. Moreover, if the polygons differ in applied textures or shaders, an overhead is introduced as different API calls are needed. In this context, instancing[1] allows applications to render a mesh multiple times in different positions and different parameters with a single draw call. This feature considerably reduces CPU overhead and enables us to efficiently exploit graphics hardware.

In this paper, we present a new method to enable large scale rendering of animated characters by performing an efficient use of GPU capabilities. Our method provides a specific combination of the three aforementioned techniques: mesh instancing, hardware palette skinning and continuous level of detail for scenes with dynamic objects. Moreover, we also offer low memory usage and we are able to render thousands of dynamic objects at interactive frame rates. Our method is also easy to be implemented in applications that contain a large number of animated characters, as it only requires a vertex shader program and two textures.

## 2   Related Work

In this section we will firstly present the latest works on GPU-based level-of-detail modeling, as this technique is key for our framework. Then, we describe and characterize recent techniques that have been developed to manage large crowded scenarios.

**Table 1.** Characterization of approaches that apply level of detail techniques for rendering large scenes of animated characters

| Work | LOD System | Use Impostors | GPU Shaders | Mesh Instancing |
|------|-----------|---------------|-------------|-----------------|
| [2]  | Discrete  | No   | No   | No  |
| [3]  | Discrete  | Yes  | Yes  | No  |
| [4]  | Discrete  | No   | Yes  | Yes |
| [5]  | Discrete  | No   | No   | No  |
| [6]  | Discrete  | No   | CUDA | No  |

## 2.1 Level of Detail

Level of detail is a technique often used to reduce complexity of animated characters. Most-utilized criterion is the distance from the viewer in a per frame decision, although there exist other criteria[7, 8].

In this state of the art we will focus on the multiresolution frameworks which make use of graphics hardware to perform their calculations. A comprehensive characterization of previous multiresolution models can be found in [7].

Discrete multiresolution modeling was lately re-oriented to offer new methods which upload the different approximations to the GPU and avoid the *popping* artifacts by applying geo-morphing [9, 10], blending [11] or hardware-related techniques[12] by means of *shaders*.

It is possible to find in the literature several approaches which maintain the fidelity to the geometry of the input mesh while performing the LOD calculations in the GPU. Ji et al. [13] encode the geometry in a quadtree based on a LOD atlas texture, with a high memory cost and a complex extraction process. Ripolles et al. proposed a fully-GPU solution which could manage continuous [14] and view-dependent resolutions [15]. More recently, and with the aim of developing a fully-GPU adaptive framework, in [16] the authors proposed a multiresolution model which required 3 rendering passes and, moreover, entailed a very high memory cost.

From a different perspective, it is worth mentioning the development of some solutions which propose uploading to the GPU a coarse mesh and using refining patterns to refine each face [17–19]. These works offer interesting results although they are not capable of retrieving the original mesh geometry.

## 2.2 Animated Characters

Some authors have previously addressed the efficient rendering of these scenes [20–22]. In table 1, we show a comparison of approaches that make use of level of detail techniques for rendering animated characters. This table takes into account several aspects, such as the level of detail system used to manage geometry, the use of impostors mixing geometry, the exploitation of GPU shaders to accelerate rendering and also mesh instancing. In general, works exploiting GPU obtain better results in terms of computational costs that other ones. However, all these solutions resort to discrete multiresolution techniques, which suppose a limitation in visual quality.

# 3   Our Method

As we can see in Table 1, all the frameworks that manage crowds by means of LOD techniques resort to discrete solutions, which are easier to implement although less accurate. In this sense, we have previously commented that continuous models offer a better granularity as the level of detail can be precisely specified, adjusting the number of visualized polygons to the requirements of the application. Moreover, exploiting graphics hardware becomes nowadays almost essential to design 3D solutions that offer competitive frame rates. In this paper, we propose developing a new method to render large scale crowded scenes with animated characters by using a GPU-suitable level of detail model. Many of the solutions presented in the previous section were developed to efficiently manage static models and we must select a fully-GPU multiresolution model which offers mesh instancing, continuous level detail and skinning. Among the possible solutions, we have selected Sliding-Tris [14].

The workflow architecture used by our approach is presented in figure 1. Our method produces a Sliding-Tris model [14] for an input animated character. More precisely, as the models are usually divided into several submeshes, we build a continuous level of detail model in the GPU for each submesh. In this sense, although in the current implementation of our framework we use the same level of detail for the entire model, it would be possible to use different levels of detail for each instance. Finally, due to the fact that we use hardware palette skinning, it is necessary to upload a texture to the GPU that contains all frames of all animations.

## 3.1   Sliding-Tris

As we have previously commented, the work we are presenting is based on the selection of an appropriate level-of-detail solution that meets the requirements. We have decided to base our framework on the work proposed in [14]. This level-of-detail technique has mainly two features:

- It uses a simplification process based on vertex collapses and stores the collapse hierarchy in a texture.
- It includes a level-of-detail update routine which alters the contents of the vertex array instead of the indices array. This update algorithm is capable of modifying the level of detail in a single rendering pass. The geometry to render is defined by means of a sliding-window which restricts from CPU the number of triangles to process and visualize. This way, only the vertices of those triangles that will be visualized will be modified on GPU.

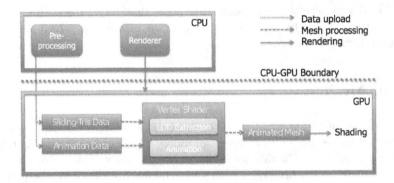

**Fig. 1.** Workflow of our method

Thus, a key aspect of Sliding-Tris is its easy integration, as a texture and a vertex shader are sufficient. Moreover, this vertex shader can be combined with the skinning technique so that all the calculations required for visualizing the mesh can be performed in the same rendering pass. Another important aspect is the fact that most of its data structures are static and can be shared by all the instances.

## 3.2 Pre-processing Step

The first part of pre-processing entails building a continuous level of detail model for each submesh that composes the animated character. This process makes use of Sliding-Tris to build the underlying model. This task is performed once for all as the resulting data are stored in a plain text file.

An application that uses our framework must prepare, before rendering the first frame, the necessary data structures in GPU. In our case these structures consist only of two textures per submesh: one to store the Sliding-Tris information and one to store the animation data. We must stress that these static data can be shared among all the instances and that these textures must only be uploaded once for each execution of the application.

Finally, in this pre-processing step we must also create the structure to manage the instances. In other words, each character contains an instance of the pieces or submeshes it is composed of.

## 3.3 Rendering

At runtime, as shown in algorithm 1, we iterate over the instances of each submesh in each character. Thus, for each instance, we determine its level of detail, and render the appropriate approximation. The decision about what level of detail to use is taken per frame on a per-instance basis. In order to adjust the level of detail, we used the distance to the camera, although other criteria could be applied. It is important to underline that we share the same level of detail for the whole character. However, our method is prepared to accept different levels of detail for each instance, and therefore to the different parts of the character providing a possible view-dependent framework.

Once instanced data are sent to the graphics pipeline, *vertex shader* units perform some fundamental tasks. First, the level of detail extraction process is performed to obtain the suitable geometry. Once completed, texture containing animation data is processed and the corresponding information about bone matrices for the current frame recovered. Thus, we finally send the resulting skinned and approximated mesh through the next stages in the pipeline. It is worth reminding that both tasks are performed in the same *vertex shader* so that the whole framework can work in one single pass.

---

**Algorithm 1.** CPU-side rendering loop

---

```
for i = 1 to numCharacters do
  SubMeshes=AnimatedCharacter[i].SubMeshes
  for j = 1 to SubMeshes.numInstances do
    SubMeshes[j].Instance.determineLOD()
    SubMeshes[j].Instance.renderInstanced()
  end for
end for
```

---

**Fig. 2.** Rendering of a large crowded scenes with 9,000 animated characters at around 30 FPS using an underlying continuous level of detail method

# 4    Results

In this section we present a set of measures taken with our method. On the one hand, we describe the results obtained from an analysis of the spatial cost. On the other hand, we also show results about the overall performance. All of our tests were performed using a Mac Pro 2.26 GHz with 8 GB of RAM and an NVidia Geforce GT 120 video card with 512 MB of video memory at a view port of 1024x768. Implementation was performed in HLSL as shader programming language; Direct3D was used as supporting graphics library.

## 4.1    Memory Cost

The memory cost is a key feature of an adequate level-of-detail solution. Table 2 compares the memory cost of Sliding-Tris [14] with two solutions: a discrete framework which uses 5 levels of detail [5] and a continuous approximation [16]. The original cost of the mesh in triangles is also presented. It can be seen how Sliding-Tris offers the best memory cost, reducing to 60% the memory needs if compared with the other fully-GPU solution.

**Table 2.** Memory cost study (in bytes)

| LOD solution | Memory cost |
| --- | --- |
| Original model (in triangles) | 60v |
| Ripolles et al. 2009 [14] | 80v |
| Rodriguez et al. 2010 [5] | 105v |
| Hu et al. 2010 [16] | 125v |

## 4.2    Performance

In order to analyse performance of our method we created a scene with 9,000 animated characters (see Figure 2).

In Figure 3a, we can observe the existing difference, in terms of frames per second, when comparing the resulting overhead produced by animating a large number of characters. Normally, animating characters is usually a heavy computational cost, but by performing this task at a GPU level this cost remains almost unaffected. Our results show improvements of around 3% of the total time required to compute animation.

Using level of detail is also an essential technique to take into consideration in our method. We tested our method by comparing the triangle throughput when enabling and disabling the underlying continuous level of detail model, while maintaining visual quality of the scene. As shown in figure 3b, geometry sent to through the graphics pipeline noticeably varies. Although the obtained visual quality is sufficient, we could improve the quality of the approximations by using

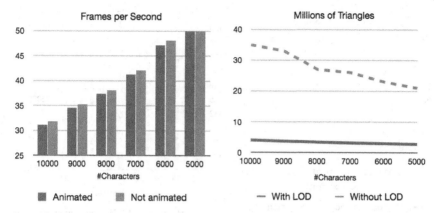

(a) Comparison of overhead produced by animating the characters by applying hardware palette skinning.

(b) Millions of triangles per number of characters in a scene by enabling or disabling the continuous level-of-detail system.

**Fig. 3.** Analysis of Performance with level of detail

a more accurate level of detail, although performance would be affected. Thus, depending on the final application, adjustments are necessaries for the criterion applied to select the different levels of detail.

Instancing becomes very important when considered on top of the level of detail model. Figure 4a shows great improvements in frame rate when instancing is active. If we focus on a scene with 10,000 animated characters with continuous level of detail, it renders around 30 frames per second when instancing, and around 7 frames per second when not using instantiation. This difference is enough for an application to be interactive or not. It is important to underline that using instantiation also offers improvements on the CPU side, that is, we free the CPU to employ processing time for other operations such as physics or artificial intelligence. Thus, the importance of our method is proportional to the CPU load of the final application where it is implemented. Moreover, continuous level of detail becomes fundamental in scenes with many animated characters as discrete solutions can produce visual disturbances while a continuous multiresolution system provides enough granularity to offer a balance between performance and perceived visual quality.

Finally, Figure 4b shows a draw calls comparison when using instancing in our method. This figure needs two Y-axis as the difference in draw calls is very noticeable. In general, each draw call removed allows a reduction in CPU overhead, and also a possible increase in performance. We obtained 123 draw calls to render around 10,000 characters. In contrast, if instancing is not active, 46,100 draw calls are necessary. Thus, there exists a significant difference in final frame rate as Figure 4a showed.

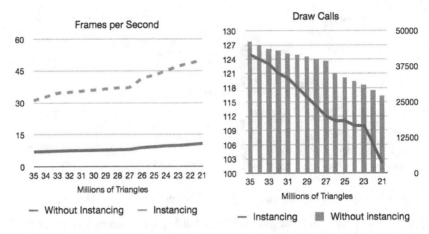

(a) Frames per second per millions of tri-  (b) Draw calls produced in our method
angles by using instancing and not using  by using instancing and no instancing.
it. Animation and level of detail are ac-  Animation and level of detail are active
tive in this test.                          in this test.

**Fig. 4.** Analysis of Performance with instancing

## 5    Conclusions and Future Work

We have presented a method for rendering large crowded scenes with animated
characters at interactive frame rates. We successfully combined hardware palette
skinning, mesh instancing and continuous level of detail. It is important to mention that our framework offers continuous approximations, while all the previous
works use discrete solutions which are less accurate. Our results show low storage
cost, a minimization of the overhead produced by animations and also competitive rendering times.

Some lines of future research might be supporting view-dependent capabilities
across the different submeshes that compose the character and introducing some
variations in submeshes to obtain more homogeneousness in the scene.

**Acknowledgements.** This work was supported by the Spanish Ministry of
Science and Technology (Project TIN2010-21089-C03-03), Bancaixa (Project
P1.1B2010-08) and Generalitat Valenciana (Project PROMETEO/2010/028).

## References

1. Dudash, B.: Mesh instancing. Technical Report 00000-001-v00, NVIDIA (2004)
2. Pratt, D.R., Pratt, S.M., Barham, P., Barker, R.E., Waldrop, M.S., Ehlert, J.F.,
   Chrislip, C.A.: Humans in large-scale networked virtual environments. Presence 6(5),
   547–564 (1997)

3. Dobbyn, S., Hamill, J., OConor, K., OSullivan, C.: Geopostors: a real-time geometry impostor crowd rendering system. In: Proc. of Interactive 3D Graphics and Games, pp. 95–102 (2005)
4. Dudash, B.: Animated crowd rendering. GPU Gems 3, 39–52 (2004)
5. Rodriguez, R., Cerezo, E., Baldassarri, S., Seron, F.J.: New approaches to culling and lod methods for scenes with multiple virtual actors. Computers & Graphics 34(6), 729–741 (2010)
6. Feng, W.-W., Kim, B.-U., Yu, Y., Peng, L., Hart, J.: Feature-preserving triangular geometry images for level-of-detail representation of static and skinned meshes. ACM Trans. Graph. 29, 11:1–11:13 (2010)
7. Luebke, D.: Level of detail for 3D graphics, vol. 1. Elsevier Science Inc. (2002)
8. Ahn, J., Oh, S., Wohn, K.: Optimized motion simplification for crowd animation. Comput. Animat. Virtual Worlds 17, 155–165 (2006)
9. Sander, P.V., Mitchell, J.L.: Progressive buffers: View-dependent geometry and texture for lod rendering. In: Symposium on Geometry Processing, pp. 129–138 (2005)
10. Borgeat, L., Godin, G., Blais, F., Massicotte, P., Lahanier, C.: Gold: interactive display of huge colored and textured models. Trans. Graph. 24(3), 869–877 (2005)
11. Southern, R., Gain, J.E.: Creation and control of real-time continuous level of detail on programmable graphics hardware. Comput. Graph. Forum 22(1), 35–48 (2003)
12. Giegl, M., Wimmer, M.: Unpopping: Solving the image-space blend problem for smooth discrete lod transitions. Computer Graphics Forum 26(1), 46–49 (2007)
13. Ji, J., Wu, E., Li, S., Liu, X.: Dynamic lod on GPU. In: Proceedings of the Computer Graphics International, pp. 108–114 (2005)
14. Ripolles, O., Ramos, F., Chover, M.: Sliding-tris: A sliding window level-of-detail scheme. In: CGGM 2008 (2008)
15. Ripolles, O., Gumbau, J., Chover, M., Ramos, F., Puig-Centelles, A.: View-dependent multiresolution modeling on the GPU. In: WSCG (2009)
16. Hu, L., Sander, P.V., Hoppe, H.: Parallel view-dependent level-of-detail control. IEEE Transactions on Visualization and Computer Graphics 16, 718–728 (2010)
17. Lorenz, H., Döllner, J.: Dynamic mesh refinement on GPU using geometry shaders. In: WSCG (February 2008)
18. Schwarz, M., Stamminger, M.: Fast GPU-based adaptive tessellation with CUDA. Computer Graphics Forum 28(2), 365–374 (2009)
19. Dyken, C., Reimers, M., Seland, J.: Real-time GPU silhouette refinement using adaptively blended bézier patches. Computer Graphics Forum 27(1), 1–12 (2008)
20. Savoye, Y., Meyer, A.: Multi-layer level of detail for character animation (2008)
21. Pilgrim, S., Steed, A., Aguado, A.: Progressive skinning for character animation. Comput. Animat. Virtual Worlds 18(4-5), 473–481 (2007)
22. Pettre, J., de Heras Ciechomski, P., Maim, J., Yersin, B., Laumond, J.-P., Thalmann, D.: Real-time navigating crowds: scalable simulation and rendering. Computer Animation and Virtual Worlds 17(3-4), 445–455 (2006)

# A New Image Dataset on Human Interactions

Wenjuan Gong[1], Jordi Gonzàlez[1],
João Manuel R.S. Tavares[2], and F. Xavier Roca[1]

[1] Dep. Computer Science & Computer Vision Centre
Edifici O, Universitat Autònoma de Barcelona, 08193, Bellaterra, Spain
[2] Instituto de Engenharia Mecânica e Gestão Industrial,
Departamento de Engenharia Mecânica, Faculdade de Engenharia,
Universidade do Porto, Rua Dr. Roberto Frias, S/N - 4200-465 Porto, Portugal

**Abstract.** This article describes a new collection of still image dataset which are dedicated to interactions between people. Human action recognition from still images have been a hot topic recently, but most of them are actions performed by a single person, like running, walking, riding bikes, phoning and so on and there is no interactions between people in one image. The dataset collected in this paper are concentrating on human interaction between two people aiming to explore this new topic in the research area of action recognition from still images.

**Keywords:** Human action recognition, human interaction, dataset.

## 1 Introduction

Human action recognition and tracking from video sequences has been widely studied [4,5] while there are relatively fewer research on action recognition from still images. The fact that human motion variations along time can provide useful information for recognizing human actions results the difficulties in action recognition from still images. Also, other difficulties from image processing like cluttered background, illumination changes and occlusion makes this a harder problem.

**Fig. 1.** Example images from [1]. From left to right, actions are running, walking, kicking, crouching, throwing, and catching.

F.J. Perales, R.B. Fisher, and T.B. Moeslund (Eds.): AMDO 2012, LNCS 7378, pp. 204–209, 2012.
© Springer-Verlag Berlin Heidelberg 2012

Although this is a hard problem, the need to automatically understand huge amount images from Internet makes human action recognition from still images an interesting topic that attract attention of more and more researchers. For example, authors in [1] collect a dataset of 467 images on action recognition from still images which include running, walking, catching, throwing, crouching and kicking. Samples from this dataset is shown in figure 1.

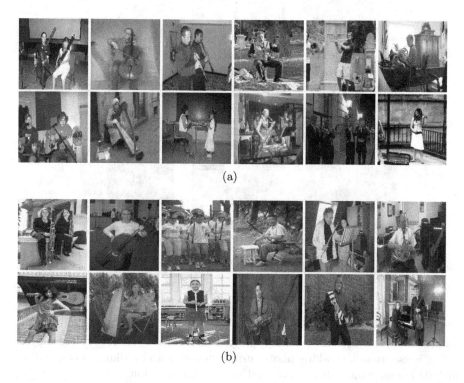

(a)

(b)

**Fig. 2.** Example images from people-playing-musical-instrument dataset [2], including positive 2(a) and negative examples 2(b). Operated instruments include bassoon, cello, clarinet, erhu, flute, French horn, guitar, harp, recorder, saxophone, trumpet, and violin.

Some dataset of still images even include interactions between human and operated objects. For example, authors in [2] collect a dataset of people playing instruments. Operated instruments include bassoon, cello, clarinet, erhu, flute, French horn, guitar, harp, recorder, saxophone, trumpet, and violin. Each class has 200 images. Example images are shown in figure 2.

Dataset from [3] is dedicated to people playing sports, shown in figure. The dataset are composed of 180 training images and 120 test images including six actions: cricket defensive shot, cricket bowling, croquet shot, tennis forehand, tennis serve, and volleyball smash. Example images are shown in figure 3.

**Fig. 3.** Example images from [3]

Pascal challenge also includes a tester for action recognition from 2010[1]. The dataset include 9 actions: phoning, playing instrument, reading, riding bicycle, riding horse, running, taking photo, using computer and walking. These actions include human-object interaction and single human action.

Although there are several dataset on action recognition dedicated to human interactions, they are only concentrating on human object interactions, and as far as we know, there are not yet published dataset on action recognition from still images including human-human interaction. This paper is going to explain the newly collected dataset which aim to open this topic.

The main contributions of this work are:

- Collection of a new dataset for action recognition from still images dedicating human-human interaction
- Discussion of possible human-human interactions which could be included in the dataset.

In the next section, we will explain the rules according to which we collect images. Section 3 explains the source and the composition of the dataset. We conclude in section 4 with a discussion of the dataset and future work.

---

[1] http://pascallin.ecs.soton.ac.uk/challenges/VOC/voc2010/

**Fig. 4.** Example images from Pascal challenge 2010

## 2    Rules for Collecting Images

The collection of still images on action recognition dedicating to human-human interactions are aiming to include as many different actions as possible while recognizing them from images are still solvable. The followings are specification for collecting the dataset.

- All images are natural humans performing actions. No cartoon figures, no drawing are included. Also we try to include images taken under natural conditions. The less post processing the better.
- Range of images. The collected images are the range of about the size of interacting people, which means if we think too much background is included, we would crop the image and take the bounding box of interacting humans. The reason we do this is interacting between humans is already a difficult problem, we want to collect a dataset that allow researchers to deal with this problem directly instead of other steps like detecting human performers.
- Consistency within one action class. To distinguish one action class from another, images from one action class must have different characteristics with the other. For example, we include hugging and kissing actions in the dataset, so we exclude case of kissing while hugging to distinguish between these two classes.
- Variance within one action class. To make the dataset more applicable, we include as much variances in one action class as possible while following the previous rule. For example, in hugging class, we include cases in which more than two people are hugging. Also images are collected within variant scenes, under different illumination conditions and different view point.

**Table 1.** Compositions of the dataset

| Actions | Number of Images |
|---|---|
| Shaking hands | 70 |
| Hugging | 70 |
| Kissing | 70 |
| Punching | 70 |

**Fig. 5.** Example images from the dataset. Images from the first row to the fourth correspond to the four action classes: shaking hands, hugging, kissing and punching.

## 3 Dataset

The dataset are collected from Flicker. We consider four actions in this version of the dataset: shaking hands, hugging, kissing and punching. Example images from different action classes are shown in figure 5. Image numbers of different action classes in the dataset is shown in table 1.

## 4 Future Work

This paper collects a dataset to provide experimental images for action recognition from still images with human-human interaction. We include four different actions in this version. Future work include:

- To add more actions into this dataset. For example, one person serving food to another person or couple dancing.
- To develop a baseline method for action recognition. One possibility is to apply the state-of-the-art classification method on action recognition to this dataset.
- To include more than one class of human-human interaction in an image and provide bounding boxes information. Like in action recognition tester of Pascal challenge 2010, in which one image might contain more than one human action type, we would like to include more than one human-human interaction in an image. We would also provide bounding boxes information for positions of each human-human interaction.

**Acknowledgements.** The authors acknowledge the support of the Spanish Research Programs Consolider-Ingenio 2010: MIPRCV (CSD200700018); Avanza I+D ViCoMo (TSI-020400-2009-133) and DiCoMa (TSI-020400-2011-55); along with the Spanish projects TIN2009-14501-C02-01 and TIN2009-14501-C02-02.

## References

1. Nazli, I., Ramazan, G.C., Selen, P., Pinar, D.: Recognizing actions from still images. In: 19th International Conference on Pattern Recognition, Tampa, FL, pp. 1–4 (2008)
2. Bangpeng, Y., Fei-Fei, L.: Grouplet: a Structured Image Representation for Recognizing Human and Object Interactions. In: The Twenty-Third IEEE Conference on Computer Vision and Pattern Recognition, San Francisco, CA (2010)
3. Bangpeng, Y., Fei-Fei, L.: Modeling Mutual Context of Object and Human Pose in Human-Object Interaction Activities. In: The Twenty-Third IEEE Conference on Computer Vision and Pattern Recognition, San Francisco, CA (2010)
4. Cedras, C., Shah, M.: Motion-Based Recognition: A Survey. Image and Vision Computing 13(2), 129–155 (1995)
5. Gavrila, D.M.: The Visual Analysis of Human Movement: A Survey. Computer Vision and Image Understanding 73, 82–98 (1999)

# Experimental Results
# on Fingerprint Liveness Detection

Luca Ghiani, Paolo Denti, and Gian Luca Marcialis

Department of Electrical and Electronic Engineering,
University of Cagliari,
Piazza d'Armi, Cagliari, Italy
{luca.ghiani,marcialis}@diee.unica.it, paolode@hotmail.com

**Abstract.** Fingerprint liveness detection is aimed to detect if a fingerprint image, sensed by an electronic device, belongs to an alive fingertip
or to be an artificial replica of it. Recent studies have shown that a fingerprint can be replicated and, if a clever attacker tries to evade the system,
this is an issue. Accordingly, several countermeasures in terms of fingerprint liveness detection algorithms have been proposed, but never compared on a benchmark data set, internationally accepted by the research
community. In this paper, we present some recent experimental results on
several state-of-the-art fingerprint liveness detection algorithms on the
datasets available at Second International Fingerprint Liveness Detection Competition (LivDet 2011). The results we proposed help assessing
which are the more effective approaches used so far.

## 1 Introduction

Biometry measures allow us to perform the identification of a person based on his
physical (fingerprints, face, iris) or behavioural (gait, signature) attributes and
to establish an identity based on who that person is, rather than what he/she
possesses (e.g. a card that can be lost or stolen) or remembers (e.g. a password
that can be forgotten) [1]. Nowadays, more than ever, it is very important to
be able to tell if an individual is authorized to perform actions like entering a
facility, access privileged information or even cross a border. Therefore, biometric
systems are considered to be more reliable for the recognition of a person than
traditional methods.

During the past decade we have seen a significant growth in biometric research
resulting in the development of innovative sensors, novel feature extraction and
matching algorithms. A biometric system is a pattern recognition system that
acquires biometric data from an individual, extracts a features set from the
data, compares these features against those stored in a database and executes
an action based on the comparison result.

Fingerprints are the most used, oldest and well-known biometric measurements [2]. Everybody has them and each one is different from the other since
ridges formation is a combination of factors both environmental and genetic.
Fingerprints are composed of epidermic ridges and valleys that usually run in

F.J. Perales, R.B. Fisher, and T.B. Moeslund (Eds.): AMDO 2012, LNCS 7378, pp. 210–218, 2012.
© Springer-Verlag Berlin Heidelberg 2012

parallel. On the images obtained through sensors ridges are dark lines while the valleys are bright lines. Obviously their uniqueness depends on the type and number of features extracted (basically less features means less details and therefore less information obtained).

However, as recently shown, fingerprints can be forged and that is the subject of this work. The main fingerprints characteristic is that, each one of them is considered unique. If fingerprints can be replicated, this uniqueness is no longer valid. It is possible to create an artificial replica through several methods and using several materials, and the related images can be indistinguishable from alive ones (see for example Figures 1 and 2). Therefore, the development of liveness detection techniques is important to try to distinguish if a fingerprint image is coming from an alive person or from a replica. Liveness detection seeks additional data to verify if a biometric measure is authentic. Fingerprint liveness detection, with either hardware-based or software-based systems, is used to check if a presented fingerprint originates from a live person or an artificial finger [3]. It is based on the principle that additional information can be obtained from the data acquired by a standard verification system. This additional data can be used to verify if an image is authentic.

To detect liveness, hardware-based systems use additional sensors to gain measurements outside of the fingerprint image itself while the software-based ones use image processing algorithms to gather information directly from the collected fingerprint. These systems classify images as either live or fake.

(a) Digital     (b) Biometrika          (c) Italdata          (d) Sagem

**Fig. 1.** Examples of live fingerprints acquired with the 4 sensors

In this paper, we focus our attention on the software-based approaches, which are cheapest than hardware-based, since these require additional and invasive hardware to measure the liveness directly from the fingertip of people. Instead, software-based must detect liveness from features extracted from the fingerprint images captured by the sensor. In other words, the liveness detection problem is treated as a pattern recognition problem, where a set of features must be selected in order to train an appropriate classifier. Although several feature sets have been proposed to this aim, it is difficult to assess the state-of-the-art appropriately, due to the lack of data sets. In order to cover this gap, we considered a large set

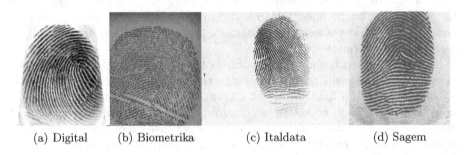

(a) Digital      (b) Biometrika      (c) Italdata      (d) Sagem

**Fig. 2.** Examples of fake fingerprint acquired with the 4 sensors

of liveness measurements at the state-of-the-art and tested to the data sets made available for the two editions of the fingerprint liveness detection competition, held in 2009 and 2011 [4, 5]. We compared the state-of-the-art results with the LivDet competition results and made a first point about the real performances of these approaches on realistic data sets.

This paper is organized as follows. Section 2 briefly describes the investigated algorithms. Section 3 shows the experimental results and performance with respect to the LivDet results. Section 4 concludes the paper.

## 2    Investigated Algorithms

In fingerprint liveness detection there are two different types of algorithms: the live-based ones look for characteristics of a living person's fingerprint, while the fake-based ones take advantage from the fact that, during the fake production, some details are lost and some defects are introduced.

We studied the fingerprint liveness detection state-of-the-art and we selected two live-based (pores detection and ridges wavelet) and six fake-based algorithms (local binary patterns, power spectrum, wavelet energy, valleys wavelet, curvelet energy and curvelet GLCM).

- LBP: local binary patterns were first employed for two-dimensional textures analysis and excellent results were obtained due to their invariance with respect to grey level, orientation and rotation. It extracts certain uniform patterns corresponding to micro-features in the image. The histogram of these uniform patterns occurrence is capable of characterize the image as it combines structural (it identify structures like lines and borders) and statistical (micro-structures distribution) approaches [6].
- Pores detection: since the pores presence in live fingerprints determines the perspiration effect, the pores detection algorithm analyzes pores distribution in order to discriminate between fake and live fingerprint images. By scanning the image along the fingerprint ridges[7] it extracts the pores number and the average distance between pores.

- Power spectrum: Coli *et al.* [8] analyzed fingerprints images in terms of high frequency information loss. In the artificial fingerprint creation, the ridge-valley periodicity is not altered by the reproduction process but some micro-characteristics are less defined. Consequently, high frequency details can be removed or strongly reduced. It is possible to analyze these details by computing the image Fourier transform modulus also called power spectrum.
- Wavelet energy signature: wavelet decomposition of an image [9] lead to the creation of four sub-bands: the approximation sub-band containing global low frequency information, and three detail sub-bands containing high frequency information. The image is decomposed in 4 levels using 3 different wavelet filters (Haar, Daubechies (db4) and Biorthogonal (bior2.2)) and the approximation image is not considered, hence the sub-bands number is $3 \times 4 = 12$.
- Ridges wavelet: after his extraction, a fingerprint skeleton can be used as a mask to obtain the gray level values along the ridges and these values are united into a signal. A wavelet multiresolution decomposition is applied to that signal with seven decomposition levels [10].
- Valleys wavelet: in this case the skeleton of the valleys is obtained. As for the ridges wavelet analysis, the skeleton is used as a mask to extract a signal representing the gray level values along the valleys. As for the ridges wavelet analysis a wavelet multiresolution decomposition is applied to that signal with seven decomposition levels [11].
- Curvelet [12] transform partitions curves into a collection of ridge fragments and then uses ridgelet transform to represent each of them. It is very efficient for representing edges and other singularities along curves due to his high directional sensitivity and his high anisotropy. We consider two different curvelet signature:
  - Curvelet energy signature: the energies of the 18 sub-bands are measured by computing means and variances of curvelet coefficients.
  - Curvelet co-occurrence signature: for each of the 18 sub-bands, the GLCM (Gray Level Co-occurrence Matrix) is calculated together with 10 corresponding features.

# 3   Experimental Results

## 3.1   The LivDet 2011 Data Sets

Two editions of the International Fingerprint Liveness Detection Competition (LivDet) have been held in 2009 and in 2011 [4, 5].

In particular, the four LivDet 2011 datasets consist of images acquired with four different devices; Biometrika, Digital Persona, Italdata and Sagem. There are 4000 images for each of these devices, 2000 live images and 2000 spoof images.

All the fake fingerprints have been created with the consensual method, by following these steps: the volunteer releases his fingerprint on a mould of plasticine or silicon-like material; the chosen material is poured or applied over the mould and after a certain time interval, this cast is removed from the mould, and can be used as fingerprint replica. Each replica in sensed by the sensor, that provide a "fake fingerprint image".

Spoof materials used were gelatine, latex, PlayDoh, silicone and wood glue for Digital Persona and Sagem; gelatine, latex, liquid silicon, silicone and wood glue for Biometrika and Italdata (400 of each of 5 spoof materials in both cases).

Each dataset of 4000 images per scanner was divided into two equal parts, training and testing. The first part had to be used to train the algorithm, and the second part to test them on independent data. In this paper, we follow the same protocol in order to compare the results with those of the competition.

## 3.2 Results

The classifier output is a posterior probabilty estimation of the live class given the feature set, thus included in the $[0, 1]$ real interval. This can be considered as a measurement of the "liveness" of the data received as input. Once a threshold $t$ is selected, if this probability $s$ is higher than $t$, the fingerprint is considered as alive, otherwise it is considered as fake. These results can be presented with a ROC curve: by varying the $t$ value from 0 to 1, we can plot the correspondent percentage of fake fingerprints misclassified as alive ones, and the percentage of live fingerprints misclassified as fake ones. According to the LivDet terminology, these values are called FerrFake and FerrLive, respectively [4, 5].

ROC curves are shown in Figures 3, 4, 5, 6. We notice that usually the results with the Italdata sensor are worse than the others (except for the pores detection and valleys wavelet algorithms) and that, for each of the four datasets, the best performance is always the one obtained with the LBP algorithm. However, in general, the performance on LivDet 2011 data set is worse than that reported in several papers [7–12], for many algorithms. The results worsening can be due to the quality improvement of the artificial fingers produced for the LivDet competition. As a matter of fact, some feature sets, as the one based on the power spectrum or on the wavelet transform, aimed to measure the image liveness at high frequencies, show several limitation in the performance. On the contrary, a texture classification algorithm as the LBP based one, preserves its discriminatory power. This is probably because its capability in describing some image peculiarity continues to work no matter what the quality of the fakes is. We are currently better investigating the properties of this feature set, in order to understand the motivation of his "robustness" with respect to the fake quality. Anyway, this is certainly an important advantage, which, if confirmed theoretically and experimentally, could set that the best way to improve a liveness detection algorithm is to follow the LBP paradigm.

Table 1 shows the rate at which each algorithm produces a false acceptance of a spoof image (FerrFake) and Table 2 shows the rate at which each algorithm produces a false rejection of a live subject (FerrLive). The threshold $t$ used is set to 0.5, that is, the Bayesian error is computed according to the posterior probabilities estimated by the SVM. These results are paired with those obtained by the three LivDet 2011 participants (in the last three rows of both tables). Once again the LBP emerges as the best algorithm even when its results are compared with those of the three participants. In fact, if the LBP's FerrFake value is higher than that of LivDet 2011 participants (for example, Dermalog), the corresponding FerrLive value is much lower. This also holds for the FerrLive value, and clearly shows that, on overall, the Bayesian error of LBP is the lowest one. The only performance really comparable with that of LBP is the one of the "Federico" participant, but only for the Digital sensor. On average, we notice that all algorithms exhibit, with some variations, the same performance, which makes current fingerprint liveness detection algorithms unacceptable if integrated on a fingerprint matching system as a separated module, due to their high FerrLive value which is not adequately counterbalanced by a low enough FerrFake value.

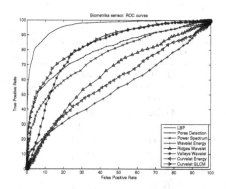

**Fig. 3.** Biometrika sensor ROC curves

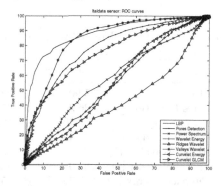

**Fig. 4.** Italdata sensor ROC curves

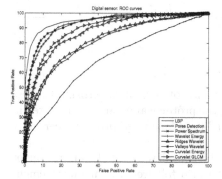

**Fig. 5.** Digital sensor ROC curves

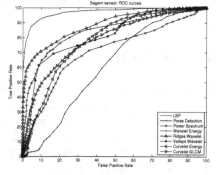

**Fig. 6.** Sagem sensor ROC curves

**Table 1.** FerrFake calculated with the Biometrika, Italdata, Digital and Sagem sensors

|                      | Biometrika | Italdata | Digital | Sagem |
|----------------------|------------|----------|---------|-------|
| LBP [6]              | 16.40      | 15.10    | 8.70    | 4.34  |
| Pores Detection [7]  | 27.80      | 22.00    | 30.50   | 49.90 |
| Power Spectrum [8]   | 23.90      | 29.40    | 23.50   | 21.81 |
| Wavelet Energy [9]   | 73.00      | 51.80    | 15.10   | 16.22 |
| Ridges Wavelet [10]  | 47.10      | 63.10    | 37.00   | 18.15 |
| Valleys Wavelet [11] | 48.60      | 39.10    | 12.40   | 55.12 |
| Curvelet Energy [12] | 55.10      | 40.70    | 27.40   | 39.58 |
| Curvelet GLCM [12]   | 16.40      | 25.20    | 22.00   | 25.00 |
| Dermalog [5]         | 29.00      | 28.50    | 6.20    | 12.50 |
| Federico [5]         | 42.00      | 40.10    | 11.60   | 13.10 |
| CASIA [5]            | 38.10      | 2.80     | 34.70   | 23.60 |

**Table 2.** FerrLive calculated with the Biometrika, Italdata, Digital and Sagem sensors

|                      | Biometrika | Italdata | Digital | Sagem |
|----------------------|------------|----------|---------|-------|
| LBP [6]              | 5.90       | 22.00    | 12.60   | 12.70 |
| Pores Detection [7]  | 26.90      | 35.30    | 41.70   | 30.40 |
| Power Spectrum [8]   | 37.40      | 56.20    | 30.80   | 41.20 |
| Wavelet Energy [9]   | 27.40      | 41.80    | 13.00   | 27.90 |
| Ridges Wavelet [10]  | 30.50      | 50.80    | 18.10   | 22.90 |
| Valleys Wavelet [11] | 9.40       | 8.20     | 13.70   | 9.00  |
| Curvelet Energy [12] | 35.30      | 55.10    | 16.40   | 17.50 |
| Curvelet GLCM [12]   | 29.40      | 36.30    | 14.70   | 31.10 |
| Dermalog [5]         | 11.00      | 15.10    | 66.00   | 15.10 |
| Federico [5]         | 38.00      | 39.90    | 6.20    | 13.80 |
| CASIA [5]            | 29.70      | 50.60    | 16.10   | 22.10 |

## 4    Conclusions

In this paper, we investigated the performance of several fingerprint liveness detection algorithms, by testing them using the protocol and data sets adopted in the LivDet 2011 competition, where the quality of fake fingerprint was certainly higher than that of the previous edition.

Like a "cops and robbers game", it must be considered that the improvement of the liveness detection algorithms will be also followed by an improvement of the falsification techniques. In this continuous struggle it is mandatory to introduce novel feature sets, intrinsically robust to the quality of the fingerprint replica.

Reported analysis clearly suggests that there is much work to do on fingerprint liveness detection, in order to design algorithms and features sets whose integration with fingerprint verification systems can be considered "acceptable" in terms of overall verification performance.

Our future works are related to these mentioned problems: the study of materials peculiarities, and the spoof creation process by non consensual methods, and focusing on a robust enough fingerprint liveness detection algorithm to be integrated on fingerprint verification systems.

**Acknowledgments.** This work was partly supported by the Tabula Rasa project, 7th FRP of the European Union (EU), grant agreement number: 257289; by the PRIN 2008 project "Biometric Guards - Electronic guards for protection and security of biometric systems" funded by the Italian Ministry of University and Scientific Research (MIUR). The authors also thank Zahid Akthar and Valerio Mura for collecting part of the LivDet 2011 data sets.

# References

1. Jain, A.K., Flynn, P., Ross, A.: Handbook of Biometrics. Springer (2007) ISBN 978-0-387-71040-2
2. Maltoni, D., Maio, D., Jain, A.K., Prabhakar, S.: Handbook of Fingerprint Recognition. Springer, New York (2003) ISBN 0387954317
3. Coli, P., Marcialis, G.L., Roli, F.: Vitality Detection from Fingerprint Images: A Critical Survey. In: Lee, S.-W., Li, S.Z. (eds.) ICB 2007. LNCS, vol. 4642, pp. 722–731. Springer, Heidelberg (2007) ISBN 978-3-540-74548-8, doi:10.1007/978-3-540-74549-5_76
4. Marcialis, G.L., Lewicke, A., Tan, B., Coli, P., Grimberg, D., Congiu, A., Tidu, A., Roli, F., Schuckers, S.: First International Fingerprint Liveness Detection Competition—LivDet 2009. In: Foggia, P., Sansone, C., Vento, M. (eds.) ICIAP 2009. LNCS, vol. 5716, pp. 12–23. Springer, Heidelberg (2009)
5. Yambay, D., Ghiani, L., Denti, P., Marcialis, G.L., Roli, F., Schuckers, S.: LivDet 2011 - Fingerprint Liveness Detection Competition 2011. In: 5th IAPR/IEEE Int. Conf. on Biometrics, New Delhi (India), March 29, April 1 (in press, 2012)
6. Ojala, T., Pietikäinen, M., Mäenpää, T.: Multiresolution gray-scale and rotation invariant texture classification with local binary patterns. IEEE Trans. on Pattern Analysis and Machine Intelligence, 971–987 (2002), doi:10.1109/TPAMI.2002.1017623
7. Marcialis, G.L., Roli, F., Tidu, A.: Analysis of Fingerprint Pores for Vitality Detection. In: Proc. of 20th IEEE/IAPR International Conference on Pattern Recognition (ICPR 2010), Instanbul (Turkey), August 23-26, pp. 1289–1292 (2010) ISBN 978-1-4244-7542-1, doi:10.1109/ICPR.2010.321
8. Coli, P., Marcialis, G.L., Roli, F.: Power spectrum-based fingerprint vitality detection. In: Tistarelli, M., Maltoni, D. (eds.) IEEE Int. Workshop on Automatic Identification Advanced Technologies AutoID 2007, Alghero (Italy), June 7-8, pp. 169–173 (2007)

9. Nikam, S.B., Agarwal, S.: Texture and Wavelet-Based Spoof Fingerprint Detection for Fingerprint Biometric Systems. In: First International Conference on Emerging Trends in Engineering and Technology, ICETET 2008, Nagpur, Maharashtra, July 16-18, pp. 675–680 (2008) ISBN 978-0-7695-3267-7, doi:10.1109/ICETET.2008.134

10. Tan, B., Schuckers, S.: Liveness Detection for Fingerprint Scanners Based on the Statistics of Wavelet Signal Processing. In: Computer Vision and Pattern Recognition Workshop, CVPRW 2006, June 17-22, pp. 26–26 (2006) ISBN 0-7695-2646-2, doi:10.1109/CVPRW.2006.120

11. Tan, B., Schuckers, S.: New approach for liveness detection in fingerprint scanners based on valley noise analysis. J. Electron. Imaging 17, 011009 (2008), doi:10.1117/1.2885133

12. Nikam, S.B., Agarwal, S.: Fingerprint Liveness Detection Using Curvelet Energy and Co-occurrence Signatures. In: Fifth International Conference on Computer Graphics, Imaging and Visualization 2008 IEEE, pp. 217–222 (2008) ISBN 978-0-7695-3359-9, doi:10.1109/CGIV.2008.9

# Modeling Deformable Filament Bundles
# by Means of Mass-Spring Systems
# for the Design of Carbon Reinforced Materials

Alejandro Mesejo-Chiong[1,*], Angela León-Mecías[1], and Patrick Shiebel[2]

[1] University of Havana, Faculty of Mathematics and Computer Science,
San Lázaro y L, 10400 Havana, Cuba
{mesejo,angela}@matcom.uh.cu
[2] Faserinstitut Bremen e.V., Am Biologischen Garten 2,
28359 Bremen, Germany
patschie@uni-bremen.de

**Abstract.** The construction and design of textile reinforcement elements offer great potential for efficient production of load-designed components out of fiber reinforced composites materials.

Tailored fiber placement (TFP) is a promising new technology that contributes to the development of carbon fiber reinforced composites by reducing structural weight at safe design. The TFP process allows a filament bundle positioning in almost any orientation. This way the fiber reinforcement can be aligned as closely as possible to the optimal mechanical direction. However, the flexibility of orientation can result in high deformation grades of the filament bundles; this may result in vulnerable regions of the fiber's reinforced structure.

This contribution presents a mass-spring system for physical numerical simulation of the three-dimensional deformation behavior experienced by carbon-tows by the TFP process including filament interaction and collision. Trough simulation we attempt to predict the deformation grade of the filament bundles by the TFP process. The advantages and shortcomings of this approach are presented by numerical results obtained for different number of filaments in the bundle.

**Keywords:** physics based modeling, mass-spring system, filament bundle simulation, collision detection.

# 1    Introduction

The construction and design of textile reinforcement elements offer great potential for an efficient production of load-designed components out of fiber-reinforced composites materials. Carbon fibers offer the highest specific modulus and highest specific strength of all reinforcing fibers; therefore are carbon fiber reinforcement

---

* Corresponding author.

F.J. Perales, R.B. Fisher, and T.B. Moeslund (Eds.): AMDO 2012, LNCS 7378, pp. 219–229, 2012.
© Springer-Verlag Berlin Heidelberg 2012

composites such as, carbon fiber reinforced plastics, carbon fiber reinforced cement ideally suited for applications in which strength, stiffness, lower weight, and outstanding fatigue characteristics are critical requirements.

Tailored fiber placement (TFP) [5], [9] and [13], based on the well-known embroidery technique, is a promising technology, which contributes to this aim by reducing structural weight at safe design. The TFP process, used for the deposition of dry carbon fiber tows (carbon-tows are multifilament yarns that can be described by number of filaments, 1K = 1000 filaments per tows) on a stitching base, allows a tow positioning in almost any orientation. This way fiber reinforcement can be aligned as closely as possible to the optimal mechanical direction to tailor the local stiffness and strength of the composite material. However, the flexibility of orientation can result in high deformation grades of the tows. This may result in vulnerable regions of fiber's reinforced structure which may weaken the mechanical properties of the components, see Figure 1. The three-dimensional deformation behavior of the roving in place along curved paths should be examined.

**Fig. 1.** Vulnerable regions, the void parts between the curved filament bundles, of the fiber's reinforced structure can appear due to the deformation grades of the tows

This contribution presents a mass-spring system for physical numerical simulation of the three-dimensional deformation behavior experienced by carbon-tows by the TFP process including filament interaction and collision; we attempt to simulate as many individual filaments as possible. In a mass-spring system, deformable objects are represented by a set of mass points, mechanical springs and dampers [11].

Mass-spring systems are very often used in computer graphics to simulate the behavior of deformable bodies. Reasons include the straightforward implementation and the relatively low computational requirements arising from such systems. Nevertheless, a mass-spring system lacks a clear correspondence between the physical properties of the object under study and the properties of the masses and springs constituting the system.

## 2     Mass-Spring-Systems for the Simulation of the Tows

Filament bundles or tows have been generally modeled as one-dimensional flexible part such as cables or hoses, covering different kinds of applications, for example in the automotive industry, or in the simulation of the behavior of yarn used for sutures or to the simulation of hairs, [2], [3], [6], [7], and [8]. Such kinds of objects are often used also in computer animation. For the physical simulation different kind of models have been used; for instance Kirchhoff's rod theory [2], [4], Cosserat models [10], [6], inverse kinematics [7], mass-spring systems [8], [12] or systems of uncouple particles [1]. All this models are different regarding accuracy and computational cost. Classical models for filament bundles neglect the real interaction between filaments; this approach is not enough for our purposes.

In densely packed structures like tows, the probability for filament-filament collisions is very high. Therefore, the adhesive strength, the friction and the collisions between the filaments has to be considered. A roving can be regarded as a bundle of continuous, non-twisted, stretched filaments. A filament can be considered as a flexible rod with cylindrical cross-section.

In our approach, all filaments are physically identical and each one is modeled by an identical mass-spring system. The filament bundle is consequently simulated as a set of interconnected mass-spring systems. A filament is represented by a uniform cylindrical rod with diameter $r_f$ and length $L_f$. Usual values of $r_f$ are between three and five micrometers. The filament is described through the centerline of the rod, which can be seen as a spatial curve (see Figure 2). In the following, all spatial information in respect of a filament will correspond to points along its center line.

The spring-mass scheme for one filament consists of $n_p$ mass points $P = \left\{ p_0, p_1, \ldots, p_{n_p-1} \right\}$ distributed equidistantly along the filament. Here $p_i = (x_i, y_i, z_i)$ gives the coordinates of the mass point $p_i$ in world space. The initial distance between the point masses, also termed as the rest length of the springs, is given through

$$\Delta p = \frac{L_f}{(n_p - 1)} \tag{1}$$

The mass points define the vertices of a polyline that establishes a discrete representation of the filament centerline. Each particle receives the same mass $m_p$. Given the mass density $\rho_f$ of the filaments material we obtain

$$m_p = \rho_f \frac{2\pi r_f^2 L_f}{n_p} \tag{2}$$

**Fig. 2.** Filament representation as a cylindrical rod. Centerline in black

Between the point masses, virtual massless springs are positioned so that the elastic behavior of a filament can be approximated by application of Hooke's law and Newton's second law. Two main physical properties of the filaments should be modeled, stretching and bending. To counteract the stretching of the filaments, linear elastic springs are used. They are placed between two adjacent mass points $p_{i-1}$ and $p_i$ for $i = 1, \ldots, n_p - 1$. To simulate the bending behavior of the filament we will also use linear elastic springs, this case between mass points $p_{i-1}$ and $p_{i+1}$ for $i = 1, \ldots, n_p - 2$. Therefore, $n_p - 1$ springs are used to simulate the elastic stretching behavior of one filament while $n_p - 2$ springs are used to simulate the bending behavior.

A linear elastic spring works according to the Hooke's law. A spring interposed between the mass points $p_{i-1}$ and $p_i$ exerts the force $F_{S_{i-1}}$ over $p_{i-1}$ where

$$F_{S_{i-1}} = -k_s \left( \| p_{i-1} - p_i \| - \Delta p \right) \frac{p_{i-1} - p_i}{\| p_{i-1} - p_i \|} \tag{3}$$

while for the force $F_{S_i}$ exerted over $p_i$ we have $F_{S_i} = -F_{S_{i-1}}$. In equation (2) $k_s$ is the spring constant and $\Delta p$ is the rest length of the springs as given by (1).

If linear elastic springs are employed to simulate the bending behavior we obtain, similar to (2), the following forces acting over mass points $p_{i-1}$ and $p_{i+1}$

$$F_{B_{i-1}} = -k_b \left( \| p_{i-1} - p_{i+1} \| - 2\Delta_p \right) \frac{p_{i-1} - p_{i+1}}{\| p_{i-1} - p_{i+1} \|} \tag{4}$$

and $F_{B_{i+1}} = -F_{B_{i-1}}$. Here $k_b$ is another spring constant.

The spring constants $k_s$ and $k_b$ have to be determined so that the physical properties of the filament are best approximates by the acting forces. This is a difficult task in the formulation of a mass-spring system, since no procedure is known to achieve a proper correspondence between the physical properties of the filament and the spring constants. We then attempt to tackle this problem by setting

$$k_s = \frac{EA}{\Delta p} \tag{5}$$

where $E$ is the tensile modulus (Young's Modulus) of the filament material, $A$ the cross-sectional area of the filament and $\Delta p$ the rest length of the spring. In our case $A$ is given by $2\pi r_f^2$. Also, according to the Euler-Bernoulli bending theory, we choose

$$k_b = 3\frac{EI}{(\Delta p)^3} \tag{6}$$

here $I$ represents the area moment of inertia of the cross-section and for a cylindrical beam it is given by $I = (\pi r_f^4)/4$.

We build the mass-spring system of the tow with single filament's mass-spring systems. The number $n_f$ of filaments in a carbon tows ranges between 3000 and 24000. In order to simplify the calculations we attach two indices to the mass points, i.e. a mass point is denoted by $p_{ij}$. The first index refers to the filament where the mass point is located, then $i = 1, ..., n_f$. The second index refers to the positioning of the mass point in the filament, therefore $j = 1, ..., n_p$. We have a total of $n_f n_p$ mass points that also will be called particles.

We determine also an initial configuration of the roving that resembles, so good as possible, the positioning of resting filaments in a tow. We assume that all filaments in this initial configuration are straight and parallel to each other. Without loss of generality it is also assume that all filaments in the tow are parallel to the y-axis and all have one end on the $XZ$ plane. Therefore, we need only a initial distribution of the filaments in a bounded closed region of the $XZ$ plane.

To resemble the distribution of filaments in the tow the initial distribution is random within a region $G \subset \mathbb{R}^2$ bounded by two half ellipses $E_O$ and $E_U$. Both ellipses have equal major axis and the endpoints of $E_O$ and $E_U$ coincide. The parameters for this construction are the width $w_R$ and the height $h_R$ of the tow and the ratio $\alpha_{OU}$ between the semi-minor axis of $E_O$ and $E_U$ where $0 < \alpha_{OU} < 1$. The region $G$ is then determined by the union of $E_O$ and $E_U$.

For the distribution of filaments within $G$ is necessary to know the minimum distance $d_{min}$ between filaments, which is determined by the thickness of the filament's coating. A filament has diameter $r_f$ and should maintain a minimum distance $d_{min}$ to any other filament; therefore the centerlines of two filaments cannot be at a distance less than $2r_f + d_{min}$. Figure 3 shows a typical initial distribution of filaments centerlines.

The mass-spring system of the roving is only completely described when the interaction between closely situated filaments is considered. To replicate this interaction we consider linear elastic springs between mass points of different filaments, which are in close neighborhood. These springs, called adhesion springs, possess a spring constant $k_a$ that resembles the properties of the coating. The mechanical properties of the coating are one of the production secrets of fiber tows manufacturers; therefore, the adhesive physical properties between the filaments are unknown. We simply choose an $k_a$ equal to $10^{-n_a}k_s$. The value of $n_a$ is taken between one and ten, the precisely value can only be determined by simulation. The adhesion springs act only if their length does not exceed a certain value $d_{max}$.

Throughout a simulation run is necessary to keep track of which particles are close enough to demand an adhesion spring between then and which ones of the existing springs are elongate beyond $d_{max}$ in order to eliminate then.

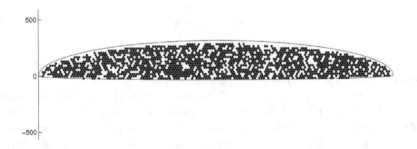

**Fig. 3.** Initial cross-section of one filament tow. Filaments centerlines are represented as black dots and the half ellipses are represented in blue. Here $w_R = 1600$, $h_R = 300$ and $\alpha_{OU} = 0.95$. Measurements are in micrometer and the number of filaments $n_f$ is equal to 1250.

## 3    Simulation of Three-Point Flexural Test for a Carbon Tow Specimen

The three-point flexural test, also know as bending test, is commonly used in engineering practice to provide values for the modulus of elasticity in bending, flexural stress, flexural strain and the flexural stress-strain response of one material. In this test, a specimen of the material is supported (near the extremes) on two static bases while a measuring device descends over the center of the specimen and exerts a force on it. The acting counterforces are measured together with the bending degree of the material.

In order to validate the potentials of the simulation of carbon fiber tows trough particle systems we try to simulate the three point bending test with our mass-spring system. Three cylinders simulate the three point loading conditions. Two of them, as support for the carbon tow specimen, are immovable and perpendicular to the tow course. The other one slowly descends over the center of the tow. The cylinders are, as the filaments, defined by them centerlines and them radius. Therefore for the simulation we need to prescribe the radius of the cylinders and the velocity of descend of the moving one. Both support cylinders should have equal radius $r_{fc}$ and the other one have radius $r_{mc}$. The velocity of the moving cylinder is set to $v_{mc} = (0,0,-v)$ and is supposed to be in millimeters per second.

The dynamical behavior of the mass-spring system is determined by the consecutive positions (in time) of the $n_f n_p$ particles and is given trough application of Newton's second law of motion. We obtain a second order system of ordinary differentials equivalent to the following system of first order ODEs:

$$
\dot{p}_{ij}(t) = v_{ij}(t)
$$
$$
\dot{v}_{ij}(t) = \frac{1}{m_p} F_{ij}(p_{ij}(t), v_{ij}(t))
\tag{7}
$$

where $\dot{p}_{ij}(t) = dp_{ij}(t)/dt = v_{ij}(t)$, $\dot{v}_{ij}(t) = dv_{ij}(t)/dt = a_{ij}(t)$. The forces $F_{ij}$ are given by the interaction of all particles $p_{kl}$ connected to $p_{ij}$ as described in equations (3), (4) and also considering the action of the adhesion springs.

The notation of (7) is very compact but for each particle $p_{ij}$ there are six equations, three of then for the position of the particle and the other three for the velocity. Therefore, the number of equations in (7), equal to $6n_f n_p$, is very large even for moderate number of particles. In fact simulating a filament with only three particles (bare minimum) and taking only 500 filaments in the tow we obtain a system with 9000 equations.

The initial conditions for the integration of (7) are given by the positions $p_{ij}(0)$ of the particles in the initial configuration of the tow. Since it is assumed that the tow is resting over two static cylinders the initial velocities are all equal to cero.

The probability of (7) to be a stiff system of differential equations is very high due to the very different orders of magnitude of the spring constants. In fact, $k_a$ is at least $1/10$ of $k_s$. Stiff differential equations systems are usually solve with implicit numerical integrators. These ones allow large step sizes at the expense of solving nonlinear systems of equations. Despite of the larger step sizes allowed, the high number of equations to integrate in (7) makes stiff integrators slow. Our choice of integrator come then to one-step explicit methods likes, for example, the Euler method. This imposes severe restrictions on the step sizes but, as will be seen later, small step sizes are more suitable for a successful collision handling procedure.

### 3.1    Dynamic Evolution of the Simulation and Damping

We start the simulation with a resting particle system where the only acting forces are external ones. In the three-point bending test, the descending cylinder is the only source of external forces since others, like gravity, can safely be omitted.

At the beginning of the simulation, the descending cylinder is located right above the top filaments in the particle system. The down motion of the cylinder causes collisions with the top filaments and these should bend as a result. The bending of some filaments in a densely packed filament structure, as the one depicted in Figure 3, causes filament-filament collisions. As a result, the positions of the particles changes and inner forces begin to work. Filament-filament collisions and filament-cylinders collisions determine the dynamic evolution of the particle system. Therefore, methods for robust collision detection and response are upmost important.

Before we address the collision detection and response problem we refer to another issue of mass-spring system, namely the oscillatory character of systems driven by spring forces. From classical mechanics we know that a system, where only ideal springs forces are working, simple harmonic motion undergoes. This motion is characterized by sinusoidal oscillations about the equilibrium point and is known as a harmonic oscillator. To avoid this behavior frictional forces proportional to the velocity, known as damping forces, should be introduced.

Depending on the damping coefficient, the system can oscillate with smaller frequency or decay exponentially to the equilibrium position without oscillations. For this last case we set the damping coefficient $c$ to

$$c = 2\sqrt{mk} \qquad (8)$$

where $k$ the spring constant and $m$ the mass of the particle is.

We then introduce damping forces according to

$$F_{D_{i-1}} = -c \left( \frac{(v_{i-1} - v_i) \cdot (p_{i-1} - p_i)}{\|p_{i-1} - p_i\|} \right) \frac{p_{i-1} - p_i}{\|p_{i-1} - p_i\|} \qquad (9)$$

for to particles $p_{i-1}$ and $p_i$ connected by a spring where $c$ is given by (8) and $F_{D_i} = -F_{D_{i-1}}$. To each spring force a term of the form (9) is added. The force defined by (9) restrains only the motion of the particles along the line of action of the spring.

## 3.2    Collision Detection and Solving

As mentioned above the detection and resolution of collisions is an important step of the simulation but also a complicated and time consuming one. For the treatment of collisions, i.e. detection and response, there are not known good overall approach. Common methods detect first collisions and after that, existing ones are solve. Consequently, particles of a filament can go inside another filament or inside a cylinder. Interpenetration can not be avoided. We follow such an approach.

We should then detect interpenetrations between filaments and between filaments and cylinders. Filaments are represented by polylines and a radius $r_f$, we can then reduce the problem of filament-filament interpenetration to the search for the closest points between two segments in space.

Given two filaments $F_1 = \left\{ p_{11}, ..., p_{1n_p} \right\}$ and $F_2 = \left\{ p_{21}, ..., p_{2n_p} \right\}$ we have the set of segments $S_1 = \left\{ s_{11}, ..., s_{1(n_p-1)} \right\}$ and $S_2 = \left\{ s_{21}, ..., s_{2(n_p-1)} \right\}$ where $s_{ij} = p_{ij} + \alpha \left( p_{i(j+1)} - p_{ij} \right)$, $\alpha \in [0,1]$. The filaments $F_1$ and $F_2$ are in collision, if at least one pair $j, k \in \{1, ..., n_p - 1\}$ exist such that $d(s_{1j}, s_{2k}) < 2r_f$. The distance $d(s_{1j}, s_{2k})$ is given as the solution of the minimum problem

$$d(s_{1j}, s_{2k}) = \min_{\alpha, \beta \in [0,1]} \left\| p_{1j} - p_{2k} + \alpha \left( p_{1(j+1)} - p_{1j} \right) - \beta \left( p_{2(k+1)} - p_{2k} \right) \right\|. \qquad (10)$$

Finding the collision between two filaments would require to solve $(n_p - 1)^2$ minimum problems like (10). The need for a better method is obvious.

To avoid the solution of minimum problems like (10) we use a hierarchical decomposition of the colliding objects with bounding volumes called Axis Aligned Bounding Box (AABB). The AABB of each filament's segment is calculated and stored in a tree that can be easily traverse to detect intersection. Only by intersection of two AABBs we solve the time consuming problem (10). For collision with the cylinders we follow a similar approach.

To solve the collisions we use following two steps algorithm:

1.  If the AABBs of two segments $s_{1j}$ and $s_{2k}$ intersects, then find $\alpha^*$ and $\beta^*$ such that $d(s_{1j}(\alpha^*), s_{2k}(\beta^*)) = \min_{\alpha, \beta \in [0,1]} d(s_{1j}(\alpha), s_{2k}(\beta))$,

2.  Introduce a virtual spring, with spring constant equal to $k_s$, between $s_{1j}(\alpha^*)$ and $s_{2k}(\beta^*)$.

The described algorithm solves the collision problem only segment against segment. Consequently, we do not consider information about the overall interpenetrations of two filaments. As a result we cannot guarantee, for geometrically complex filaments intersections, the solution to all collisions after a relatively small number of time steps. The best way to achieve a collisions free system after a few iterations steps is to keep the integration time step small enough. This last statement is confirmed trough our experiments.

## 4     Results of the Experiments

For the solution of (7) we employ the first order integration methods known as Euler and Euler-Cromer. As a first step we calibrate the simulation parameters trough simple experiments with a limited number of particles. The calibration step starts with the values of the simulation parameters given by (1), (2), (5), (6) and (8) among others. We compare the results obtained by the Euler and Euler-Cromer methods in this step against the ones of the ode15s method for stiff systems in the MATLAB ODE suite. The initial values of the simulation parameters are suitably modified until the results of the Euler and Euler-Cromer methods, with a time step of minimally $10^{-3}$, to those of ode15s coincide.

**Table 1.**  Average running times for a simulation (in hours) corresponding to certain products of particles per filament with number of filaments

| $n_p \times n_f$ | Average computing time (h) |
|:---:|:---:|
| $5 \times 500$ | 0.17 |
| $11 \times 500$ | 0.56 |
| $5 \times 1500$ | 2.53 |
| $11 \times 1500$ | 7.98 |
| $11 \times 3500$ | 18.25 |

After the calibration step we start the tow simulation by determining the values of $n_p$ and $n_f$ and the velocity of de descending cylinder. Experiments with $n_p \in \{5,7,9,11\}$ and $n_f$ from 500 up to 3500 in steps of 500 were done. In Table 1 the average running times in hours for a few simulations are given. A simulation runs until the moving cylinder five times the width of the carbon tow descends. All experiments were conducted on a desktop computer with an Intel Core2 Quad Processor Q6600 (8M Cache, 2.40 GHz, 1066 MHz FSB), 6 GB RAM and Windows 7 operating system.

One objective of this work was the comparison of the simulation of tows by mass-spring systems with other deformable bodies modeling methods like FEM. In this regard, the only argument to favor particle systems could be extreme low computing times by great number of filaments. As it is shown in Table 1 this is not our case. The approach followed by us for the mass-spring simulation is, for high number of filaments, very time consuming. Nevertheless, the results were coherent with the expected mechanical behavior as shown in figure 4.

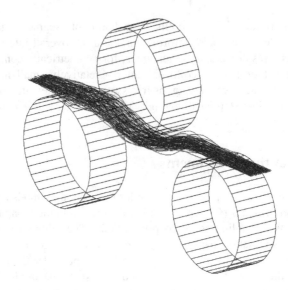

**Fig. 4.** Illustration of the results of the three-point flexural test simulation for 500 filaments with 11 particles per filament

## 5     Conclusions

In this work we investigate the suitability of the simulation with mass-spring systems of the bending behavior of densely packed deformable objects like carbon tows. The running times achieved by our implementation, again those of others methods like the Finite Element Method, are not much better. The causes of this result are the huge number of collisions to handle. In addition, collisions propagate as a wave that only dissipates after many simulation steps. In order to achieve better running times new collision detection methods for densely packed filament structures are to be developed.

Nevertheless, simulations by mass-spring systems holds advantages like the ease of implementation. If a calibration step as the one we outlined in section 4 is employed the simulation parameters can be easily adjusted to yield the expected mechanical behavior.

**Acknowledgments.** This work was supported by project HE 2574/11-1 of the DFG (German Research Foundation) and MAEC-AECID A/030033/10 and MAEC-AECID A2/037538/11 of the Spanish Government.

## References

1. Bando, Y., Chen, B.-Y., Nishita, T.: Animating Hair with Loosely Connected Particles. In: Brunet, P., Fellner, D. (eds.) Eurographics 2003, vol. 22(3), The Eurographics Association and Blackwell Publishers, 108 Cowley Road, Oxford OX4 1JF, UK and 350 Main Street, Malden, MA 02148 (2003)

2. Bergou, M., Wardetzky, M., Robinson, S., Audoly, B., Grinspun, E.: Discrete Elastic Rods. ACM Transactions on Graphics 27(3), Article 63, 12 pages (2008)
3. Bertails, F., Basile, A., Querleux, B., Leroy, F., Lévêque, J.-L., Cani, M.-P.: Predicting Natural Hair Shapes by Solving the Statics of Flexible Rods. In: Dingliana, J., Ganovelli, F. (Guest eds.) Eurographics 2005. Short Presentation. The Eurographics Association and Blackwell Publishers, 108 Cowley Road, Oxford OX4 1JF, UK and 350 Main Street, Malden, MA 02148 (2005)
4. da Fonseca, A.F., de Aguiar, M.A.: Solving the boundary value problem for finite Kirchhoff rods. Physica D 181, 53–69 (2003)
5. Gliesche, K., Orawetz, H.: Nutzung des Tailored Fibre Placement Verfahrens zur Low-cost-Herstellung von beanspruchungsgerechten Spantstrukturen. Präsentation des Institut für Polymerforschung e. V. Dresden auf dem Critical Design Review des Verbundprojektes EMIR CFK-Rumpf, Bremen (2004)
6. Grègoire, M., Schömer, E.: Interactive simulation of one-dimensional flexible parts. Computer-Aided Design 39, 694–707 (2007)
7. Hergenröther, H., Dähne, P.: Real-time virtual cables based on kinematic simulation. In: 8th International Conference in Central Europe on Computer Graphics, Visualization and Interactive Digital Media, Conference Proceedings, University of West Bohemia, Pilsen, pp. 402–409 (2000)
8. Loock, A., Schömer, E.: A Virtual Environment for Interactive Assembly Simulation: From Rigid Bodies to Deformable Cables. Research Report. Computer Science Department of the Universität des Saarlandes (2002)
9. Mattheij, P., Gliesche, K., Feltin, D.: Tailored Fiber Placement-Mechanical Properties and Applications. Journal of Reinforced Plastics and Composites 17, 774 (1998), doi:10.1177/073168449801700901
10. Pai, D.K.: Interactive Simulation of Thin Solids using Cosserat Models. In: Drettakis, G., Seidel, H.-P. (Guest eds.) Eurographics 2002, vol. 21(3). The Eurographics Association and Blackwell Publishers, 108 Cowley Road, Oxford OX4 1JF, UK and 350 Main Street, Malden, MA 02148 (2002)
11. Plath, J.: Realistic modeling of textiles using interacting particle systems. Computers & Graphics 24, 897–905 (2000)
12. Selle, A., Lentine, M., Fedkiw, R.: A Mass Spring Model for Hair Simulation. ACM Transactions on Graphics 27(3), Article 64, 11 pages (2008)
13. Temmen, H., Degenhardt, R., Raible, T.: Tailored Fiber Placement optimization Tool. In: 25th International Congress of Aeronautical Sciences (2006), http://www.dlr.de/fa/Portaldata/17/Resources

# An Avatar Acceptance Study
# for Home Automation Scenarios

Cristina Manresa-Yee[1], Pere Ponsa[2], Diana Arellano[1], and Martin Larrea[3]

[1] UGIVIA, Math. and Computer Science Department,
Universitat Illes Balears, Ed. Anselm Turmeda, Crta.
Valldemossa, km. 7.5, Palma, Spain
[2] Automatic Control Department, Barcelona Tech. Unviersity, EPSEVG,
Av. Victor Balaguer s/n, 08800 Vilanova i la Geltrú, Spain
[3] Laboratorio de Investigación y Desarrollo en Visualización y Computación Grafica
(VyGLab), Departamento de Ciencias e Ingeniería de la Computación,
Universidad Nacional del Sur, Argentina
{cristina.manresa,diana.arellano}@uib.es,
pedro.ponsa@upc.edu, mll@cs.uns.edu.ar

**Abstract.** In this paper we present a graphical user interface (GUI) for home automation which includes an avatar interface as a help-system. The work aims at analysing the user-home automation system interaction to model the user control over the system and the level of assistance required. We have developed high-fi prototypes to test the avatar-based help system with incremental functionalities embedded in the home GUI. Preliminary results suggest the acceptance of the system and its use in share control systems in smart and assistive home scenarios.

**Keywords:** Avatar, Emotion, Home Automation, Usability.

## 1 Introduction

Research is analyzing the use of avatars for interfacing smart homes [1] as face-to-face communication is natural for humans. Different works study the use of avatars and talking heads in assistive homes and intelligent ambient for elderly people with cognitive impairments, alzheimer or normal aging [2, 3, 4, 5]. The objective is to bind the user emotionally towards the system and to develop a user-friendly interaction. Avatars can manifest emotions by changing the tone of the voice, or their postures, or showing different facial expressions. Nevertheless, facial expressions are one of the most powerful ways to handle non-verbal communication; indeed it is said that in natural interaction only 7% of the meaning of a communicative message is transferred vocally while 55% is transferred by facial expressions [6].

To produce affective states many applications use basic metaphors such as the Pleasure-Arousal-Dominance scale [7] to measure the user's emotional state, while performing a task that is being evaluated. Other approaches use affective agents to create a knowledge model in which conceptual models describe emotions, and these

F.J. Perales, R.B. Fisher, and T.B. Moeslund (Eds.): AMDO 2012, LNCS 7378, pp. 230–238, 2012.
© Springer-Verlag Berlin Heidelberg 2012

are shown in the avatar through facial expressions, improving the communication with the user [8].

The use of realistic virtual characters searches for empathy with the user, which according to [9] is a necessary quality to develop products that meet customer needs.

In this paper, we present a graphical user interface (GUI) for home automation which includes an avatar interface as a help-system and we assess its use and acceptance. The paper is organized as follows. Section 2 describes the integration of all the factors in this multidisciplinary research. Section 3 evaluates the use of this interface in order to assess user satisfaction at early stages of the design and development of prototypes in formative usability evaluation. This will allow us to find a more effective communication in the interaction between people and systems. Finally, the last section discusses the main conclusions and future work.

## 2    Interactive System Design

In this work, we combined a set of factors to develop an effective, empathic and satisfactory home automation system.

First, we designed a home automation interface display following ergonomics guidelines. The home display interface was a graphical interface designed to allow users to carry out control tasks in a home. Therefore, the interface was developed following the design recommendations from the 'Ergonomic Guideline for Supervisory Control Interface Design', which is a method that helps to take into account all the aspects of the interface design, in order to improve the effectiveness of human-computer interaction (HCI) in supervision tasks [10].

There was also a scale model of a smart home with home automation and energy control domotics: opening/closing doors/windows, switching on/off lights, controlling heating. The scale model had five rooms (garage, dining room, kitchen, bathroom and bedroom), and several domotic devices (blinds, light, temperature control, garage's door).

As a help system for the interface, we used an emotional, multimodal and communicative avatar -the avatar Alice [11]- to represent 16 different emotions and 8 emotional states or moods [12, 13]. Besides the basic emotions (joy, sadness, anger, fear, disgust, and surprise) [14], we used intermediate emotions, which results from the combination of the basic emotions based on their activation values. These activation values are provided by the activation-evaluation classification performed by Whissell [15]. In this way, emotions such as gratitude or resentment can be expressed [6]. The avatar was embedded in the GUI to provide general information on the home, the rooms and devices, and to appear when particular events occurred, triggered by the user or by an internal state of the automation system. In the initial prototypes, we used four face expressions. In Table 1 images of the four selected emotions (neutral, joy, surprise and fear) can be seen and a description on when and why they appear.  The avatar provided information to the user and suggested the actions to carry out.

An important requirement was to analyze the mapping among facial expressions, emotional states and operating states of the system. We had to associate the avatar's facial expression with each of the possible scenario situation: normal operation, alarm condition, device failure or emergency situation. For the initial tests, emotions like disgust and sadness were discarded because we considered them not adequate to give information on system control performance.

The avatar provided textual, visual and audio information. The user chose the language and the vocal response of the avatar, using the voice functionality of Loquendo Text to Speech software; we are still working in a text library in order to classify the home automation states and dynamically associate to each situation a speech response of the system.

**Table 1.** Mapping between facial expression and emotional states of the help avatar of the home automation system and the user's interaction

| Emotional state | Facial expression | System state and user action |
|---|---|---|
| Neutral | | Alice informs on the devices and general properties of the home The user asks explicitly information on the system |
| Joy | | Alice shows a satisfaction face due to the user's action. The user carries out an operation on the system (an action on a device). |
| Surprise | | An unexpected event occurs (device failure) and Alice informs on an alarm situation (low, moderate or critical risk). The user decides to perform an action to reset the normal situation |
| Fear | | An unexpected event occurs and Alice informs about the high risk of danger and tries to mitigate the problem. The user must press the emergency stop button and leave the home |

In laboratory conditions, we carried out rapid prototyping and usability testing to achieve a usable system accepted by the user. We developed diverse scenarios to test the integration of all the components and specially to assess the help of the avatar. In the first scenario, there was human-computer interaction and human-machine interaction (Fig 1a): the input devices were a mouse and a panel. The controller gave the user feedback (an action of the user in the panel activated a light in the panel; an action of the user on the screen activated simulated functions). The panel allowed switching between manual or automatic control (traded control). The avatar provided information on the control mode, general home information and abnormal situation management of the simulated scenario.

In the second scenario, there was human supervisory control (Fig 1b). In this case we had the human, the controller and the scale model. In monitoring tasks, the human supervised the information on the screen while the programmable controller was controlling the scale model. The user decided to intervene inside the scale model and change from supervisory control mode to manual control mode. The avatar provided information about the current state of the scale model and allowed the human a continuous transition from supervisory control to manual control.

The levels of automation are an issue to analyze, whether manual, automatic or traded control is more appealing for the user.

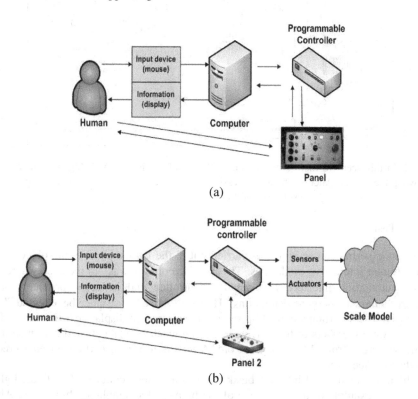

(a)

(b)

**Fig. 1.** The experimental scenarios tested in this work

## 3    Experimental Test

In order to test each change in the system, usability tests were performed from the beginning of the design process of a home automation interface with an assistant avatar (see Fig. 2). The aims of the experimental sessions were:

a) Test 1: to assess the interactive modalities between the user and the avatar during abnormal situations management.

b) Test 2: to assess the integration of the avatar-based help system in the graphical interface of a scale model.

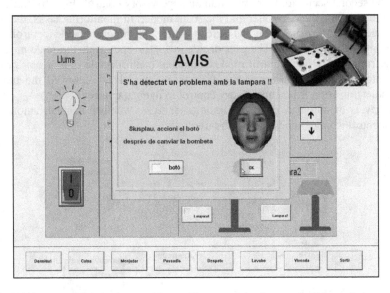

**Fig. 2.** In this scenario there is a problem with one of the lamps. A dialog window appears showing the avatar Alice with an expression of low fear and a warning message. Alice recommends the user how to solve the problem.

### 3.1    Test 1

The first experimental session was carried out in the laboratory with the objective to test different interactive modalities. The work hypothesis was "In the case where the home automation interface is manually controlled and a set of problems arise (failures, alarms, emergency situations). How will Alice's assistance be assessed?"

Twelve users participated testing the home automation display and the panel. The subjects were members of the university among teachers, students and administrative staff, with ages from 20 to 45 years old. After the test each participant answered a satisfaction questionnaire.

The task was divided into 6 subtasks (navigation, temperature, TV, blinds, lights, doors). An example of a task is: one of the bulbs in the simulation blows and Alice suggests the user to change the bulb and close the incidence. Other task example is when the user is navigating through the application and an unexpected event occurs:

there is fire in the corridor, a pop up warning screen appears and the avatar suggests the user to close the door, activate the extinguisher, press the emergency stop (which will alarm an external tele-assistance system) and leave the house.

The estimated duration of the task was 300 seconds, although no time duration was specified and users did not receive any instruction of doing the tasks as fast as they could.

The questions considered in a 4-Likert scale questionnaire (low (1), fair (2), good (3), very good (4)) were:

1. The task was difficult to understand
2. The task was long
3. I was confused, without having a clear idea what to do
4. I had to concentrate very much to carry out the task efficiently
5. Assess the Alice agent
6. Is it helpful?
7. Is Alice pleasant?
8. Assess speech information
9. Assess abnormal situations (fault, alarm, critical situation)
10. Did Alice warn the user promptly?
11. Do you prefer another kind of help? (yes, no)
12. Open question regarding the user's opinion of Alice
13. Assess the quality of the panel

High effectiveness is considered when the user successfully completes 75% of the 6 subtasks. In this experimental session, 11 out of 12 users completed all the subtasks.

In regard to efficiency, the minimum duration needed to perform the task was 232.5 seconds, the maximum was 314.3 seconds, and the average time was 272.38 seconds with a standard deviation of ± 24.01 seconds. 5 out of the 12 users completed the experimental session with a duration above the average.

During the execution of the tasks we observed that users not always followed the avatar's instructions in the actions to carry out. For instance, when the avatar recommended lowering the temperature of the cooking hob, in some cases users did not decrease the temperature or they navigated to other areas of the house without turning off the hob. To avoid ambiguities and confusion we are redesigning the interface and the help information module to make the actions to carry out clearer for the user.

Regarding the user's satisfaction, in Question 5 "Assess the Alice agent", 7 out of the 12 users evaluated the avatar Alice as very good, and 5 out of this 12 evaluated the avatar as good. In Question 6 "Has Alice been helpful?" 5 out of the 12 users evaluated Alice's assistance as very good, and 7 out of 12 users as good. In Question 10 "Does Alice warn the user promptly?", 9 out of 12 users rated her as very good and 3 out of 12 users as good.

Concerning Question 7 "Is Alice pleasant?", 2 out of 12 users evaluated Alice as a very pleasant avatar, 9 out of 12 as a good avatar and 1 out of 12 as fair. For the users, this was the first time they interacted with Alice in a domotic assistance context.

As for Question 11 "Do you prefer another kind of help?", 9 out of 12 users agreed with the current help system and 3 out of 12 users commented they would prefer another help system, although they did not specified the features of a new help system.

In addition, some users expressed surprise when the avatar Alice first appeared. Also, they did not have problems with the integrated use of the mouse, the panel and the interaction with the avatar. The next step will be to prepare an experimental test with the computer, the programmable controller and the scale model home

## 3.2    Test 2

For this context the avatar Alice shows relevant information about the state of the house and the user plans, decides and executes a set of actions. A user's action is transmitted to the scale model.

The experimental session was also carried out in the laboratory and the aim was to test the complete integrated system. The work hypothesis was "In the case of human supervisory control of a home automation system where the avatar informs about the home situation: how will be Alice's assistance assessed?"

Seven users participated testing the home automation display and the scale model. The participants were university members (engineering students) with ages between 20 and 23 years old. After the experiment they answered a satisfaction questionnaire.

The task was presented to the user as an instruction with 8 subtasks (save energy, adjust the bath temperature, warm up the food, fill the bath, write a post-it, close the blinds, set the clock and exit). This scenario is close to a real scenario following a cognitive walkthrough with a set of daily user tasks. An example:

*"You just get out of bed and start to use the application:*
- *To take advantage of daylight, go to the general supervision and ACTIVATE "Save energy" once this is made, you must DEACTIVATE.*
- *Go to work and when you return home, change and adjust the temperature of the bath, go to current state screen and go to the bathroom. Choose 25°"*

The estimated duration of the task was 500 seconds, although no time duration was specified and users did not receive any instruction of doing the tasks as fast as they could.

The 4-Likert questionnaire is similar to the questionnaire of the previous section with an additional question about the quality of the scale model.

High effectiveness is achieved when the user successfully completes the 8 subtasks. In this experimental session, 4 out of 7 users completed all the subtasks with success. 3 out of 7 users completed four to seven tasks with success.

Regarding to efficiency, the minimum duration needed to perform the task was 420 seconds, the maximum was 540 seconds, and the average time with standard deviation was $480 \pm 42.4$ seconds. Five out of the seven users completed the experimental session with a duration above the average.

In Question 5 "Assess the Alice agent", 4 out of 7 users evaluated the avatar Alice as very good and 3 out of 7 users evaluated her as good.

In Question 6 "Is Alice helpful?, 3 out of the 7 users evaluated Alice's assistance as very good, 3 out of 7 evaluated Alice's assistance as good and 1 out of 7 evaluated Alice's assistance as neutral.

In the Question 7 "Is Alice pleasant?", 3 out of 7 users evaluated Alice as a very pleasant, 3 out of 7 users evaluated Alice as pleasant and just 1 evaluated Alice as little pleasant. However, in the Question 11 "Do you prefer another kind of help?", there was no doubt and no one preferred another kind of help.

To the Question "Assess the quality of the scale model", 1 out of 7 users assessed the quality as very good, 3 out of 7 assessed the quality as good and 2 out of 7 as neutral.

From section 3.1 to section 3.2 we have substituted the simulated scenario by a scale model scenario. Nevertheless, this fact does not increase the user's perception that the task was more difficult to understand. In general, the avatar Alice inside the scale model had a high level of acceptance.

# 4    Conclusions

This work presents a home automation system design that takes into account the user's experience at early stages of the development process. We highlight the integration of the graphical interface and the affective avatar Alice for help assistance. In the experimental tests (simulated scenario, scale model scenario) many different abnormal events appeared in a short period of time (warning, fire alarm, critic situation). In this context, many users understand the abnormal situation and the steps to drive the system to a safe state with the help of the avatar.

In the evaluation, special attention was paid to the interaction between the avatar and the user, to observe whether the communication was effective or rather forced and artificial. In general, assessment was very positive. Users also evaluated positively the assistance offered by the avatar Alice in problematic situations in order to restore them. It was also important to analyze the acceptance of Alice, regarding to the empathy between the user and the avatar to work in a cooperative system. Most of the opinions were good and results did not show rejections regarding Alice's appearance. However, additional tests with more users and with different capabilities (age, disabilities) must be carried out and it would be interesting to analyze whether differences appear in the acceptance of Alice due to gender.

In conclusion, the preliminary results in experimental sessions show that the integration between the GUI and the avatar-based help system is well accepted. Finally, the future work is to explore a new concept: the assistive home, a home that focuses on the accessibility and the usability of a smart home for children, young and elderly people, and to take the results of the experimental study from the laboratory to a real smart home environment and assess the satisfaction of people with special needs in real environments.

**Acknowledgments.** This work is partially supported by Spanish MAEC- AECID FRIVIG A1/037910/11, by MINECO TIN2010-16576 and by the Barcelona Tech University "Human-centred design approach in supervisory control systems" project.

# References

1. Kühnel, C., Weiss, B., Wechsung, I., Fagel, S., Möller, S.: Evaluating talking heads for smart home systems. In: International Conference ICMI 2008, Crete, Greece, pp. 81–84 (2008)
2. Morandell, M.M., Hochgatterer, A., Fagel, S., Wassertheurer, S.: Avatars in Assistive Homes for the Elderly: A User-Friendly Way of Interaction? In: Holzinger, A. (ed.) USAB 2008. LNCS, vol. 5298, pp. 391–402. Springer, Heidelberg (2008)
3. Morandell, M.M., Hochgatterer, A., Wöckl, B., Dittenberger, S., Fagel, S.: Avatars@Home. In: Holzinger, A., Miesenberger, K. (eds.) USAB 2009. LNCS, vol. 5889, pp. 353–365. Springer, Heidelberg (2009)
4. Morandell, M.M., Fugger, E., Prazak, B.: The Alzheimer avatar–caregivers' faces used as GUI component. In: Eizmendi, E., et al. (eds.) Challenges for Assistive Technology, pp. 243–247. IOS Press (2007)
5. Ortiz, A., del Puy Carretero, M., Oyarzun, D., Yanguas, J.J., Buiza, C., Gonzalez, M.F., Etxeberria, I.: Elderly Users in Ambient Intelligence: Does an Avatar Improve the Interaction? In: Stephanidis, C., Pieper, M. (eds.) ERCIM Ws UI4ALL 2006. LNCS, vol. 4397, pp. 99–114. Springer, Heidelberg (2007)
6. Peter, C., Herbon, A.: Emotion representation and physiology assignments in digital systems. Interacting with Computers 18, 139–170 (2006)
7. Bradley, M., Lang, P.: Measuring emotion: the self assessment Manikin and the semantic differential. Journal of Behavior Therapy and Experimental Psychiatry 25, 49–59 (2004)
8. Arellano, D., Lera, I., Varona, J., Perales, F.J.: Integration of a semantic and affective model for realistic generation of emotional states in virtual characters. In: International Conference on Affective Computing & Intelligent Interaction (ACII 2009), Amsterdam (2009)
9. Kouprie, M., Visser, F.J.: A framework for empathy in design: stepping into and out of the user's life. Journal of Engineering Design 20(5), 437–448 (2009)
10. Ponsa, P., Díaz, M.: Creation of an Ergonomic Guideline for Supervisory Control Interface Design. In: Harris, D. (ed.) HCII 2007 and EPCE 2007. LNCS (LNAI), vol. 4562, pp. 137–146. Springer, Heidelberg (2007)
11. Balci, K.: Xfaced: authoring tool for embodied conversational agents. In: ICMI, pp. 208–213 (2005)
12. Arellano, D., Varona, J., Perales, F.J.: Why do I feel like this? The importance of context representation for emotion elicitation. International Journal of Synthetic Emotions 2(2), 28–47 (2011)
13. Arellano, D.: Visualization of affect in faces based on context appraisal. Ph D. Thesis. Universitat de les Illes Balears (2012)
14. Ekman, P.: Basic emotions. In: Dalgleish, T., Power, M. (eds.) Handbook of Cognitive and Emotion. Wiley, New York (1999)
15. Whissell, C.M.: The dictionary of affect in language. In: Plutchik, R., Kellerman, H. (eds.) Emotion: Theory, Research and Experience, pp. 113–131. Academic Press, New York (1989)
16. Sabini, J., Silver, M.: Ekman's basic emotions: why not love and jealousy? Cognition and Emotion 19(5), 693–712 (2005)

# A Tennis Training Application
# Using 3D Gesture Recognition

Cristian García Bauza[1,2], Juan D'Amato[1,2], Andrés Gariglio[1], María José Abásolo[3,4], Marcelo Vénere[1,5], Cristina Manresa-Yee[6], and Ramon Mas-Sansó[6]

[1] Instituto PLADEMA, Universidad Nacional del Centro de la Provincia de Buenos Aires, Tandil, 7000 Argentina
[2] CONICET, Argentina
[3] Universidad Nacional de La Plata, La Plata, 1900 Argentina
[4] Comision de Investigaciones Científicas de la Provincia de Buenos Aires, Argentina
[5] CNEA, Argentina
[6] Universitat de les Illes Balears, Palma, 07122 España
{crgarcia,jpdamato}@exa.unicen.edu.ar,
andres.gariglio@gmail.com, mjabasolo@lidi.info.unlp.edu.ar,
venerem@exa.unicen.edu.ar, {cristina.manresa,ramon.mas}@uib.es

**Abstract.** This paper presents a sport training system which recognizes user movements from data of the Wiimote device with accelerometer technology. Recognizing a new gesture involves the normalization of the Wiimote data and searching in a gesture templates database. The Dynamic Time Warping (DTW) comparison algorithm is used as a correlation function to compare the new gesture with every template. Based on prior training, the system can successfully recognize different sport shots. Particularly the system is instantiated for tennis training. The user visualizes the trajectory of the ball in a three-dimensional environment and he can interact with virtual objects that follow Newton dynamics.

**Keywords:** Gesture recognition, Wiimote, Videogames, Sport training, Tennis training, Accelerometer, Computer graphics, Dynamic Time Warping.

## 1 Introduction

The keyboard, the mouse and the monitor continue being the standard configuration for the human-computer interaction (HCI). Nevertheless, during the last years diverse technologies have appeared that try to change the way how users interact with the computer and other electronic devices. Recently there have been big advances that allow the use of 3D gestures to interact in virtual environments, doing tasks as selection, manipulation, navigation and system control [1]. Though great quantity of developments exists focused on recognizing user gestures, most of them use conventional tracking devices [2][3][4][5]. The recognition of gestures from information given by gyroscopes or accelerometers is an emerging technology in HCI [6]. With the rapid development and mass-production of the technology in mobile

F.J. Perales, R.B. Fisher, and T.B. Moeslund (Eds.): AMDO 2012, LNCS 7378, pp. 239–249, 2012.
© Springer-Verlag Berlin Heidelberg 2012

phones and video consoles, people have access to one or more devices equipped with an accelerometer, for example, the Apple iPhone or the Nintendo Wiimote. These devices with wireless capability offer new possibilities to interact and to be used in a wide range of applications, such as domestic appliances control, home automation, special education, rehabilitation, augmented reality and sports training.

The present work focuses on a sport training system that recognizes 3D gestures by analyzing the Wiimote's accelerometer information. The application uses 3D technology to represent game scenes and simulate the physical behavior of virtual objects that can interact with the ball. User movements are compared to previously generated templates. The developed tools can help sports trainers to detect the weaknesses and strengths of each user. Particularly the system is instantiated in a tennis training application that is called *WiiSimTennis*.

The paper is organized as follows: section 2 reviews the literature on sport training systems; section 3 describes the gestures recognition process of our system; section 4 describes the system architecture and interaction; section 5 presents some experiments and results with the tennis training application and finally section 6 presents the conclusions and future work.

## 2    Related Work

Successful performances in sports games require not only efficient and correctly executed techniques but also a high level of perceptual skills. Müller et al [7] comment that sports training aims at minimizing the mistakes to improve the performance-precision relationship. This demands a complete analysis of the athlete's movements, who will then receive a feedback on how to improve the technique or information to compare his or her performance with previous evaluations.

To be able to evaluate specific stimuli is necessary to be able to control the training conditions. Commonly video presentations or presentations on natural size screens are used. In [8] the behavior of the handball archers was analyzed. In [9] video is used to carry out visual searches of a football player's strategies. Clearly, the training systems based on three-dimensional virtual environments are better than the video-based, since they give more versatility in the creation of scenes and situations for training [10][11][12][13].

Trained user immersion is enhanced by using a device such as the Wiimote and by virtually recreating the user gestures on a screen [14]. Siemon et al [15] show that sports like bowling (or tennis) can take advantage of this kind of virtual reality systems to obtain a basic trainer. Although the player performance is not analyzed in a professional way, the user receives information across the graphs on the screen (for example, a curve of his forehand shot or the speed achieved in his service). Principally the beginners can obtain improvements in their performance by receiving feedback in every shot and trying it repeatedly.

## 3    Gesture Recognition

The Wiimote is a part of the Nintendo Wii video games console, but it can be used as a PC input device by means of a Bluetooth connection. This device is a wireless control with form of remote control which is hold by the user's hand. It allows the detection of movement in the 3D space. It includes an accelerometer that gives accelerations in three ordinal axes every certain interval of time. It also includes an infrared built-in camera that can provide information about its position, including the distance up to the PC. However, to use the position information, a more complex configuration is needed not being viable for the recognition of gestures in general cases. For this reason our work is only based on the accelerometer information.

The typical movements in sports, for example a drive or reverse shot in tennis, are what we can call a gesture. In this work we represent a shot or gesture as a movement in a certain direction in the three-dimensional space with a certain speed.

In this section we explain the fundamentals of the gestures recognition software module of our system, where the gesture concept means a sport shot or a movement.

## 3.1    Gesture Description

The information provided by the Wiimote accelerometer must be compiled and interpreted. The gestures realized with the Wiimote are described with three acceleration values $(a_x, a_y, a_z)$ at every instant of time, each value corresponding to acceleration in $X$, $Y$ and $Z$ axis respectively.

There exists more than one way of representing it. One way could be a 3D path that recreates the movement performed by the user in the 3D space. To obtain a realistic curve, additional information such as position and initial orientation are necessary, but the results are not always the desired ones. Several works such as in [16] propose to carry out an estimation of the position in the 3D by means of Kalman's filters. This is effective to follow the path of the Wiimote, but fails to detect the user's movement.

In this work, we interpret the Wiimote data as three acceleration curves $Ax$, $Ay$ and $Az$, corresponding to accelerations in $X$, $Y$ and $Z$ axis respectively at each instant.

It is easy to see that the curves of a gesture can be performed with different amplitude and different time or speed by different users. Leong et al. [17] observed that for a particular gesture (e.g. to draw a circle) different speeds of execution were obtained for different users and small variations were found in samples done by the same person. Due to this, the number of obtained values increases if the gesture is performed slower, whereas the number decreases if the gesture is faster than the average speed. These facts can obstruct the compilation of information and the later comparison of two gestures.

To solve the differences in speed, the sequence of information is normalized in a normalized interval of time equal to the total duration of the gesture. We follow the one proposed by Leong et al. [17] that use 50 values for the representation of every gesture. The fixed-size vector of $(a_x, a_y, a_z)$ data is obtained by linear interpolation, and is what we call a sample. Fig. 1 shows an example of the two sets of X acceleration data: the original one with 40 values and the re-sampled or normalized one with 50 values. It can be seen that re-sampling preserves the curve of information of the original movement.

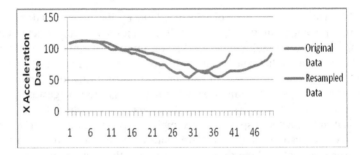

**Fig. 1.** Example with the original acceleration in x-axis (from time 0 to 40) and the normalized information (from time 0 to 50)

To obtain a more precise representation for every gesture we use the idea of templates such as Leong et al proposed in [17]. A template is built from a set of samples corresponding to a certain type of movement. The process of creation of a template follows the following steps. First several samples of the movement recreated by the user must be obtained; then these samples are normalized by re-sampling; finally the $Ax$, $Ay$ and $Az$ curves of the template are built with the mean value of the normalized samples at each instant of time. Fig. 2 shows an example of template built from five samples.

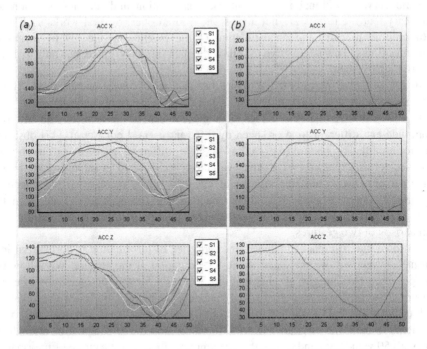

**Fig. 2.** Example of a template built from five samples: (a) Graphic of X, Y and Z accelerations of the five samples; (b) Graphic of X, Y and Z accelerations of the template

This template generation process can be seen as a stage of training of the system. In our system a database of the different tennis shots are built at prior. In Fig. 3 the process of creation of templates from N samples is shown. To recognize a new gesture, the vector or gesture sample is compared against the stored templates by means of the *Dynamic Time Warping* algorithm which is presented in the next section.

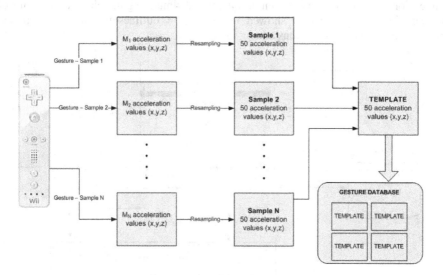

**Fig. 3.** Template generation process

## 3.2    Gestures Comparison

The *Dynamic Time Warping (DTW)* is an algorithm to measure similarity between two sequences that can change in time or speed [18]. This algorithm has gained popularity for being extremely efficient, as can be seen in [19][20][21]. It minimizes the effects of change and distortion in time, allowing elastic transformations of the series in order to detect similar forms with different phases. With an adjustment it can also be used in multidimensional gestures [22].

The utilization of the *DTW* algorithm is a correlation strategy to find the most similar template to an unknown gesture. The *DTW* determines a measure of similarity between them. The following three *DTW* values are computed between the new sample $N$ obtained from the Wiimote data and every template $T_i$ stored in the database: $DTW(N^{Ax}, T_i^{Ax})$, $DTW(N^{Ay}, T_i^{Ay})$ and $DTW(N^{Az}, T_i^{Az})$.

Senin [18] proposes to analyze the *DTW* values of every axis and if every value does not overcome a certain threshold of similarity, one concludes that the two gestures are similar.

If a new sample is compared with several templates it can happen that more than one template fulfill this previous condition. In this case the most similar template is the nearest one based on the Euclidean distance between every pair of tuplas ($N^{ax}$, $N^{ay}$, $N^{az}$) and ($T_i^{ax}$, $T_i^{ay}$, $T_i^{az}$).

## 4    System Description

### 4.1    System Architecture

The developed system is formed by different components for every task such as obtaining data from the Wiimote, recognizing sport shots, visualizing of the three-dimensional scene of the virtual environment and simulating the physical behavior of virtual objects. The graphic showed in the Fig. 4 outlines the above mentioned components and the interactions among them.

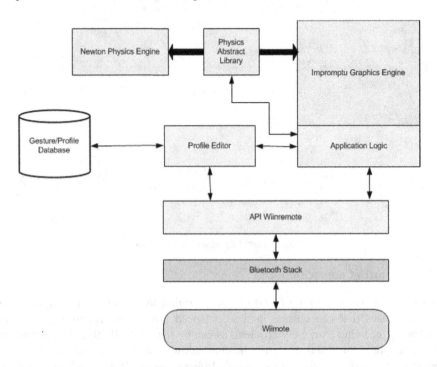

**Fig. 4.** System architecture

The system is based on an event-guided architecture over our Impromptu Graphics Engine [23]. This graphical engine provides a complete support to easily create and visualize three-dimensional scenes. For every scene a set of 3D models was prior created and a graphic resource administrator loads them at runtime. The profile edition module administrates the user profile, allowing the creation and edition of shots and templates. Fig. 5 shows an example of a tennis shot introduced by the user. To simulate the physical behavior of the virtual objects that compose the scene the Newton physics engine called Newton Game Dynamics [24] is used across an abstraction level that we define in [25], which allows a transparent communication between both software packages. The condition of every physic primitive is defined by its position and orientation in a certain time. The physical engine is the manager that calculates the new condition of the objects and updates it. The graphical engine requests this information for every object and applies the new values of position and orientation visualizing them on the screen.

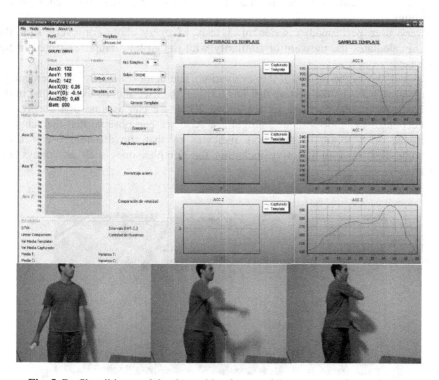

**Fig. 5.** Profile edition module: three video frames of the sequence of a tennis shot

### 4.2    Interaction

The application supports different modes of use and interaction: the training mode and the obstacles mode. In the training mode (Fig. 6) the user can execute different shots being able to check a series of statistical information as speed and place of rebound. It can compare his current training condition with a database of historical statistics. It can also compare his shot with a different user profile (for example one of a trainer or a professional tennis player). In the obstacles mode (Fig. 7) the application raises different fictitious situations with virtual objects to allow the training of directional shots. In these scenes the player must knock down objects in specific positions or succeed shots in different strategic points.

## 5    Experiments and Results

Our system is instantiated in a tennis training application that is called *WiiSimTennis*. To test the application we experiment with ten different users which already have experience in the use of the Wiimote. The experiment consists in the practice of five tennis shot: forehand, backhand, volley, smash and service [26].

The system was trained with 10 users to create a gestures database. The profile was also stored to uniquely identify each user. The first test consists in comparing a user shot with the gestures in his profile. This test evaluates the consistency of the algorithm.

Every user performed a series of 3 tests of every shot. For every shot the system calculates the measure of similarity with the gesture templates stored in the database.

Table 1 shows the results of this evaluation. The numbers indicate the percentage of similarity between the gesture that has fulfilled the user and the existing one in the database. As all the percentages are above 70 % we can assume that the system can recognize the shot without ambiguities. Also we can observe that the range of difference of 5 % in all the shots indicates us that the different users repeat the same shot in a similar way including the complex ones such as volleys and smash.

**Fig. 6.** Screen capture of the *WiiSimTennis* application: training mode

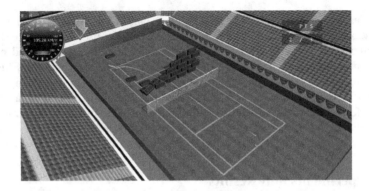

**Fig. 7.** Screen capture of the *WiiSimTennis* application: obstacles mode

**Table 1.** Percentage of similarity between the different tennis shots performed by ten different users with the existing template in the database

|       | Forehand | Backhand | Volley | Smash | Service |
|-------|----------|----------|--------|-------|---------|
| U1    | 84%      | 83%      | 78%    | 80%   | 81%     |
| U2    | 81%      | 81%      | 81%    | 80%   | 81%     |
| U3    | 83%      | 81%      | 82%    | 79%   | 80%     |
| U4    | 83%      | 80%      | 79%    | 78%   | 78%     |
| U5    | 82%      | 79%      | 80%    | 79%   | 80%     |
| U6    | 84%      | 80%      | 81%    | 82%   | 80%     |
| U7    | 85%      | 82%      | 79%    | 81%   | 79%     |
| U8    | 83%      | 81%      | 78%    | 77%   | 81%     |
| U9    | 82%      | 80%      | 79%    | 78%   | 82%     |
| U10   | 80%      | 80%      | 79%    | 80%   | 81%     |
| **Mean** | **83%** | **81%** | **80%** | **80%** | **80%** |

We conducted a second test, where an experienced tennis player was chosen as reference. The remaining nine participants made each kind of tennis shot and the system tried to identify them. In Table 2 we show a confusion matrix with the obtained results

**Table 2.** Number of movements detected by the system according to the ones performed by the users

|           |          | Actual Class | | | | | |
|-----------|----------|--------------|----------|--------|-------|---------|---------|
|           |          | *Forehand*   | *Backhand* | *Volley* | *Smash* | *Service* | *unknown* |
| **Predicted class** | *Forehand* | **9** | 0 | 0 | 0 | 0 | 0 |
|           | *Backhand* | 0 | **8** | 1 | 0 | 0 | 0 |
|           | *Volley*   | 0 | 2 | **7** | 0 | 0 | 0 |
|           | *Smash*    | 0 | 0 | 0 | **6** | 2 | 1 |
|           | *Service*  | 0 | 0 | 0 | 2 | **7** | 0 |

The results seem acceptable. Some false positives that arise are "reasonable." For example, a *volley* and *backhand* are quite similar between them, so is the "service" and "smash". As shown in Table 1, the similarity is high in any situation and is true for both cases. When "false negatives" appear, the system applies a default movement.

Some other data can be extracted from the system. The percentage of similarity regarding a professional tennis player can indicate the level of tennis experience for each user. Additionally, these values can be analyzed to know the evolution of the user performance over the time.

# 6     Conclusions and Future Work

This paper presents a sport training system instantiated in a tennis training game called *WiiSimTennis*. The user interacts by means of the Wiimote in the 3D environment that represents the scene of the game and includes virtual object with Newton physic dynamics. The system can recognize the different user shots and presents information such as speed, place of bound and comparisons with historical information. Provided that the process of generation and validation of gestures is generic the system is applicable to a family of applications. Besides the tennis training application our system can be easily instantiated to other sports such as golf, bowling, basket and also a rehabilitation application. The instantiation implies the definition of the adapted 3D scene and the specific training of the application.

At present we are adjusting the system to be able to use a more complete input device such as the Microsoft Kinect.

As a future work we mention the inclusion of biomechanics to the system.

**Acknowledgments.** This research was partially supported by project A1/037910/11 FRIVIG. Formación de Recursos Humanos e Investigación en el Área de Visión por Computador e Informática Gráfica, granted by MAEC-AECID (Programa de Cooperación Interuniversitaria e Investigación Científica entre España e Iberoamérica).

# References

1. Bowman, D.A., Kruijff, E., LaViola, J.J., Poupyrev, I.: 3D User Interfaces: Theory and Practice. Addison Wesley Longman Publishing Co., Inc., Redwood City (2004)
2. Perrin, S., Cassinelli, A., Ishikawa, M.: Gesture recognition using laser-based tracking system. In: FGR, pp. 541–546 (2004)
3. Turk, M.: Gesture recognition. Handbook of Virtual Environments, pp. 223–238 (2001)
4. Vafadar, M., Behrad, A.: Human Hand Gesture Recognition Using Motion Orientation Histogram for Interaction of Handicapped Persons with Computer. In: Elmoataz, A., Lezoray, O., Nouboud, F., Mammass, D. (eds.) ICISP 2008. LNCS, vol. 5099, pp. 378–385. Springer, Heidelberg (2008)
5. Caridakis, G., Karpouzis, K., Pateritsas, C., Drosopoulos, A., Stafylopatis, A., Kollias, S.: Hand trajectory-based gesture recognition using self-organizing feature maps and markov models. In: 2008 IEEE International Conference on Multimedia & Expo., ICME (2008)
6. Ruffaldi, E., Filippeschi, A., Avizzano, C.A., Bardy, B., Gopher, D., Bergamasco, M.: Feedback, Affordances and Accelerators for Training Sports in Virtual Environments. Presence, Teleoperations and virtual environments 20(1), 33–46 (2011)
7. Müller, H., Schumacher, B., Blischke, K., Daugs, R.: Optimierung sportmotorischen Technik-Trainings durch computergestutzte Videosysteme. In: Perl, J. (ed.) Sport und Informatik, pp. 37–47. Hofmann, Schorndorf (1990)
8. Schorer, J.: Eine Studie zur Identifikation, den Mechanismen und Entwicklung senso-motorischer Expertise. Dissertation. Universität Heidelberg (2006)

9. Savelsbergh, G.J.P., Williams, A.M., Van der Kamp, J., Ward, P.: Visual search, anticipation and expertise in soccer goalkeepers. Journal of Sports Sciences 20, 279–287 (2002)
10. Liu, X., Sun, J., He, Y., Liu, Y., Cao, L.: Overview of Virtual Reality Apply to Sports. JCIT: Journal of Convergence Information Technology 6(12), 1–7 (2011)
11. Bideau, B., Kulpa, R., Vignais, N., Brault, S., Multon, F., Craig, C.: Using Virtual Reality to Analyze Sports Performance. IEEE Computer Graphics and Applications 30(2), 14–21 (2010)
12. Ruffaldi, E., Filippeschi, A., Avizzano, C.A., Bardy, B., Gopher, D., Bergamasco, M.: Feedback, Affordances and Accelerators for Training Sports in Virtual Environments. Presence, Teleoperations and virtual environments 20(1), 33–46 (2011)
13. Christian, J., Krieger, H., Holzinger, A., Behringer, R.: Virtual and Mixed Reality Interfaces for e-Training: Examples of Applications in Light Aircraft Maintenance. In: Stephanidis, C. (ed.) HCI 2007, Part III. LNCS, vol. 4556, pp. 520–529. Springer, Heidelberg (2007)
14. Tanaka, K.: Virtual Training System using feedback for sport skill learning. Int. J. of Computer Science in Sport. 8(2), 1–7 (2009)
15. Siemon, A., Wegener, R., Bader, F., Hieber, T., Schmid, U.: Video Games can Improve Performance in Sports. An Empirical Study with Wii Sports Bowling. In: Wallhoff, F., Rigol, G. (Hrsg.) Proceedings of the KI 2009 Workshop on Human-Machine-Interaction (2009)
16. Chow, Y.: 3D Spatial Interaction with the Wii Remote for Head-Mounted Display Virtual Reality. World Academy of Science, Engineering and Technology 50, 377–383 (2009)
17. Leong, T., Lai, J., Panza, J., Pong, P., Hong, J.: Wii Want to Write: An Accelerometer Based Gesture Recognition System. In: International Conference on Recent and Emerging Advanced Technologies in Engineering, pp. 4–7. Carnegie Mellon University (2009)
18. Senin, P.: Dynamic time warping algorithm review. Technical Report CSDL-08-04, Department of Information and Computer Sciences. University of Hawaii, Honolulu, Hawaii 96822 (2008)
19. Niezen, G., Hancke, G.: Gesture recognition as ubiquitous input for mobile phones. In: International Workshop on Devices that Alter Perception (DAP 2008), Conjunction with Ubicomp (2008)
20. Liu, J., Wang, Z., Zhong, L., Wickramasuriya, J., Vasudevan, V.: uWave: Accelerometer based Personalized Gesture Recognition and Its Applications. In: IEEE PerCom (2009)
21. Wilson, D.H., Wilson, A.: Gesture Recognition using the XWand. Technical Report CMURI-TR-04-57. CMU Robotics Institute (2004)
22. Holt, G.A., Reinders, M.J.T., Hendriks, E.A.: Multi-Dimensional Dynamic Time Warping for Gesture Recognition. In: Thirteenth Annual Conference of the Advanced School for Computing and Imaging (2007)
23. D'amato, J.P., García Bauza, C.: Simulación de Escenarios Tridimensionales Dinámicos, Grade thesis dissertation. Universidad Nacional del Centro de la Pcia de Buenos Aires, Tandil, Argentina (2004)
24. Newton Game Dynamics - Physics Engine, http://newtondynamics.com/forum/newton.php
25. García Bauza, C., Lazo, M., Vénere, M.: Incorporación de comportamiento físico en motores gráficos. In: Mecánica Computacional, vol. XXVII, pp. 3023–3039 (2008)
26. Wikipedia, Tennis Shots, http://en.wikipedia.org/wiki/Tennis_shots

# Real-Time 4D Reconstruction of Human Motion

József Hapák, Zsolt Jankó, and Dmitry Chetverikov

MTA SZTAKI and Eötvös Loránd Univeristy
Budapest, Hungary
http://vision.sztaki.hu

**Abstract.** A studio for real-time 4D reconstruction of moving actors and deformable objects has been recently created at the Computer and Automation Research Institute of the Hungarian Academy of Sciences (MTA SZTAKI). The studio uses 13 synchronised, calibrated high-resolution video cameras and a GPU to build dynamic 3D models providing free-viewpoint video in real-time. We give a brief overview of advanced studios operating around the world, then discuss the GPU implementation details of the reconstruction pipeline. Finally, a performance comparison of the offline and real-time versions of the system is given.

## 1 Introduction

In this paper, we present the GPU-based spatio-temporal (or 4D) reconstruction studio created by the Geometric Modelling and Computer Vision Lab of MTA SZTAKI. Recently, we have reported on the main operation principles of the original, off-line version of our studio [4]. In the offline mode, the video data is stored on disc before being processed. The main contribution of this paper is a description of the fast GPU implementation of the algorithms. This development allows for the real-time operation of the studio: a dynamic 3D model of the moving actor is built from videos on-line without storing the video data. The GPU-based solution provides the capability to view the dynamic model from any viewpoint during capture, called free viewpoint video [1].

A typical spatio-temporal reconstruction studio is a room with uniform background and appropriate illumination, equipped with multiple calibrated and synchronised video cameras. Its main objectives are capturing videos of a scene from multiple viewpoints and creating dynamic 3D models of articulated objects moving in the scene. The main application domains of 4D studios are computer games, interactive media, film production, and motion analysis in different areas. TV production of sports events also uses similar techniques.

A number of studios exist in some countries of Western Europe and in the United States. The studios share main operation principles but differ in technical solutions. Below, we briefly discuss a few advanced 4D studios. To save space, we will refer the reader to the web pages of the projects, where relevant publications, demos and applications can be found.

Most systems mentioned in this paper use the visual hull [7] as the initial volumetric 3D model. Images are first segmented into object and background. Object silhouettes obtained by the cameras are then back-projected to 3D space as the generalised cones whose intersection gives the visual hull, a bounding geometry of the actual 3D object.

F.J. Perales, R.B. Fisher, and T.B. Moeslund (Eds.): AMDO 2012, LNCS 7378, pp. 250–259, 2012.

Using more cameras results in a finer volumetric model, but some concave details may be lost anyway.

The volumetric visual hull is usually transformed into a surface mesh which is textured by selecting the most appropriate view for each unit of the mesh based on visibility, or by combining several views. The mesh is typically obtained from the hull using the standard Marching Cubes algorithm [8], while texturing techniques show greater variety. As the local geometry of the visual hull may significantly differ from the true one, various methods are used to enhance the shape.

Our project is related to similar projects at INRIA [3,10], MIT [9], MPI Informatik [11] and University of Surrey [12]. An essential difference between our approach and INRIA, MIT and MPII is that they go beyond independent frame-by-frame modelling we currently use. They take advantage of the continuity of motion and exploit the high redundancy of video sequences. Working in the spatio-temporal domain results in better geometry and texturing, but needs much more computing power.

In the 4D studio created by the Computer Graphics Group at the Massachusetts University of Technology, USA, the dynamic reconstruction process is initialised by a high-quality static 3D model obtained by a laser scanner. Articulated mesh animation from multiview silhouettes [9] is achieved using a simplified skeleton model of human body. Manual correction is applied to improve the mesh. The skeleton model facilitates motion transfer from human to model and animation of 3D human models.

Similarly to the Computer Graphics Group of MIT, the Graphics, Vision and Video Group [11] of the Max Planck Institut Informatik, Germany, also uses a laser-scanned shape to initialise the dynamic reconstruction process. However, the approach [11] does not apply skeleton model of human body. Instead, feature points detected in surface texture are used to support handling the shape deformations. Similar to INRIA, photo-consistency [6] is used for fine tuning of the result.

The Centre for Vision, Speech and Signal Processing at the University of Surrey, UK, has developed an advanced 4D studio [12]. The initial 3D model obtained from the silhouettes is enhanced using shape-from-shading [13]. A skeleton model of human body is applied. The software developed at the Centre provides free-viewpoint video, that is, allows one to view the recorded event from any viewpoint during video capture.

The Institute of Computer Science (FORTH, Crete, Greece) has created a smaller studio [2] for smaller articulated objects such as human hands. The cameras and lights are set around a table. All processing steps are implemented on a GPU, which provides real-time operation for relatively slow hand motion. The project primarily aims at markerless hand pose recovery in 3D for applications such as human-computer interaction and virtualised reality. We aim at reconstructing the motion of complete human body, which requires a different setup and GPU-based solutions.

In the next section, we present the main hardware and software components of the real-time 4D reconstruction studio. The section concludes with performance evaluation of the real-time reconstruction in terms of speed compare to the offline implementation [4]. The experience we gained to date, including the current problems and their possible remedies, is discussed in section 3, where our future plans are also presented.

## 2    4D Reconstruction Studio at SZTAKI

Our 4D reconstruction studio is a 'green box': green curtains and carpet provide homo-
geneous background. The massive, firm steel frame is a cylinder with dodecagon base.
The size of the frame is limited by the size of the room. The diameter is around five
meters; originally, a seven-meter studio was planned. The frame carries 12 CCD video
cameras (JAI CB-200GE) placed uniformly around the scene and one additional camera
on the top in the middle. Figure 1 shows an interior panoramic view and a sketch of the
studio.

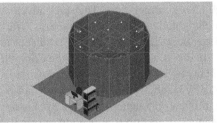

**Fig. 1.** A panoramic view (left) and a sketch (right) of the 4D studio

The cameras are equipped with wide-angle lenses (L-SV-0814H) to cope with relatively close views. This necessitates careful calibration against radial distortion. The
resolution of the cameras is $1624 \times 1236$ pixels; they operate at 25 fps and use GigE
(Gigabit Ethernet). The studio uses seven conventional PCs: Intel i5-760 CPU, 2GB
RAM (8GB in the main PC). Each of the PCs but one handles two cameras. Innovative
lighting has been designed for the studio to achieve better illumination. The graphics
card is NVIDIA GTX 580 with 1536 MB memory.

The studio has two main software blocks: the image acquisition software for video
recording and the 3D reconstruction software for creation of dynamic 3D models. The
image acquisition software configures and calibrates the cameras and selects a subset
of the cameras for video recording. The easy-to-use, robust and efficient Z. Zhang's
method [14] is used for intrinsic and extrinsic camera calibration and calculation of the
parameters of radial distortion.

The images captured by the cameras are transmitted to the PCs at full resolution.
Since the full-resolution images are too large to process in real time, in the real-time
mode they are always resized. (Optionally, in the offline mode they can be resized as
well.) In section 2.3, we will discuss how the processing speed depends on image size.
The image format conversion and size reduction are performed on each PC separately
for the cameras connected to the PC.

The main steps of the 3D reconstruction process are as follows: image segmentation
into foreground and background; creation of volumetric model using the Visual Hull algorithm; transforming the volumetric model into triangulated mesh using the Marching

Cubes algorithm; texturing, that is, adding texture to the triangulated mesh. Below, we discuss the first three steps as geometry processing, the last step as appearance processing. Figure 2 illustrates the overall workflow of the GPU-based processing.

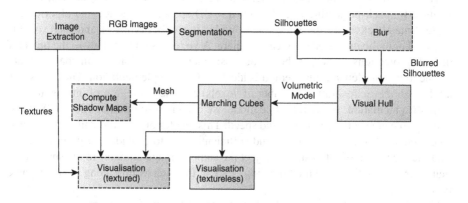

**Fig. 2.** The workflow of the GPU-based processing

## 2.1  Geometry Processing

We use a shape-from-silhouettes technique to obtain a volumetric model of the dynamic shape. A novel image segmentation method has been developed for this project. The method uses the spherical colour representation that improves robustness to illumination changes. Given the $R,G,B$ values of a pixel, these coordinates are defined as

$$\rho = \sqrt{R^2 + G^2 + B^2}$$
$$\theta = \arctan\left(\frac{G}{R}\right) \tag{1}$$
$$\phi = \arcsin\left(\frac{\sqrt{R^2 + G^2}}{\sqrt{R^2 + G^2 + B^2}}\right)$$

The angles $\theta, \phi$ are less sensitive to illumination changes, shadow and shading. (See [4] for details.)

Difference between the reference background image and the processed image is calculated pixel-by-pixel and stored in a greyscale difference image. In the GPU, the reference background and the processed images are stacked in a 3D array. Each processor of the GPU calculates and thresholds the difference for a pixel. The threshold can be tuned in runtime. To speed up the operation, we use the texture samplers of the GPU as their caches facilitate efficient access to the data.

A surface reconstructed from a binary silhouette mask tends to be rugged. This effect can be reduced by either blurring the mask or smoothing the volumetric model. Since 3D smoothing is costly, we blur the mask before back-projecting the silhouettes. In the offline mode, this operation is straightforward. In the real-time mode, we use a separable box filter. A kernel run by the GPU processes a pixel. The size of the kernel cannot be modified in runtime; it can only be modified by re-compiling the program. This allows the compiler to optimise the generated code. The caches of the texture samplers play here a greater role since during the filtering the same data is accessed several times.

The volumetric Visual Hull [7] is defined as the intersection of the generalised cones obtained by back-projecting the silhouettes to 3D space. In practice, the algorithm is implemented backwards: the 3D space is divided into cubes (voxels), and each voxel is projected onto the image plane of each camera. A voxel is said to belong to the object if all of its projections are within the silhouettes; otherwise, it belongs to the background.

Due to its parallelism, this method is ideal for GPU implementation. The key issues are the volumetric resolution (number of voxels) and the 3D region of interest to constrain the calculation. In the real-time mode, we use the resolution of $128 \times 128 \times 128$ voxels to balance between quality and speed. This resolution is sufficiently high to produce models of acceptable quality and sufficiently low to provide fast processing. To limit the 3D region of interest, we project the camera image domains to 3D space, take their intersection, then find the bounding block of the intersection along the coordinate axes.

Using the inherently parallel Marching Cubes algorithm [8], we transform the volumetric model into a triangulated surface model whose visualisation is supported by video cards. For real-time operation, we have tailored an existing CUDA-optimised solution to our needs. To increase speed, we utilise the Graphics Interoperability of CUDA with the OpenGL graphics library. In the memory of the video card, the result of the Marching Cubes appears as a Vertex Buffer Object easy to visualise by OpenGL.

## 2.2  Appearance Processing

In the offline mode, the algorithm for texturing the triangulated surface [5] minimises a cost function based on triangle visibility and texture smoothness.

Texturing was the most difficult part of the processing pipeline to implement on a GPU. Contrary to the offline mode, one cannot generate a texture atlas in real time because of limitations in processing time and resources. The program applies a pixel-wise texturing procedure that uses the input images in a direct way. Instead of utilising CUDA, our implementation is based on the graphics API of OpenGL, more specifically, on its shading language, GLSL.

To calculate the colour of a given pixel, we have first to decide if the point is visible to a given camera at all. The visibility problem is solved using the shadow maps. Viewing the cameras as lighting sources, we create the corresponding shadow maps. In this way, occlusion can be handled by shadowing. A 'shadowed' pixel is not visible to a camera.

Two methods for pixel colour calculation were implemented; the final outcome is a combination of them. Both methods are based on mapping the input images onto the surface model from the viewpoint of the camera.

In the first method, the normal vector of the surface determines the camera from which the pixel is best visible. (The vector 'points' at the camera.) Sampling for the pixel colour calculation is done in the image captured by that camera. In practice, however, this method yields a very noisy result because of drastic switches between cameras.

The second texturing method obtains much smoother result by selecting the cameras closest to the current virtual viewpoint of the user, as illustrated in figure 3. We use the images of the three closest cameras. Because of the occlusion problem, the selection can only be done on the pixel level, since the visibility is determined at this level. To speed up the operation, on the CPU we sort the cameras depending on how close they are to the current viewpoint of the user. The result is passed to the fragment shader that uses it along with the occlusion data to attempt selecting the three closest cameras.

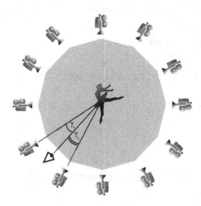

**Fig. 3.** Camera selection for texturing

If the attempt is successful, the virtual viewing direction of the user is expressed as a linear combination of the viewing vectors of the three cameras. The coefficients are used as weights for the sampling of pixel colour from the three images. If the user's viewpoint coincides with that of a camera, the image of that camera is only used; otherwise, pixels of the three best images are interpolated. If the attempt fails, the first method is applied. This can only happen when too few cameras are used, or when the pixel is not sufficiently visible. The second texturing method is summarised in Algorithm 1.

Figure 4 shows a sample input image and the reconstructed textureless 3D model viewed from a different direction, to illustrate the capablity of free-viewpoint video. Figure 5 shows another sample input image and the reconstructed textured 3D model placed in a virtual environment.

## 2.3   Performance of the GPU Implementation

In the offline mode, the complete recorded data of each camera is stored on a separate disc of a computer. The reconstruction program needs about 30 minutes to process a ten-second video at full resolution. That is, processing a multiframe (13 synchronised images) and creating a single, instantaneous 3D shape requires over 7000 milliseconds. A relevant part of this time is taken by disc operations.

---

**Algorithm 1.** Texturing

---

**Require:**
  $n$: number of cameras,
  $I_i, i \in [1..n]$: input images,
  $P_i, c_i, i \in [1..n]$: projection matrix, direction of camera $i$,
  $P, v$: projection matrix, direction of current view
**Ensure:**
  $I_{\text{out}}$: output image

  **for all** pixel $u \in I_{\text{out}}$ **do**
    /* Compute angles between cameras and current view */
    $\gamma_i := \cos^{-1}(\frac{v^T c_i}{\|v\|\|c_i\|}), i \in [1..n]$
    /* Select 3 best cameras */
    $i_1, i_2, i_3 := \arg\min_{i \in [1..n]}(\gamma_i)$
    /* Compose $3 \times 3$ transformation matrix */
    $B := [c_{i_1}, c_{i_2}, c_{i_3}]$
    /* Compute weights */
    $w := B^{-1} v$
    /* Normalise weights */
    $w := \frac{w}{w[1] + w[2] + w[3]}$
    /* Compute 3D point and projections */
    $X := \text{backproject}_P(u)$
    $u_{i_j} := P_{i_j} X, j = 1, 2, 3$
    /* Compute colour of current pixel */
    $I_{\text{out}}(u) := w[1] I_{i_1}(u_{i_1}) + w[2] I_{i_2}(u_{i_2}) + w[3] I_{i_3}(u_{i_3})$
  **end for**

---

**Fig. 4.** A sample input image and the reconstructed textureless 3D model

**Fig. 5.** A sample input image and the reconstructed textured 3D model in a virtual environment

In the GPU mode, only two multiframes are stored in the memory of the main computer. Table 1 presents the processing times, in milliseconds, for the stages of the GPU-based reconstruction. In the table, 'Seg.' is Segmentation, 'Blur.' Blurring, 'VH' Visual Hull, 'MC' Marching Cubes, 'SM' Shadow Maps, and 'Tex.' Texturing. Note that the processing time of segmentation includes transmitting the data to the GPU memory; the short transmission time was not measured separately.

**Table 1.** Processing times of the GPU-based reconstruction (in ms)

| Resolution | Seg. | Blur. | VH | MC | SM | Tex. | Total |
|---|---|---|---|---|---|---|---|
| 320 × 244 | 5.1 | 5.7 | 1.5 | 1.6 | 1.5 | 1.5 | 16.9 |
| 480 × 364 | 11.9 | 12.8 | 1.6 | 1.5 | 1.5 | 1.5 | 30.7 |
| 640 × 484 | 20.5 | 22.5 | 1.6 | 1.5 | 1.5 | 1.5 | 49.0 |
| 1624 × 1236 | 129.1 | 147.8 | 1.6 | 1.5 | 1.5 | 1.5 | 282.9 |

The most time-consuming part of the pipeline is image processing, namely, segmentation and blurring. Here, the computational load grows linearly with the number of pixels, while for the 3D operations it mainly depends on the number of voxels which is fixed ($128^3$).

Sending the data from the cameras to the computer takes 40 ms per multiframe. Adding this delay to the reconstruction time, we see that for image resolution of 320 × 244 and 480 × 364 pixels the latency is less than 2 frames at 25 fps video rate; for 640 × 484, the latency is about 2 frames. A latency of $1 - 2$ frames is practically real-time, and we observed that acceptable quality of reconstruction can still be achieved at the resolution of 480 × 364 pixels. In other words, our studio provides dynamic 3D reconstruction in real time.

# 3   Conclusion

We have presented the main current features of the 4D reconstruction studio being developed at the MTA SZTAKI. As far as the studio's hardware is concerned, we are basically satisfied with its operation and performance. The quality of texturing depends on the precision of surface geometry which is not perfect. The Visual Hull and the Marching Cube algorithms may yield imprecise surface normals, which may in turn deteriorate the calculation of visibility and lead to incorrect texture mapping. Along with some concave shape details, texture details may be lost or distorted. In addition, the frame-by-frame processing may lead to quick small-size temporal variations in texture called texture flickering, which are minor but still perceived by human eye.

Our reconstruction system is now capable of producing dynamic 3D models in real time. Besides traditional applications such as computer games and movies, real-time modelling can be useful in another area: it has the potential of extending telecommunication to a new dimension. During a 'video call', one would be able to see not only a video stream of the conversation partner, but the partner's 3D model as well. With a suitable facility (e.g., a 3D monitor or a CAVE), dynamic 3D models would add more realism to the conversation.

We are now working on improving the quality of the model. This includes better segmentation as well as better shape and texturing, in particular, by utilising the spatio-temporal coherence. As a part of this plan, we are developing a program for interactive correction of the triangulated mesh, which will result in better shape and consistent handling of topological changes. Such programs are used by other studios as well, e.g., at the MIT.

**Acknowledgments.** This work was supported by the NKTH-OTKA grant CK 78409, by the European Union and the European Social Fund under the grant agreement TÁMOP 4.2.1./B-09/KMR-2010-0003, and by the HUNOROB project (HU0045, 0045/NA/2006-2/ÖP-9), a grant from Iceland, Liechtenstein and Norway through the EEA Financial Mechanism and the Hungarian National Development Agency.

# References

1. Carranza, J., Theobalt, C., Magnor, M., Seidel, H.: Free-viewpoint video of human actors. ACM Transactions on Graphics 22, 569–577 (2003)
2. FORTH ICS: From multiple views to textured 3D meshes: a GPU-powered approach (2010), www.ics.forth.gr/~argyros/research/gpu3Drec.htm
3. INRIA Rhône-Alpes: The Grid and Image Initiative (2012), http://grimage.inrialpes.fr/
4. Jankó, Z., Chetverikov, D., Hapák, J.: 4D Reconstruction Studio: Creating dynamic 3D models of moving actors. In: Proc. Sixth Hungarian Conference on Computer Graphics and Geometry, pp. 1–7 (2012), http://athos.vision.sztaki.hu/~mitya/publ/publ.html

5. Janko, Z., Pons, J.P.: Spatio-temporal image-based texture atlases for dynamic 3-D models. In: Proc. ICCV Workshop 3DIM 2009, pp. 1646–1653 (2009)
6. Kutulakos, K., Seitz, S.: A theory of shape by space carving. In: Proc. International Conference on Computer Vision, vol. 1, pp. 307–314 (1999)
7. Laurentini, A.: The visual hull concept for silhouette-based image understanding. IEEE Trans. Pattern Analysis and Machine Intelligence 16, 150–162 (1994)
8. Lorensen, W., Cline, H.: Marching cubes: A high resolution 3D surface construction algorithm. In: Proc. ACM SIGGRAPH, vol. 21, pp. 163–169 (1987)
9. MIT CGP: Dynamic Shape Capture and Articulated Shape Animation (2011), http://people.csail.mit.edu/drdaniel/
10. Morpheo Team: Capture and Analysis of Shapes in Motion (2012), http://morpheo.inrialpes.fr/
11. MPI Informatik: Dynamic Scene Reconstruction (2012), www.mpi-inf.mpg.de/~theobalt/
12. University of Surrey: SurfCap: Surface Motion Capture (2008), http://kahlan.eps.surrey.ac.uk/Personal/AdrianHilton/Research.html
13. Zhang, R., Tsai, P., Cryer, J., Shah, M.: Shape-from-shading: a survey. IEEE Trans. Pattern Analysis and Machine Intelligence 21, 690–706 (1999)
14. Zhang, Z.: A flexible new technique for camera calibration. IEEE Trans. Pattern Analysis and Machine Intelligence 22, 1330–1334 (2000)

# Human Context: Modeling Human-Human Interactions for Monocular 3D Pose Estimation

Mykhaylo Andriluka[1] and Leonid Sigal[2]

[1] Max Planck Institute for Informatics, Saarbrücken, Germany
[2] Disney Research, Pittsburgh, USA

**Abstract.** Automatic recovery of 3d pose of multiple interacting subjects from unconstrained monocular image sequence is a challenging and largely unaddressed problem. We observe, however, that by tacking the interactions explicitly into account, treating individual subjects as mutual "context" for one another, performance on this challenging problem can be improved. Building on this observation, in this paper we develop an approach that first jointly estimates 2d poses of people using multi-person extension of the pictorial structures model and then lifts them to 3d. We illustrate effectiveness of our method on a new dataset of dancing couples and challenging videos from dance competitions.

## 1   Introduction and Related Work

Human pose estimation and tracking have been a focal point of research in vision for well over 20 years. Despite much progress, most research focuses on estimation of pose for single well separated subjects. Occlusions and part-person ambiguities, that arise when two people are in close proximity to one another, make the problem of pose inference for interacting people a very challenging task. We argue that the knowledge of pose for one person, involved in an interaction, can help in resolving the pose ambiguities for the other, and vice versa; in other words, two people involved in an interaction (e.g., dance, handshake) can serve as mutual context for one another.

Recent tracking-by-detection (TbD) methods [1] have shown impressive results in real world scenarios, but with a few exceptions [2], are restricted to individual people performing simple cyclic activities (e.g., walking). Despite successes, TbD methods ignore *all* contextual information provided by the scene, objects and other people in it. As a result, in close interactions, independent pose estimates, ignorant of one another, compete and significantly degrade the overall performance. In contrast, [3, 4] argue that context is an important cue for resolving pose ambiguities, and show that human-object context improves pose estimation. Inspired by these recent advances, in this paper, we advocate the use of human-to-human context to facilitate 3d pose inference of multiple interacting people. This differs from prior work where interactions are either ignored [1, 5] or are only considered in the form of partial occlusions [6].

F.J. Perales, R.B. Fisher, and T.B. Moeslund (Eds.): AMDO 2012, LNCS 7378, pp. 260–272, 2012.

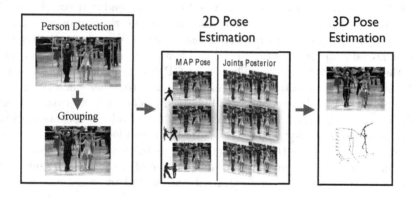

**Fig. 1.** Complete overview for the proposed method illustrated through an actual result obtained with our framework on a real competition dance sequence

**Contributions:** Our key contribution is an automatic framework for estimating 3d pose of interacting people performing complex activities from monocular observations. In developing this hierarchical framework we incorporate and analyze the role of modeling interactions, in the form of human-human context, at all levels. We introduce a novel multi-aspect flexible pictorial structure (MaFPS) model to facilitate joint 2d inference over pairs of people. The aspects encode the modes of interaction and result in non-tree structured model for which we introduce efficient approximate inference. We show results on challenging monocular sequences that contain dancing couples. The couples in our dataset (to be made publicly available) appear on cluttered background and are engaged in considerably more challenging and diverse set of motions than is typical of state-of-the-art methods (e.g., walking people in street scenes [1]).

## 2   Method

To achieve our goal of estimating 3d poses of interacting people in images of realistic complexity we leverage the recent progress in people detection, tracking and pose estimation. We rely on layered hierarchical framework that combines *bottom-up* and *top-down* information. At a high level, the approach can be expressed as a generative model for 3d human pose that combines rich *bottom-up* likelihood with a *top-down* prior:

$$p(Y_1, Y_2|I) \propto p(I|Y_1, Y_2)p(Y_1, Y_2),  \tag{1}$$

where $I$ is a set of image observations and $Y_i = \{y_i, d_i\}$ correspond to the parameters of 3d pose, $y_i$, and camera parameters required to project the pose into the image, $d_i$, for the $i$-th person. The inference amounts to searching for a *maximum a posteriori* (MAP) estimate of $Y_1$ and $Y_2$ with respect to the model in Eq. (1). In our model we incorporate interactions at different levels and take them into account both in the prior and likelihood terms.

The 3d pose prior, $p(Y_1, Y_2)$, captures the activity-induced correlations between poses of the two subjects and also models the relative orientation and position of the subjects with respect to one another. We rely on the Gaussian Process Dynamical Model (GPDM) [7] and learn parameters of the prior model from the motion capture data. The use of GPDM also allows us to learn the model of dynamics for stitching individual 3d poses together when tracking.

To avoid depth and observation ambiguities, typical in monocular inference, we define a rich likelihood model, $p(I|Y_1, Y_2)$, that encodes consistency between the projected 3d poses and 2d posteriors over body part locations. Characterizing 2d posteriors, and hence the likelihood, involves inference over 2d pose of the body that takes into account spatial configuration of parts and discriminatively learned part appearances. For further robustness and temporal consistency of 2d pose estimates, we condition the 2d model on position and scale of person detections.

Formally, we introduce a set of auxiliary variables $L_i = \{L_i^t\}$ which correspond to 2d configuration of the body and $D_i = \{D_i^t\}$ which correspond to position and scale of the $i$-th subject in each frame of the sequence; with $t$ being the frame index. We make a first-order Markov assumption over $D_i$ and assume conditional independence of 2d poses $L_i$ given positions of people in each frame so that:

$$p(L_1, L_2, D_1, D_2|I) = \prod_t p(L_1^t, L_2^t|D_1^t, D_2^t, I)$$
$$p(D_1^t, D_2^t|I)p(D_1^t, D_2^t|D_1^{t-1}, D_2^{t-1}). \tag{2}$$

The posterior, $p(L_1^t, L_2^t|D_1^t, D_2^t, I)$, on the right-hand side of the equation corresponds to the joint multi-aspect flexible pictorial structure (MaFPS) model for the two interacting subjects, which we describe in detail in Sec. 2.2.

To properly account for uncertainty in the 2d pose estimates we define the likelihood in Eq. (1) by evaluating the projection of the 3d pose under the posterior distribution given by Eq. (2). We define the likelihood of the pose sequence as:

$$p(I|Y_1, Y_2) = \prod_{t,n} p_{L1,n}(\pi_n(Y_1^t))p_{L2,n}(\pi_n(Y_2^t)), \tag{3}$$

where $p_{L1,n}$ denotes the marginal posterior distribution of the $n$-th body part of the configuration $L_1$ and $\pi_n(Y_1^t)$ corresponds to the projection of the $n$-th part into the image.

In order to obtain a MAP estimate for the posterior in Eq. (1) we adopt a multi-stage approach in which we first infer auxiliary variables $D_i$ and $L_i$ and then infer the 3d poses using local optimization, while keeping the auxiliary variables fixed. To further simplify inference we make an observation that in most sequences person detection and our tracking and grouping procedure are reliable enough to allow us to infer $D_i$ first by obtaining modes of $p(D_1^1, D_2^1)p(D_1^1, D_2^1|I) \prod_{t=2}^T p(D_1^t, D_2^t|I)p(D_1^t, D_2^t|D_1^{t-1}, D_2^{t-1})$ before inferring posterior over $L_i$ conditioned on $D_i$.

## 2.1   Person Detections and Grouping

As a first step towards inferring 3d poses of people we proceed with recovering positions of potentially interacting people and tracking them over time. This corresponds to estimating the values of the variables $D_1$ and $D_2$ in Eq. (2).

We employ the tracking-by-detection approach described in [1] and find tracks of people by connecting hypothesis obtained with the person detector [8]. We then identify pairs of tracks that maintain close proximity to one another over all frames, and use them as estimates for $D_1$ and $D_2$.

Denoting the set of people detection hypothesis in frame $t$ by $h^t$ and a track corresponding to a sequence of selected[1] hypothesis over $T$ frames by $h_\alpha = \{h_{\alpha_t}^t; t = 1, \ldots, T\}$, we are looking for two such tracks that are both consistent over time (with respect to position and scale) and at the same time are likely to correspond to the interacting persons. In this work we use spatial proximity of detections as the main cue for interaction and focus of finding two tracks that maintain close proximity to one another over all frames. Ideally, we would like to jointly estimate the assignment of hypothesis to both tracks. However, we found that the following greedy procedure works well in practice. We first identify tracks of individual people by optimizing the following objective with Viterbi-decoding[2]:

$$p(h_\alpha) = p(h_{\alpha_1}^1) \prod_{t=2}^{T} p(h_{\alpha_t}^t) p(h_{\alpha_t}^t, h_{\alpha_{t-1}}^t), \qquad (4)$$

where the unary terms correspond to the confidence score of the person detector and the binary terms are zero-mean Gaussian with respect to the relative distance in position and scale.

Given a set of single person tracks we associate two tracks using the closest distance. We define the distance between two tracks $h_{\alpha_1}$ and $h_{\alpha_2}$ as the average distance between corresponding track hypothesis:

$$D(h_{\alpha_1}, h_{\alpha_2}) = \frac{1}{t_2 - t_1} \sum_{t=t_1}^{t_2} \|x(h_{\alpha_{1,t}}) - x(h_{\alpha_{1,t}})\|, \qquad (5)$$

where $x(\cdot)$ is the centroid of detection and $t_1$ and $t_2$ are the first and last frame contained in both tracks. We only link two tracks with distance less than a predefined threshold and link tracks with the smallest distance if multiple tracks are sufficiently close to each other. Finally we merge all the tracks that were assigned to each other into disjoint groups and independently infer poses of people for each such group.

---

[1] The index of selected hypothesis at frame $t$ is denoted by $\alpha_t$.

[2] We extract multiple tracks by stopping the Viterbi inference once at least one of the transition probabilities between frames falls below a predefined threshold and repeat the optimization using hypothesis have not been assigned to a track yet. Following the initial optimization we filter all the tracks that are too short or have too low score.

**Fig. 2. Flexible body model:** Traditional 10-part PS model [9] on left, and the proposed 22-part flexible PS model in the middle; half-limbs for all body parts, that are allowed to slide with respect to one another, are illustrate in red and yellow; torso is modeled using 4 flexible parts in green

## 2.2    2D Pose Estimation

In our approach we define the likelihood of 3d body pose using estimates of the 2d projections of the body joints. This allows us to leverage the recent results in 2d pose estimation and rely on the discriminativly trained body part detectors and robust local appearance features [9–11].

**Basic Pictorial Structures Model:** We denote the 2d configuration of subject $i$ in frame $t$ by by $L_i^t = (l_{i0}^t, \ldots, l_{iN}^t)$, where $l_{ij}^t = (x_{ij}^t, \theta_{ij}^t, s_{ij}^t)$ correspond to the image position, rotation and scale of the $j$-th body part; $N = 10$ denotes the total number of parts, which are traditionally chosen to correspond to torso, head, lower and upper legs, forearms and upper arms [12, 11, 9]. Given the image evidence $I^t$ the posterior over 2d body configuration is proportional to the product of likelihood and prior terms: $p(L_i^t|I) \propto p(I^t|L_i^t)p(L_i^t)$.

In the absence of interactions, one can rely on the tree-structured pictorial structures model to represent the posterior over $L_i^t$. In addition, we assume that the likelihood term factorizes into the product of individual part likelihoods $p(I^t|l_i^t)$, which we model using boosted body part detectors as in [9]. Since representing joint posterior over 2d configurations is intractable, for 3d likelihood in Eq. (3), we approximate this posterior as a product over posterior marginals of individual body parts: $p(L_i^t|I) \approx \prod_n p(l_{in}^t|I)$.

**Flexible Pictorial Structure Model:** The use of traditional 10-part PS model commonly employed in the literature [3, 9, 11, 13] presents a number of challenges when applied in our setting. Focusing on individual people, traditional PS model: (i) does not properly model foreshortening of parts because parts are represented with rigid rectangles of fixed size and (ii) is not effective in inference of poses across variety of camera views. To address (ii) view-based [1] and multi-pose [3] models have been introduced. These amount to a collection of PS models trained with view-specific or pose-specific spatial priors. In our case, where we are after jointly modeling multiple people, such mixture models will result in an exponential number of PS models. Instead, following [14, 15] we propose a more flexible extension that is able to deal with both (i) foreshortening and (ii) diverse camera views using one coherent PS model.

In our model we represent human body with an extended 22-part pictorial structures model shown on Fig. 2. In this model each of the body limbs is represented with two parts (half limbs) attached to the ends of the limb. These parts are allowed to slide along the part axis with respect to each other, capturing the foreshortening of the limb. In addition, we model the torso with 4 parts attached to shoulders and hips so that the model is capable of representing various torso orientations by shifting this parts with respect to each other. The 4 torso parts are connected in a star-shape pattern. In Fig. 2 (right) shows example of body configuration inferred with our 22-part model on the "People" dataset from [11]. Note, that the model could properly adjust to the orientation of the torso which also resulted in better estimate of the other body parts (for more see Fig. 3).

**Conditioning on Person Detection:** One of the challenges of recovering pose of multiple people using pictorial structures is *double-counting*. The double-counting problem, in this context, refers to the fact that since the two subjects are conditionally independent[3] the model is likely to find location of the two subjects one on top of another situated on the most salient person in the image. While we use posterior for the 3d pose likelihood, weak modes that appear on the less salient subject still cause problems. To address the double-counting issue one can use: (1) repulsive potentials that penalize substantial overlap between parts [16], or (2) resort to pixel-wise occlusion reasoning by introducing and marginalizing over image layers [17].

We take a different approach, that stems from an observation that our person detection and grouping works remarkably well in separating out interacting couples. To ensure that body-part hypothesis of both subjects are well represented and have substantial probability mass in the posteriors we condition 2d pose inference process on the estimated positions of both people given by $D_1^t$ and $D_2^t$. This bares some similarity to the progressive search approach of [18]. We assume that positions of body parts are conditionally independent of $D_i^t$ given the position of the root node $l_{i0}^t$, so that conditioning the model on $D_i^t$ corresponds to replacing the uniform prior on position of root part $p(l_{i0}^t)$ with conditional distribution $p(l_{i0}^t | D_i^t)$, which we assume to be Gaussian centered on the image position given by $D_i^t$.

**Multi-person Pictorial Structure Model:** Our joint model incorporates interactions as a form of constraints on positions of the body parts of the interacting people. Clearly, depending on the type of the interaction, positions of different body parts of people involved will be dependent on each other. For example, during the waltz arms of both subjects are typically close together, whereas during the crossover motion in cha-cha partners will only hold one hand. In order to accommodate these modes of interaction we introduce an interaction

---

[3] Same is true for models with weak conditional dependence between parts as those imposed by interaction aspects.

aspect variable $a^t$ which will specify the mode of interaction for the frame $t$. Given the interaction aspect, the joint posterior distribution over configurations of interacting people is given by

$$p(L_1^t, L_2^t | I^t, a^t) \propto p(I^t | L_1^t) p(I^t | L_2^t) p(L_1^t, L_2^t | a^t), \qquad (6)$$

where we have assumed independence of the appearance of both people allowing us to factorize the joint likelihood into the product of likelihoods of each person. The joint prior on configurations of people is given by

$$p(L_1^t, L_2^t | a^t) = \prod_{i=1}^{2} p(L_i^t) \prod_{(n,m) \in W} p(l_{1n}^t, l_{2m}^t)^{a_{nm}^t}, \qquad (7)$$

where $p(L_i^t)$ is a tree structured prior, $W$ is a set of edges between interacting parts and $a_{nm}^t$ is a binary variable that turns the corresponding potential on and off depending on the type of interaction. The interaction potential are given by $p(l_{1n}^t, l_{2m}^t) = \mathcal{N}(x_{1n}^t - x_{2m}^t | \mu_{nm}, \Sigma_{nm})$, and specify the preferred relative distance between the positions of the interacting parts.

We model 4 aspects that correspond to hand holding; these include: (1) no hand holding, (2) left hand of one subject holding right hand of the other subject, (3) left hand of one subject holding left hand of the other subject, and (4) two-hand hold. These interaction aspects are motivated by our target application of looking at dancing couples. That said, we want to emphasize that our joint 2d pose estimation model is general and applicable to most interactions.

**Inference in the Multi-person Model:** Modeling dependencies between subjects comes at a cost of more expensive inference. In tree-structured model inference can be made efficient with the use of convolution [12]. The dependencies between subjects can introduce loops (as is the case with the two-hand hold that we model) which makes exact inference prohibitively expensive. In order to make the inference tractable, we rely on the following two-stage procedure. In the first stage we ignore interaction factors and perform the inference in the tree-structured model only. We then sample a fixed number[4] of positions for each body part of each subject from the marginal of the tree-structured model, and repeat the inference with the full model using the sampled positions as a state-space. This inference procedure relates to branch and bound method proposed by Tian et al. [19].

## 2.3   3D Pose Estimation

To estimate 3d poses of interacting people we rely on a prior model that incorporates three types of dependencies between subjects: dependencies between body pose, relative orientation and position between subjects. To capture these

---

[4] In our implementation we sample positions 2000 times for each part and remove the repeating samples.

dependencies we rely on a joint Gaussian process dynamical model (GPDM) [7] trained using motion capture sequence of couples dancing. We train one GPDM model for each dance move, performed by 3 to 4 couples.

**Joint 3d Prior Model:**  Typically, GPDM is used to learn a latent model of motion for a single subject. In our case, we are interested in learning a joint model over two interacting people. To do so, we express our training samples as $Y = (Y_1, Y_2, Y_\delta, Y_{\theta_1}, Y_{\theta_{1\to 2}})$, where $Y_1$ and $Y_2$ are 3d poses of the two subjects, $Y_\delta$ is relative position of subject 2 with respect to 1, $Y_{\theta_1}$ is the root orientation of first subject in a canonical frame of reference and $Y_{\theta_{1\to 2}}$ is the orientation of subject 2 with respect to 1. For convenience, we collect all training samples in our dataset $\mathcal{D}$ into $\mathbf{Y} = \{Y \in \mathcal{D}\}$. We learn a joint GPDM model by minimizing negative log of posterior $p(\mathbf{X}, \bar{\alpha}, \bar{\beta}|\mathbf{Y})$ with respect to latent positions $\mathbf{X} \in \mathbb{R}^{d \times |\mathcal{D}|}$ and hyperparameters $\bar{\alpha}$ and $\bar{\beta}$ [5].

**MAP Pose Inference:** In our approach the 3d pose estimation corresponds to finding the most likely values for $Y_1$ and $Y_2$ and the parameters of their projection into the image, $Q$, given the set of image observations, $I$, and the GPDM prior model learned above – $\mathcal{M}_{GPDM} = (\mathbf{X}, \mathbf{Y}, \bar{\alpha}, \bar{\beta})$.

The projection parameters are given by $Q = \{r^t, \delta^t, \gamma_1^t, \gamma_t^2, \phi^t\}$, where $r^t$ is the position of the first person in frame $t$, the $\gamma_1^t$ and $\gamma_t^2$ are the scales of first and second person, $\phi^t$ is the absolute rotation of the canonical reference frame for the couple (with respect to which $Y_{\theta_1}$ is defined) and $\delta^t$ is the deviation in the image position of the second person with respect to the position predicted by the projection of $Y_\delta$ into the image. Note, $\delta^t$ allows us to deviate from the GPDM prior in order to generalize across closer and more distant embraces that we were not able to explicitly model using few mocap sequence samples.

Assuming there is negligible uncertainty in the reconstruction mapping [20], the 3d pose of both subjects in the canonical space, given a latent pose $X$, is given by the mean of the Gaussian process: $\mu_Y(X) = \mu + \mathbf{Y}\mathbf{K}_Y^{-1}\mathbf{k}_Y(X)$ where $\mathbf{K}_Y^{-1}$ is the inverse of a kernel matrix, and $\mathbf{k}_Y(X)$ is a kernel vector computed between training points and the latent position $X$. With this observation the likelihood in Eq. (1) can be expressed directly as a function of latent position $X$ and projection parameters $Q$. With slight abuse of notation, we can hence re-write Eq. (1) as:

$$p(\mu_Y(X), Q|I) \propto p(I|\mu_Y(X), Q)p(Y|X, \mathcal{M}_{GPDM}) \tag{8}$$

where $p(Y|X, \mathcal{M}_{GPDM}) = \frac{d}{2}\ln\sigma^2(X) + \frac{1}{2}\|X\|^2$ and $\sigma^2(X)$ is a covariance of a GPDM model defined as $\sigma^2(X) = k_Y(X, X) - \mathbf{k}_Y(X)^T\mathbf{K}_Y^{-1}\mathbf{k}_Y(X)$.

We approach the inference by directly optimizing Eq. (8) with respect to $X$ and $Q$ using gradient-based continuous optimization (scaled conjugate gradients). In order to define the gradients of the likelihood function Eq. (3) we represent the posteriors of the 2d configurations $L_i$ using the kernel density estimate given by $p_{L_1,n}(l) = \sum_k w_k exp(\|l - l_{nk}\|) + \epsilon_0$, where $l_{nk}$ are the samples

---

[5] For details of learning we refer the reader to [7].

**Table 1. Quantitative performance of 2d pose estimation:** three models are compared in all cases conditioned on the person detections. Numbers indicate percentage of body parts correctly found by the model.

| Method | Torso | Upper leg | Lower leg | Upper arm | Forearm | Head | Total |
|---|---|---|---|---|---|---|---|
| Cond. PS [9] (10 parts) | 96.1 | 88.2 89.5 | 72.4 64.5 | 26.3 23.7 | 18.4 13.2 | 72.4 | 56.4 |
| Flexible Cond. PS (22 parts) | 100.0 | 92.1 96.1 | 75.0 89.5 | 46.1 42.1 | 32.9 25.0 | 96.1 | 69.4 |
| MaFPS (joint model, 44 parts) | 100.0 | 92.1 96.1 | 76.3 89.5 | 46.1 47.4 | 39.5 27.6 | 96.1 | 71.0 |

from the posterior of part $n$ used in the second stage of the inference procedure described in Sec. 2.2 and $w_k$ are the value of posterior distribution for this sample; $\epsilon_0 = 0.02$ is a uniform outlier probability to make the likelihood robust.

**Implementation Details:** We found that good initialization is important for quick convergence of the optimization. In order to obtain a set of good initial hypothesis we initialize the projection parameters $Q$ from the estimates of people positions given by $D_i$ and select a set of candidate poses from the training set with the highest likelihood. We also found that the converges can be significantly sped up by first optimizing the projection parameters $Q$ while keeping the latent positions $X$ constant, and then jointly optimizing the pose and projection parameters.

## 3   Experiments

We conduct experiments to validate modeling choices and show the role of encoding interactions at all levels.

**Dataset:** We collected a dataset of dancing couples consisting of 4 amateur couples performing latin ballroom, mainly *cha-cha*. We first recorded mocap of the subjects for training of GPDM models in mocap suites and video in their natural clothes using 2 synchronized video cameras. Video recordings were then annotated with 3d poses by clicking on joints in two views and optimizing 3d pose to match 2d projections using a continuous optimization. We annotated every 3-rd frame of the selected 3 sequences (corresponding to 3 common cha-cha moves[6] 60 frames each) from 2 couples. Our dataset hence comprises of 120 annotated 3d frames. We use a subset of 40 frames from two of the cameras with their 2d annotations for 2d experiments.

**Learning:** We learn appearance for part detectors and spatial priors for PS model from a public dataset of [13] to avoid overfitting to 8 people present in our dataset.

**Error:** We conduct experiments on two levels with 2d pose and 3d pose estimation. For experiments in 2d we use a well established percentage of parts correct (PCP) metric introduced in [18]. In 3d we measure error using average

---

[6] This included new yorker, underarm turn and basic enclosed. We train one GPDM for each across couples.

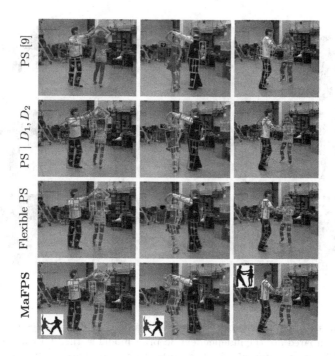

**Fig. 3. 2D pose estimation:** Comparison of results obtained with extensions proposed in Sec. 2.2 on our dance dataset; corresponding quantitative results are in Table 1. Top row: traditional cardboard PS [9] model – note the over-counting issue; second row: [9] model but conditioned on the person detection; third row: conditional model but with flexible parts; last row: our complete MaFPS model with interaction aspects – note the difference in the arms. Aspects chosen for the image are illustrated by inlay icons.

Euclidean distance between joints. In all cases we report error average over both interacting subjects.

**Person Detection:** Person detector had a nearly perfect 100% true positive rate (with few deviations in scale) on our dataset of 60 frames/seq. × 3 seq. × 2 couples × 2 views = 720 images. The false positive rate was on average $2 - 3$ detections per frame, but all false positives were removed during grouping. In the interest of space we forgo more formal evaluation.

**2D Pose Estimation:** We first evaluate extensions we make to the pictorial structures (PS) model in Sec. 2.1 to support 2d inference of interacting people. We illustrate typical behavior of the 4 models we consider and visual improvements that we gain by conditioning on person detection, adding flexibility and interaction aspects to the model in Fig. 3. Quantitatively, based on results in Table 1, we gain 23% by adding flexibility to parts and 2.3% on average by adding aspects. It is worth noting that even though the improvements that result from modeling interaction aspects are marginal on average, they are large

(a)                                    (b)

**Fig. 4. Results of our method:** (a) Several examples of 3D poses estimated by our approach. Compared are the independent 3d prior model learned for each person individually (left) and our joint 3d prior (right), both based on the same 2d pose estimates. (b) 3D poses estimated from challenging monocular dance competition videos; notice motion blur, variations in appearance, clothing, lighting, and pose.

for the parts that are affected by the interaction (e.g., up to 20% improvement for the forearm). We only report quantitative results for models conditioned on detections; unconditioned PS model [9] lost one of the persons completely in more then half of the frames due to double-counting (see Fig. 3 top left).

**3d Pose Estimation:** We also compare the role of modeling 3d pose prior jointly over the two subjects. Estimating poses of each subject independently we achieve average joint error of 25 cm. Joint model that includes interactions between subjects improves this result to 19 cm. Qualitative results are illustrated in Fig. 4 (a). The joint prior model is particularly instrumental in determining the proper global view of the subjects (see Fig. 4 (a) second and third row), and resolving depth ambiguities (see Fig. 4 (a) first row).

**Real Sequences:** Lastly, we illustrate performance on real image sequence obtained at dance competition in Fig. 4 (b). Note, that dancers in these sequence were more professional then those in our dataset. Despite this and variations in performance style, we are still able to recover meaningful 3d motions in this extremely challenging scenario.

## 4    Conclusions

We explore the role of human-human context in estimating 3d pose of dancing couples from monocular video. To model interactions, we introduce a novel layered model that leverages latest advances in person detection, 2d pose estimation, and latent variable models for encoding 3d priors over pose trajectories. In the process, we introduce extensions to the traditional PS model that are able to account for aspects of human-human interactions and better deal with foreshortening and changing viewpoint. We illustrate performance on very challenging monocular images that contain couples performing dance motions. These sequences go beyond what has been shown in state-of-the-art. In the future, we intend to look at further extending the current model to also take into account occlusions among the interacting subjects.

## References

1. Andriluka, M., Roth, S., Schiele, B.: Monocular 3d pose estimation and tracking by detection. In: CVPR (2010)
2. Pellegrini, S., Edd, A., Schindler, K., van Gool, L.: You'll never walk alone: Modeling social behaviour for multi-target tracking. In: ICCV (2009)
3. Yao, B., Fei-Fei, L.: Modeling mutual context of object and human pose in human-object interaction activities. In: CVPR (2010)
4. Kjellström, H., Kragic, D., Black, M.J.: Tracking people interacting with objects. In: CVPR (2010)
5. Ionescu, C., Bo, L., Sminchisescu, C.: Structured svm for visual localization and continuous state estimation. In: ICCV (2009)
6. Eichner, M., Ferrari, V.: We Are Family: Joint Pose Estimation of Multiple Persons. In: Daniilidis, K., Maragos, P., Paragios, N. (eds.) ECCV 2010. LNCS, vol. 6311, pp. 228–242. Springer, Heidelberg (2010)
7. Wang, J.M., Fleet, D.J., Hertzmann, A.: Gaussian process dynamical models for human motion. PAMI 30 (2008)
8. Felzenszwalb, P., Girshick, R., McAllester, D., Ramanan, D.: Object detection with discriminatively trained part based models. PAMI 32 (2010)
9. Andriluka, M., Roth, S., Schiele, B.: Pictorial structures revisited: People detection and articulated pose estimation. In: CVPR (2009)
10. Eichner, M., Ferrari, V.: Better appearance models for pictorial structures. In: BMVC (2009)
11. Ramanan, D.: Learning to parse images of articulated objects. In: NIPS (2006)
12. Felzenszwalb, P., Huttenlocher, D.: Pictorial structures for object recognition. International Journal of Computer Vision (2005)
13. Johnson, S., Everingham, M.: Clustered pose and nonlinear appearance models for human pose estimation. In: BMVC (2010)
14. Sapp, B., Weiss, D., Taskar, B.: Parsing human motion with stretchable models. In: CVPR (2011)
15. Yang, Y., Ramanan, D.: Articulated pose estimation with flexible mixtures-of-parts. In: CVPR (2011)
16. Ferrari, V., Marin-Jimenez, M., Zisserman, A.: Pose search: retrieving people using their pose. In: CVPR (2009)

17. Sigal, L., Black, M.J.: Measure locally, reason globally: Occlusion-sensitive articulated pose estimation. In: CVPR (2006)
18. Ferrari, V., Marin-Jimenez, M., Zisserman, A.: Progressive search space reduction for human pose estimation. In: CVPR (2008)
19. Tian, T.P., Sclaroff, S.: Fast globally optimal 2d human derection with loopy graph models. In: CVPR (2010)
20. Urtasun, R., Fleet, D., Fua, P.: 3d people tracking with gaussian process dynamical models. In: CVPR (2006)

# Motion Capture for Clinical Purposes, an Approach Using PrimeSense Sensors

Gabriel Sanmartín, Julián Flores, Pablo Arias, Javier Cudeiro, and Roi Méndez

[1] CoGRADE, Instituto de Investigacións Tecnolóxicas
Constantino Candeira s/n
15782 Santiago de Compostela, A Coruña, Spain
gabriel.sanmartin@usc.es
[2] Neuroscience and Motor Control Group (NEUROcom), Department of Medicine-INEF
Galicia, University of A Coruña, A Coruña, Spain
pabloarias@udc.es

**Abstract.** Virtual Reality (VR) is the computer recreation of simulated environments that create on the user a sense of physical presence on them. VR provides the advantages of being highly flexible and controllable, allowing experts to generate the optimal conditions for any given test and isolating any desired variables in the course of an experiment. An important characteristic of VR is that it allows interaction within the virtual world. Motion capture is one of the most popular technologies, because it contributes to creating in the subject the required sense of presence. There are several methods to incorporate these techniques into VR system, with the challenge of them not being too invasive. We propose a method using PrimeSense sensors and several well-known computer vision techniques to build a low-cost mocap system that has proven to be valid for clinical needs, in its application as a support therapy for Parkinson's disease (PD) patients.

**Keywords:** motion capture, prime sense, Kinect, Parkinson, inverse kinematics, virtual reality.

## 1    Introduction

In this work we introduce a low cost VR motion capture system designed as a support therapy for patients suffering Parkinson's Disease. VR has been extensively used as a therapy for several pathologies, namely for treating phobias such as acrophobia [13], arachnophobia [14], or social phobia [15], and also in other mental disorders such as post traumatic stress disorder [16].

Parkinson's Disease is a very common idiopathic neurodegenerative disorder, and it is regarded as the second most frequent motor disorder, with around 1-2% of the elder population (over 65 years) suffering from this disease.

The system we have developed is based on multiple tests designed by the NEUROcom research group [26]. We describe the nature of these tests (specifically test 2, involved in the current development), targeted specifically to evaluate and

F.J. Perales, R.B. Fisher, and T.B. Moeslund (Eds.): AMDO 2012, LNCS 7378, pp. 273–281, 2012.

potentially treat patients with PD in section 2. A brief description of both tests involved in the development is included, followed by a set of requirements derived from them, in terms of motion capture.

We introduce two different approaches with regard to the motion capture technology used to translate the subject's moves into the virtual world. The first approach was to incorporate a classic mocap system based on optical markers using specific cameras, but this turned out to be not valid for this particular test. For this reason, there was a move towards trying to find new computer vision methods to improve the operation of the system, so we developed a new system based purely on computer vision over a conventional RGB camera, plus a cheap depth sensor, a combo currently being built by PrimeSense in devices such as Microsoft's Kinect [23] or ASUS' Xtion PRO live [24].

The first approach we took focused on the analysis made initially for test 1 [2] only, which was based on a classical mocap approach, using optical infrared devices and retro reflective markers. We detail this method and explain why a new system was needed in section 3.

Section 4, exposes our new approach based solely on computer vision algorithms for segmentation, then integrating the depth sensor of PrimeSense (specifically, we used both Kinect and ASUS Xtion models).

Lastly, on Section 5 we draw conclusions as a result of a comparison between the two methods.

## 2    Experimental Design

The design of the experiment is based on arm reaching movement. This movement is defined as the arm projection towards an object [22]. Several studies have shown that aging may impair this ability [18][19], impairment which is of greater impact in the case of Parkinson's disease [20][21]. The alterations in the movement include slowness (bradikinesia) or reduction of movement amplitude (hypokinesia), and both lead to a loss in the quality of life because of the importance of the arm reaching in several daily living activities, for instance dressing or transfers [17]. It is therefore of great interest to develop tools aimed at studying the physiological and pathological substrates of arm reaching and therefore to propose new therapeutic approaches to improve the motor function.

This particular test experiment is carried out as follows: the patient will sit on a chair, in a comfortable, relaxed position, with his hands leaning on a table. He wears a HMD which provides him with a first person view of a virtual 3D environment similar to that he is actually on when running the tests: a square room, clean and aseptic, with a generic virtual depiction of himself (the "avatar"). At any given moment of the test, one of two colored panels in front of the patient (chosen at random) will show up. These panels are designed to look like targets and the subject is required by the expert to reach with his arms and touch them with a specific hand. After "touching" it, the target will change color and disappear, and the subject must go back to his original resting position. The process is repeated with the active target being reselected randomly.

**Fig. 1.** Screencap of the virtual scene

A series of data is collected during the course of the experiment, like response times, speed of movement, and other neurological and physiological information, that is used later by the expert for further analysis after the test is finished.

### 2.1 Motion Capture

From the initial description of the experiment, it is evident that the system should translate the subject's movements in real life into the virtual environment, with the least possible delay, in order to create a sufficient sense of presence to support the validity of the tests.

We created a 3D mesh of a generic human using Maya, with enough detail to guarantee a sense of immersion in the subject. This mesh has been provided with an articulated rigging to properly transfer the information from motion capture to the virtual character. For this particular test, the conclusion is that the hands positions should be registered and passed on to the VR application in real time in order to translate the movements of the patient into the 3D world. Although other joints are involved in the actions required by the test (like the arms and forearms), they can be inferred by the use of inverse kinematics techniques from the end position of the hands, especially since the range of movement is not significantly wide.

## 3   First Approach

We drew a first VR approach for these requirements by focusing the first of the tests ("finger-tapping", described in [2]) and designed an experimental setting. In this experiment, the user kept his hand still over a table, and then he was required to tap his finger continuously, so the only tracked element was essentially the phalanges of the index finger, from a stationary position. With that in mind, the following motion capture system was considered.

In this solution, the system provides rotational and positional information of the tracked elements through a series of passive markers distributed carefully along the elements of interest. For this data acquisition we used a number of infrared cameras (model Natural Point TrackIR 4:PRO [25]), and markers made with either retro reflective adhesives, or small balls covered with retro reflective film. Positional information is mapped directly to the 3D environment after the coordinate transformation, while rotational info is inferred from pairs of markers. Position, mass and height/width ratio is provided directly by the API included with the cameras (which is closed), so integrating computer vision into the tracking itself is limited to post-processing of positional information (like for instance, a temporal correspondence algorithm), and not to a proper work over the raw image provided by the cameras.

This method has proved to be a good solution for the first experiment, with effective results in terms of presence, validity and clinical reliability, the outcomes of which were indistinguishable from those obtained in the real environment [2], and it is in fact being used today by the researchers of NEUROcom to study real cases of Parkinson's disease patients.

### 3.1    Problems with This Approach

When the system was used with the second experiment tests (described in section 2), it turned out to be much less adequate, and it was obvious a new approach was needed.

In this case, the XYZ position of the hands is needed, so we needed to be able to track in a much wider area. We tried the method used in the previous test, with two markers on each hand, one of them placed on the index finger tip, the other in the outer knuckle. We used two markers to prevent occlusion of one of them when crossing the hands, although in principle only one would have been needed.

Initially three cameras were used for this test (two on the sides, one overhead). However, while this approach would have been better for off-line capture (where the animator can correct errors due to occlusion or marker-swapping), getting an error-free result in real time is too hard due to occlusion problems on the side cameras, especially when crossing hands occur. This is a crucial issue because an error in the capture might cause the hand to hop unrealistically thus breaking the suspension of disbelief and the sense of presence. This layout was then discarded, in favor of a single overhead camera, using each marker mass as the height coordinate, instead of the side cameras.

While markers and motion capture provide the position of the hands, the rest of the joints are inferred through inverse kinematic techniques. A slightly altered revision of the Cyclic-Coordinate Descent method [1] was used, which is an iterative algorithm that was designed to solve inverse kinematic problems on robotic manipulators. It is a fast and reliable method for smooth and continuous movements like those involved in motion capture.

It was concluded that this system was too unstable for the needs of the experiment 2. On one hand, using a single camera with 4 markers which are very similar makes it very difficult to preserve spatial and temporal correspondence, especially when total occlusion or "marker-swapping" occur. The system is also highly dependent of light conditions and the state of the retro reflective material. Also, with the use of the marker mass as the height coordinate, the values are highly variable and their reliability and precision is low, since two markers apparently of the same size are perceived as very different in size by the cameras, due to defective materials or optical conditions. The result is very noisy values with limited reliability.

Lastly, the system is highly invasive and unpleasant to the subject, since markers must be fixed on the hand by using adhesive tape or several Velcro stripes.

For all these reasons, it was evident that a change in the approach was needed, to be more fitting with the specific characteristics of the environment in this particular experience (since using infrared cameras was a legacy from a previous project).

# 4    Second Approach

Unlike other work situations in computer vision, in this case the environment is controllable, both in light conditions and with regard to the environmental setting. In the previous approach, the background was static, with a fixed camera in an overhead position, and it consisted of a wooden table covered with a black matte fabric. The light conditions do not change during the execution of the tests. All of this makes working with color feasible.With all this in mind, we thought about how to achieve a capture with three degrees of freedom with a single camera, and the PrimeSense devices are good candidates.

## 4.1    PrimeSense Technology

PrimeSense sensors like Microsoft Kinect [23] or ASUS Xtion PRO live [24]  are devices that have a RGB conventional camera working at 8-bit color depth and a depth camera with 11 bits of resolution, providing up to 2048 non-linear depth levels in a range from 0.5 to approximately 7 meters of distance from the camera. This sensor works by emitting a series of infrared light points in a pattern known by the device. By comparing the perceived pattern with the one memorized, the sensor can figure out the distance of that particular point.

The RGB and infrared cameras are separated by a small distance (around 2.5cm). By using a chessboard pattern and a standard stereo calibration, it is possible to determine the difference between them. For that purpose, the cameras must first be calibrated individually, using a zero distortion for the IR camera and a distortion and de-centering model for the RGB camera. Then, with all internal camera parameters fixed (including focal length), we calibrate the external transform between the two [9] [10].

We have used the ASUS Xtion Pro LIVE installation of the PrimeSense technology, mainly because it supports up to 60fps of temporal resolution, thus ensuring more precision in real-time capture than Microsoft's Kinect, although both of them can be used with the system we have developed.

For further computer vision processing, we integrated the image streaming of the device with OpenCV [26] using these parameters, creating a small wrapper that simplifies the acquisition of both depth and RGB images from the cameras.

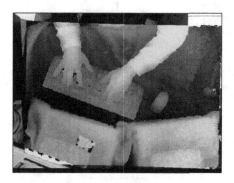

**Fig. 2.** Combination of both depth and RGB images after calibration

## 4.2     Camshift

We used a color based algorithm called Camshift for segmentation, that is, to detect, locate and segment the elements to track, in this case the hands of the patient.

In a previous section the environmental conditions and restrictions were analyzed, this being a controlled setting with a static background of a single color, so it was concluded that it is acceptable to make use of color based algorithms. Specifically, we have chosen the Camshift algorithm (Continuously Adaptive Mean Shift) a well-known algorithm for tracking objects in image sequences introduced in [3], which has been previously used in hand tracking in [7] or [8]. Camshift is a target tracking method based on an adaptation of the Mean Shift algorithm to deal with dynamic probability distributions (variable size and position), associated with objects in motion. It is fast and robust, ignores partial occlusions and is highly tolerant to lighting changes [3].

In our case, we have decided the application of two independent instances of Camshift, one for each hand, covering these with a pair of gloves of different, bright color, or with two cardboard pieces of different color. This is to enhance the robustness of the system (compared to using only the skin color for segmentation) and also to allow the differentiation of the two hands, avoiding problems with occlusion of one hand with the other. The process is summarized below, and also schemed in the diagram on fig. 3.

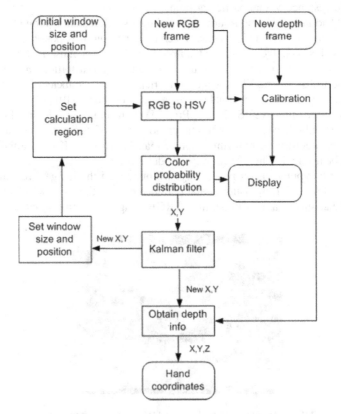

**Fig. 3.** Block diagram of the tracking process

When a new RGB frame arrives, it first is converted into HSV color space, which corresponds to a projection of the RGB color space over its main diagonal from white to black. Because values with low or high saturation make it difficult to recognize the chromatic information, since hue becomes very unstable, we first discard values close to black or white.

Then, the colors of both hands are determined in a first step either by a previously stored histogram, or by placing each hand in a designated area. The color information in the chosen method is sampled to build a color histogram. This is used to convert each pixel to a probability of the selected color as seen in fig. 4.

As mentioned before, Camshift is an extension of the Meanshift algorithm. Details on Meanshift are found on [11] [12]. It basically is an optimization technique that climbs the gradient of a probability distribution. It works by first selecting a search window size and position, then calculating the mean location of the search window based on the probability distribution, and then relocating the window on that mean position, and repeating these steps until convergence. Camshift adapts this algorithm for dynamically changing distribution (as in video sequences, where size and location might change over time) by adjusting the window size over each incoming frame, based on the zeroth moment of the distribution.

If the tracking element is lost, the system readjusts itself by simply setting the search window size to the image width and height. Given that the background is aseptic with a constant color, it quickly finds the hand again and the system stabilizes itself automatically.

**Fig. 4.** Original image (left) and color probability distribution (right)

From operation of Camshift, we obtain a blob representation of each element of interest. The centroid of this blob is calculated and used as the (x,z) position of the hand. This 2D position is then used to obtain the distance of the object from the camera by projecting the same pixel over the aligned depth image after calibration of both streams.

To smooth the motion capture and eliminate noise, a Kalman filter is applied over the whole process (in the three coordinates). This enhances the robustness over potential errors when movement is too fast or diffuse and the tracker might lose the hand, but find it immediately thereafter.

## 5　Conclusion

We presented two methods to reproduce motion capture keeping a low cost profile.

The first one used conventional optical motion capture that, although valid for a previous test, was not producing the desired results, due mainly to it being too prone to errors, too sensitive to external conditions and too invasive.

The second approach was a new method using a regular RGB camera and a depth sensor, combining several computer vision techniques. The result is a reliable and fast system that tracks both hands precisely and provides valid motion capture information for clinical needs in a test designed for Parkinson's disease patients.

The new system is more robust than the previous one and more resistant to capture errors and marker occlusion, also avoiding marker-swapping. Also, we have reduced invasiveness considerably by using loose gloves or a single adhesive of lightweight cardboard. Environmental conditions are more flexible, reducing the dependency of light conditions and only demanding the use of bright unique colors in the scene for the tracking elements.

We analyzed physiological and neurological parameters on the term of the first method when proving experiment 1, and concluded that presence was guaranteed. On our future plans remains ensuring that this new method is also valid under the same conditions and using the same tests.

**Acknowledgements.** This work was done under the Virtual Reality for Parkinson's disease patients project which is carried on by the Cograde group (Universidade de Santiago de Compostela) along with the NEUROcom group of Universidade da Coruña.

It would not have been possible without the help of the Computer graphics and vision unit at Universitat de les Illes Balears.

## References

1. Wang, L.-C.T., Chen, C.C.: A combined optimization method for solving the inverse kinematics problems of mechanical manipulators. IEEE Transactions on Robotics and Automation 7(4), 489–499 (1991)
2. Arias, P., Robles-García, V., Sanmartín, G., Flores, J., Cudeiro, J.: Virtual Reality as a Tool for Evaluation of Repetitive Rhythmic Movements in the Elderly and Parkinson's Disease Patients. PLoS ONE 7(1), e30021, doi:10.1371/journal.pone.0030021
3. Bradski, G.R.: Computer Vision Face Tracking for Use in a Perceptual User Interface. Intel Technology Journal, Q2 1998 (1998)
4. Zhang, C., Qiao, Y., Fallon, E., Xu, C.: An improved CamShift algorithm for target tracking in video surveillance
5. Xiangyu, W., Xiujuan, L.: The Study of Moving Target Tracking Based on Kalman-CamShift in the Video
6. Dae-Sik, J., Gye-Young, K., Choi-Hyung, I.: Kalman Filter incorporated model updating for real-time tracking. In: Proc. 1996 IEEE TENCON, Digital Signal Processing Applications, pp. 878–882 (1996)

7. Varona, J., Buades, J.M., Perales, F.: Hands and face tracking for VR applications. Computers & Graphics 29(2), 179–187 (2005)
8. Manresa, C., Varona, J., Mas, R., Perales, F.: Hand tracking and Gesture Recognition for Human-Computer Interaction
9. Burrus, N.: Kinect Calibration, http://nicolas.burrus.name/index.php/Research/KinectCalibration
10. Konolige, K., Mihelich, P.: Technical description of Kinect calibration, http://www.ros.org/wiki/kinect_calibration/technical
11. Fukunaga, K.: Introduction to Statistical Pattern Recognition. Academic Press, Boston (1990)
12. Cheng, Y.: Mean shift, mode seeking and clustering. IEEE Trans. Pattern Anal. Machine Intell. 17, 790–799 (1995)
13. Hodges, L., Kooper, R., Orothbaum, B., Opddyke, D.: Virtual environments for treating the fear of heights. IEEE Computer, 28–84 (1995)
14. Carlin, A.S., Hoffman, H.G., Weghorst, S.: Virtual reality and tactile augmentation in the treatment of spider phobia: A case report. Behaviour Research and Therapy 35(2), 153–158 (1997)
15. Pertaub, D.P., Slater, M., Barker, C.: An experiment on public speaking anxiety in response to three different types of virtual audience. Presence-Teleoperators and Virtual Environments 11(1), 68–78 (2002)
16. Difede, J., Hoffman, H., Jaysinghe, N.: Innovative use of virtual reality technology in the treatment of PTSD in the aftermath of September 11. Psychiatric Services 53(9), 1083–1085 (2002)
17. Granger, C.V., Hamilton, B.B., Sherwin, F.G.: Guide for the use of uniform data set for medical rehabilitation. Uniform Data System for Medical Rehabilitation. Buvalo General Hospital, New York
18. Bennett, K.M., Castiello, U.: Reach to grasp: changes with age. J. Gerontol. 49(1), 1–7 (1994)
19. Carnahan, H., Vandervoort, A.A., Swanson, L.R.: The influence of aging and target motion on the control of prehension. Exp. Aging. Res. 24(3), 289–306
20. Majsak, M.J., Kaminski, T., Gentile, A.M., Flanagan, J.R.: The reaching movements of patients with Parkinson's disease under self-determined maximal speed and visually cued conditions. Brain 121(Pt 4), 755–766
21. Negrotti, A., Secchi, C., Gentilucci, M.: Effects of disease progression and L-dopa therapy on the control of reaching-grasping in Parkinson's disease. Neuropsychologia 43(3), 450–459
22. Jeannerod, M.: Intersegmental coordination during reaching at natural visual objects. In: Long, J., Baddeley, A. (eds.) Attention and Performance IX, pp. 153–168. Lawrence Erlbaum, Hillsdale
23. Microsoft Kinect for Windows, http://www.microsoft.com/en-us/kinectforwindows/
24. ASUS Xtion PRO live, http://us.estore.asus.com/index.php?l=product_detail&p=4001
25. Natural Point TrackIR 4: PRO, http://www.naturalpoint.com/trackir/02-products/product-TrackIR-4-PRO.html
26. Neuroscience and Motor Control Group (Neurocom), http://www.udc.es/dep/medicina/neurocom.htm
27. OpenCV. Open Source Computer Vision, http://opencv.willowgarage.com/

# Human Behavior Analysis from Depth Maps

Sergio Escalera[1,2]

[1] Dept. Matemàtica Aplicada i Anàlisi,
Universitat de Barcelona, Gran Via de les Corts Catalanes 585,
08007, Barcelona, Spain
[2] Computer Vision Center, Campus UAB, Edifici O, 08193, Bellaterra, Spain
sergio@maia.ub.es

**Abstract.** Pose Recovery (PR) and Human Behavior Analysis (HBA) have been a main focus of interest from the beginnings of Computer Vision and Machine Learning. PR and HBA were originally addressed by the analysis of still images and image sequences. More recent strategies consisted of Motion Capture technology (MOCAP), based on the synchronization of multiple cameras in controlled environments; and the analysis of depth maps from Time-of-Flight (ToF) technology, based on range image recording from distance sensor measurements. Recently, with the appearance of the multi-modal RGBD information provided by the low cost Kinect™ sensor (from RGB and Depth, respectively), classical methods for PR and HBA have been redefined, and new strategies have been proposed. In this paper, the recent contributions and future trends of multi-modal RGBD data analysis for PR and HBA are reviewed and discussed.

**Keywords:** Pose Recovery, Human Behavior Analysis, Depth Maps, Kinect™.

## 1 Introduction

Pose Recovery (PR) uses to be a first step of most Human Behavior Analysis (HBA) systems. However, detecting humans and recovering their pose in images or videos is a challenging problem due to the high variety of possible configurations of the scenario (such as changes in the point of view, illumination conditions, or background complexity) and the human body (because of its articulated nature). In the past few years, some research on PR has focused on the use of Time-of-Flight range cameras (ToF) [1–4]. Nowadays, several works related to this topic have been published because of the emergence of inexpensive structured light technology, reliable and robust to capture the depth information along with their corresponding synchronized RGB image. This technology has been developed by the PrimeSense [5] company and released to the market by Microsoft® XBox® under the name of Kinect™.

F.J. Perales, R.B. Fisher, and T.B. Moeslund (Eds.): AMDO 2012, LNCS 7378, pp. 282–292, 2012.
© Springer-Verlag Berlin Heidelberg 2012

With the recent wide use of the depth maps introduced by the Microsoft®️ Kinect™️ device, a new source of information has emerged. With the use of depth maps, 3D information of the scene from a particular point of view is easily computed, and thus, working with consecutive frames, we obtain RGBDT information, from Red, Green, Blue, Depth, and Time data, respectively. This motivates the use of multi-modal data fusion strategies to benefit from the new data representation in PR and HBA applications. While these tasks could be achieved by inter-frame feature tracking and matching against predefined gesture models, there are scenarios where a robust segmentation of human limbs are needed, e.g. observing upper limb anomalies or distinguishing between finger configurations while performing a gesture. In that respect, depth information appears quite handy by reducing ambiguities due to illumination, colour, and texture diversity. Many researchers have obtained their first results in the field of human motion capture using this technology. In particular, Shotton et al. [6] presented one of the greatest advances in the extraction of the human body pose from depth images, an approach that also is the core of the Kinect™️ human recognition framework. Moreover, new devices offering multi-modal RGBD + audio information are appearing [7], improving the $320\times240$ and $640\times480$ resolution of Kinect™️ Depth and RGB images, consolidating the field of research, and opening the possibilities for a new broad range of applications.

Currently, there exists a steady stream of updates and tools that provide robustness and applicability to the device. In December 2010, OpenNI [8] and PrimeSense [5] released their own Kinect™️ open source drivers and motion tracking middleware for PCs runningWindows (7, Vista, and XP), Ubuntu, and MacOSX. Then, the middleware FAAST (Flexible Action and Articulated Skeleton Toolkit) was developed at the University of Southern California (USC) Institute for Creative Technologies to facilitate the integration of full-body control within virtual reality applications and video games when using OpenNI-compliant depth sensors and drivers [9, 10]. In June 2011, Microsoft®️ released a non-commercial Kinect™️ Software Development Kit (SDK) forWindows that includes Windows 7-compatible PC drivers for the Kinect™️ device [11]. Microsoft®️ SDK allows developers to build Kinect™️ enabled applications in Microsoft®️ Visual Studio 2010 using C++, C# or Visual Basic. Microsoft®️ has released a commercial version of the Kinect™️ for Windows SDK with support for more advanced device functionalities. There is also a third set of Kinect™️ drivers for Windows, Mac and Linux PCs by the OpenKinect (libFree- Nect) open source project [12], adapted by libraries commonly used on Computer Vision as OpenCV. Code Laboratories CL NUI Platform offers a signed driver and SDK for multiple Kinect™️ devices on Windows XP, Vista, and 7 [13]. As a consequence of the new data representation obtained from Microsoft®️ Kinect™️, new libraries to process depth maps have emerged, such as the Point Cloud Library (PCL) [14].

Some examples of applications that have benefited from RGBD representation are: reconstruction of dense surfaces and 3D object detection [15], improved descriptors and learning for object recognition [16, 17], augmented reality [18], SLAM [19], or PR-HBA, just to mention a few. In this paper, recent literature on PR and HBA using depth maps is reviewed. Once PR is robustly performed using RGBD representation, standard techniques for HBA can be consequently improved. HBA is extremely challenging because of the huge number of possible configurations of the human body that defines human motion. Common approaches to model sequential data for gesture recognition are based on Hidden Markov Model (HMM) [20], which consist of learning the transition probabilities among different human state configurations, and, more recently, there has been an emergent interest in Conditional Random Field (CRF) [21] for the learning of sequences. However, all these methods assume that we know the number of states for every motion. Other approaches make use of templates or global trajectories of motion, being highly dependent of the environment where the system is built. In order to avoid all these situations, Dynamic Time Warping framework (DTW) [22] allows to align two temporal sequences taking into account that sequences may vary in time based on the subject that performs the gesture. The alignment cost can be then used as a gesture appearance indicator. In comparison to classical 2D approaches, the authors of [23] show that an improved PR description based on 3D skeletal model from RGBD data allows to compute feature variability, and include this measure in DTW for improved HBA recognition.

The rest of the paper is organized as follows: Section 2 reviews the most recent achievements and proposals in PR based on depth maps to improve the accuracy of standard HBA systems and Section 3 concludes the paper, discussing future trends in this field.

## 2    Pose Recovery Using Depth Maps

One of the main advantages of the Kinect™ device is its ability to obtain an aligned representation of RGBD data using a cheap and reliable sensor. Different technologies for capturing depth maps, including the structured light technology of Microsoft® Kinect™, are summarized in Figure 1. The Kinect™ infrared sensor displays a structured/codified matrix of points through the environment. Then, each depth pixel is computed by sampling the derivative of the higher resolution infrared image taken in the infrared camera. This value is inversely proportional to the radius of each gaussian dot, which is linearly proportional to the actual depth. Given the extra image dimension offered by the Kinect™ sensor, new approaches taking benefit of this issue have been proposed for improving PR. The most recent and relevant approaches are described below.

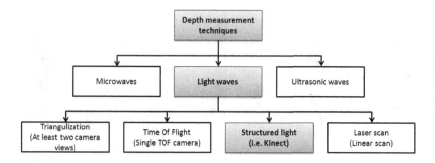

**Fig. 1.** Different technologies for the acquisition of depth maps

One of the first contributions for PR in depth maps is the approach of [6], which also is part of the core of the Kinect™ device software. The method is based on inferring pixel label probabilities through Random Forest (RF) based on learning offsets of depth features. Then, mean shift is used to estimate human joints and representing the body in skeletal form. An example of the synthetic generated samples for training the system and two trees of the forest are shown in Fig. 2(a). Using the same philosophy, the authors of [24] optimize the results of [6] including a second optimization layer to the RF probabilities in a multi-label Graph Cuts optimization procedure. The scheme and results of this approach are shown in Fig. 2(b). The Graph Cuts theory was previously applied to PR in RGB computer vision approaches [25, 26] as well as other image modalities [27] with successful results.

The skeletal model defined by previous approaches is being used in combination with other techniques in different HBA approaches. For instance, the authors of [28] use the skeletal model in conjunction with computer vision techniques to detect complex poses in situations where there are many interacting actors.

The authors of [29] propose an hybrid approach as an alternative to the Graph Cuts optimization of [24] to static pose estimation, called Connected Poselets. This representation combines aspects of part-based and example-based estimation, first detecting poselets extracted from the training data. The method applies a modified Random Decision Forest to identify Poselet activations. By combining keypoint predictions from poselet activations within a graphical model, the authors infer the marginal distribution over each keypoint without using kinematic constraints. An example of the procedure is illustrated in Fig. 2(c).

In the scope of Probabilistic Graphical Models, different approaches have been proposed. In [33], the authors propose a method for learning shape models enabling accurate articulated human pose estimation from a single image. The authors learn a generative model of limb shape which can capture the wide variation in shape due to varying anatomy and pose. The model is learnt from silhouette, depth, and 3D pose data.

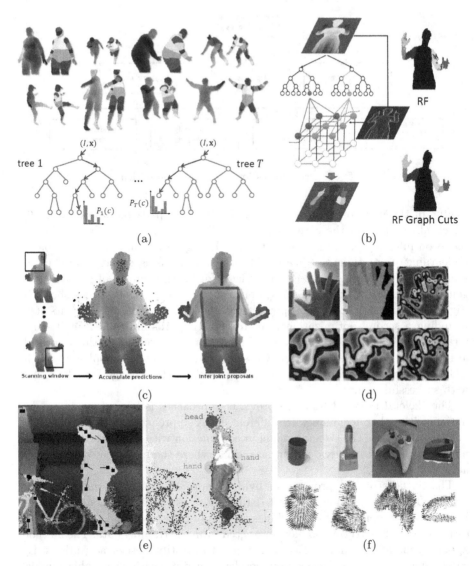

**Fig. 2.** Different approaches for PR. (a) Random Forest (RF) [6]; (b) Graph Cuts optimization of RF probabilities [24]; (c) Multiscale scanning window. Each window is evaluated by a Random Forest classifier to detect poselet activations [29]. Each activated poselet makes local predictions for the body parts it was trained on. The overall configuration is inferred by combining keypoint predictions within a graphical model, and finding the maximum over the marginal distributions; (d) Gabor filter over depth maps at multiple scales for hand detection in a multi hand pose Random Forest approach for American Sign Language (ASL) recognition [30]; (e) Left: keypoint detection over depth map. Right: inferred body parts from a graphical model [31]; and (f) Normal vectors of segmented objects from depth maps [32].

Obviously, a relevant aspect of the RGBD representation is the definition of new descriptors based on 3D point clouds. On the one hand, recent publications regarding image descriptions are related to the distribution of surface normal vectors [14]. On the other hand, standard computer vision descriptors are used over depth maps instead of RGB data. For instance, the authors of [30] have recently proposed an approach for American Sign Language recognition applying Gabor filters over depth maps of hand regions. Hand-shapes corresponding to letters of the alphabet are characterized using appearance and depth images and classified using Random Forests. An example of the descriptors is shown in 2(d). The authors of [31] propose a novel keypoint detector based on saliency of depth maps which is stable to certain human poses and they include this novel detector in a probabilistic graphical model representation of the human body. The interest points, which are based on identifying geodesic extrema on the surface mesh, can be classified as, e.g., hand, foot, or head using local shape descriptors. This approach also provides a natural way of estimating a 3D orientation vector for a given interest point. This can be used to normalize the local shape descriptors to simplify the classification problem as well as to directly estimate the orientation of the body parts in space. An example of the use of this approach is illustrated in Fig. 2(e). The surveillance system proposed in [32] uses the orientation-invariant Fast Point Feature Histogram [14] based on distribution of normal vectors to identify the robbery of objects in outdoor and indoor environments. An illustration of normal vectors computed from depth maps of image objects is shown in 2(f). In citeKD and [34] the authors use Kernel Descriptors (KD) and Hierarchical Kernel Descriptors (HKD) to avoid the need for pixel attribute discretization, being able to turn any pixel attribute into compact patch-level features. Using KD over multi-modal RGBD, the similarity between two patches is based on a kernel function, called match kernel, that averages over the continuous similarities between all pairs of pixel attributes in the two patches. This method has been recently applied to multiple object recognition in RGBD data with successful results [34]. With a similar idea, the authors of [35] propose the Wave Kernel Signature (WKS) descriptor for 3D keypoint matching, where WKS is represented as the average probability of measuring a quantum mechanical particle at a specific location.

Following the description based on the Geodesic maps from [31], the authors of [36] compute 3D geodesic maps in depth maps for learning distances corresponding to body parts. First, the approach detects anatomical landmarks in the 3D data and, then, a skeleton body model s fitted using constrained inverse kinematics. Instead of relying on appearance-based features for interest point detection, which can vary strongly with illumination and pose changes, the authors build upon a graph-based representation of the depth data that allows the measurement of geodesic distances between body parts. As these distances do not change with body movement, one can localize anatomical landmarks independent of pose. For differentiation of body parts that occlude each other, the authors also use motion information obtained from optical flow. An example of the computed geodesic maps are shown in Fig. 3(a).

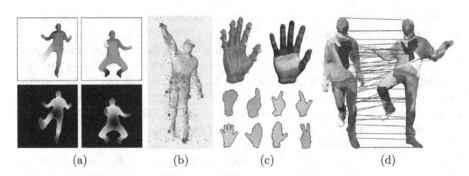

(a)                    (b)                    (c)                    (d)

**Fig. 3.** Different approaches for PR. (a) Geodesic maps over segmented subjects in [36]; (b) Probabilistic graphical model of [37]; (c) Up: Hand labeled model of [38]. Down: Hand Shape Templates of [39]; (d) Linear Programming matching based on kernel descriptors of [40].

Another approach in the scope of graphical models is the probabilistic MO-CAP approach of [37]. The authors combine a generative model with a discriminative model that feeds datadriven evidence about body part locations. In each filter iteration, the authors apply a type of local model-based search that exploits the nature of the kinematic chain. As fast movements and occlusion can disrupt the local search, they utilize a set of discriminatively trained patch classifiers to detect body parts. This noisy evidence about body part locations is propagated up the kinematic chain using the unscented transform. The resulting distribution of body configurations allows to reinitialize the model-based search, which in turn allows the system to recover from temporary tracking drift. An example of the graphical model and the inferred pose configuration for a test sample is shown in Fig. 3(b).

Since the description of body posture may vary from each particular application, it is common to find methods that focus on particular limbs to perform a more detailed local description. This is the case of head and hand regions, which described using RGBD data become a very useful tool for different real applications, such as Human Computer Interaction systems (HCI). In the top Fig. 3(c) an example of a hand parts model defined in [38] to train a Random Forest approach is shown. The bottom of Fig. 3(c) shows the shape templates proposed in [39] to look for different hand configurations in a HCI system.

Although most of previous approaches do not require from a previous background extraction step, several methods in literature use to start with an initial background extraction step based on depth information. However, background substraction can lead with several foreground objects from which persons should be identified. In this sense, the authors of [41] present a method for human detection and segmentation based on contouring depth images, applying 2D Chamfer match over silhouettes. Other classical and recent approaches used for shape analysis and matching of point clouds are Active Shape Models, Shape Context, Template Matching, or Linear Programming Approaches [40]. Fig. 3(d) shows an example of body shape matching using the linear programming approach of [40].

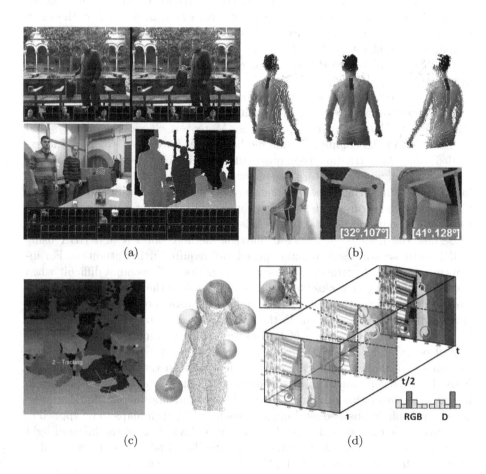

**Fig. 4.** Some applications of the Human Pose Recovery and Behavior Analysis group (HuPBA) [42]. (a) Multi-modal surveillance system of [32]. Up: Outdoor scenario, user is identified, theft is recognized, and different objects, included a small cup, are detected. Down: Users and objects are correctly identified and classified/recognized. User-object membership relations are defined. Different users can be identified simultaneously by the system; (b) System for static pose and range of movement estimation in physiotherapy, rehabilitation, and fitness condition; (c) Behavior modeling of children with Attention Deficit Hyperactivity Disorder diagnosis; And (d) General modeling of actions and gestures by multi-modal spatio-temporal Bag-of-Visual-and-Depth-Words model. Left: Salient points based on depth maps are detected and labeled to different clusters. Right: Depth descriptors are combined with RGB data descritors, and a Spatio-Temporal Bag-of-Visual-and-Depth-Words for action recognition is defined.

## 3   Conclusion

In this paper, the recent literature related to Pose Recovery and Human Behavior Analysis from multi-modal RGBD data was reviewed. In particular, the main benefits from the multi-modal RGBD from Microsoft® Kinect™ were described. Among the broad range of applications related to the devices, those particular methodologies related to PR for improved Human Behavior Applications were discussed.

We saw recent approaches based on background substraction and body part models detection and segmentation, using both discriminative and generative approaches, including hybrid approaches. Moreover, classical descriptors and techniques from 2D computer vision methodologies have been redefined and extended using the extra dimension provided by the Kinect™ device. This has lead to the design of new descriptors, use of normal vectors of surfaces, geodesic paths in 3D spaces, clustering of point clouds, etc. As a result, several non-invasive applications have become real. In Fig. 4 some applications of our research group using RGBD data representation are briefly described [42].

Besides the high performance of current methods for PR and HBA using RGBD data, several issues remain opened and require further attention. For instance, background extraction in complex scenarios still becomes difficult when the foreground object is close to artifacts belonging to the background. In those cases, the use of depth information is not straightforward, and more sophisticated approaches are required. In the case of PR, though one can benefit from the high discriminative power of RGBD representation, more accurate recognition of poses under different appearance and points of view are also necessary for some real applications. This requires dealing with the whole set of human body deformations, including occlusions and changes in appearance produced, for example, by clothes and non-controlled environmental factors. Furthermore, some real applications also need higher resolution of depth maps to be applied in real environments and deal with the reflectance deviations of the infrared light for particular materials. On the other hand, significant advances are expected to appear in the next years regarding the hardware capabilities.

## References

1. Jain, H., Subramanian, A.: Real-time upper-body human pose estimation using a depth camera, HP Technical Reports
2. Rodgers, J., Anguelov, D., Hoi-Cheung, P.: Object pose detection in range scan data. In: CVPR, pp. 2445–2452 (2006)
3. Ganapathi, V., Plagemann, C., Koller, D., Thrun, S.: Real time motion capture using a single time-of-flight camera. In: CVPR, pp. 755–762 (2010)
4. Sabata, B., Arman, F., Aggarwal, J.: Segmentation of 3d range images using pyramidal data structures. CVGIP: Image Understanding 57(3), 373–387 (1993)
5. Primesensor™, http://www.primesense.com/?p=514
6. Shotton, J., Fitzgibbon, A., Cook, M., Sharp, T., Finocchio, M.: Real-time human pose recognition in parts from single depth images (2011)
7. Dephsense ds311,
   http://www.softkinetic.com/Solutions/DepthSensecameras.aspx

8. Openni, http://www.openni.org
9. Flexible action and articulated skeleton toolkit (faast),
   http://projects.ict.usc.edu/mxr/faast/
10. Suma, E., Lange, B., Rizzo, A., Krum, D.M.: FAAST: the flexible action and articulated skeleton toolkit. In: Virtual Reality, Singapore, pp. 245–246 (2011)
11. Kinect for windows sdk from microsoft research,
    http://research.microsoft.com/en-us/um/redmond/projects/kinectsdk/
12. Openkinect (libfreenect), http://openkinect.org/
13. Code laboratories cl nui platform - kinect driver/sdk,
    http://codelaboratories.com/nui/
14. Point cloud library (pcl), http://pointclouds.org/
15. Rusu, R.B.: Semantic 3D Object Maps for Everyday Manipulation in Human Living Environments. Articial Intelligence (KI-Kuenstliche Intelligenz) (2010)
16. Lai, K., Bo, L., Ren, X., Fox, D.: Sparse distance learning for object recognition combining rgb and depth information. In: ICRA
17. Bo, L., Ren, X., Fox, D.: Depth kernel descriptors for object recognition. In: IROS, pp. 821–826 (2011)
18. Koch, R., Schiller, I., Bartczak, B., Kellner, F., Koser, K.: Mixin3d: 3d mixed reality with tof-camera, pp. 126–141 (2009)
19. Castaneda, V., Mateus, D., Navab, N.: Slam combining tof and high-resolution cameras. In: WACV, pp. 672–678 (2011)
20. Gehrig, D., Kuehne, H.: HMM-based human motion recognition with optical flow data. In: IEEE International Conference on Humanoid Robots, Humanoids 2009 (2009)
21. Sminchisescu, C., Kanaujia, A., Metaxas, D.: Conditional models for contextual human motion recognition. CVIU 104(2-3), 210–220 (2006)
22. Zhou, F., la Torre, F.D., Hodgins, J.K.: Aligned cluster analysis for temporal segmentation of human motion. In: IEEE Conference on Automatic Face and Gestures Recognition, FG (2008)
23. Reyes, M., Dominguez, G., Escalera, S.: Feature weighting in dynamic time warping for gesture recognition in depth data. In: ICCV, Barcelona, Spain (2011)
24. Hernandez-Vela, A., Zlateva, N., Marinov, A., Reyes, M., Radeva, P., Dimov, D., Escalera, S.: Graph cuts optimization for multi-limb human segmentation in depth maps. In: CVPR (2012)
25. Hernandez-Vela, A., Reyes, M., Escalera, S., Radeva, P.: Spatio-temporal grabcut human segmentation for face and pose recovery. In: IEEE International Workshop on Analysis and Modeling of Faces and Gestures, CVPR (2010)
26. Hernandez-Vela, A., Primo, C., Escalera, S.: Automatic user interaction correction via multi-label graph cuts. In: 1st IEEE International Workshop on Human Interaction in Computer Vision HICV, ICCV (2011)
27. Igual, L., Soliva, J., Hernandez-Vela, A., Escalera, S., Jimenez, X., Vilarroya, O., Radeva, P.: A fully-automatic caudate nucleus segmentation of brain mri: Application in volumetric analysis of pediatric attention-deficit/hyperactivity disorder. In: BioMedical Engineering OnLine (2011)
28. Liu, Y., Stoll, C., Gall, J., Seidel, H.: Markerless motion capture of interacting characters using multi-view image segmentation. CVPR 14(1), 1249–1256 (2011)
29. Holt, B., Ong, E.-J., Cooper, H., Bowden, R.: Putting the pieces together: Connected poselets for human pose estimation. In: ICCV (2011)
30. Pugeault, N., Bowden, R.: Spelling it out: Real-time asl fingerspelling recognition. In: ICCV (2011)

31. Plagemann, C., Ganapathi, V., Koller, D., Thrun, S.: Real-time identification and localization of body parts from depth images. In: ICCV, pp. 3108–3113 (2011)

32. Clapes, A., Reyes, M., Escalera, S.: User Identification and Object Recognition in Clutter Scenes Based on RGB-Depth Analysis. In: Perales, F.J., Fisher, R.B., Moeslund, T.B. (eds.) AMDO 2012. LNCS, vol. 7378, pp. 1–11. Springer, Heidelberg (2012)

33. Charles, J., Everingham, M.: Learning shape models for monocular human pose estimation from the microsoft xbox kinect. In: ICCV, pp. 1202–1208 (2011)

34. Bo, L., Lai, K., Ren, X., Fox, D.: Object recognition with hierarchical kernel descriptors. In: CVPR (2011)

35. Aubry, M., Schlickewei, U., Cremers, D.: The wave kernel signature: A quantum mechanical approach to shape analysis. In: ICCV (2011)

36. Schwarz, L., Mkhitaryan, A., Mateus, D., Navab, N.: Estimating human 3d pose from time-of-flight images based on geodesic distances and optical flow. In: IEEE Conference on Automatic Face and Gesture Recognition, FG (2011)

37. Ganapathiand, V., Plagemann, C., Koller, D., Thrun, S.: Real time motion capture using a single time-of-flight camera. In: CVPR, pp. 755–762 (2010)

38. Keskin, C., Racc, F., Kara, Y., Akarun, L.: Real time hand pose estimation using depth sensors. In: ICCV (2011)

39. Minnen, D., Zafrulla, Z.: Towards robust cross-user hand tracking and shape recognition. In: ICCV, pp. 1235–1241 (2011)

40. Windheuser, T., Schlickewei, U., Schmidt, F.R.: Geometrically consistent elastic matching of 3d shapes: A linear programming solution. In: ICCV (2011)

41. Xia, L., Chen, C.-C., Aggarwal, J.K.: Human detection using depth information by kinect department of electrical and computer engineering. PR, 15–22 (2011)

42. Human pose recovery and behavior analysis group,
    http://www.maia.ub.es/~sergio/

# Author Index